APPLYING COGNITIVE BEHAVIOURAL THERAPEUTIC APPROACHES IN SPORT

Cognitive-behavioural therapies (CBTs) are foundational to sport psychology. The majority of the psychological techniques employed by sport psychologists in their work with athletes stem from CBTs. However, there is a knowledge gap concerning what CBTs are and how the different types of CBTs can be applied in sport. This knowledge gap is important to fill, because CBTs are highly effective and are easily integrated into the sport setting, and thus practitioners should be aware of, if not trained in, such approaches.

Applying Cognitive Behavioural Therapeutic Approaches in Sport is the first dedicated volume to bring together the dominant cognitive-behavioural approaches to sport psychology. This book includes state-of-the-art evidence regarding the theory and practice of CBTs in sport, produced by academic and applied leaders in the area. Chapters include key historical and theoretical information about the CBTs and intricate details as to how a range of CBTs are applied in the real world of sport. Also, in each chapter, authors will cover historical and contemporary literature, and offer a hypothetical applied case study that details how the approach is applied in sport.

Practitioners (sport psychologists; psychotherapists), trainees, and students (undergraduate, and post-graduate) will for the first time receive an in-depth and sport-specific resource that includes a range of CBTs, making this book one of a kind.

Martin J. Turner, PhD (CPsychol., HCPC Reg.) is a Sport and Exercise Psychologist at Manchester Metropolitan University, UK. His main expertise are within stress and emotion management. He has worked with sporting organisations such as the FA and ECB, and is currently the psychologist for Scarlets Rugby. Martin is an award-winning researcher and teacher, and is most known for his work applying Rational Emotive Behaviour Therapy (REBT) within achievement settings, and studying the effects of stress and adversity on well-being and performance.

Marc V. Jones, PhD (CPsychol., HCPC Reg.) is a Professor of Psychology at Manchester Metropolitan University, UK. His work is focused on understanding the impact of stress on health, well-being and performance and effective leader-follower interactions. The protocols, and approach that Marc and colleagues have developed for the assessment and training of stress responses, and enhancing performance, have been utilised by professional athletes and sports teams along with business and education sectors.

Andrew G. Wood, PhD (CPsychol., HCPC Reg.) is a Senior Lecturer at Manchester Metropolitan University, UK. His main expertise is within the scientific understanding of stress and emotion, and the application of psychotherapies in high performance settings to develop psychological well-being. Andrew's most notable role was as the Lead Sport psychologist for the England B1 (Blind) Football Team.

APPLYING COGNITIVE BEHAVIOURAL THERAPEUTIC APPROACHES IN SPORT

Edited by Martin J. Turner,
Marc V. Jones, and
Andrew G. Wood

Routledge
Taylor & Francis Group
NEW YORK AND LONDON

Designed cover image: simonkr/Getty Images

First published 2023
by Routledge
605 Third Avenue, New York, NY 10158

and by Routledge
4 Park Square, Milton Park, Abingdon, Oxon, OX14 4RN

Routledge is an imprint of the Taylor & Francis Group, an informa business

ISBN: 978-0-367-75443-3 (hbk)
ISBN: 978-0-367-75432-7 (pbk)
ISBN: 978-1-003-16251-3 (ebk)

DOI: 10.4324/9781003162513

Typeset in Bembo
by KnowledgeWorks Global Ltd.

This book is dedicated to our friend Dr. Andrew G. Wood.

CONTENTS

LIST OF FIGURES

LIST OF TABLES

FOREWORD

As something of an outsider looking into the world of sport and exercise psychology, I have often noted a degree of resistance to some of the ideas and methods that have garnered the most praise and attention. They are too frequently characterised by a lack of depth, both in terms of empirical support, and in their reliance upon the superficial charm of buzzwords or personality.

Athletic performance, coaching support, and every connected pursuit is about the relationship between thought, behaviour, emotion, and physiology, with all of above being occasioned within a specific context. Limited concepts like 'mindset' seem to simply scratch the surface of this complex interaction. They evidence an over-emphasis on cognition, which often results in a reductive approach that amounts to little more than promoting the so-called power of positive thinking. I challenge the reader to consider which of the above aspects of a performance situation is most amenable to quick and easy change: cognition, behaviour, emotion, physiology, or the wider context? More than 20 years of experience as a psychologist and psychotherapist suggests to me that the answer isn't cognition. Frustratingly, the answer is probably, "It depends". Thus, the practitioner needs to approach the situation with a model that is flexibly able to address any or all of the aforementioned aspects such as the need arises. The cognitive behavioural psychotherapeutic tradition provides a number of such models, differing in emphasis, whilst all understanding the basic interactional nature of any situation.

And...don't take my word for it. That would be to fall into the 'guru' approach that I have already alluded to as problematic. The isolated genius of the guru is of little use to an underperforming athlete in the arena, in the heat of competition. An athlete needs to have been empowered to find the answers within themselves. As psychological practitioners, we might better position ourselves as 'cheerleaders' rather than 'gurus'. We will stand on the side-lines whilst the athlete engages everything they have learned. The cognitive behavioural tradition understands this. It is about helping people find their own strengths and find access to the solutions they already had within them.

In light of the above, this book is a very welcome addition to the sport and exercise psychology literature. It presents a range of models and perspectives from within the family of cognitive behavioural therapies and helps the reader to consider the practical application of each. It understands that 'CBT' is not a unitary thing, but a psychotherapeutic tradition containing related, yet distinct, viewpoints. It understands that simply changing one's thinking is not likely to be the complete answer. It understands that the necessary expertise to help a struggling athlete comes from the collaboration between the athlete and the practitioner, and does not reside in the mind of a guru. Finally, it understands that outcome data is important, and that of all the traditions within psychological therapy, the CBT tradition has amassed the best evidence for its efficacy.

I invite the reader to approach this book with humility and curiosity. Be willing to explore the different variants of CBT that are detailed herein. Consider how the application of the different models to the various case studies might relate to your own practice. Is there a model that resonates with the way that you view the world?

Is there an angle you might not have considered? Is there something you might usefully add to your practice? There may be much that is familiar to the reader in this book, and I am certain there will be something new to learn as well. I don't know of another text within sport and exercise psychology that has covered the cognitive behavioural tradition so comprehensively. Therefore, it is my hope that this book broadens and deepens the application of these models in the service of helping athletes, and everyone connected to their performance, to be the best possible versions of themselves.

Dr. Richard Bennett
Clinical Psychologist and Cognitive Behavioural Psychotherapist
Centre for Applied Psychology
University of Birmingham
30th August 2022

ACKNOWLEDGEMENTS

Martin J. Turner

I have learned a great deal in putting this book together, mainly because the chapter authors were generous in their offerings such that my own understanding of CBTs has increased. I have previously collaborated with many of the chapter authors and I thank them for their collegiate approach to our work and interactions. My chief motivation for this book was to understand more about the CBTs as applied to sport – a goal I have achieved for myself – and an endeavour I hope is shared by readers.

I also thank the wider sport and exercise psychology community for engaging with the work we have done concerning the use of CBTs in performance settings. It is the existence of a willing audience that spurs me on to continue to research and write about the application of cognitive behavioural approaches. I hope this book adds to the already keen interest in CBTs within sport and exercise psychology, and encourages readers, whatever their level of experience, to develop their understanding and competence in CBTs.

Thank you to my co-editors Marc and Andrew (Woody) who continually tolerate (and sometimes encourage) my CBT-based ramblings. Marc has been a constant source of support since I was an undergrad student, and Andrew has been my partner in crime for much of the CBT writing I have done. This book could not have come into being without a wide network of supportive colleagues - I thank anybody with whom I have conversed about CBTs in sport.

Most importantly, I thank my wife Jayne. Imagine having to listen to my daily ramblings on REBT—Jayne is a saint, and my one true constant.

Marc V. Jones

For Helen, Molly, and Jacob.

Martin J. Turner and Marc V. Jones

We are indebted to each of the contributing authors for their time and effort in writing the chapters that make up this book. During the lifespan of this project, authors and editors faced many issues related to the global pandemic as well as shifts in work and home life. We are grateful to the chapter authors for staying with the project when it would have been easier to pull-out. We offer our sincere thanks to Dr. Richard Bennett for writing the Foreword to this book – in our quest to inform the sport psychology community about cognitive behavioural approaches to practice, authentic and authoritative voices like Richard's are vital.

We also extend our gratitude to Megan Smith, David Varley, and the wider team at Routledge (Taylor & Frances Group) for supporting this book and granting us many project extensions amidst the uncertainty of the last few years.

CONTRIBUTORS

Dr. Gillian Aspin (CPsychol., HCPC Reg.) is an accredited Schema Therapist who runs GCApsychology. Gill works with people with a wide range of personal and interpersonal problems using a number of therapies, including Schema Therapy and others modes of CBT, that focus on unhelpful patterns of thinking, feeling, and behaving.

Dr. Richard Bennett (CPsychol., HCPC Reg.) is affiliaited with the Centre for Applied Psychology, University of Birmingham, and has more than 25 years' experience working as a healthcare professional within the National Health Service and in private practice, providing psychotherapy, training, and supervision. He has authored and co-authored a number of books and peer-reviewed papers on various aspects of cognitive behavioural psychotherapies. He is an Associate Fellow of the British Psychological Society, an accredited Cognitive Behavioural Psychotherapist, Trainer, and Supervisor with the British Association of Behavioural and Cognitive Psychotherapies. He is recognised as a certified Supervisor in Rational Emotive Behaviour Therapy by the Albert Ellis Institute in New York, where he is an Associate Fellow. Dr. Bennett is also a Peer-reviewed Acceptance and Commitment Therapy Trainer with the Association for Contextual Behavioural Sciences.

Dr. Hannah Butler-Coyne (CPsychol., HCPC Reg.) is affiliated with HBC Clinical & Sport Psychology; University of Central Lancashire, and Lancashire & South Cumbria NHS Foundation Trust. Hannah is a HCPC Registered and BPS Chartered Clinical Psychologist and qualified Sport Psychologist, and works in both private practice and a busy Child and Adolescent Mental Health and Children's Psychological Integrated NHS Service on the Fylde Coast. Within independent practice Hannah specialises in the application of clinical psychology in sport settings, supporting athletes and sportspeople to enhance performance and/or manage mental health difficulties. Hannah is also a Lecturer at the University of Central Lancashire and visiting Lecturer on a number of academic courses in universities and colleges in the North West.

Dr. James Collard is affiliated with the Cairnmillar Institute, and is a clinical psychologist and academic. He has expertise in areas of clinical and health psychology. James has completed advanced and supervisory training in CBT, including training in the traditional models of Cognitive Therapy (CT) and Rational Emotive Behaviour Therapy (REBT), and the more recent "3rd wave" models (e.g., ACT, MiCBT). In addition to his clinical work, James provides supervision and training in CBT. As an academic, he has conducted research into the role of cognitions and cognitive processes in mental health and on training methods for CBT practitioners.

Dr. Ulla Damgaard-Sørensen qualified as a Clinical Psychologist in 2005 from Salomons, Canterbury Christ Church University. Since then, she has mainly worked in forensic services where she has applied the schema therapy model to very diverse clients and within complex organisations. With more than 10 years' experience of working in forensic settings in England as a clinical psychologist, Ulla has worked in a variety of settings, with men and women, a range of pathologies (psychiatric, personality disordered, and psychopathic), and a wide span of ages, including children and older adults. Ulla's last post in the UK was at the Fens Unit, HMP Whitemoor, where she worked with men identified as suffering from Dangerous and Severe Personality Disorder (including psychopathy). Ulla currently works at the Telepsykiatrisk Center, where she is the Clinical Lead for Internetpsykiatrien, a national health service providing online therapy to patients.

Dr. Faye F. Didymus is a Reader in sport and exercise psychology at Carnegie School of Sport, Leeds Beckett University. Faye's research focuses on athlete welfare using theories of psychological stress and well-being. Faye's research has been funded by The Football Association, Sport Wales, UK Coaching, Funds for Women Graduates, the Sidney Perry Foundation, the Psychology Postgraduate Affairs Group, the British Psychological Society, Loughborough University Graduate School, and Leeds Beckett University. Faye is a British Association of Sport and Exercise Sciences Accredited Sport and Exercise Scientist, a Science Council Chartered Scientist (CSci), and holds primary certificates in Cognitive Behavioural Therapy and Training and Stress Management. Faye's previous and on-going applied practice includes work with organisations such as International Business Machines (IBM), the Lane4 Management Group, British Triathlon, the National Ice Skating Association of Great Britain, the Talented Athlete Scholarship Scheme, and Loughborough University Performance Sport.

Dr. Joseph Dixon (CPsychol., HCPC Reg., CSci.) is a dual-chartered Sport & Exercise and Occupational Psychologist who has worked with elite athletes and teams across a variety of different sports. From 2013, he has been Lead Psychologist with Stoke City Football Club in the English Premier League and Championship Division whilst completing a PhD focusing on challenge and threat states in athletes. In this time, he has also worked within both Men's English Premiership Rugby and with Elite Para Football teams at the English Football Association. He currently combines his work in applied practice alongside a Lecturing role in Sport & Exercise Psychology at Staffordshire University.

Ms. Jennifer A. Hobson (CPsychol., HCPC Reg.) is the Lead Academy Psychologist at Stoke City Football Club. She is also a Post Graduate Researcher exploring the Theory of Challenge and Threat States in Athletes (TCTSA) in youth academy football players to establish how TCTSA variables change over time and whether they predict performance and mental health outcomes. Jennifer is Lecturer in Applied Sport Psychology at Sheffield Hallam University.

Dr. Marc V. Jones (CPsychol., HCPC Reg.) is a Professor of Psychology at Manchester Metropolitan University in the Department of Psychology. His work is focused on understanding the impact of stress on health, well-being and performance, and effective leader–follower interactions. The protocols, and approach that Marc and colleagues have developed for the assessment and training of stress responses, and enhancing performance, have been utilised by professional athletes and sports teams along with business and education sectors. In addition to his ongoing work in sport and business, currently Marc is working on, and developing, research, and consultancy projects in stress, well-being, and health in extreme environments. These include military settings, space travel and emergency medicine groups. Marc has published widely with more than 100 publications comprising peer-review papers, books, and book chapters.

Dr. Satu Kaski (PhD), working as a sport psychologist and psychotherapist, has an extensive experience in the field of clinical sport psychology. In addition, she has long applied schema therapeutic methods in sports. She is the first Finnish certified advanced level individual schema therapist (trainer and supervisor). Among other things, she has completed research on the well- and ill-being of sport coaches and athletes. In Finland, she has a long experience working with athletes and coaches. She works as a director in UTHA (a centre of mental health for athletes, artists and those working with excellence).

Dr. Paul McCarthy (CPsychol., HCPC Reg.) is the Programme Director for the Taught Doctorate in Sport and Exercise Psychology at Glasgow Caledonian University. He is an active researcher and lecturer in applied psychology, especially sport and exercise psychology. His private practice serves clients from amateur to professional status with a specific emphasis on golf and football. His research examines issues within applied sport psychology practice, attention, emotion and resilience among athletes. He publishes peer-reviewed journals, books, and book chapters on topics in applied psychology, especially sport and exercise psychology.

Dr. Peter Olusoga (CPsychol.) is a Senior Lecturer in Psychology at Sheffield Hallam University in the United Kingdom and holds an Associate Professor II position at Inland Norway University of Applied Sciences. His PhD thesis focused on stress and coping in elite sports coaching, and his current research focuses on coach burnout, and well-being in high-performance sports environments. In addition to research, Dr. Olusoga is a Chartered Psychologist with the British Psychological Society (BPS), an experienced consultant, and host of the award-winning sport and performance psychology podcast, Eighty Percent Mental.

Dr. Martin J. Turner (CPsychol., HCPC Reg.) is a Sport and Exercise Psychologist whose main expertise are within stress and emotion management. He has worked with sporting organisations such as the FA and ECB, and is currently the psychologist for Scarlets Rugby. Martin is an award-winning researcher and teacher at Manchester Metropolitan University. He is most known for his work applying Rational Emotive Behaviour Therapy (REBT) within achievement settings, and studying the effects of stress and adversity on well-being and performance. In his research work he also examines the psychophysiology of the human stress response, and its relationship to human functioning. He is an advocate for cognitive-behavioural approaches to performance psychology.

Dr. Jo Wood (CPsychol., HCPC Reg.) is a Consultant Counselling Psychologist, who has worked for more than 17 years' in the NHS with adults, children, young people, and couples. Jo offers short to long term therapy using a number of different approaches, including Cognitive Behavioural Therapy, Schema Therapy, EMDR, and Couples' Therapy for Depression. Having completed her dual training in Sports and Exercise Psychology, she also provides consultations to individuals and teams on all areas of improving performance and motivation whether for sports or general exercise. Dr Wood combines working in her own private practice with working as an Associate for Cognacity and providing sports psychology to a GB development programme.

Ms. Shameema Yousuf (HCPC reg., MBACP) is affiliaited with Empower2Perform and is a Zimbabwean transnational UK practitioner psychologist, and mental health therapist in private practice. She works at the intersection of performance, mental health, and culture across elite sport, non-profit organizations, and the corporate sector. She is also a lecturer, published author, presenter, and keynote speaker with scholarly interest in culture and mindfulness.

INTRODUCTION

An introduction to applying cognitive behavioural therapeutic approaches in sport

Martin J. Turner and Marc V. Jones

Start at the Beginning

The genesis of this book was a paper Martin J. Turner published alongside some of the chapter authors (i.e., Aspin, Didymus, Olusoga; Turner et al., 2019; 2020) and a symposium presented at the 2019 British Psychological Society (BPS) Division of Sport and Exercise Psychology (DSEP) annual conference. The paper and symposium, entitled "One case, four approaches: The application of psychotherapeutic approaches in sport psychology", brought together a range of cognitive-behavioural therapies (CBTs) to address a single hypothetical athlete case. What we learned from these exercises is that even though the same case information was presented, each CBT offered a unique direction of work alongside distinct ways of working and technical application. We also noticed that there were many similarities across the different CBTs, which spoke to the familial relationship between the CBTs (Turner et al., 2020). In these aforementioned works, it was not possible for the authors to elaborate or provide in-depth details for the CBTs they were writing and speaking about. So, in the present book, "Applying Cognitive Behavioural Therapeutic Approaches in Sport", each CBT is given pride of place in a dedicated chapter.

This book offers practitioners, scholars, and researchers of sport psychology, theoretical and example case study accounts of experienced and qualified practitioners using CBTs with athletes. This book is for anyone who has an interest in the theory and practice of sport psychology, and particularly those who wish to learn more about how CBTs can be applied with athletes. There is certainly a need for contemporary literature reviews concerning the use of CBTs in sport. But in addition, explanatory case studies offer a unique and detailed perspective on practitioners' work, offering insights into the "at the coal face" details that are priceless for experienced practitioners and trainees alike. The chapters of this book bring theory and research in CBT to life. The authors that have contributed to this book have grappled to deliver psychological approaches and constructs in the often unpredictable and constantly changing real-world context of sport. Their insights are highly valuable, in part because practitioner insights on the application of CBTs are rare.

There are currently various books on the market that provide "how to" guides to using CBTs in clinical populations (e.g., Dryden, 2012), but none of these books address sport as a context in which to apply CBTs, and currently there is no book that brings together the perspectives and

DOI: 10.4324/9781003162513-1

case studies of prominent sport and exercise psychologists using CBTs. This is significant because CBTs as applied in clinical contexts may not be easily transferred to sport settings. In addition, whilst the field of sport psychology has some great journals in which to publish our work, few journals publish detailed accounts of professional practice. The proposed book offers much needed detail concerning how sport psychology is practiced particularly through a CBT lens.

Cognitive-Behavioural?

What is it to be "cognitive-behavioural" in your approach to practice? Put simply, taking a cognitive-behavioural approach to your work means that you understand that there is a connection between cognition, emotions, and behaviour. This relationship is such that shifts in one element (e.g., cognition) can be reflected in changes in the other elements (e.g., emotions and behaviour). When trying to understand the mechanisms through which performance, and more broadly, well-being, is affected in sport, we are often required to take a multi-layered and multivariate approach to assessment, and often apply multi-modal and eclectic solutions. Often, and inappropriately, commentators on CBT have placed too much emphasis on the "cognitive" and thus the conversation around CBTs can be too simplistic and unidimensional. In practice, most CBTs promote the utilisation of cognitive *and* emotional *and* behavioural modification as a means to alleviating dysfunction (and promoting function) and to facilitate the healthy pursuit of meaningful sport and life goals. This broad cognitive-behavioural tradition has been codified within a variety of CBTs that each have their own position on the roots of human suffering and fulfilment, and thus each have a unique set of potential solutions. The core tenets and background of CBTs are covered by James Collard early in this book, who does a much better job than we could possibly achieve here in this short introduction. But suffice it to say, that "CBT" is an umbrella term for a family of therapies and as such when we speak of "CBT", we really mean "CBTs". Or as Kuo (2019) states, "CBT should not be conceived of as one singular approach. Rather, CBT represents a large body of related interventions using a therapeutic approach with common elements" (p. 87).

Given that there are many CBTs, practitioners have a choice when it comes to practicing from a cognitive-behavioural perspective. The current book aims to inform and enlighten the reader with regards to some of the most prominent CBTs that one can learn about, train within, and implement in sport. This is a mere snapshot of the CBTs that are available to practitioners, and the CBTs chosen for this book are a result of the editors' personal proclivities and the status of the selected CBTs in the sport literature. That is, we selected CBTs for which the professional practice and research literature seems to be growing and or are well established, and for which fellow practitioner often talk to us about. Thus, the CBTs represented in this book are not the "best" or "top" CBTs, rather, they do appear to be the most prominently referenced in contemporary sport psychology literature.

What CBTs Are Covered in This Book?

Olusoga and Yousuf offer a chapter on acceptance and commitment therapy (ACT), Wood and Butler-Coyne offer a chapter concerning compassion focused therapy (CFT), Didymus and McCarthy present cognitive therapy (CT), Turner covers rational emotive behaviour therapy (REBT), Jones and Turner present stress inoculation training (SIT), and Aspin, Kaski and Damgaard-Sørensen detail schema therapy (ST). Chapter authors introduce their own hypothetical athlete case (i.e., an athlete who presents with an issue that might be considered *typical* in sport psychology practice) and then outline the use of that CBT with that case. The hypothetical case is based on a real athlete, or is an amalgamation of athletes, that the authors worked with and thus there is a real-world quality to each chapter. In doing so, the authors outline the key theoretical and practical features of the CBT and also note the professional practice considerations one might need to consider when applying that particular CBT. Alongside these specific CBT chapters, some authors have been invited to offer chapters that provide a broader perspective on CBTs per se. Collard provides a chapter on the philosophical and theoretical underpinnings of CBTs, whilst Hobson and Dixon offer details on how the cognitive-behavioural tradition can be used to inform a multi-modal approach to real-world systemic sport psychology provision.

Why Do We Need This Book?

Sport psychologists are charged with the provision of psychological support services to those working within an athletic milieu. This could be athletes, coaches, support staff, parents of athletes, for example, although in this book, the contributing chapter authors mainly focus their attention on athletes. As practitioners, we 'have to' decide on our professional philosophy, our approach to working with athletes, our models and frameworks, on the theoretical underpinnings to our work (if we are interested in evidence-based practice, which we should be), and on the methods and modes that will shape our work. As such, having an understanding of some of the psychotherapeutic approaches we can take to our work is important, because these psychotherapies (the CBTs) have a vast philosophic and scientific undergirding, and a heap of supporting evidence (e.g., David et al., 2018), and thus can provide us with many of the tools we need in our practice.

Many of the tools we use in sport psychology are derived from CBTs. Specifically, the "canon of psychological skills" (Andersen, 2009, p. 11) perhaps reflects the most prevalent techniques, namely relaxation, self-talk, imagery, goal setting, and concentration. These psychological skills come from CBTs and have been adapted for the context of sport (see Vealey, 2007). Indeed, Emily Claspell (2010) recounts a private correspondence with Andersen who remarks on the beauty of the flowers, leaves, branches, main trunk, and root system of an azalea bush, and asserts that using psychological skills training (PST) as a model "is like focussing only on the flowers" (p. 131). The flowers are a part of a broader system of CBT and Andersen questions whether practitioners working in sport really study the whole plant. In this book, we present broader systems of CBT each with their own (although similarities between CBTs are present) set of techniques and "psychological skills". Self-talk in REBT will not be the same as self-talk in CT, for example.

If CBTs are foundational to sport psychology practice, why do we not have more literature detailing the use of CBTs in sport? First, sport psychology literature often reports the use of the canon techniques in isolation and in absence of full psychotherapeutic procedures. This is fine, and it depends on the context and the case whether and what extent one applies isolated psychological skills and or one applies full psychotherapeutic procedures. However, it is in part for this reason that there is a dearth of information in published literature concerning the use of CBTs with athletes (McArdle & Moore, 2012).

Second, rarely are the origins of the canon of psychological skills recognized in sport psychology literature, and as such, we forget that CBTs are foundational to contemporary sport psychology practice. Many of the dominant theories in sport psychology, even the overly abstracted ones, have clear links to CBTs even if CBT literature is not referenced. Because CBTs are not referred to, or written about as influential to contemporary theory, they have been side-lined to an extent, or at least, they are not as prominently cited as they could and should be.

Third, and as one of us (Martin) notes in a recent book, there appears to be a shift away from PST in the sport psychology community, for reasons that are not clear. We believe that we should not be so quick to abandon PST, and should find ways to continue to adapt PST to fit the ever-changing populations we serve. "Those who are having problems with their usage of PST in their practice should look first to the user" (i.e., themselves) (Turner, 2022). The ubiquity of PST perhaps has caused the industry to forget the importance, depth, and evidence base, of the ideas nested within PST. Those ideas are reflected in the CBTs covered within this book.

Next Steps

We hope that the content contained within this book is thought-provoking, interesting, illustrative, and instructive. We also hope that the description of the CBTs and the techniques offered by them, inform the reader's practice and encourages them to seek training in one or more of the approaches presented. We also hope that readers are encouraged to write about their experiences of applying CBTs in sport, and that researchers are encouraged to undertake more scientific investigation of CBTs in sport settings. A cognitive-behavioural approach to sport psychology practice is just one option for those working in sport psychology support. But as you will hopefully gather from this book, it is an option that is broad enough to apply across many issues, but is specific enough to offer consistent conceptual underpinnings and usable frameworks, techniques, and modes of working for sport psychology provision.

References

Andersen, M. B. (2009). The "canon" of psychological skills training for enhancing performance. In K. F. Hays (Ed.), *Performance psychology in action: A casebook for working with athletes, performing artists, business leaders, and professionals in high-risk occupations* (pp. 11–34). American Psychological Association. https://doi.org/10.1037/11876-001

Claspell, E. (2010). Cognitive-behavioral therapies. In S. J. Hanrahan, & M. B. Andersen (Eds.), *Routledge handbook of applied sport psychology* (pp. 131–140). Routledge.

David, D., Cristea, I., & Hofmann, S. G. (2018). Why cognitive behavioral therapy is the current gold standard of psychotherapy. *Frontiers in Psychiatry, 9*, 4. https://doi.org/10.3389/fpsyt.2018.00004

Dryden, W. (2012). *Cognitive behaviour therapies* (1st ed.). SAGE Publications Ltd.

Kuo, C. (2019). Cognitive behavioral therapy around the globe. In D. J. Stein, J. K. Bass, & S. G. Hofmann (Eds.), *Global mental health and psychotherapy: Adapting psychotherapy for low- and middle-income countries* (pp. 87–126). Elsevier Academic Press. https://doi.org/10.1016/B978-0-12-814932-4.00005-7

McArdle, S., & Moore, P. (2012). Applying evidence-based principles from CBT to sport psychology. *The Sport Psychologist, 26*(2), 299–310. https://doi.org/10.10.1123/tsp.26.2.299

Turner, M. J. (2022). *The rational practitioner: The sport and performance psychologist's guide to practicing rational emotive behaviour therapy*. Routledge.

Turner, M. J., Aspin, G., Didymus, F., Flockhart, K., & Wood, A. G. (2019). One case, five approaches: The application of psychotherapeutic approaches in sport psychology. Symposium delivered at the Division of Sport and Exercise Psychology annual conference, Solihull.

Turner, M. J., Aspin, G., Didymus, F., Mack, R., Olusoga, P., Wood, A. G., & Bennett. R. (2020). One case, five approaches: The application of psychotherapeutic approaches in sport psychology. *The Sport Psychologist, 34*(1), 71–83. https://doi.org/10.1123/tsp.2019-0079

Vealey, R. S. (2007). Mental skills training in sport. In: G. Tenenbaum, & R. C. Eklund (Eds.), *Handbook of sport psychology* (3rd ed., pp. 287–309). Wiley.

1

COGNITIVE-BEHAVIOURAL THERAPY (CBT)

James Collard

What is Cognitive-Behavioural Therapy (CBT)?

Today, the term cognitive-behavioural therapy (CBT) is commonly referred to within the field of psychology. There can, however, be considerable confusion about what this term means and how it is used (Collard, 2019b). In essence, CBT refers to a school of psychological therapies and interventions that all adhere to a theoretical framework, which focuses on cyclical interactions between cognitions, emotions, and behaviours in understanding how people function. In this way, it is considered an "umbrella" term for a range of therapies that have been developed to assist people in overcoming and managing psychological difficulties and to enhance their functionality (Nezu & Nezu, 2016; O'Kelly, 2020). The commonality between these CBTs also extends to their focus on empirical support for psychological models of functioning and support for related interventions (David & Cristea, 2018; David et al., 2018).

As a result, CBTs also promote a scientist-practitioner mindset in approaching issues of human functioning. This encourages practitioners to collect data on functional issues, to pragmatically evaluate formulations developed to represent functional issues, and to evaluate the usefulness of intervention strategies provided to individuals (Tarrier & Johnson, 2016). Such formulations are considered from within a biopsychosocial framework. This allows for the recognition of contextual factors that contribute to an individual's functioning. These include the persons biological functioning, and the evolutionary history underpinning this, their internal psychological phenomena (i.e., thoughts and feelings), their overt behaviours, their social interactions and situations, and the interplay between these factors (Gilbert, 2019; Nezu & Nezu, 2016). It is from these formulations that cognitive-behavioural interventions are developed and selected for an individual. These can be quite varied but typically seek to influence conscious thoughts and beliefs, cognitive processes, or behavioural choices.

Background and History of CBT

While CBT is relatively young as a psychological science, emerging in the middle of the 20th century, it has philosophical and theoretical roots that are thousands of years old. In particular, CBTs incorporate Stoic, Buddhist, Tao, and existential concepts (Ellis, 2005b;

DOI: 10.4324/9781003162513-2

Murguia & Díaz, 2015). They have done so through commonalities to a constructivist philosophy, which posits that individuals interact with their experiences to construct meaning in their life (Dimeff & Linehan, 2001; Ellis, 2003; Hayes et al., 1999). This constructivist philosophy can be seen in quotes from Epictetus, "People are not disturbed by things, but by the view they take of them", and by Buddha, "We are what we think. All that we are arises with or thoughts. With our thoughts we make the world". It can also be observed in the work of Immanuel Kant who noted that reality cannot be directly experienced, but is instead "known" through "categories of thinking" (Leahy, 1996, p. 20).

The emergence of CBT as a psychological science has been suggested to have occurred in three waves over the past century. The first wave is considered to have been behaviourism, which started to identify basic learning mechanisms in the early 20th century. A key pioneer of this approach was John Watson. He rejected the subjective nature of psychology at the time and emphasised the importance of interactions with the environment as central to learning and to the development of behaviour (Wilson, 2005). Our understanding of learning principles was further developed by the works related to classical conditioning by Ivan Pavlov (1927), and operant conditioning by Burrhus Skinner (Skinner, 1938). These were later combined by O. Hobart Mowrer in his two-factor theory of fear and avoidance (Mowrer, 1947, 1956).

Pioneering the translation of such learning theory into therapeutic approaches, Mary Cover Jones, in 1924, developed behavioural strategies for helping children to overcome fears (Wilson, 2005). The advancement of behavioural theories into a formal psychological therapy then occurred through the 1950s and 1960s. A prominent proponent of this development was Joseph Wolpe (1958). He applied behavioural research to the treatment of neurotic disorders. This focused on a learning theory called reciprocal inhibition, which proposed that anxiety could be treated by engagement in behaviours that were inconsistent with it. Clinically, he first applied this to social anxiety cases, training individuals in assertive behaviour to counter their anxiety. From this work, he then developed the notion of grading exposure to anxiety provoking stimuli; this has since become known as systematic desensitisation. Another major advancement during this period arose as a result of the criticism by behaviourists for the existing psychodynamic approach to therapy and models of dysfunction. Promoting a scientifically empirical approach to understanding dysfunction and its treatment as an alternative, prominent behaviourists such as John Dollard, Neal Miller, Hans Eysenck, and B.F. Skinner reformulated psychotherapy in behavioural terms (O'Donohue & Ferguson, 2016; O'Kelly, 2020; Wilson, 2005).

The second wave of CBT occurred through the middle of the 20th century. This has been called the cognitive revolution and was due to dissatisfaction with the purely behaviourist approach to understanding human functioning. For instance, it was noted that purely behavioural perspectives were unable to explain language acquisition, developmental stages of thinking, attachment behaviour, and moral reasoning (Leahy, 1996; O'Kelly, 2020). Forerunners of this shift to a cognitive model of functioning included Alfred Adler (1932), Karen Horney (1950), and George Kelly (1955). Through the 1950s and 1960s, models of functioning based on a cognitive mediation theory were then developed. The two most prominent to emerge were Albert Ellis' (1955, 1962) rational emotive behaviour therapy (REBT) and Aaron Beck's (1963, 1967) cognitive therapy (CT). Both Ellis and Beck had been psychoanalytically trained, but based on their personal experiences, clinical work, and empirical evidence, they began to promote a move towards more active and goal focused therapy, integrating cognitive and behavioural strategies to help those they worked with (Beck, 2019; Ellis & MacLaren, 1998).

Further contributions to the understanding of cognitive-behavioural interactions through this period were made by Albert Bandura (1969) with his work on social learning theory, and by Richard Lazarus (1984) with his work on appraisal theory and coping. Other notable contributors to the early development of the clinical practice of CBT were Michael Mahoney (1974), Arnold Lazarus (1976), and Donald Meichenbaum (1977).

There have since been a range of cognitive-behavioural modalities that have been developed, often in response to perceived limitations of earlier models. These have been suggested to constitute a third wave of CBT (e.g., Fletcher & Hayes, 2005; Hayes, 2004a; Hayes et al., 2013). Some of these have focused on tailoring approaches to more complex forms of dysfunction. Examples of these are schema therapy (ST; Young et al., 2003) and dialectical behaviour therapy (DBT; Linehan, 1993a), which were both developed to treat personality disorders, and cognitive processing therapy (CPT; Resick et al., 2007), which was developed to treat post-traumatic stress disorder. Other recent models that have been developed have also emphasised the role of secondary processes, that is the reactions people have to their own cognitions, emotions, and internal sensations. These have tended to focus on mindfulness interventions and acceptance of these internal processes and experiences. Included among these are acceptance and commitment therapy (ACT; Hayes et al., 1999), metacognitive therapy (MCT; Wells, 2009), and various forms of mindfulness-based cognitive-behaviour therapy (e.g., Cayoun, 2011; Segal et al., 2002).

The suggestion by proponents of ACT that these more recent models represent a third wave of CBT has led to some tension within the field. This resulted in debate over efforts to differentiate the various models on the basis of their theory and practice, rather than focusing on their commonalities (Collard, 2019a). Interestingly, the authors of the other recent models do not self-identify as being part of a third wave, tending to view their approaches as being in line with traditional CBT approaches (David & Hofmann, 2013).

More recently, however, there have been efforts in the literature to reconcile these suggested differences, identifying the commonalities within the models, and to develop a more integrated and coherent model of CBT (Barlow et al., 2011; Collard, 2019a; David & Freeman, 2015; Hofmann & Hayes, 2018). Efforts have also been made over recent years to integrate CBT theories and research with other areas, including biology, evolutionary psychology, social psychology, developmental psychology, and neurocognition, to develop a unified model of human functioning (Beck & Bredemeier, 2016; Gilbert, 2019).

A Taxonomy of CBT

When discussing the literature and research relating to CBT, it is important to note that key terms and concepts can be separated into three categorical levels. These are (1) the general theory underpinning the school, (2) specific treatment models and packages, and (3) specific interventions (Collard, 2019b). Figure 1.1 provides a pictorial demonstration of how these taxonomical levels relate to the area of CBT but does not include all relevant models or interventions.

The underlying theoretical framework of CBT is not "owned" by any particular individual or group of individuals. It is a general theoretical framework that provides an understanding of how various psychological components (e.g., thoughts, feelings, and behaviours) relate to one another. It also explains how various functions are adaptive or maladaptive, how change occurs, and how disorder arises. While particular individuals, such as Ellis (1962) and Beck (1967), may have contributed significantly to its development, CBT is not

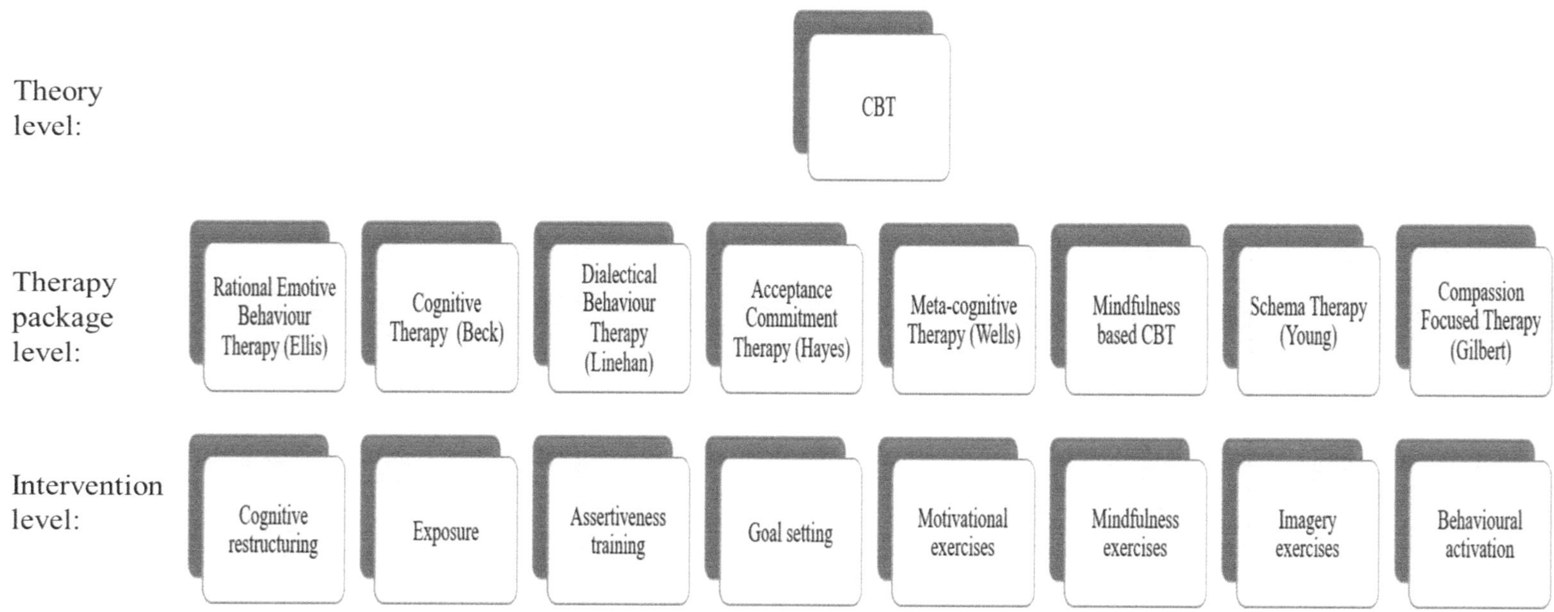

FIGURE 1.1 Taxonomical overview of the school of CBT.

fixed. It is constantly being reviewed and advanced through scientific research (David & Cristea, 2018).

Within the overarching cognitive-behavioural framework, there have now been a variety of models and packages developed by individuals or groups. These models tend to be identified with those that created them. They also often bring with them mini-theories and idiosyncratic terminology that may emphasise particular processes for helping people. Despite this, they still all maintain commonalities with more general cognitive-behavioural theory.

The intervention level, on the other hand, describes the specific cognitive-behavioural strategies that may be utilised to help improve people's functioning. Here there can be considerable overlap in the recommendations made by the various CBT models.

Misconceptions about how concepts fit within these categorical levels can cause confusion at times and can result in inappropriate comparisons between them. This is a common issue within psychology in general, and is unsurprising given the proliferation of mini-theories within the area of CBT (Buss, 1995). However, such confusion can inhibit the ability to integrate similar, and related, concepts (Zarbo et al., 2016).

Common examples include times where the term CBT itself gets misclassified. For instance, it has at times been confused with a specific treatment model within the school, being Beck's cognitive therapy. It can also be used by some to refer to the specific intervention of cognitive restructuring. Such confusion is greatly reductionistic in terms of the understanding of CBT, as the area involves so much more than just cognitive restructuring and much more than even Beck's approach to therapy. Conversely, when the term CBT is used instead of cognitive restructuring, this provides non-specific information, as there are a wide variety of cognitive-behavioural interventions that could be applied to a situation.

Misclassifications have also at times resulted in inappropriate comparisons between cognitive-behavioural concepts belonging to different levels of this hierarchy. Examples of this include comparisons between CBT and ACT (e.g., Arch et al., 2012; Ellis, 2005a; Losada et al., 2014) and between CBT and relaxation training (e.g., Donegan & Dugas, 2012; Schröder et al., 2013). Such comparisons represent a "categorical error that is analogous to comparing trees with oaks" (Herbert & Forman, 2013, p. 2). It can also result in the misunderstanding that some cognitive-behavioural models, such as ACT and DBT (e.g., DiGiorgio et al., 2010; Harris, 2008), are not part of the broader school of CBT.

Appropriate comparisons within the same taxonomical levels are instead quite important for the ongoing development and advancement of cognitive-behavioural theory and practice. It has, however, been suggested that further development of cognitive-behavioural theories and practices would be better served by focusing more on the specific theories and interventions, moving beyond the discussion of branded modalities (Collard, 2019b; Rosen & Davison, 2003).

Foundations/Philosophical Background

Philosophy and Understanding of Human Functioning

As noted above, the underlying philosophy of CBTs is based on a constructivist view of human functioning. This philosophy suggests that individuals interact with their experiences to construct meaning in their life (Ellis, 2003). This meaning is therefore a result of symbolic activity of the mind. This symbolic activity, at times labelled "human language", can be either verbal or non-verbal, and contributes to both the functional and dysfunctional outcomes that an individual may experience (Hayes et al., 1999). This model therefore places an emphasis on cognitions and cognitive processes in understanding human functioning.

As an extension of this philosophy, all human outcomes, whether functional or dysfunctional, are viewed as being within the normal range of human experience. For instance, Ellis (1962) proposed that humans are both innately rational and irrational, while Beck (2020) describes automatic thoughts as a natural part of human functioning that can be either functional or dysfunctional, and Hayes et al. (1999) notes that human language is the basis for both achievement and suffering.

Within a cognitive-behavioural framework, the functionality of a response is evaluated on a pragmatic basis, giving due consideration to the context within which it occurs. This promotes a holistic and scientific approach to understanding human functioning that is based on logical empiricism, an approach that allows for the balancing of reason with the empirical measurement of outcomes (Collard, 2019a). This is demonstrated in Ellis's definition of rationality. Within his approach to therapy, he stated that there is "no absolute, essential view of rationality" and that "rational means self-helping and irrational means self-defeating" (Ellis & MacLaren, 1998, pp. 19–20). Elaborating upon this, he noted that while a thought may be considered functional in many circumstances, it is not considered to be inherently functional under all conditions and at all time, rather that its rationality is reflected in logic, empirical support, and/or pragmatic utility (David et al., 2010; Ellis & MacLaren, 1998). Similarly, Beck has stated that when evaluating the functionality of an automatic thought, such a thought can be assessed for both "its validity and/or utility" (Beck, 2020, p. 242). Within ACT, Hayes et al. (1999) also discuss the application of a "pragmatic truth criterion" to understand human behaviour. This involves the evaluation of relevant factors contributing to a behaviour (including mental behaviour, such as thoughts), and an evaluation of whether the behaviour provides functional outcomes.

The appreciation of contextual factors when evaluating the pragmatic utility of thoughts, emotions, and behaviours is importantly highlighted in a number of ways within cognitive-behavioural models. These include the recognition of behaviours in relation to peoples' goals (Hayes, 2004b) and the recognition of our existence within an objective reality outside of ourselves (Dobson, 2013). This further allows for the appreciation of bi-directional relationships that exist between cognitions, emotions, and behaviours, and acknowledgement of the influences that social and biological factors can have on an individual (Beck & Haigh, 2014; Ellis, 1987, 1994a).

While these principles provide for an understanding of human functioning, CBTs are also underpinned by existential and humanistic principles (Ellis, 2003; Sabucedo, 2019). These principles help to inform views on healthy functioning. They include a recognition of the inherent dignity and worth of humans simply because they are alive and unique individuals (Ellis, 2003; Hayes et al., 1999). This underpins the notion of unconditional acceptance, which holds that it is not possible to rate the value of a person, thereby promoting a position of unconditional acceptance of the self and unconditional acceptance of others. The focus on acceptance is also extended to life more generally, promoting acceptance of all aspects of life, regardless of how desirable they may be, especially those outside of our control (Murguia & Díaz, 2015). At the same time, there is also an emphasis on choice and the responsibility for living an authentic and valued life, thereby promoting a eudaimonic approach to wellbeing (David et al., 2013). Together these principles recognise that while life may give rise to events outside of our control, limiting the range of our choices, we still have the ability to choose how we respond to these events. Following from this, people are said to therefore have the capacity to achieve a meaningful life by making choices that are consistent with their values (Ellis, 1962, 2003; Fletcher & Hayes, 2005; Murguia & Díaz, 2015; Ruggiero et al., 2018).

Functioning and Mental Health/Understanding Human Functioning

Put simply, cognitive-behavioural models of human functioning are information processing models. These models hold that the events (A) do not in themselves trigger responses (C) but are instead mediated by cognitions and cognitive process (B) (Dobson, 2013; Ellis, 1994b). It is important to note that these As can include external events (e.g., performing in front of an audience) and internal events (e.g., feeling nauseas). The Cs can include emotional reactions, physical sensations, behavioural response, and shifts in attentional focus. The cognitions and cognitive processes involved in B can range from being conscious and explicit to unconscious and implicit (David & Cristea, 2018). Commonly, it is recognised that there are also different levels of processing within cognitive responses to events. Typically, people are more aware of their surface thoughts about specific situations, at times called automatic thoughts (Beck, 2020) or inferences (Ellis & MacLaren, 1998). Beneath these, however, are considered to be more general beliefs. These include intermediate beliefs that act as rules or guides for life and are closely related to the deepest level beliefs that are known as core evaluations about the self, others, and life. These more generalised beliefs are sometimes grouped together under the label of "schema" (Beck & Haigh, 2014; Young et al., 2003).

Unsurprisingly, with the prominence of cognitive factors given in these models, there has been a significant focus on understanding such processes. Such literature has focused on how people develop patterns of thoughts and beliefs, on the nature of different cognitive processes (e.g., conscious vs unconscious; automatic vs reflective), and on the consequences of the various cognitive processes.

In terms of understanding how individuals acquire their cognitive patterns, learning theories have played a central role. These include classical conditioning, operant conditioning, and social learning. Classical conditioning is a simple form of associative learning. It occurs when the individual learns to associate a situation or stimulus with a conditioned response simply based on a temporal relationship despite there being no direct relationship between the stimulus and the response (e.g., a smell present during the experience of a traumatic event may later retrigger an anxiety reaction even though the smell itself is not dangerous; Pavlov, 1927). Operant conditioning processes are those that provide feedback to an individual through rewards and punishments, thereby shaping learning and behaviour due to reinforcement contingencies (e.g., a child punished for making mistakes may learn to view mistakes as threatening; Skinner, 1938). Social learning theory often relates to modelling, where the individual learns through observation of others in the world around them (e.g., a child observing an adult who hits out when frustrated may then replicate the behaviour in response to their own frustrations; Bandura, 1969). Together these learning processes contribute to the development of response sets for how to interact with the world.

Understandably, this places significant importance upon the learning individuals receive from their early life experiences. In particular, adversity, trauma, and abuse during childhood have been found to predict information processing biases in adolescent and adult years (Gibb et al., 2003; Schwartz et al., 2012). It is also important to note here that through the repeated practice of these response sets, the cognitive processes involved can become neurologically

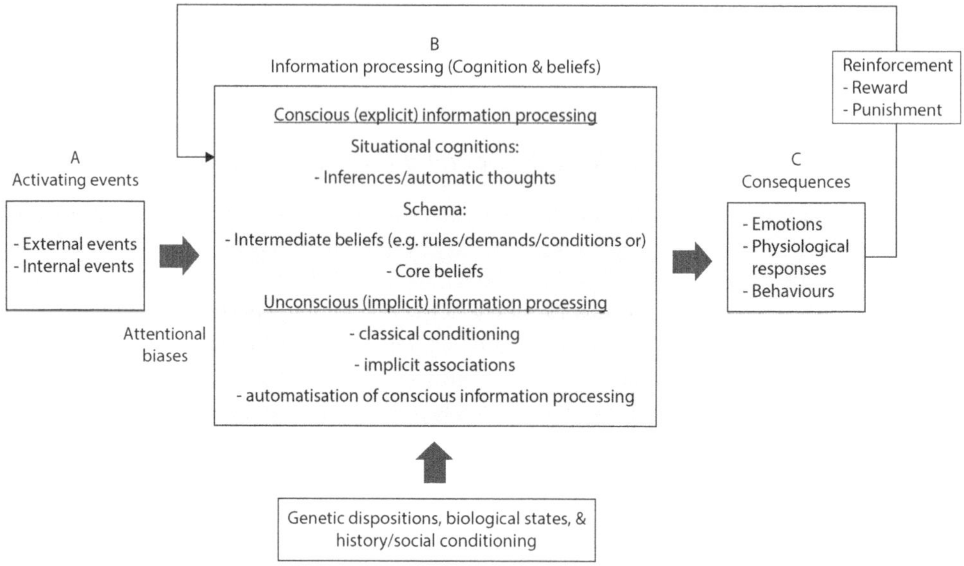

FIGURE 1.2 General CBT information processing (ABC) model. (Based on David et al., 2010.)

consolidated to the degree that they can become automatic and unconscious (Fabio et al., 2019). This is based on natural processes that help to make other repeated processes faster and more efficient. Consequently, people develop habitual ways of interpreting and responding to events that are embedded in relatively stable cognitive structures, often termed schema (Beck, 2015) (Figure 1.2).

These schemas are the individual's central beliefs about themself, others, and the world around them. They include core-evaluations that the individual holds. They then influence how individuals perceive events in their lives, giving rise to interpretations of specific events. They can also influence the individual's attentional focus in response to a situation (e.g., an individual that is anxious about making mistakes may be automatically disposed to attending to mistakes they make, regardless of the severity of the mistake). Thus, schema are responsible for the selection and interpretation of incoming data, providing the basis for personality (Beck, 2015; Ellis, 1994b). Further to this, schema can also contribute to biases in memory processes, both in terms of the consolidation of certain memories and the ability to recall memories (Beck & Haigh, 2014).

While these responses may be to events in the external world, it is also important to note that through the awareness of one's own responses, these can themselves become new activating events that the individual will process and respond to, based on underlying schema. These secondary processes, which include meta-cognitions and meta-emotions, govern how the individual relates to their own internal processes and can reinforce the initial response that was experienced (David & Freeman, 2015; Ellis, 1994b; Hayes et al., 2011; Wells, 2009).

The conscious systems can then be applied in a reflective manner to these habitual response sets. Typically, individuals will employ this reflective system in a way that leads to the conscious reinforcement of their existing habits. Thus, while people may often develop their beliefs during their early years, such beliefs are then maintained by ongoing information processing that provides further learning that reinforces the existing beliefs. However, this reflective system also provides the potential for change, when it can be applied in ways that contribute to the inhibition of the existing response sets and to the development of new learning and the practice of new response sets.

Psychopathology

Based on the model of human functioning described above, cognitive-behavioural theory tends not to view psychopathology as being based on inherently abnormal processes. Rather, it views psychopathology as being the result of the inappropriate application of a normal process to a context for which it is not well-suited, thereby resulting in dysfunctional outcomes (Beck & Haigh, 2014; Hayes et al., 1999).

A primary factor considered to contribute to much dysfunction is the use of rigid thinking patterns. Within cognitive-behavioural models, these rigid thought processes have been labelled as demand cognitions (Ellis, 1962), conditional assumptions (Beck & Haigh, 2014), and as rule governance (Hayes et al., 1999). While these simple mental heuristics are recognised as being normal and may have benefits in an imminent survival context, promoting speed of response (e.g., quickly activating an avoidant reaction if a car is about to run you over), they tend to be overly simplistic and sacrifice contextual information (LeDoux, 2019). It is due to the insensitivity of these cognitions to context and change that they result in less functional outcomes. Such rigid thought patterns are identified by the use of absolutistic language that includes "shoulds", "musts", "needs", "have tos", "ought to", "rules", "if ......then", and "unless .... then" statements (Beck & Haigh, 2014; Ellis, 1994b; Horney, 1950).

These rigid thought processes are also considered to be tightly linked to negative core beliefs and to drive further dysfunction as they tend to act as a subsequent block to acceptance of the self, others, and life more generally (Ellis, 2003; Hayes, 2004b). Along with this, negative core beliefs are thought to contribute to further cognitive issues that include negative biases, overgeneralised conclusions (including denigration and over identification/fusion), self-fulfilling prophecies, low frustration tolerance, rumination, and worry (Alloy et al., 2000; Beck, 2020; Cross et al., 2021; Ellis, 2003; Hayes et al., 1999; Koerner et al., 2015; Robinson & Alloy, 2003; Szentagotai et al., 2005). Behaviourally, they have also been linked to inflexible patterns that block adaptation and emotionally they have been shown to contribute to distress (Ellis, 2003; Hayes, 2004b). For instance, a person who believes they must always succeed at tasks they take on may view themselves as a failure in an overgeneralised manner if they fail to achieve a desired outcome, may worry about failing prior to an event, and may ruminate over experiences where they have failed a task. They may then avoid reminders of the event or engage in unhelpful forms of self-punishment that prevent them from effectively learning from the incident.

However, it is also important to note that the context within which such cognitions occur is also of consequence for the experience of dysfunction. This is at times described in terms of the level of belief the person holds in a cognition (Beck, 2020), and/or the way in which the person relates to it (Fletcher & Hayes, 2005; Hayes, 2004b). For instance, Beck (2015) notes that the level of belief in a dysfunctional cognition influences the level of dysfunction that it will promote. Thus, if a person experiences a dysfunctional cognition but views it as merely a spurious and fleeting event, it would not be expected to drive dysfunction. If instead they believe the thought (i.e., perceiving subjective thoughts as a statement of fact) or judge the experience of the cognition itself as "good" or "bad", these processes will turn the cognition into more than a fleeting mental event and will empower it to drive dysfunction. This also implies that dysfunctional cognitions do not occur in isolation and will also occur within the context of further dysfunction, be that emotional or behavioural (Collard, 2019a). Hence, a self-deprecating thought that is not held as a truth and is experienced in a humorous context would not typically be viewed as pathological, whereas the same self-deprecating thought when viewed as a truth and associated with depressed mood and behavioural withdrawal would be considered to be dysfunctional.

As noted above, occurring along with the activation of distressing emotional experiences tend to be behavioural urges to act in particular ways. For instance, anxiety will often be accompanied by safety behaviours (e.g., reassurance seeking, checking, distraction, avoidance, hypervigilance, escape, and rituals; Beck & Haigh, 2014; Pittig et al., 2018), anger will be accompanied with aggressive behavioural drives (Cox & Harrison, 2008), and depression with behavioural drives to withdraw (Beck & Bredemeier, 2016). While such behaviours often provide some short-term relief or gratification in their expression, these behavioural responses tend to strengthen the dysfunctional system in the longer term. Such behaviours are suggested to provide for an initial de-energisation of the dysfunctional schema, but prevent the individual from gaining new learning that would inhibit activation of the schema, instead reinforcing the schema and its underlying neurological processes (Beck & Haigh, 2014; Bushman, 2002; Craske et al., 2014; Swerdlow et al., 2020).

As noted previously, secondary processes can then be activated to further complicate the experience of dysfunction. This means that not only do people have a tendency to apply these dysfunctional responses to external stimuli but also to internal stimuli (i.e., thoughts, feelings, sensations). As a result, they often try to solve dysfunction with further dysfunction. This was highlighted by Ellis, who noted that individuals can lack acceptance for their imperfect internal experiences, and that this can act as a maintaining factor for dysfunction (David & Freeman, 2015; Ellis, 1987). This can include when people become depressed about being depressed, judging themselves negatively for such experiences (Ellis, 1987), or when they get anxious about feeling anxious, triggering panic attacks (Clark, 1986), or feel anxious and judge themselves for intrusive thoughts, contributing to obsessive-compulsive patterns (Myers & Wells, 2005), or try to avoid memories of traumatic events (Ehlers & Clark, 2000). In particular, efforts to control thoughts, memories, and emotions for the purpose of suppressing and avoiding them are accepted as having a paradoxical effect that over time increases their frequency and intensity, resulting in greater levels of dysfunction (Dimeff & Linehan, 2001; Hayes et al., 2013; Wells, 2009). This avoidance of unpleasant internal experiences is often considered to be the result of perfectionistic demands with regard to the individual's own functioning, and it has been noted that such beliefs can result in the awfulizing of emotional experiences, negative self-evaluations, negative beliefs about one's ability to cope with such experiences, and a lack of self-acceptance (Beck et al., 1992; Ellis, 1987; Myers & Wells, 2005).

CBT Interventions

Theory of Change

Based on the cognitive-behavioural understanding of human functioning, the focus of intervention is not simply just on helping people to feel better in the moment, but is instead to help them to become more functional (Ellis, 2003). Such interventions generally address either attention control, behavioural choices, deliberate reasoning, or a combination of these (Beck & Haigh, 2014). From a theoretical perspective, cognitive change is considered to be a primary focus of intervention to increase mental flexibility, thereby allowing for effective adaptation to life challenges. It is proposed that by changing cognitive content and/or cognitive processes, related emotional and behavioural responses will then be changed. However, the model also recognises that by changing behavioural responses, reinforcement processes that maintain dysfunction can be broken and new learning can be provided that promotes cognitive and emotional changes, promoting more adaptive functioning in the longer term (Craske et al., 2014; Ellis, 2003; Hofmann et al., 2013). From a neurological perspective, these strategies can be seen to utilise the aspects of psychological functioning that are considered to be under the control of the conscious mind. Typically, they engage the frontal cortex in a top-down manner to either upregulate or downregulate other psychological processes that are contributing to dysfunction from other parts of the brain (Brown et al., 2021; Hofmann et al., 2013; Pittig et al., 2018).

It is also important to note that this model of change not only emphasises the role of new insight and learning as a requirement for change, but also the application of reinforcement processes to strengthen and maintain such change. As such, cognitive-behavioural change requires the active participation of the individual to place effort into working to inhibit dysfunctional ways of operating and to practice more functional patterns, which can in turn provide experiential learning (Beck, 2020; Ellis, 1994b; Hayes et al., 1999; Wells, 2009). Through such efforts, the neural mechanisms underpinning these changes are consolidated and reinforced, promoting greater automaticity of the new cognitive, emotional, and behavioural patterns (Boswell, 2013; Craske et al., 2014; Davis et al., 2017). Without such efforts at reinforcement, the chance of experiencing a resurgence in the older dysfunctional patterns is increased (Craske et al., 2014; Pittig et al., 2018).

Cognitive Interventions

A key cognitive strategy to empower clients to be able to manage themselves better over time is psycho-education. A major goal of CBT is to help clients to better understand themselves so that they can be more functional (Beck, 2020). This can be on any area that may be relevant to their current difficulties, including the provision of information on cognitive-behavioural theory, on models of particular problems or disorders, on the rationale behind interventions, on the evolutionary and biological nature of emotions, on health behaviours, and on the influence of substances.

Self-reflection is also cultivated through a variety of strategies to increase self-awareness and insight for individuals, so that they can be mindfully aware of their responses (Boswell, 2013). This can include the use of self-monitoring exercises, reflective journaling, guided discovery, and mindfulness exercises.

Once these bring to light unhelpful cognitions or cognitive processes, other interventions may be applied to alter these. One key intervention here is known as cognitive restructuring (Beck, 2020), but can also be called disputing (Ellis, 1994b) and acceptance interventions (Hayes et al., 1999). While there may be differences in how directly these identify problematic beliefs, a primary focus of these techniques is to help individuals to challenge their rigid thinking patterns and to develop acceptance (Collard, 2019a). They can also be applied to address other, related, problematic cognitions, such as catastrophising, all-or nothing thinking, labelling/fusion, negative predictions, personalising, cognitive biases, and absolutes (Beck, 2020; Ellis, 2003; Hayes et al., 1999). Such discussions can involve empirical, pragmatic, logical, and values based/philosophical challenges to highlight issues with these cognitions. They may also be delivered in a variety of manners, including the didactic provision of information, through Socratic dialogues, through the use of metaphors, through imaginal techniques, and through the use of humour.

Other techniques that address cognitive processes, in terms of how the client may relate to their beliefs, include cognitive distancing techniques, affect labelling, and deliteralisation techniques. Cognitive distancing techniques may include phrasing of statements to reduce over identification with a thought (e.g., rephrasing the statement "I'm a failure" to "I'm having a thought that I'm a failure") or the externalising of cognitions to a symbolic entity (e.g., a dark cloud representing the individual's depression). Affect labelling is when the individual puts language to their emotional experiences. These two strategies are thought to work by requiring the individual to "step outside" of their experience and reflect on it, rather than being immersed by it (Ayduk & Kross, 2010; Powers & LaBar, 2019; Torre & Lieberman, 2018). Similarly, deliteralisation strategies, or defusion, can be used when an individual has a strong emotional reaction to a particular cognition. This involves them repeating the statement, and possibly changing the expression of it (e.g., singing it, saying it in a silly voice). By changing the context in which the cognition is experienced, the association to the emotional reaction is thought to be altered (Orsillo et al., 2016).

Value-based interventions are also common to CBT. This can involve assessment and establishment of key values for individuals, using values to give direction and set goals, and the questioning of the alignment between an individual's decision-making and their values. This focus on values can assist with the development of purpose and meaning, helping individuals to accept discomfort and adversity (Ellis, 2003; Hayes et al., 1999). It is also consistent with the development of recent interventions for savouring positive experiences and aspects of life, which are thought to help reduce negative biases and to help cultivate more positive emotional experiences (Bryant & Veroff, 2007; Craske et al., 2019).

Behavioural Interventions

Emotionally driven behaviours often include withdrawal, avoidance, and unhelpful coping strategies that act to maintain dysfunctional cycles. Consequently, behavioural interventions are important to breaking these cycles. A prominent area of focus for this is often behavioural activation (BA). This can start simply with goal setting for activities but can develop in complexity with graded task assignment being used to set activities of increasing challenge or activity scheduling being used to add more structure for planning of behaviours (Farmer & Chapman, 2016; Papageorgiou & Wells, 2008). These more advanced strategies also tend to involve detailed planning of the activities to manage possible barriers and can be paired with reflections on the satisfaction taken from the task and on the emotion experienced in relation to it (Beck, 2020).

Behavioural experiments and exposure interventions are also commonly used as a method of hypothesis testing and as a method for experientially gaining and reinforcing new learning (Craske et al., 2014; Hofmann et al., 2013). Particularly for anxiety, these interventions are considered an important method for reducing avoidance and improving an individual's ability to tolerate emotional discomfort. This helps to reduce the focus and importance given to such emotional experiences and to promote acceptance of uncomfortable internal experiences while engaging in behaviours that help the individual to function in a way that is more adaptive and meaningful for them (Beck & Haigh, 2014; Ellis, 1994b; Harley, 2015). For instance, exposure interventions have the individual deliberately approach the trigger for their anxiety to test whether the feared outcome will eventuate and/or whether they can cope with the experience (e.g., a person with a fear of heights going up a tall building to test how safe the situation is and their ability to cope with the related anxiety).

The development of skills for coping with challenging situations can also be important to improve functionality. Skills training activities can relate to problem-solving, planning, communication, effective use of body language, management of attention, and arousal control (Hofmann, 2007; Linehan, 1993b; Speed et al., 2018; Wells, 2009). Such interventions are employed to help individuals to develop greater competency in managing interpersonal issues, to be more effective in their planning and time management, to be better at managing impulsivity, and to cope more effectively with high levels of distress. For instance, problem-solving strategies may include conflict resolution skills, communication strategies may include assertiveness training, and body language skills may include shaping exercises to work on eye contact.

Arousal control strategies can be quite varied. These can include relaxation training strategies, diaphragmatic breathing, grounding techniques, and mindfulness interventions. These exercises can also at times be used as a form of attention training. Such techniques typically have a focus on bringing awareness into the present, helping the individual to disengage from intrusive and repetitive cognitive processes, including worry and rumination, especially when paired with ideas of acceptance for such internal processes (Cayoun, 2011; Fletcher & Hayes, 2005; Segal et al., 2002; Wells, 2009). Some also directly influence functioning of the autonomic nervous system, which can help with self-calming and to mitigate hyperarousal of the stress response, promoting improved biological functioning and performance (Hopper et al., 2019; Ma et al., 2017; McCraty & Childre, 2010). However, it is important to note these strategies can at times be counter indicated, as they may provide methods of avoidance or could heighten attentional biases that could maintain dysfunction (Baer et al., 2019; Taylor, 2001).

Empirical Support

Cognitive-behavioural therapy is currently the most extensively studied form of psychological therapy. This has found support both for its theory and its practice. The underlying premise of CBT, being that cognitions drive emotional responses, is perhaps the best supported theory in the field of psychology (David & Cristea, 2018; Hofmann et al., 2013), also being consistent with cognitive research paradigms, including Goss' emotion processing theory (Ford & Gross, 2018; Gross, 1998). The proposed models of dysfunction have also received consistent support for a range of psychologically dysfunctional factors and reinforcement processes at both clinical and sub-clinical levels (e.g., Deffenbacher et al., 2000; Gagnon et al., 2013; Himle et al., 1989; Oltean & David, 2018; Pittig et al., 2018; Vîslă et al., 2016; Zettle & Hayes, 1982). Cognitive-behavioural models of particular disorders and clinical presentations are also typically well-supported, explaining how such difficulties are developed and maintained (e.g., Ehlers & Clark, 2000; Hofmann, 2007; Myers & Wells, 2005; Taylor et al., 2010).

In terms of support for the proposed mechanisms of change, there is a strong level of support for processes of cognitive change in promoting improved emotional and behavioural functioning (Cristea et al., 2015; Dobson, 2013; Hofmann & Hayes, 2018; Papageorgiou & Wells, 2008), and for the role of behavioural strategies in also helping to create or reinforce functional improvements (Ahmed & Lawn, 2012; Craske et al., 2014; Ekers et al., 2008; Farmer & Chapman, 2016). While there is disparity in the support for particular cognitive-behavioural approaches to the treatment of disorders (e.g., greater support of CT programs than for ACT programs; David et al., 2018), the collective research supports the use of cognitive-behavioural interventions for helping people to learn to manage mental health disorders, psychological difficulties, health conditions (Beck & Haigh, 2014; Butler et al., 2006; Cuijpers et al., 2013; Hofmann et al., 2012; Linardon et al., 2017; Olatunji et al., 2013), and to improve mental wellbeing (van Agteren et al., 2021). In recent years, cognitive-behavioural interventions have also been associated with positive neurological and anatomical changes in brain functioning associated with psychological difficulties (Collerton, 2013; Hofmann et al., 2013; Månsson et al., 2016; Porto et al., 2009).

Despite the success of the cognitive-behavioural theories and practices to date, its scientific orientation towards understanding human functioning is ever evolving. It provides a framework that allows for the integration of a diverse range of psychological fields (e.g., learning theory, cognitive science, evolutionary psychology, neuropsychology, clinical psychology) to develop a unified psychological model of human functioning (Beck & Haigh, 2014; David & Cristea, 2018; Hofmann & Hayes, 2018). It is hoped that with advances in understanding from such research programs that cognitive-behavioural technologies will be further developed to better target and address issues of human functioning.

Conclusions

Cognitive-behavioural therapy has emerged as a psychological science since the middle of the 20th century. It is based on a constructivist philosophy that overlaps with a number of prominent philosophical traditions. This has given rise to a school of psychological therapies to help people with managing distress and enhancing their functioning. These therapies can be drawn together based on their underlying theory, which all propose a cognitive mediation model. These propose that cognitions and cognitive processes have a primary role in the generation of emotional and behavioural outcomes for individuals. Learning and reinforcement models are also highlighted within the CBT framework, to explain how habitual processes are developed and maintained, often giving rise to cyclical interactions between cognitions, emotions, and behaviours. It applies a scientific model of enquiry to the investigation of these and to understand how they influence human functioning. Common factors identified as giving rise to dysfunction are rigidity in cognitions and cognitive processes and emotionally driven behaviours that are incongruent with the pursuit of longer-term goals. Functionality is instead considered to be based upon a philosophy of acceptance, which allows for flexibility in the application of cognitive processes and behaviours to promote adaptation to situations. Frequently used strategies within this framework include psycho-education, cognitive restructuring, goal setting, BA, exposure interventions, and skills training exercises. CBT has now become the most empirically supported model of human functioning, both in terms of its underlying theory and its models of change. Its framework also provides opportunities for the further advancement in the understanding of human functioning.

References

Adler, A. (1932). *The Practice and Theory of Individual Psychology*. K. Paul, Trench, Trubner & Co. Ltd. Retrieved from http://books.google.com.au/books?id=NmBfyet9cK0C

Ahmed, N. Y., & Lawn, S. (2012). Does starting with the behavioural component of cognitive behavioural therapy (CBT) increase patients' retention in therapy? *Behaviour Change, 29*(4), 238–257. https://doi.org/DOI: 10.1017/bec.2012.23

Alloy, L. B., Abramson, L. Y., Hogan, M. E., Whitehouse, W. G., Rose, D. T., Robinson, M. S., ... Lapkin, J. B. (2000). The Temple-Wisconsin cognitive vulnerability to depression project: Lifetime history of Axis I psychopathology in individuals at high and low cognitive risk for depression. *Journal of Abnormal Psychology, 109*(3), 403–418. https://doi.org/10.1037/0021-843X.109.3.403

Arch, J. J., Eifert, G. H., Davies, C., Plumb Vilardaga, J. C., Rose, R. D., Craske, M. G., ... Craske, M. G. (2012). Randomized clinical trial of cognitive behavioral therapy (CBT) versus acceptance and commitment therapy (ACT) for mixed anxiety disorders. *Journal of Consulting and Clinical Psychology, 80*(5), 750–765. https://doi.org/10.1037/a0028310

Ayduk, Ö., & Kross, E. (2010). From a distance: Implications of spontaneous self-distancing for adaptive self-reflection. *Journal of Personality and Social Psychology, 98*(5), 809–829. https://doi.org/10.1037/a0019205

Baer, R., Crane, C., Miller, E., & Kuyken, W. (2019). Doing no harm in mindfulness-based programs: Conceptual issues and empirical findings. *Clinical Psychology Review, 71*(March 2018), 101–114. https://doi.org/10.1016/j.cpr.2019.01.001

Bandura, A. (1969). Social learning of moral judgments. *Journal of Personality and Social Psychology, 11*(3), 275–279. https://doi.org/10.1037/h0026998

Barlow, D. H., Farchione, T. J., Fairholme, C. P., Ellard, K. K., Boisseau, C. L., Allen, L. B., & Ehrenreich-May, J. (2011). *Unified Protocol for Transdiagnostic Treatment of Emotional Disorders: Therapist Guide*. Oxford University Press.

Beck, A. T. (1963). Thinking and depression: I. Idiosyncratic content and cognitive distortions. *Archives of General Psychiatry, 9*, 324–333. https://doi.org/10.1001/archpsyc.1963.01720160014002

Beck, A. T. (1967). *Depression: Clinical, Experimental, and Theoretical Aspects*. Harper and Row.

Beck, A. T. (2015). Theory of personality disorders. In A. T. Beck, D. D. Davis, & A. Freeman (Eds.), *Cognitive Therapy of Personality Disorders* (3rd ed., pp. 19–62). Guilford Press.

Beck, A. T. (2019). A 60-year evolution of cognitive theory and therapy. *Perspectives on Psychological Science, 14*(1), 16–20. https://doi.org/10.1177/1745691618804187

Beck, J. S. (2020). *Cognitive Behavior Therapy: Basics and Beyond* (3rd ed.). Guilford Press. https://doi.org/10.1017/CBO9781107415324.004

Beck, A. T., & Bredemeier, K. (2016). A unified model of depression: Integrating clinical, cognitive, biological, and evolutionary perspectives. *Clinical Psychological Science, 4*(4), 596–619. https://doi.org/10.1177/2167702616628523

Beck, A. T., & Haigh, E. A. P. (2014). Advances in cognitive theory and therapy: The generic cognitive model. *Annual Review of Clinical Psychology, 10*, 1–24. https://doi.org/10.1146/annurev-clinpsy-032813-153734

Beck, A. T., Sokol, L., Clark, D. A., Berchick, R., & Wright, F. (1992). A crossover study of focused cognitive therapy for panic disorder. *American Journal of Psychiatry, 149*(6), 778–783. https://doi.org/10.1176/ajp.149.6.778

Boswell, J. F. (2013). Intervention strategies and clinical process in transdiagnostic cognitive-behavioral therapy. *Psychotherapy, 50*(3), 381–386. https://doi.org/10.1037/a0032157

Brown, V. M., Zhu, L., Solway, A., Wang, J. M., McCurry, K. L., King-Casas, B., & Chiu, P. H. (2021). Reinforcement learning disruptions in individuals with depression and sensitivity to symptom change following cognitive behavioral therapy. *JAMA Psychiatry, 78*(10), 1113–1122. https://doi.org/10.1001/jamapsychiatry.2021.1844

Bryant, F. B., & Veroff, J. (2007). Savoring: A new model of positive experience. *Savoring: A New Model of Positive Experience*. Lawrence Erlbaum Associates Publishers.

Bushman, B. J. (2002). Does venting anger feed or extinguish the flame? Catharsis, rumination, distraction, anger, and aggressive responding. *Personality and Social Psychology Bulletin, 28*(6), 724–731. https://doi.org/10.1177/0146167202289002

Buss, D. M. (1995). Evolutionary psychology: A new paradigm for psychological science. *Psychological Inquiry, 6*(1), 1–30. https://doi.org/10.1207/s15327965pli0601_1

Butler, A. C., Chapman, J. E., Forman, E. M., & Beck, A. T. (2006). The empirical status of cognitive-behavioral therapy: A review of meta-analyses. *Clinical Psychology Review, 26*(1), 17–31. https://doi.org/10.1016/j.cpr.2005.07.003

Cayoun, B. A. (2011). *Mindfulness-Integrated CBT: Principles and Practice.* John Wiley & Sons Inc, https://doi.org/10.1002/9781119993162

Clark, D. M. (1986). A cognitive approach to panic. *Behaviour Research and Therapy, 24*(4), 461–470. https://doi.org/10.1016/0005-7967(86)90011-2

Collard, J. J. (2019a). ACT vs CBT: An exercise in idiosyncratic language. *International Journal of Cognitive Therapy, 12*(2), 126–145. https://doi.org/10.1007/s41811-019-00043-9

Collard, J. J. (2019b). Conceptual confusion in psychological therapy: Towards a taxonomy of therapies. *Journal of Rational - Emotive and Cognitive - Behavior Therapy, 37*(4), 325–337. https://doi.org/10.1007/s10942-019-00313-7

Collerton, D. (2013). Psychotherapy and brain plasticity. *Frontiers in Psychology, 4*(September), 2–6. https://doi.org/10.3389/fpsyg.2013.00548

Cox, D. E., & Harrison, D. W. (2008). Models of anger: Contributions from psychophysiology, neuropsychology and the cognitive behavioral perspective. *Brain Structure & Function, 212*(5), 371–385. https://doi.org/10.1007/s00429-007-0168-7

Craske, M. G., Treanor, M., Conway, C., Zbozinek, T., & Vervliet, B. (2014). Maximizing exposure therapy: An inhibitory learning approach. *Behaviour Research and Therapy, 58*(310), 10–23. https://doi.org/10.1016/j.brat.2014.04.006

Craske, M. G., Treanor, M., Dour, H., Meuret, A., & Ritz, T. (2019). Positive affect treatment for depression and anxiety: A randomized clinical trial for a core feature of anhedonia. *Journal of Consulting and Clinical Psychology, 87*(5), 457–471. https://doi.org/10.1037/ccp0000396

Cristea, I. A., Kok, R. N., & Cuijpers, P. (2015). Efficacy of cognitive bias modification interventions in anxiety and depression: Meta-analysis. *The British Journal of Psychiatry, 206*(1), 7–16. https://doi.org/10.1192/bjp.bp.114.146761

Cross, B. J., Collard, J. J., & Levidi, M. D. C. (2021). Core self-evaluation, rumination and forgiveness as an influence on emotional distress. *Current Psychology,* (1997), 391–393. https://doi.org/10.1007/s12144-021-01628-4

Cuijpers, P., Berking, M., Andersson, G., Quigley, L., Kleiboer, A., & Dobson, K. S. (2013). A meta-analysis of cognitive-behavioural therapy for adult depression, alone and in comparison with other treatments. *The Canadian Journal of Psychiatry/La Revue Canadienne de Psychiatrie, 58*(7), 376–385.

David, D., & Cristea, I. (2018). The new great psychotherapy debate: Scientific integrated psychotherapy vs. plurality. Why cognitive-behavior therapy is the gold standard in psychotherapy and a platform for scientific integrated psychotherapy. *Journal of Evidence-Based Psychotherapies, 18*(2), 1–18. https://doi.org/10.24193/jebp.2018.2.11

David, D., & Freeman, A. (2015). Overview of cognitive-behavioral therapy of personality disorder. In A. T. Beck, D. D. Davis, & A. Freeman (Eds.), *Cognitive Therapy of Personality Disorders* (3rd ed., pp. 3–18). Guilford Press.

David, D., & Hofmann, S. G. (2013). Another error of Descartes? Implications for the "third wave" cognitive-behavioral therapy. *Journal of Cognitive and Behavioral Psychotherapies, 13*(1), 115–124.

David, D., Cotet, C. D., Szentagotai, A., McMahon, J., & Digiuseppe, R. (2013). Philosophical versus psychological unconditional acceptance: Implications for constructing the unconditional acceptance questionnaire. *Journal of Cognitive and Behavioral Psychotherapies, 13*(2 A), 445–464.

David, D., Lynn, S. J., & Ellis, A. (2010). Rational and irrational beliefs: A historical and conceptual perspective. In A. Ellis, D. David, & S. Lynn (Eds.), *Rational and Irrational Beliefs: Research, Theory, and Clinical Practice* (pp. 3–22). Oxford University Press.

David, D., Lynn, S. J., & Montgomery, G. H. (Eds.). (2018). Evidence-based psychotherapy: The state of the science and practice. *Evidence-Based Psychotherapy: The State of the Science and Practice.* Wiley-Blackwell.

Davis, M. L., Witcraft, S. M., Baird, S. O., & Smits, J. A. J. (2017). Learning principles in CBT. *The Science of Cognitive Behavioral Therapy.* Elsevier Academic Press. https://doi.org/10.1016/B978-0-12-803457-6.00003-9

Deffenbacher, J. L., Dahlen, E. R., Lynch, R. S., Morris, C. D., & Gowensmith, W. N. (2000). An application of Beck's Cognitive Therapy to general anger reduction. *Cognitive Therapy & Research, 24*(6), 689.

DiGiorgio, K. E., Glass, C. R., & Arnkoff, D. B. (2010). Therapists use of DBT: A survey study of clinical practice. *Cognitive and Behavioral Practice, 17*(2), 213–221. https://doi.org/10.1016/j.cbpra.2009.06.003

Dimeff, L., & Linehan, M. M. (2001). Dialectical behavior therapy in a nutshell. *The California Psychologist, 34*, 10–13.

Dobson, K. S. (2013). The science of CBT: Toward a metacognitive model of change? *Behavior Therapy, 44*(2), 224–227. https://doi.org/10.1016/j.beth.2009.08.003

Donegan, E., & Dugas, M. J. (2012). Generalized anxiety disorder: A comparison of symptom change in adults receiving cognitive-behavioral therapy or applied relaxation. *Journal of Consulting and Clinical Psychology, 80*(3), 490–496. https://doi.org/10.1037/a0028132

Ehlers, A., & Clark, D. M. (2000). A cognitive model of posttraumatic stress disorder. *Behaviour Research and Therapy.* https://doi.org/10.1016/S0005-7967(99)00123-0

Ekers, D., Richards, D., & Gilbody, S. (2008). A meta-analysis of randomized trials of behavioural treatment of depression. *Psychological Medicine, 38*(5), 611–623. https://doi.org/DOI: 10.1017/S0033291707001614

Ellis, A. (1955). New approaches to psychotherapy techniques. *Journal of Clinical Psychology, 11*(3), 207–260.

Ellis, A. (1962). *Reason and Emotion in Psychotherapy. Reason and Emotion in Psychotherapy.* Lyle Stuart.

Ellis, A. (1987). The impossibility of achieving consistently good mental health. *American Psychologist, 42*(4), 364–375. https://doi.org/10.1037/0003-066X.42.4.364

Ellis, A. (1994a). Post-traumatic stress disorder (PTSD): A rational emotive behavioral theory. *Journal of Rational-Emotive & Cognitive-Behavior Therapy, 12*(1), 3–25. https://doi.org/10.1007/BF02354487

Ellis, A. (1994b). *Reason and Emotion in Psychotherapy. Reason and Emotion in Psychotherapy.* Carol Publishing Group.

Ellis, A. (2003). Similarities and differences between rational emotive behavior therapy and cognitive therapy. *Journal of Cognitive Psychotherapy, 17*(3), 225–240. https://doi.org/10.1891/jcop.17.3.225.52535

Ellis, A. (2005a). Can rational-emotive behavior therapy (REBT) and acceptance and commitment therapy (ACT) resolve their differences and be integrated? *Journal of Rational-Emotive & Cognitive-Behavior Therapy, 23*(2), 153–168. https://doi.org/10.1007/s10942-005-0008-8

Ellis, A. (2005b). Rational emotive behavior therapy. In R. J. Corsini & D. Wedding (Eds.), *Current Psychotherapies.* Brooks/Cole: Thomson Learning.

Ellis, A., & MacLaren, C. (1998). *Rational Emotive Behavior Therapy : A Therapist's Guide.* Impact Publishers.

Fabio, R. A., Caprì, T., & Romano, M. (2019). From controlled to automatic processes and back again: The role of contextual features. *Europe's Journal of Psychology, 15*(4), 773–788. https://doi.org/10.5964/ejop.v15i4.1746

Farmer, R. F., & Chapman, A. L. (2016). *Behavioral Interventions in Cognitive Behavior Therapy: Practical Guidance for Putting Theory into Action* (2nd ed). American Psychological Association. https://doi.org/10.1037/14691-000

Fletcher, L., & Hayes, S. C. (2005). Relational frame theory, acceptance and commitment therapy, and a functional analytic definition of mindfulness. *Journal of Rational-Emotive and Cognitive-Behavior Therapy, 23*(4), 315–336. https://doi.org/10.1007/s10942-005-0017-7

Ford, B. Q., & Gross, J. J. (2018). Emotion regulation: Why beliefs matter. *Canadian Psychology/ Psychologie Canadienne, 59*(1), 1–14. https://doi.org/10.1037/cap0000142

Gagnon, J., Daelman, S., & McDuff, P. (2013). Correlations of impulsivity with dysfunctional beliefs associated with borderline personality. *North American Journal of Psychology, 15*(1), 167–178.

Gibb, B. E., Butler, A. C., & Beck, J. S. (2003). Childhood abuse, depression, and anxiety in adult psychiatric outpatients. *Depression and Anxiety, 17*(4), 226–228. https://doi.org/10.1002/da.10111

Gilbert, P. (2019). Psychotherapy for the 21st century: An integrative, evolutionary, contextual, biopsychosocial approach. *Psychology and Psychotherapy, 92*(2), 164–189. https://doi.org/10.1111/papt.12226

Gross, J. J. (1998). The emerging field of emotion regulation: An integrative review. *Review of General Psychology, 2*(3), 271–299. https://doi.org/10.1037/1089-2680.2.3.271

Harley, J. (2015). Bridging the gap between Cognitive Therapy and Acceptance and Commitment Therapy (ACT). *Procedia - Social and Behavioral Sciences, 193*, 131–140. https://doi.org/10.1016/j.sbspro.2015.03.252

Harris, R. (2008). *The Happiness Trap: How to Stop Struggling and Start Living*. Trumpeter.

Hayes, S. C. (2004a). Acceptance and commitment therapy, relational frame theory, and the third wave of behavioral and cognitive therapies. *Behavior Therapy, 35*(4), 639–665. https://doi.org/10.1016/S0005-7894(04)80013-3

Hayes, S. C. (2004b). Acceptance and commitment therapy and the new behavior therapies: Mindfulness, acceptance, and relationship. *Mindfulness and Acceptance. Expanding the Cognitive-Behavioral Tradition* (pp. 1–30). Guilford Press.

Hayes, S. C., Follette, V. M., & Linehan, M. M. (2011). *Mindfulness and Acceptance: Expanding the Cognitive-Behavioral Tradition*. Guilford Press. Retrieved from http://dx.doi.org/10.1002/erv.665

Hayes, S. C., Levin, M. E., Plumb-Vilardaga, J., Villatte, J. L., & Pistorello, J. (2013). Acceptance and commitment therapy and contextual behavioral science: Examining the progress of a distinctive model of behavioral and cognitive therapy. *Behavior Therapy, 44*(2), 180–198. https://doi.org/10.1016/j.beth.2009.08.002

Hayes, S. C., Strosahl, K. D., & Wilson, K. G. (1999). *Acceptance and Commitment Therapy: An Experiential Approach to Behavior Change*. Guilford Press.

Herbert, J. D., & Forman, E. M. (2013). Caution: The differences between CT and ACT may be larger (and smaller) than they appear. *Behavior Therapy, 44*(2), 218–223. https://doi.org/10.1016/j.beth.2009.09.005

Himle, J. A., Himle, D. P., & Thyer, B. A. (1989). Irrational beliefs and the anxiety disorders. *Journal of Rational Emotive Cognitive Behavior Therapy*, 7(3), 155–165. https://doi.org/10.1007/BF01076187

Hofmann, S. G. (2007). Cognitive factors that maintain social anxiety disorder: A comprehensive model and its treatment implications. *Cognitive Behavioural Therapy, 36*(4), 193–209.

Hofmann, S. G., Asmundson, G. J. G., & Beck, A. T. (2013). The science of cognitive therapy. *Behavior Therapy, 44*(2), 199–212. https://doi.org/10.1016/j.beth.2009.01.007

Hofmann, S. G., Asnaani, A., Vonk, I. J. J., Sawyer, A. T., & Fang, A. (2012). The Efficacy of cognitive behavioral therapy: A review of meta-analyses. *Cognitive Therapy and Research, 36*(5), 427–440. https://doi.org/10.1007/s10608-012-9476-1

Hofmann, S. G., & Hayes, S. C. (2018). The future of intervention science: Process-based therapy. *Clinical Psychological Science*, 7(1), 2167702618772296. https://doi.org/10.1177/2167702618772296

Hopper, S. I., Murray, S. L., Ferrara, L. R., & Singleton, J. K. (2019). Effectiveness of diaphragmatic breathing for reducing physiological and psychological stress in adults: A quantitative systematic review. *JBI Evidence Synthesis, 17*(9), 1855–1876.

Horney, K. (1950). *Neurosis and Human Growth; the Struggle toward Self-Realization. Neurosis and Human Growth; the Struggle toward Self-Realization*. W. W. Norton.

Kelly, G. (1955). *The Psychology of Personal Constructs*. Norton.

Koerner, N., Tallon, K., & Kusec, A. (2015). Maladaptive core beliefs and their relation to generalized anxiety disorder. *Cognitive Behaviour Therapy, 44*(6), 441–455. https://doi.org/10.1080/16506073.2015.1042989

Lazarus, A. A., et al. (1976). *Multimodal Behavior Therapy: I*. Springer.

Lazarus, R. S. (1984). On the primacy of cognition. *American Psychologist*. American Psychological Association. https://doi.org/10.1037/0003-066X.39.2.124

Leahy, R. (1996). *Cognitive-Behavioral Therapy : Basic Principles and Applications*. Jason Aronson.

LeDoux, J. (2019). *The Deep History of Ourselves: The Four-Billion-Year Story of How We Got Conscious Brains*. Viking.

Linardon, J., Wade, T. D., De La Piedad Garcia, X., & Brennan, L. (2017). The efficacy of cognitive-behavioral therapy for eating disorders: A systematic review and meta-analysis. *Journal of Consulting and Clinical Psychology, 85*(11), 1080–1094. https://doi.org/10.1037/ccp0000245

Linehan, M. M. (1993a). *Cognitive-Behavioral Treatment of Borderline Personality Disorder*. Guilford Press.

Linehan, M. M. (1993b). *Skills Training Manual for Treating Borderline Personality Disorder*. Guilford Press.

Losada, A., Márquez-González, M., Romero-Moreno, R., López, J., Fernández-Fernández, V., & Nogales-González, C. (2014). Cognitive behavioral therapy (CBT) versus acceptance and commitment therapy (ACT) for dementia family caregivers: Follow-up results of a randomized clinical trial. *European Geriatric Medicine, 5*, S46.

Ma, X., Yue, Z. Q., Gong, Z. Q., Zhang, H., Duan, N. Y., Shi, Y. T., ... Li, Y. F. (2017). The effect of diaphragmatic breathing on attention, negative affect and stress in healthy adults. *Frontiers in Psychology, 8*(June), 1–12. https://doi.org/10.3389/fpsyg.2017.00874

Mahoney, M. J. (1974). Cognition and behavior modification. *Cognition and Behavior Modification*. Ballinger.

Månsson, K. N. T., Salami, A., Frick, A., Carlbring, P., Andersson, G., Furmark, T., & Boraxbekk, C. J. (2016). Neuroplasticity in response to cognitive behavior therapy for social anxiety disorder. *Translational Psychiatry, 6*(July 2015), e727. https://doi.org/10.1038/tp.2015.218

McCraty, R., & Childre, D. (2010). Coherence: Bridging personal, social, and global health. *Alternative Therapies in Health and Medicine, 16*(4), 10–24.

Meichenbaum, D. (1977). *Cognitive-Behavior Modification : An Integrative Approach/by Donald Meichenbaum*. Plenum Press.

Mowrer, O. H. (1947). On the dual nature of learning—A re-interpretation of "conditioning" and "problem-solving". *Harvard Educational Review, 17*, 102–148.

Mowrer, O. H. (1956). Two-factor learning theory reconsidered, with special reference to secondary reinforcement and the concept of habit. *Psychological Review, 63*(2), 114–128. https://doi.org/10.1037/h0040613

Murguia, E., & Díaz, K. (2015). The philosophical foundations of cognitive behavioral therapy: Stoicism, Buddhism, Taoism, and existentialism. *Journal of Evidence-Based Psychotherapies, 15*(1), 37–50.

Myers, S. G., & Wells, A. (2005). Obsessive-compulsive symptoms: The contribution of metacognitions and responsibility. *Journal of Anxiety Disorders, 19*(7), 806–817. https://doi.org/10.1016/j.janxdis.2004.09.004

Nezu, C. M., & Nezu, A. M. (2016). Introduction. In C. M. Nezu & A. M. Nezu (Eds.), *The Oxford Handbook of Cognitive and Behavioral Therapies* (pp. 1–4). Oxford University Press.

O'Donohue, W. T., & Ferguson, K. E. (2016). Historical and philosophical dimensions of contemporary cognitive-behavioral therapy. In C. M. Nezu & A. M. Nezu (Eds.), *The Oxford Handbook of Cognitive and Behavioral Therapies* (pp. 7–27). Oxford University Press.

O'Kelly, M. (2020). *CBT in Action : Practitioner's Toolkit*, (3rd Editio). CBT Australia.

Olatunji, B. O., Davis, M. L., Powers, M. B., & Smits, J. A. J. (2013). Cognitive-behavioral therapy for obsessive-compulsive disorder: A meta-analysis of treatment outcome and moderators. *Journal of Psychiatric Research, 47*(1), 33–41. https://doi.org/10.1016/j.jpsychires.2012.08.020

Oltean, H.-R., & David, D. O. (2018). A meta-analysis of the relationship between rational beliefs and psychological distress. *Journal of Clinical Psychology, 74*(6), 883–895. https://doi.org/10.1002/jclp.22562

Orsillo, S. M., Danitz, S. B., & Roemer, L. (2016). Mindfulness- and acceptance-based cognitive and behavioral therapies. *The Oxford Handbook of Cognitive and Behavioral Therapies*. Oxford University Press.

Papageorgiou, C., & Wells, A. (2008). *Depressive Rumination: Nature, Theory and Treatment*. Wiley. https://doi.org/10.1002/9780470713853

Pavlov, I. P. (1927). *Conditioned Reflexes: An Investigation of the Physiological Activity of the Cerebral Cortex*. Oxford University Press.

Pittig, A., Treanor, M., LeBeau, R. T., & Craske, M. G. (2018). The role of associative fear and avoidance learning in anxiety disorders: Gaps and directions for future research. *Neuroscience and Biobehavioral Reviews, 88*(March), 117–140. https://doi.org/10.1016/j.neubiorev.2018.03.015

Porto, P. R., Oliveira, L., Mari, J., Volchan, E., Figueira, I., & Ventura, P. (2009). Does cognitive behavioral therapy change the brain? A systematic review of neuroimaging in anxiety disorders. *Journal of Neuropsychiatry and Clinical Neurosciences, 21*(2), 114–125. https://doi.org/10.1176/jnp.2009.21.2.114

Powers, J. P., & LaBar, K. S. (2019). Regulating emotion through distancing: A taxonomy, neurocognitive model, and supporting meta-analysis. *Neuroscience and Biobehavioral Reviews, 96*, 155–173. https://doi.org/10.1016/j.neubiorev.2018.04.023

Resick, P. A., Monson, C. M., & Chard, K. M. (2007). *Cognitive Processing Therapy: Veteran/Military Version*. Department of Veteran Affairs.

Robinson, M., & Alloy, L. (2003). Negative cognitive styles and stress-reactive rumination interact to predict depression: A prospective study. *Cognitive Therapy and Research, 27*(3), 275–292. https://doi.org/10.1023/A:1023914416469

Rosen, G. M., & Davison, G. C. (2003). Psychology should list empirically supported principles of change (ESPs) and not credential trademarked therapies or other treatment packages. *Behavior Modification, 27*(3), 300–312. https://doi.org/10.1177/0145445503253829

Ruggiero, G. M., Spada, M. M., Caselli, G., & Sassaroli, S. (2018). A historical and theoretical review of cognitive behavioral therapies: From structural self-knowledge to functional processes. *Journal of Rational - Emotive and Cognitive - Behavior Therapy, 36*(4), 378–403. https://doi.org/10.1007/s10942-018-0292-8

Sabucedo, P. (2019). Acceptance and commitment therapy (ACT) and humanistic psychotherapy: An integrative approximation. *British Journal of Guidance & Counselling, 49*(3), 347–361.

Schröder, A., Heider, J., Zaby, A., & Göllner, R. (2013). Cognitive behavioral therapy versus progressive muscle relaxation training for multiple somatoform symptoms: Results of a randomized controlled trial. *Cognitive Therapy and Research, 37*(2), 296–306. https://doi.org/10.1007/s10608-012-9474-3

Schwartz, O. S., Dudgeon, P., Sheeber, L. B., Yap, M. B. H., Simmons, J. G., & Allen, N. B. (2012). Parental behaviors during family interactions predict changes in depression and anxiety symptoms during adolescence. *Journal of Abnormal Child Psychology, 40*(1), 59–71. https://doi.org/10.1007/s10802-011-9542-2

Segal, Z. V, Williams, J. M. G., Teasdale, J. D., & Gemar, M. C. (2002). Mindfulness-based cognitive therapy for depression: A new approach to preventing relapse. *Clinical Psychology & Psychotherapy, 9*(2), 123–125. https://doi.org/10.1080/713869628

Skinner, B. F. (1938). *The Behavior of Organisms: An Experimental Analysis*. Appleton-Century.

Speed, B. C., Goldstein, B. L., & Goldfried, M. R. (2018). Assertiveness training: A forgotten evidence-based treatment. *Clinical Psychology: Science and Practice, 25*(1), 1–20. https://doi.org/10.1111/cpsp.12216

Swerdlow, B. A., Pearlstein, J. G., Sandel, D. B., Mauss, I. B., & Johnson, S. L. (2020). Maladaptive behavior and affect regulation: A functionalist perspective. *Emotion, 20*(1), 75–79. https://doi.org/10.1037/emo0000660

Szentagotai, A., Schnur, J., DiGuiseppe, R., Macavei, B., Eva, K., David, D., … David, D. (2005). The organization and the nature of irrational beliefs. *Journal of Cognitive and Behavioral Psychotherapies, 5*(2), 139–158.

Tarrier, N., & Johnson, J. (2016). Introduction. In *Case Formulation in Cognitive Behaviour Therapy: The Treatment of Challenging and Complex Cases* (2nd ed., pp. 1–13). Routledge/Taylor & Francis Group.

Taylor, S. (2001). Breathing retraining in the treatment of panic disorder: Efficacy, caveats and indications. *Scandinavian Journal of Behaviour Therapy, 30*(2), 49–56. https://doi.org/10.1080/02845710118895

Taylor, S., Coles, M. E., Abramowitz, J. S., Wu, K. D., Olatunji, B. O., Timpano, K. R., … Tolin, D. F. (2010). How are dysfunctional beliefs related to obsessive-compulsive symptoms? *Journal of Cognitive Psychotherapy, 24*(3), 165–176. https://doi.org/10.1891/0889-8391.24.3.165

Torre, J. B., & Lieberman, M. D. (2018). Putting feelings into words: Affect labeling as implicit emotion regulation. *Emotion Review, 10*(2), 116–124. https://doi.org/10.1177/1754073917742706

van Agteren, J., Iasiello, M., Lo, L., Bartholomaeus, J., Kopsaftis, Z., Carey, M., & Kyrios, M. (2021). A systematic review and meta-analysis of psychological interventions to improve mental wellbeing. *Nature Human Behaviour, 5*(5), 631–652. https://doi.org/10.1038/s41562-021-01093-w

Vîslă, A., Flückiger, C., Grosse Holtforth, M., & David, D. (2016). Irrational beliefs and psychological distress: A meta-analysis. *Psychotherapy and Psychosomatics, 85*(1), 8–15. https://doi.org/10.1159/000441231

Wells, A. (2009). *Metacognitive Therapy for Anxiety and Depression*. Guilford Press.

Wilson, G. T. (2005). Behavior therapy. In R. J. Corsini & D. Wedding (Eds.), *Current Psychotherapies* (pp. 202–237).Thomson Brooks/Cole Publishing Co.

Wolpe, J. (1958). *Psychotherapy by Reciprocal Inhibition*. Stanford University Press.

Young, J. E., Klosko, J. S., & Weishaar, M. E. (2003). *Schema Therapy: A Practitioner's Guide*. Guilford Press.

Zarbo, C., Tasca, G. A., Cattafi, F., & Compare, A. (2016). Integrative psychotherapy works. *Frontiers in Psychology, 6*(January), 2015–2017. https://doi.org/10.3389/fpsyg.2015.02021

Zettle, R., & Hayes, S. (1982). Rule-governed behavior: a potential theoretical framework for cognitive–behavioral therapy. *Advances in Cognitive–Behavioral Research and Therapy* (pp. 73–118). Academic Press Inc https://doi.org/10.1016/B978-0-12-010601-1.50008-5

2

ACCEPTANCE AND COMMITMENT THERAPY (ACT)

Peter Olusoga and Shameema Yousuf

Foundations of ACT

Acceptance and commitment therapy (ACT) is a "third-wave" behavioural therapy, based on relational frame theory (RFT; Hayes, 2004; Hayes et al., 2004) and grounded in functional contextualism (Hayes et al., 1988), which was first conceptualised and developed by Steven Hayes in the 1980s (Hayes & Brownstein, 1986; Zettle & Hayes, 1986). Zettle et al. (2016) provide detail on RFT and functional contextualism that goes beyond the scope of this chapter, yet it *is* important to acknowledge here that ACT has emerged from previous traditions in behavioural psychology.

Traditionally, applied sport psychology has drawn mostly from cognitive-behavioural approaches to psychotherapy (Turner et al., 2020). Using psychological "skills" such as self-talk, imagery, relaxation, and goal-setting, these cognitive-behavioural therapy (CBT)-based approaches seek to challenge unwanted "negative" thoughts, emotions, and sensations. Sports performers are taught strategies to help them reduce or eliminate "faulty" cognitions or undesirable internal experiences in pursuit of an "ideal" performance state (i.e., no anxiety, high self-confidence, relaxed, and thinking "positively").

Acceptance and commitment therapy, rooted in functional contextualism, proposes a different approach in that it is a philosophical approach in which thoughts, feelings, memories, and sensations that we might perceive to be "negative" are not actually problematic by definition. Instead, it is the way that they *function* in certain contexts that might be problematic. When an athlete can dispassionately observe a thought as nothing more than a mental event for example (i.e., cognitive defusion), rather than believe the thought within a particular context to be absolute truth (i.e., cognitive fusion), the particular thought is no longer a problem to be eradicated. The thought might still be unpleasant and unwanted, but it does not prevent the athlete from performing to their potential. More on cognitive fusion and defusion will be discussed later.

In applying ACT to sport and performance contexts, the goal of the work is to change the relationship that performers have with internal experiences of human suffering and not remove, replace, or lessen them. Changing the context in which the athlete experiences a

DOI: 10.4324/9781003162513-3

thought or feeling, from one of labelling it as a problem and attempting to avoid it to one of acceptance of it as a normal part of the human experience, changes the *function* of the thought or feeling, rather than the experience or event itself.

Mindfulness-acceptance-commitment approaches (MAC; Gardner & Moore, 2004; 2006) are well-established in sport and performance psychology research and practice. MAC models, derived from ACT, suggest that there is no "ideal" performance state to be achieved. This makes sense, given that individuals have reported optimal performance in a variety of cognitive, affective, and physiological states (Gardner & Moore, 2012). Rather, mindfulness-acceptance approaches contend that optimal performance requires:

a. a non-judgemental, moment-to-moment awareness and acceptance of one's internal state, whatever that may be;
b. an attentional focus on task-relevant external stimuli instead of a focus on internal processes that include judgement and direct efforts and control/modulation; and
c. a consistent and effortful personal values-driven commitment to behaviour actions/choices that support one's athletic endeavour

(Gardner & Moore, 2012).

Psychological Flexibility

At the core of ACT lies the notion of *psychological flexibility*. This refers to an individual's ability to stay in contact with all present moment experiences (rather than seeking to pursue pleasant or avoid unpleasant ones), and to choose behaviours that move them in a direction dictated by personal values. Six *core processes* underpin psychological flexibility: *cognitive defusion, acceptance, flexible attention to the present moment, self-as-context, values, and committed action* (see Hayes et al., 2012).

Each of the six processes is linked with each other process as per the "Hexaflex" (Hayes et al., 2006) depicted in Figure 2.1. The key to psychological flexibility therefore is to maintain an open, centred, and engaged response style where individuals can accept and make room for unpleasant thoughts, emotions, and sensations, by paying conscious attention to their present moment experiences, and staying connected to chosen values through daily life actions. Deficits in any of these six core processes can result in "psychological rigidity".

To take an example, an athlete might as well believe that getting rid of her anxious thought (that she is not good enough to compete at this level) would allow her to be more successful on the field, and so her goal for consultancy might therefore be anxiety reduction. She is unwilling to make room for her anxious thoughts, is avoidant of them, and therefore seeks to avoid the situations that usually elicit them. For example, she might seek instant relief from the discomfort experienced by withdrawing effort. However, the long-term consequences of withdrawing might be unfulfilled goal achievement, performance detriment, and longer-term feelings of disillusionment. Psychological rigidity and, thus, experiential avoidance, means the athlete is putting herself in a position where she is no longer pursuing chosen values that could potentially lead to a sense of happiness (Hayes, 2019), and is demonstrating poor decision-making, lack of engagement, and poor execution of tasks, all of which might all impede performance. A brief description of ACT core processes can be seen in Figure 2.2.

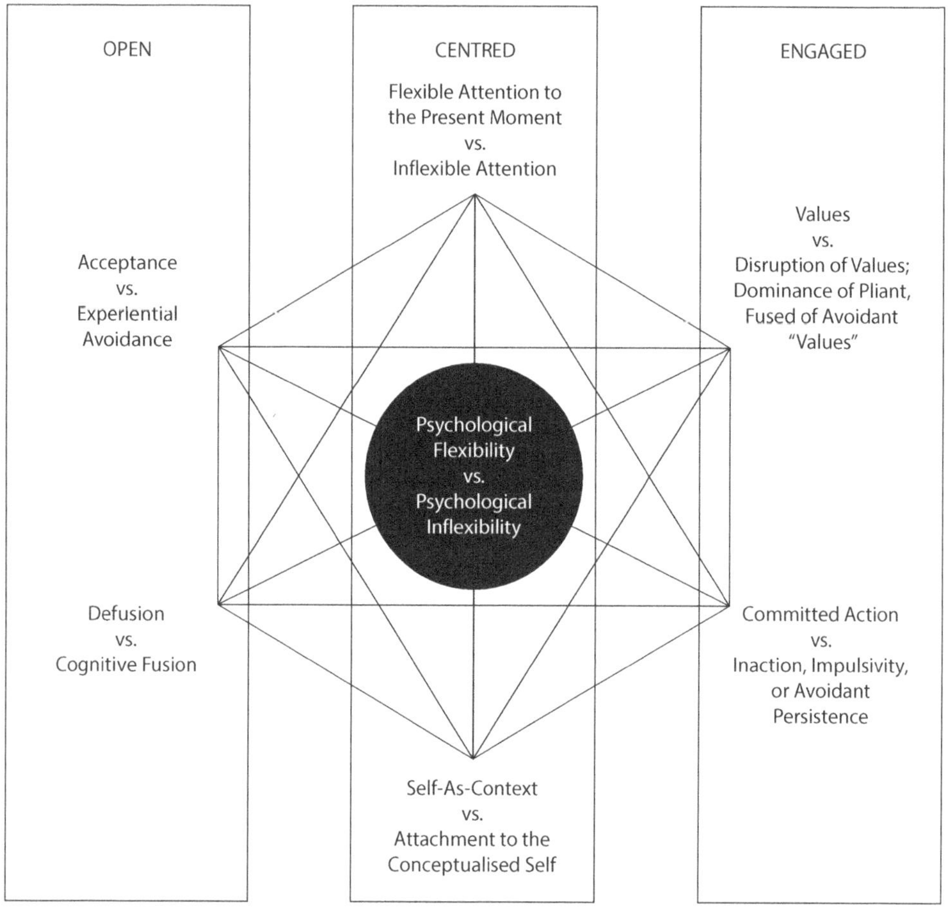

FIGURE 2.1 The Hexaflex model of ACT for psychological flexibility and inflexibility. (Adapted from Luoma et al., 2017.)

ACT-Based Intervention Research

Research evaluating the efficacy of traditional psychological skills training (PST) programmes is plentiful, but when scrutinised, there appears to be a lack of consistent, definitive evidence supporting the impact on performance outcomes (Birrer & Morgan, 2010; Gardner & Moore, 2004). Indeed, it has been posited that due to ironic processes of mental control (Wegner, 1994), suppression of "negative" cognitions and emotions shifts focus away from the task at hand (Gardner & Moore, 2012). Largely as a response to the limitations of PST, mindfulness and acceptance approaches in sport psychology have gained popularity since Gardner and Moore's (2001) application in performance contexts.

Mindfulness-based interventions (MBIs) in sport date as far back as 1985 when John Kabat-Zinn et al. (1985) offered mindfulness practice to optimise the performance of collegiate rowers. Other MBIs are also based heavily on mindful meditation, such as Kaufman et al.'s (2009) Mindful Sport Performance Enhancement (MSPE) programme and Baltzell and Akhtar's (2014) Mindfulness Meditation Training for Sport (MMTS) intervention. MAC approaches combine mindfulness practices and ACT by incorporating acceptance and commitment, and

- ***Cognitive defusion*** is the process by which an individual becomes aware of the automaticity of thoughts. They are able to let go of following and becoming entangled with their thoughts, and instead can merely observe them as mental events.
- ***Acceptance*** is the process of turning towards difficult thoughts, emotions, and sensations, and being open to experiencing them in a non-judgemental way, rather than seeking to escape from or avoid potential distressing content.
- ***Flexible attention to the present moment*** involves *mindful* focus to the here and now, as opposed to being pulled into the conceptualised past or worrying about what will happen in the future, thus allowing an individual to appreciate the full range of choices in front of them.
- ***Self as concept*** is unconcerned with ego and is instead about the individual focusing on what matters. It is viewed from the perspective of "I", *the transcendent self.* One is able to experience anxious thoughts and simply observe them in the here and now with awareness. This alleviates the need to lie or hide to protect one's self-esteem, or seek approval from others and one's own self-evaluation, which only gives rise to constructing stories to defend one's ego, *the conceptualised self.* While an individual's self-esteem is important, their quest for it in an effort to belong, may render them more pressured, stressed, anxious and less resilient to facing challenges (Hayes, 2019). Focusing on the transcendent self, frees and pivots the individual to greater connection by building a sense of healthy belonging and self.
- ***Values*** direct individuals to pursue activities that align with providing true meaning. Hayes (2019) suggests that individuals yearn for meaning and that when they are free to pick their life direction, they are self-directed and motivated.
- ***Committed action*** refers to the specific steps taken in specific moments (i.e., specific moment-to-moment *behaviours*) that move individuals in valued-directions.

FIGURE 2.2 Brief description of the ACT core processes.

values-driven behaviour. For clarity, although both ACT and MAC approaches incorporate mindfulness exercises, ACT is largely focused on improving psychological flexibility through six core processes, whereas MAC incorporates ACT techniques with a goal of enhancing performance and improving psychological wellbeing.

Several reviews have summarised the findings from MBI research in sport and performance contexts. Sappington and Longshore (2015), for example, carried out a systematic review of 19 MBI studies, including interventions based upon MAC and MSPE protocols. They concluded that the evidence was supportive of the idea that MBI's might "be effective in improving performance and characteristics associated with well-being (e.g., psychological flexibility, anxiety, flow)" (p. 256). Bühlmayer et al. (2017) conducted a meta-analysis exploring the effects of mindfulness practice, but only two of the studies included specifically examined MAC approaches. In another systematic review, Noetel et al. (2017) highlighted 66 studies that adopted mindfulness-acceptance approaches to sport performance, although again this review included studies that adopted mindfulness-only interventions, transcendental meditation, and self-compassion, with only a handful of the studies using ACT-specific approaches. Given limitations of space and the focus of this chapter, discussion is limited to literature on MAC and ACT as applied to sport performance, and the reader is directed to the reviews mentioned above for an overview of other MBI research in sport.

Only a handful of randomised control trials (RCTs) have explored the effects of mindfulness-acceptance interventions with athlete populations. Ivarsson et al. (2015) explored the use of MAC protocols for injury prevention with 41 female soccer players. While no statistically significant differences were found between the MAC group and a group receiving sport psychology presentations, 67% of athletes in the MAC group remained injury-free through the season, compared with 40% in the control group (a moderate effect size) and the MAC group also had 50% fewer injuries than controls. It is difficult to pinpoint the direct link between

MAC and injury prevention, but the authors suggested that the mindfulness element of the programme might have improved athletes' ability to pay attention to relevant stimuli, thus reducing their risk of injury during competition.

Zhang et al. (2016) demonstrated the use of an 8-week MAC protocol for skill development with 43 first-year college students on a dart throwing task. Not only did dart throwing performance improve more in the MAC group than in controls, but participants also reported improvements in mindfulness, experiential acceptance, and flow post-intervention and at follow-up. Finally, lending further support to the idea that ACT-based interventions are beneficial for athletes, Josefsson et al. (2019) found that athletes from a multitude of sports assigned to a MAC group showed a greater level of improvement on dispositional, sport-specific mindfulness skills, emotion regulation abilities, and perceived performance than athletes allocated to a traditional PST group. Taken together, these studies provide encouraging evidence that mindfulness-acceptance approaches based on ACT might be beneficial for performance enhancement, as well as the development of skills, abilities, and qualities likely related to improved performance.

Although RCTs are rare, evidence from other experimental studies and non-RCTs demonstrates that mindfulness-acceptance approaches can have positive effects on performance. Elite golfers (e.g., Bernier et al., 2009) and chess players (Ruiz & Luciano, 2012) have improved their performances/national rankings following ACT-based interventions, while Wolanin and Schwanhausser (2010) demonstrated improved performance of field-hockey and volleyball athletes (compared to controls) after a 7-week MAC protocol.

A number of case studies also provide evidence for the efficacy of ACT and MAC interventions. Gardner and Moore (2004), for example, examined the impact of a MAC intervention with two individual sport athletes (swimming and powerlifting). Both athletes experienced improvements in their performance after 12 weeks of one-to-one sessions (extended to 16 weeks for the swimmer). The swimmer reported his best competitive season with two wins with personal best times and the powerlifter reported her best ever performance, lifting 15% beyond her best previous masters efforts. Other case studies have highlighted performance improvements following interventions based on ACT (e.g., Bernier et al., 2014, Lutkenhouse, 2007, Schwanhausser, 2009), though it is difficult to say with certainty that any of these interventions specifically drove these changes.

As Gardner and Moore (2017) suggested, "athletes and other performers do not perform in a bubble...they are people first... sport psychologists can and need to strive beyond an impact on performance alone" (p. 182). Taken together, evidence from a broad range of studies points to the positive impact of mindfulness-acceptance approaches for athletes across a range of issues that can be but are not necessarily performance related. Individual athletes have, for example, reported personal growth and self-improvement in a number of areas such as the ability to handle frustration, rejection, mistakes, conflict, and a greater sense of personal wellbeing (Lutkenhouse, 2007), reduced distractibility, worry, anxiety, and less experiential avoidance (Gardner & Moore, 2004), and increased mindful awareness, attention, acceptance, and flow (Schwanhausser, 2009). Track and field athletes have reported improvements in goal-directed energy and perceived stress compared with controls following MAC interventions (Goodman et al., 2014), while other improved or enhanced performance-related factors include increased mindfulness skills, non-reactivity to inner experience, increased experiential acceptance, increased ability to take action towards goals, reductions in believability and interference of general unpleasant private events during competitions, and improved goal-directed behaviour (Hasker, 2010, Kettunen &Välimäki, 2014, Ruiz & Luciano, 2012). Finally, athletes have also discussed improved awareness and acceptance of bodily sensations as being important for their performances (Bernier et al., 2009) and improved consistency of training, overall sense of enhanced wellbeing, focus, and values-driven effort (Yau et al., 2021).

Limitations of Existing Literature

While the literature certainly suggests that ACT-based interventions might have positive impacts on both performance- and non-performance-related outcomes, there are also some important considerations for future research and practice. For example, Si et al. (2016) noted that Chinese culture and the emphasis on collective interests in the Chinese sports system can make it more difficult for Chinese athletes to connect with personal values. Consequently, integrating conceptualisations of values and commitments in line with the cultural values and beliefs of the participants would increase the effectiveness of MAC training (Si et al., 2016). Roychowdhury et al. (2021) conducted a narrative review of articles in sport and exercise psychology published between 2008 and 2020, and contended that Eurocentric assumptions have pervaded spiritual and eastern philosophical practices, requiring greater need for culturally sensitive and competent research and practices. Indeed, the authors acknowledge that they may need to exercise cultural reflexivity given that their own practices and applications slant towards Eurocentric research. Additionally, they contend that before applying such interventions, practitioners must examine whether the interventions are culturally appropriate for the clients they support. Finally, Noetel et al.'s (2017) systematic review concluded that while many studies found positive effects for mindfulness and acceptance interventions, it is difficult to make strong causal claims about the performance benefits for athletes, and that further well-designed RCTs are needed in order to strengthen the research base.

In the next section, we consider a case study and provide a scripted intervention of how we might work with a client in consultation about their performance detriments, by working through the six core processes of the Hexaflex model.

Case Study

Amelia is a 20-year-old professional soccer player who has just been offered a full-time contract with the club she has been with since the age of 10 years. She is also halfway through her degree in sport psychology at university and is keen to implement what she is learning. However, now that she is training and competing full-time, Amelia finds the demands of the game challenging and far greater than she imagined. She has been in the starting line-up on a few occasions, but the coaches notice her getting flustered in the moment when pressed by an opponent, and she therefore loses possession of the ball or mistimes her pass. Recently, coaches have noticed that Amelia is cutting corners in her gym work and seems to lose focus in training. At training one day, while warming up, she shares that she feels like she's just there to make up the numbers and says "how can I improve and gain confidence if I get benched for making one mistake?" She books in for a session to discuss her concerns in which she expresses that her goal is to start and finish matches.

Initial Intake and Identifying Problems

During the initial stages of consultancy, the goal is to formulate the client's issue in ACT terms. We might start by getting the client to explain, in their own words, some of the challenges they are facing (e.g., "I wonder if we might start with you just telling me a little bit about what you're struggling with at the moment?"). We already know from the case study information that Amelia is struggling to make decisions under pressure and would like to be more confident. We might explore a little bit more about what that is actually like for her:

CONSULTANT: So Amelia, I'd like to try and understand a little more about what's going on for you when you feel under pressure. Can you think of an example of when that's happened recently?

AMELIA: I just feel a little lost when I'm out there. I've only been playing at this level for a few months really, and I'm still getting used to the pace of everything. It's a real step up, and you just have to think so much more quickly. I have less time to make a pass as everything is quicker and so I get flustered and I don't have time to look where I want to pass the ball and I think I'm going to make a mess of it anyway. I feel like I'm letting my team down.

CONSULTANT: So when you're out there playing, it sounds like there are some other unhelpful thoughts when you get the ball…

AMELIA: Yeah, there's some self-doubts, I guess… just about my ability to make the right pass. I'm questioning everything and I lose concentration and tighten up. It's like sometimes when the ball is coming to me, I'm thinking "don't mess up again! Coaches won't be happy, the team will get frustrated", and sometimes I don't even want the ball because I know I'll just lose it. I need to appear perfect to them and I know I'm not that good. I was always good at reading the game, but I'm mostly just trying to *not* mess up at the minute. I feel like if I could just get the confidence back I'd be alright, but it's just not there, and I'm not really sure what to do about it.

CONSULTANT: Tell me if I'm getting this wrong, but it sounds like when you're out there trying to play in the moment and read the game, your mind is actually giving you all these thoughts… "don't let your team down, don't waste time on the ball, the coaches are watching you, maybe it's best if you just stay out of the way so you don't look bad?"

AMELIA: To be fair, it's got to the point where I stay out of the way on the pitch. Even though I get told off because I'm out of position, it's a relief not to feel the anxiety anymore. But then it's like I'm just losing interest and can't seem to do anything right. I know I'm going to keep messing up and keep getting benched, so what's the point? Maybe I should just focus on University.

This interaction between Amelia and the consultant requires an open poise, utilising helping/counselling skills, which include open-ended questions such as asking her to think of an experience, active listening that enables paraphrasing, and confirmation to establish whether the consultant has understood Amelia correctly. These skills allow Amelia to feel empowered to correct the consultant if needed, and feel that she is being heard, which all builds relational trust.

By referring to Amelia's mind as a separate entity that is giving her thoughts, we have already begun the process of defusion. We might also find out whether there are any other physical sensations, emotions, or feelings that Amelia is avoiding (e.g., "when you're experiencing these thoughts, what shows up in your body?"), but we should also explore what the client really wants from the consultancy. She has already described wanting to be more confident, but drawing out the perhaps complex combination of goals and values that is driving the client to seek help is important for the next stage of the consultancy.

CONSULTANT: Let's say I had a magic pill that you could take, and tomorrow morning you could be the most confident athlete in the world… what would that enable you to do differently?

AMELIA: Well, I suppose I'd just be able to focus on playing and not have to worry about what everyone else was thinking.

CONSULTANT: And if you could be free of that worry, if you could be free of those unhelpful thoughts... how would things be different?

AMELIA: I'd be able to focus on my job on the pitch. I'd see the game more clearly. I'd probably play a lot better and not be worried about being benched again. I'd feel more free...... right now I feel constantly tense.

CONSULTANT: Okay. And let's say that happened. What would be different then?

AMELIA: Uh... I suppose I'd be enjoying football again... looking forward to matches, enjoying training, having a laugh with the girls, but at the minute, I just don't really want to be there.

There are two things to note here. Amelia is describing several things that are important to her (*values*), but that seem out of reach to her right now: staying present and her role ("focus on my job"), improving her performance, enjoying training, and socialising ("having a laugh"). Amelia also explains that she doesn't really want to be there at the minute, which might shed some light on the behaviours her coaches have observed (cutting corners in the gym). If we explore the function of the behaviour rather than the form, her cutting corners could be a way for her to avoid being in a situation which produces all of the unwanted sensations and thoughts that she has described (***experiential avoidance***).

In ACT terms, we have learnt, via this relatively short exchange, that Amelia is finding it difficult to stay present (***mindful awareness***) and is instead being hooked by unhelpful thoughts about her and other's expectations and judgements. Her ***conceptualised self*** is reliant on external validation and acceptance. Furthermore, rather than experiencing thoughts as fleeting and passing cognitive events (***acceptance***), Amelia believes the literal truth of her thoughts, that she isn't good enough (***cognitive fusion***). Her self-descriptive language (e.g., she "was" good at reading the game and "knows" she's going to mess up) is in absolute terms (***attachment to conceptualised self***), and she is "not sure what the point of playing is anymore" (***lack of contact with values***). Instead, she avoids getting involved when on the pitch (***inaction***), is beginning to lose motivation to continue in football altogether, and questions herself as to why she is playing (***lack of values clarity***).

Creative Hopelessness

The next step is to expose the fallibility of the "system" of thinking within which the client is working. That is, highlighting the ultimate unworkability of control-reduce-eliminate strategies when it comes to unwanted thoughts, feelings, and sensations, while remaining non-judgemental in exploring *with* the client whether their strategies have worked. Indeed, her strategies may have helped in the short term, but the long-term workability of control attempts can be questioned given some of her observed avoidance behaviours.

CONSULTANT: Let's run through some of the things that you've tried already. What sort of things have you tried to help the situation?

AMELIA: Well... I suppose I've tried just thinking positively. Like when I get those thoughts, trying to block them out and think about something more positive, like my positioning.

CONSULTANT: Okay, so one strategy is to block unhelpful thoughts to get rid of them so that you can play much better. That seems like a perfectly reasonable strategy for your mind to come up with. How has that worked when you've tried to do that?

AMELIA: It works sometimes. But sometimes the negative thoughts either won't go away, or keep coming back a few minutes later, and then I'm annoyed at myself for not being able to concentrate. So then I'm having that thought, and it just kind of spirals and I can't get out of my own head!

The consultant is doing two important things here. First, reinforcing the idea that the client's strategies are perfectly reasonable, logical things to try. Second, referring again to the client's mind as if it is separate from the client. This is *defusion* in practice and is useful when we contrast the solutions that the client's mind is telling them will work, with their direct experience of whether or not they are actually working.

CONSULTANT: So we should add getting mad at yourself to the list too?

AMELIA: (laughs) I suppose so.

CONSULTANT: And I think it's pretty clear from what you've just said, that that isn't really working out for you. Even though you listen to your own mind, which seems to work for a bit, you just end up in a worse place stuck in your own head.

AMELIA: Yup.

The idea is to continue in this vein (and this may take some time), exploring all of the strategies that the client has used to try and solve the problem and then presenting the contrast between what their mind is telling them will work, and their direct experiences. Ultimately, we are trying to establish the unworkability of logical, analytical, problem-solving strategies for dealing with internal experiences. The client has tried to remove, reduce, or otherwise get rid of unwanted thoughts and sensations, but with little success. In Amelia's case, the more she has tried, the more of these unwanted experiences she has. The client is "stuck".

CONSULTANT: We've covered a lot of ground here, Amelia, and we've got a pretty long list of things that you've tried to do to help with this situation. And they are all pretty logical things. You've clearly put a lot of effort into this and I can see that working on this is something that's really important to you. I want you to take a moment though, to just look at the difference between what your mind is telling you to do and what your experience is telling you. If one of your lecturers was giving you ideas about how to revise, and none of them ever worked, you might, at some point, stop going to them for advice. But your mind seems to keep giving you these ideas about how to deal with the issue, and because it's your own mind, you want to trust it. It's really tempting to keep on trying your mind's ideas, even though your own experience is showing you that they aren't really helping. So I guess the question really becomes what is more reliable here, your mind or your experience?

AMELIA: So, what am I supposed to do then?

CONSULTANT: At this point, I think it might be important for us to really notice that you're feeling a bit stuck in all of this. Have you ever seen a Chinese finger trap?

As Hayes et al. (1999) assert, a state of hopelessness is not what we might ordinarily strive towards. However, the goal of *creative hopelessness* is not to make the client feel as though there is no hope. It is to help the client shift their stance, notice that their agenda of trying to change their internal experiences is what is hopeless, and potentially give up unworkable strategies in the service of moving towards their values.

There are several popular ACT metaphors that are useful here (e.g., person in the hole, tug-of-war with the Monster; see Strosahl et al. (2004) for explanations of many other ACT exercises/metaphors), but we suggest using an actual Chinese finger trap because it allows the client to directly experience the feeling of "stuckness" and how "pulling away" actually makes the situation worse. The use of metaphor is prevalent in ACT. Once we begin to describe or explain the core processes to clients, or engage in logical, analytical discussions about the problem, we are no longer "doing ACT". Appropriately considered metaphors and physical exercises allow the client to directly experience and connect with the principles of ACT "in-the moment" and help to avoid the problem of over-intellectualising.

CONSULTANT: So this is a Chinese finger trap. It's a child's toy really. You put one finger in each end (demonstrates and passes to client). Are your fingers in good and tight? Okay, what do you notice?

AMELIA: Uh... yeah my fingers are stuck.

CONSULTANT: Oh, well can you pull them out?

AMELIA: (tries to pull her fingers out). Nope. Stuck.

CONSULTANT: This feels a bit like the situation you're in. You're having a bunch of unhelpful thoughts and your mind is telling you to get rid of them, to pull away from them, and that's a reasonable and logical response. What happens if you try to pull your fingers out of the trap?

AMELIA: (tries harder). Ugh. It's getting tighter.

CONSULTANT: And isn't that just like what you described earlier? The more you try to pull away from your unhelpful thoughts and situations, the more of them you end up having and you just end up feeling even more stuck? Your mind is telling you that you need to pull away, to get out, and look at all of the efforts you've put into doing that. But what's happened is that it makes the trap tighter. What if it wasn't the strategies that were the problem?

AMELIA: What do you mean?

CONSULTANT: Well, what if your situation was a trap too? What if it's not that the strategies aren't working? What if it's that the strategies *can't* work? Just like the finger trap. What if it was the struggle that was the problem?

AMELIA: So what can I do now?

CONSULTANT: Let's see what happens if you push your fingers further into the trap.

At this stage, the client might wonder what the alternative is, and it might be necessary to elucidate somewhat, while also reinforcing the idea of letting go of the struggle. Together we notice that the trap loosens if Amelia pushes her fingers further into it. If the client is insistent on having some tangible strategy, the consultant can gently point out that this is their mind telling them that there must be something they can *do* to help, and again reinforce the idea that just noticing the struggle is what's important right now. Having engaged with the client and explored her willingness to try something new, we would continue to work more deliberately on the six ACT core processes that might be a cause of psychological inflexibility. The number of experiential exercises and metaphors that can be used is vast, so we provide an example or two in each of the following sections:

Mindful Breathing and Noticing (*Acceptance, Defusion, and Flexible Attention*)

To help Amelia notice thoughts without judgement or the impulse of the mind wanting to solve the problem, several methods might be used (Hayes, 2019). Here the consultant asks

Amelia to consider the thoughts she had during a recent performance and notes them down on a piece of paper.

CONSULTANT (holding the paper right in front of Amelia's face): What do you see?
AMELIA: Absolutely nothing. I can't see anything up that close!

The consultant moves the paper back, until Amelia can read what it says. Moving the paper to the side means Amelia now has vision out in front too.

CONSULTANT: But you can still see the paper, right? It hasn't gone anywhere. Your thoughts are still there, written on it, but if we just draw it back a little, we can notice and recognise the thoughts, but our vision is no longer dominated by them. You can see what's really in front of you and decide on a course of action.

This is the pivot towards *cognitive defusion* and it is a process where Amelia begins to release herself from believing her thoughts. The "Leaves on a Stream" exercise (a thought enters your mind, briefly observe it, place it on a leaf, watch it float down the stream), or similar, might also be introduced, along with the practice of labelling thoughts as they are noticed (i.e., worrying, concerned). The exercise is a technique used in ACT to help clients cope with uncomfortable thoughts and feelings. Just as leaves float by on a stream, in this exercise, the client lets thoughts float on. In addition, breath awareness exercises would help to strengthen Amelia's attentional focus (on the physical sensations of breathing), while still being aware and accepting of thoughts, feelings, or any other physical sensations experienced. Unlike rhythmic breathing, this exercise does not involve counting breaths but emphasises attending to the sensations of breathing without any attempt at conscious control. Amelia would be encouraged to continue a daily 10-minute practice before her next session. At the start of each subsequent session, the consultant would recap on the session before, enquire how the practices assigned are going, and explore any challenges and struggles.

Accessing the Transcendent Self (*Self as Context, Defusion*)

While it has been noted that psychological flexibility processes are connected and do not necessarily follow a fixed approach, the next step in the consultation may be about helping Amelia to raise awareness to access the *transcendent self* and strengthen the connection to her authentic self and others.

CONSULTANT: I'd like to explore some of the difficult feelings you've been experiencing and some of the statements you've made. I know it isn't always easy for you, but I'm hoping it will help you access a part of yourself you may not have realised is there. Would you be willing to give this a try?
AMELIA: Sure, but I normally just try to shut out feelings. I am so anxious, the only way out is when I avoid the situation and don't have the eyes of everyone watching to see whether I am any good.

The consultant asks Amelia to write down "I am" statements as noted above (e.g., I am anxious, I am rubbish, I am the problem). The consultant then asks Amelia to add the words "or not" to the end of each statement and to read them out loud slowly and deliberately. This helps her notice her fusion with the statement and when the client repeats the statement with "or not", she can take note of any unhelpful thoughts that arise.

CONSULTANT: Let's try something here. If we cross out everything before "or not", are you still you?
AMELIA (frustrated): Uh that doesn't make sense, it just says "or not".
CONSULTANT: "I notice you had a reaction to my question..."
AMELIA: Well yeah because I am somebody, I am something, I'm me!
CONSULTANT: Okay. Well let's try something else then. Circle the I am in your statements. Now let's see if we can simply rest on "I am".

This process helps to bring her closer to just being, rather than rely on the distorted story that she tells herself; rubbish, not good.

CONSULTANT: I'd like us to try something else here too. Instead of "I am anxious" could we try, "I am having the thought that..."
AMELIA: Like... I am having the thought that my teammates think I'm no good?
CONSULTANT: Exactly. And I wonder if whenever we're talking about your thoughts whether we can try to use that language. "I am having the thought that... I am experiencing the sensation of..."

This change in language allows Amelia to describe the situation, her behaviour, and how she is thinking and feeling without being drawn into self-judgments and her conceptualised self. The idea is to help Amelia pivot away from becoming the story of her ego and help her to move in the direction of greater awareness and perspective.

Mindful Noticing, Body Scanning, and Labelling Emotions (Flexible Attention, Defusion, Acceptance)

As Amelia continues to work on raising awareness, it is also important that she becomes aware of physical sensations of feelings held in her body that are stimulated by activating events and inferred by certain cognitions that had become fused. Still using breath technique between sessions and at the start of a new session, she is now introduced to body scanning and the Plutchik's (1980) emotion wheel to explore a range of feelings and accurately label them to provide understanding around her survival behaviours and explore the range of emotions accessible to her. The idea is to not suppress her feelings or judge them but to gain more understanding around her suffering.

Mindful Breathing, Attention Refocusing, and Concentration (Acceptance, Commitment)

It is important to recap on Amelia's breathing and noticing "homework", reinforcing that breathing can be difficult and that simply noticing distractions takes practice. This is a good opportunity to reinforce and encourage Amelia to take a non-judgmental stance and to simply notice and label any feelings of frustration during these exercises. She is now also introduced to another 10-minute breathing exercise that introduces acceptance and attention refocusing with a comparative, sport-specific example. On a football pitch, her mind may wander during training, but being able to refocus her attention back on the ball and her power stance is what she begins to train for through her breathing. In breathing ladders, the count is now introduced as the attention "refocuser" as we demonstrate to Amelia that she can choose to refocus her attention.

CONSULTANT: Amelia, I want you to recognise where we place our attention is a choice, and while we do become distracted by noises, thoughts, and any number of different things, I wonder if you would try a breathing exercise that helps you to focus your attention, just as you would need to when in a match. You mentioned that you often say to yourself "Don't mess up, I don't want the ball" which results in you being distracted by thoughts that lead you to be out of position to receive the ball. What would it help you to think about so that you are in position?

AMELIA: I want to think about where the ball is and be able to follow it into position and then I need to open up and scan the pitch, hold a strong body stance to hold off any opponent. Yeah, I can think about that.

The athlete comes to a realisation that she has been placing her attention elsewhere, which has not been helping. By exploring what it takes to be in position, her technique, and body posture in receiving the ball, she is led to specific points that she can choose to intentionally focus on in training, and the cues that intentionally bring her attention back to the task.

CONSULTANT: How about if we help you practice placing your attention in a place of choice and holding it there with a breathing exercise. Think of it as a training exercise that helps you place your mind on what you choose to attend to.

AMELIA: Ha! If you can help me do that would be ace!

CONSULTANT: Okay let's try a breathing exercise. It's called a ladder because our aim is to help you count up like a ladder and place your attention on the count just like you would the contact with the ball you are receiving. Remember before you were simply breathing in whatever way that came to you. Now we want to help you place attention on your breathing and count as you exhale after taking a breath in. But before we start, let's try to make sure we have a quiet place.

Let's begin… (slowly and deliberately)… Breathe in, and breathe out, and as you exhale silently say one. Remember to place your attention on your breath and the count as you exhale. Breathe in, and breathe out, and silently say two. Don't worry if you lose your count, just come back, and begin again.

The consultant continues to lead by reminding Amelia to lean into self-compassion and kindness towards self. We might remind her to say something as simple as "you're ok" to herself when she loses her focus while breathing, and to exercise this same compassion towards "self" when on the pitch too.

Amelia is also introduced to another breathing technique called pyramid breathing. This technique may incorporate placing attention on other parts of the body as she breathes, moving from the belly upwards to the chest, and through her mouth, thereby incorporating other factors to pay attention to. This is similar to when she needs to pay attention to receiving a ball *and* then shifting it to hold her body position while she holds off an opponent. Amelia is asked to continue practising these techniques, committing to 10 minutes of breathing meditation daily before her next session. She is also reminded to choose to place her attention on receiving the ball and her body positioning in training and we would ask her to write this down on a card as a reminder of her week's focus. When Amelia returns the following week for her session, we would, as usual, recap on the week's practices and how she has fared on refocusing her attention on the task at hand.

Value-Driven Actions and Value-Driven Goal Behaviours for Practice and Competition (*Values, Committed Action*)

In the initial consultation, Amelia had highlighted values of presence ("staying present"), her role ("focus on my job"), improving her performance, enjoying training, and socialising ("having a laugh"). We might now explore more deeply what matters to Amelia and what motivates her to play football. Amelia explains that she has always loved competing and what it means to her is that she likes to prove herself and fight; she has never been one to give up and has always loved being challenged to learn. However, of late, she has been finding it hard. She acknowledges that external obstacles to her living her inspired values include the coach not playing her, and internal obstacles of fear, and self-criticism. She also explains that she is a team player which matters to her and the reason for playing the sport. This provides the basis for then working to establish how she wishes to demonstrate those behaviours through her actions in practice and competition. See Table 2.1 for an example of value-driven actions and goal behaviours.

If helpful to the client, these behaviours and actions may be written down in a worksheet to provide a visual representation for the client. It is important here to spend time working on a shared plan to monitor Amelia's commitment to these actions with a scale that measures how well she has managed during the week and going forward. This can be discussed with Amelia so that she is able to monitor her own progress, although it is important to emphasise that it is simply a tool to help her raise awareness and to not think of it as a constraint.

TABLE 2.1 Example value-driven actions and goal behaviours

Value	*Practice behaviour & action*	*Competition behaviour & action*
Focus on my job/Improving performance – Learn, Challenge, fight	Following my gym program and complete each repetition Study past games and learn from mistakes – watch video clips and analyse the tactical aspects Sit down with the coaches to discuss my video observations and training difficulties to gain better understanding of the game Study set plays and understand my role in those set plays .... (and any others)	Prepare for the game by studying the game plan and watch video clips in performance analysis Whether on the bench or not, study the set plays book for the game Constantly scan the play and my position on pitch Focus my attention on the ball and my body shape/power stance as I receive the ball and fight off opposition .... (and any others)
Enjoyment and socialising	Laughing and joking at training during warm up while staying focused on the warm up exercises	Getting into the spirit with my teammates on the coach Supporting and cheering my teammates if on the bench ....

Drawing Together Values Commitment and Avoidance, Feelings, Goal-Directed Committed Actions in Service of Long-Term Goals

The Lighthouse analogy (Larsen et al., 2017) depicts a road journey towards a lighthouse as the ultimate goal. On this journey, the client can find themselves taking a different path at a fork in the road that is referred to as the "Emotion Driven Way". The athlete might take this action in response to difficult thoughts and emotions when faced by a difficult situation, which might provide short-term relief and reward, but long-term consequences of being further away from the lighthouse. Instead, by connecting values back to their game plan of actions and behaviours, with awareness and acceptance of their emotions and processes of cognitive defusion, the athlete continues on "The Values Driven Way" and their journey towards the lighthouse. The Lighthouse analogy specifically allows joint exploration of the client's path along the road towards a lighthouse (outcome). Discussing what Amelia wants her outcome to be (a consistent starter on the team), and, using the values and action-driven behaviours from the previous session, we might discuss how Amelia has managed any difficulties, thoughts, and feelings faced.

Examining her avoidance and inactions, she is able to recognise that they have been taking her down a different road (the "Emotion Driven Way""). Amelia begins to understand that the behaviours and past inactions provided more instant relief and release from suffering, though resulted in consequences of being benched, not developing power and strength as a result of cutting out of the gym early, all the while moving further away from the lighthouse (i.e., the starting line-up).

Remembering that ACT processes require that the individual lean into the suffering and difficulty, Amelia is then able to explore what that might look like. Short-term consequences of her struggle may indeed feel uncomfortable, be extremely challenging, and might require several hours reviewing difficult video content of her performance struggles. While initially difficult and requiring a lot of effort, the long-term rewards are growth in confidence, better team relationships with players and staff, and more enjoyment, as she becomes more able to maintain her attention on improvement and development in her performance.

We would also discuss how she can commit to her actions in training by working with the coaches on some extra drills that draw out her technique, physical stance, and positioning. Amelia agrees that having this approach will help her refocus on what matters in service of her longer-term goal and thereby allow her to still be on the path towards the lighthouse.

Modes of Working

As with many forms of consultancy, it is difficult to give a precise or even an imprecise indication of how long an ACT intervention might take, or how many sessions might be appropriate. For some clients, it might be necessary to spend weeks just working on loosening their grip over control strategies with creative hopelessness exercises, while others might reach that willingness to abandon control in favour of acceptance much more quickly. It is important to go at the client's pace here and to remember that we are not trying to convince the client of anything, only afford them opportunities to access their direct experience and contrast that to what their mind is telling them. Once the client is open to trying what might seem like a counterintuitive strategy (leaning into rather than away from their discomfort), we can begin working on developing psychological flexibility, but again this is not a linear process and we might revisit the notion of control many times over the course of the consultancy as we notice the client falling back on logical, problem-solving thinking (e.g., "yes, but I wish I could be less anxious!").

We can though, as we have seen in the case study, begin the work of ACT immediately, through our early interactions with the client by discussing what is important to them (values), talking about the mind as a separate entity (defusion), pausing to ask what they are experiencing right now (mindfulness, acceptance), and so on. There is also no set structure through which to progress an ACT consultancy, or any order that core processes might be approached in. Indeed, each core process is linked with each other process, so experiential exercises or metaphors often tap into pairs of, or multiple, processes at once (e.g., flexible attention to the present moment *and* acceptance, or defusion *and* self-as context). However, case formulation might result in the consultant and client agreeing upon a set of treatment goals, and the consultant deciding course of action or set of interventions that target relevant areas of psychological flexibility (see Hayes et al., 2004).

When the client is consistently engaging in committed action based on chosen values, and demonstrating the open, centred, and engaged response style discussed at the start of this chapter, we might as well have reached a point where we can think about bringing the consultancy to a close.

There is evidence to suggest that due to its experiential nature, ACT can work well if delivered in a group format. Hearing how other people have experienced exercises or interpreted metaphors might be useful, and client-generated metaphors can also be shared in group formats. Being among others who are displaying willingness, expressing their openness to experience, and publicly committing to action based on personal values can create a powerful social context for change (see Walser & Pistorello, 2004, for an extended discussion).

The therapeutic relationship itself is at the heart of the ACT intervention. It is accepting and focused on values, with the therapist modelling and reinforcing the psychological flexibility being taught. While a detailed discussion about the therapeutic relationship in ACT is beyond the scope of this chapter, Hayes et al., (2012) provide a useful chapter that examines the powerful nature and challenges of this relationship in ACT.

References

Baltzell, A. & Akhtar, V. L. (2014). Mindfulness Meditation Training for Sport (MMTS) intervention: Impact of MMTS with Division I female athletes. *The Journal of Happiness and Well-being, 2*(2), 160–173.

Bernier, M., Thienot, E., Codron, R., & Fournier, J. F. (2009). Mindfulness and acceptance approaches in sport performance. *Journal of Clinical Sport Psychology, 3*(4), 320–333. https://doi.org/10.1123/jcsp.3.4.320

Bernier, M., Thienot, E., Pelosse, E., & Fournier, J. F. (2014). Effects and underlying processes of a mindfulness-based intervention with young elite figure skaters: Two case studies. *The Sport Psychologist, 28*(3), 302–315. https://doi.org/10.1123/tsp.2013-0006

Birrer D. & Morgan G. (2010). Psychological skills training as a way to enhance an athlete's performance in high-intensity sports. *Scandinavian Journal of Medicine and Science in Sports, 20*(s2), 78–87. https://doi.org/10.1111/j.1600-0838.2010.01188.x

Bühlmayer, L., Birrer, D., Röthlin, P., Faude, O., & Donath, L. (2017). Effects of mindfulness practice on performance-relevant parameters and performance outcomes in sports: a meta-analytical review. *Sports Medicine, 47*(11), 2309–2321. https://doi.org/10.1007/s40279-017-0752-9

Gardner, F. L. & Moore. Z. E. (2001). The Multi-level Classification System for Sport Psychology (MCS-SP): Toward a structured assessment and conceptualization of athlete-clients. Workshop presented at the annual conference of the Association for the Advancement of Applied Sport Psychology, Orlando, FL.

Gardner, F. L. & Moore, Z. E. (2004). A mindfulness-acceptance-commitment-based approach to athletic performance enhancement: Theoretical considerations. *Behavior Therapy, 35*(4), 707–723. https://doi.org/10.1016/S0005-7894(04)80016-9

Gardner, F. L. & Moore, Z. E. (2006). *Clinical Sport Psychology*. Human Kinetics.

Gardner, F. L. & Moore, Z. E. (2012). Mindfulness and acceptance models in sport psychology: A decade of basic and applied scientific advancements. *Canadian Psychology, 53*(4), 309–318. https://doi.org/10.1037/a0030220

Gardner, F. L. & Moore. Z. E. (2017). Mindfulness-based and acceptance-based interventions in sport and performance contexts. *Current Opinion in Psychology, 16*, 180–184. https://doi.org/10.1016/j.copsyc.2017.06.001

Goodman, F. R., Kashdan, T. B., Mallard, T. T., & Schumann, M. (2014). A brief mindfulness and yoga intervention with an entire NCAA division I athletic team: An initial investigation. *Psychology of Consciousness: Theory, Research, and Practice, 1*(4), 339–356. https://doi.org/10.1037/cns0000022

Hasker, S. M. (2010). Evaluation of the Mindfulness-Acceptance-Commitment (MAC) approach for enhancing athletic performance. *Dissertation Abstracts International, 71*(9-B), 57–90.

Hayes, S. C. (2004). Acceptance and commitment therapy, relational frame theory, and the third wave of behavioral and cognitive therapies. *Behaviour Therapy, 35*(4), 639–665. https://doi.org/10.1016/S0005-7894(04)80013-3

Hayes, S. C. (2019). *A Liberated Mind: How to Pivot toward What Matters*. Avery.

Hayes, S. C. & Brownstein, A. J. (1986). Mentalism, behavior-behavior relations and a behavior analytic view of the purposes of science. *The Behavior Analyst, 9*(2), 175–190. https://doi.org/10.1007/BF03391944

Hayes S. C., Hayes L. J., & Reese H. W. (1988). Finding the philosophical core: A review of Stephen C. Pepper's World Hypotheses. *Journal of the Experimental Analysis of Behavior, 50*(1), 97–111. https://doi.org/10.1901/jeab.1988.50-97

Hayes, S. C., Luoma, J. B., Bond, F. W., Masuda, A., & Lillis, J. (2006). Acceptance and commitment therapy: Model, processes and outcomes. *Behaviour Research and Therapy, 44*(1), 1–25. http://dx.doi.org/10.1016/j.brat.2005.06.006

Hayes, C., Strosahl, K. D., Luoma, J., Smith, A. A., & Wilson, K.G. (2004). ACT Case Formulation. In S. Hayes & K. D. Strosahl (Eds.), *A Practical Guide to Acceptance and Commitment Therapy* (pp. 59–73). Springer.

Hayes, S. C., Strosahl, K. D., & Wilson, K. G. (1999). *Acceptance and Commitment Therapy: An experiential approach to behaviour change* (2nd Ed). The Guilford Press.

Hayes, S. C., Strosahl, K. D., & Wilson, K. G. (2012). *Acceptance and Commitment Therapy: The process and Practice of Mindful Change* (2nd Ed). The Guilford Press.

Ivarsson, A., Johnson, U., Andersen, M. B., Fallby, J., & Altemyr, M. (2015). It pays to pay attention: A mindfulness-based program for injury prevention with soccer players. *Journal of Applied Sport Psychology, 27*(3), 319–334. https://doi.org/10.1080/10413200.2015.1008072

Josefsson, T., Ivarsson, A., Gustafsson, H., Stenling, A., Lindwall, M, Tornberg, R., & Böröy, J. (2019). Effects of Mindfulness-Acceptance-Commitment (MAC) on sport-specific dispositional mindfulness, emotion regulation, and self-rated athletic performance in a multiple-sport population: An RCT study. *Mindfulness, 10*(3), 1518–1529. https://doi.org/10.1007/s12671-019-01098-7

Kabat-Zinn, J., Beall, B., & Rippe, J. (1985, June). A systematic mental training program based on mindfulness meditation to optimize performance in collegiate and Olympic rowers. Poster session presented at the World Congress in Sport Psychology, Copenhagen.

Kaufman, K. A., Glass, C. R., & Arnkoff, D. B. (2009). Evaluation of Mindful Sport Performance Enhancement (MSPE): A new approach to promote flow in athletes. *Journal of Clinical Sport Psychology, 25*(4), 334–356. https://doi.org/10.1123/jcsp.3.4.334

Kettunen, A. & Välimäki, V. (2014). Acceptance and value-based psychological coaching intervention for elite female floorball players. Jyväskylä: (Unpublished master's thesis), University of Jyväskylä.

Larsen, C. H., Diment, G., Hansen, J., & Henrikson, K. (2017, April, 26). *Daring to ACT at the Olympic Games: Why and how we integrate mindfulness in high pressure competitions* [Workshop]. Mindfulness and Acceptance Summit, Copenhagen, Denmark.

Luoma, J. B., Hayes, S. C., & Walser, R. D. (2017). *Learning ACT: An Acceptance and Commitment Therapy skills training manual for therapists* (2nd Ed.). New Harbinger Publications Inc.

Lutkenhouse, J. M. (2007). The case of Jenny: A freshman collegiate athlete experiencing performance dysfunction. *Journal of Clinical Sport Psychology, 1*(2), 166–180. https://doi.org/10.1123/jcsp.1.2.166

Noetel, M., Ciarrochi, J., Van Zanden, B., & Lonsdale, C. (2017). Mindfulness and acceptance approaches to sporting performance enhancement: a systematic review. *International Review of Sport and Exercise Psychology, 12*(1), 139–175. https://doi.org/10.1080/1750984X.2017.1387803

Plutchik, R. K. H. (1980). *Theories of Emotion*. Academic Press.

Roychowdhury, D., Ronkainen, N., & Guinto, M. L. (2021). The transnational migration of mindfulness: A call for reflective pause in sport and exercise psychology. *Psychology of Sport and Exercise, 56.* DOI: https://doi.org/10.1016/j.psychsport.2021.101958

Ruiz, F. J. & Luciano, C. (2012). Improving international-level chess players' performance with an acceptance-based protocol: Preliminary findings. *The Psychological Record, 62*, 447–462. https://doi.org/10.1007/BF03395813

Sappington, R. & Longshore, K. (2015). Systematically reviewing the efficacy of mindfulness-based interventions for enhanced athletic performance. *Journal of Clinical Sport Psychology, 9*(3), 232–262. https://doi.org/10.1123/jcsp.2014-0017

Schwanhausser, L. (2009). Application of the Mindfulness–Acceptance–Commitment (MAC) Protocol with an adolescent springboard diver: The case of Steve. *Journal of Clinical Sports Psychology, 3*(4), 377–396. https://doi.org/10.1123/jcsp.3.4.377

Si, G., Lo, C. & Zhang, C. (2016). Mindfulness training program for Chinese athletes and its effectiveness. In A. L. Baltzell (Ed.), *Mindfulness and Performance* (pp. 235–267). Cambridge University Press. https://doi.org/10.1017/CBO9781139871310.012

Strosahl, K. D., Hayes, S. C., Wilson, K. G., & Gifford, E. V. (2004). An ACT primer: Core therapy processes, intervention strategies, and therapist competencies. In: S. C. Hayes & K. D. Strosahl (Eds.), *A Practical Guide to Acceptance and Commitment Therapy* (pp. 31–58). Springer Science and Business Media.

Turner, M. J., Aspin, G., Didymus, F. F., Mack, R., Olusoga, P., Wood, A. G., & Bennett, R. (2020). One case, five approaches: The application of psychotherapeutic approaches in sport psychology. *The Sport Psychologist, 34*(1), 71–83. https://doi.org/10.1123/tsp.2019-0079

Walser, R. D., & Pistorello, J. (2004). ACT in group format. In S. Hayes & K. D. Strosahl (Eds.), *A Practical Guide to Acceptance and Commitment Therapy* (pp. 347–372). Springer.

Wegner, D. M. (1994). Ironic processes of mental control. *Psychological Review, 101*(1), 34–52. https://doi.org/10.1037/0033-295X.101.1.34

Wolanin, A. T. & Schwanhausser, L. A. (2010). Psychological functioning as a moderator of the MAC approach to performance enhancement. *Journal of Clinical Sport Psychology, 4*(4), 312–322. https://doi.org/10.1123/jcsp.4.4.312

Yau, E. K. B., Ping, N. P. T., & Kuan, G. (2021). The use of Mindfulness Acceptance Commitment (MAC) approach for Malaysian elite triathletes. *Journal of Sport Psychology in Action, 12*(4), 1–9. https://doi.org/10.1080/21520704.2021.1920522

Zettle, R. D. & Hayes, S. C. (1986). Dysfunctional control by client verbal behavior: The context of reason giving. *The Analysis of Verbal Behavior, 4*, 30–38. https://doi.org/10.1007/BF03392813

Zettle, R. D., Hayes, S. C., Barnes-Holmes, P. M. D., & Biglan, A. (2016). *The Wiley Handbook of Contextual Behavioral Science*. Wiley-Blackwell.

Zhang, C., Si, G., Duan, Y., Lyu, Y., Keatley, D. A., & Chan, D. K. (2016). The effects of mindfulness training on beginners' skill acquisition in dart throwing: A randomized controlled trial. *Psychology of Sport and Exercise, 22*, 279–285.

3

COMPASSION FOCUSED THERAPY (CFT)

Jo Wood and Hannah Butler-Coyne

Introduction

Cultivating compassion as an antidote to suffering and distress has long been discussed within various religious and philosophical schools of thought (Lama, 1995). More recently, there has been scientific interest in this proposition with evolving psychological, neuro-physiological, and social understanding of compassion and its importance to wellbeing. As a result, various forms of training and therapy have emerged, enabling clients to nurture compassion to manage a range of difficulties and mental health problems (Gilbert, 2020; Basran et al., 2022). Compassion focused therapy (CFT), developed by Paul Gilbert, provides an evolution-informed, biopsychosocial approach to deal with the human condition (Gilbert, 2010; 2014). Less of a third-wave approach and more of an integrative therapy, CFT incorporates processes and techniques from a wide range of therapies, including other CBT approaches and experiential therapies. Drawing upon Buddhist psychology and defining compassion as "a sensitivity to the suffering of self and others, with a deep commitment to try to relieve it" (Gilbert, 2014, p. 19), CFT stresses the two different mindsets or psychologies of compassion. The first mindset turns towards and engages with suffering (as opposed to avoiding it) with the second mindset focused on the suffering in ourselves and others. Developed from the clinical observations of clients who presented with high levels of shame and self-criticism, together with those who failed to improve utilising traditional Beckian or Ellisian CBT, CFT looks to the evolution of the human mind to help explain these difficulties (Gilbert, 2009a).

Compassion focused therapy acknowledges that the human brain is complex or "tricky" consisting of a range of different motives, emotions, and cognitive competencies, which result in a potential conflict between the "old" and "new" areas of the brain. The old (emotional) brain oversees our basic desires, feelings, and needs necessary for survival, including avoiding harm, finding food and shelter, developing relationships, and being part of groups, and the "new" sophisticated human brain governs our ability to think, reflect, fantasise, plan for the future, and develop a sense of self-identity (Gilbert, 2009a). As our new thinking brain needs to interact with old brain emotions and motives that organise our minds and bodies, this can result in us responding emotionally and biologically to our thoughts and imaginations

DOI: 10.4324/9781003162513-4

as if they were genuine, trapping us within complex emotional states such as depression and anxiety (Kolts, 2016). For example, any perceived criticism we receive is likely to activate our threat system, regardless of whether we are being criticised or not, potentially trapping us in a cycle of overthinking and depression. Equally, our once evolved adaptive mechanisms are now within a "different (and fast changing) age" no longer *as* effective. For instance, according to social rank theory, depression evolved to encourage submission following a defeat in competing for resources, etc. (Gilbert, 2001). However, our ability to self-criticise and living in a socially disconnected modern world that values competition has rendered depression more maladaptive than adaptive (Simos, 2022).

To help clients understand their emotions and experiences through the lens of evolution, CFT emphasises three emotional-motivational systems. Responsible for our survival as a species and underpinned by social mentality theory, these systems organise our minds (in terms of attention, thinking, imagery, behaviour, motivation, and emotional experience) and work together to regulate our emotional experiences:

- The threat and protection system.
- The drive and excitement system.
- The soothing-affiliative system.

While the threat protection system detects threats, giving us surges of anxiety, anger, or disgust, and allows us to respond in a way to self-protect (e.g., flight, flight, freeze), the drive and excitement system engenders positive feelings of arousal and pleasure to direct us towards resources and goals. In comparison, the soothing-affiliative system encourages feelings of containment and peace, linked with affiliation and social connectedness, when we are not defending ourselves or pursuing goals, and calms the other systems (Depue & Morrone-Strupinsky, 2005). Evolving from attachment and our capacity to care, compassion plays a part in stimulating this safety system. CFT aims to encourage clients to cultivate the three flows of compassion (compassion to self, others, and from others) through the competencies and attributes of a compassion-focused mindset, allowing them to replace competition-based social mentalities with caring ones (Gilbert, 2010).

Initially developed for working with complex mental health problems maintained by shame and self-criticism (Gilbert, 2010), CFT has shown positive outcomes in both clinical and non-clinical populations across a wide range of conditions and difficulties, including depression, anxiety, anger, shame, and self-criticism (see Beaumont & Hollins, 2015; Kirby, 2017; Craig et al., 2020, for an overview; Simos, 2022). More recently, there has been interest in applying the approach to competitive sporting contexts, with concerns about the impact of elite sporting performance on mental health (Gulliver et al., 2015; Foskett & Longstaff, 2018; Walton et al., 2021). Some studies suggest that elite athletes may be more susceptible to mental health problems than the general population (Gouttebarge et al., 2019; Reardon et al., 2019) and that depression and anxiety are prevalent across various sports, including rugby union (Gouttebarge et al., 2017). In addition, various vulnerability factors appear to contribute to poor athlete wellbeing and mental health in highly competitive environments, including the impact of concussion and musculoskeletal injury (Kiliç et al., 2018), inflexible athlete identity (Brewer & Petitpas, 2017), irrational beliefs (Turner et al., 2019), perfectionism (Jensen et al., 2018) and self-criticism (Powers et al., 2009; Sutherland et al., 2014). Self-compassion could play a role in reducing these factors by supporting elite athletes to adapt to inevitable adverse events (e.g., injury and failure; Ceccarelli et al., 2019), to counteract unhelpful negative emotional and cognitive responses such as self-criticism and rumination (Mosewich et al., 2011; 2013; Doorley et al., 2022), and to potentially improve performance (Killham et al., 2018).

This case study will focus on applying Gilbert's CFT to a professional rugby player struggling with poor mental health following a period of injury.

Practice

Case Study

Luke is a 23-year-old professional rugby player and an established Hooker in a premier league team which he joined approximately 6 months ago. Luke moved to the other end of the country to fulfil his rugby dreams. He currently shares a flat with some of his teammates. He lives and breathes rugby and has done since 6 years old. Luke's number one fan is his dad, who himself had a premature end from the sport due to injury. Growing up, Luke often felt as though he had a "hard time" from his dad both within his sport and schoolwork. He rarely gave praise, constantly pushed him to "do better", and at times questioned his commitment to rugby (or his schoolwork) if performance was ever perceived to be lacking. Luke did "ok" academically but always felt he could do better, suspecting also, that his dad felt this too.

During a recent pivotal game, Luke sustained a serious shoulder injury requiring several operations. Luke's medical team advised 8 months' rehabilitation. Luke had experienced several injuries in the past; however, this was the first provoking uncertainty about his rugby career. Luke became extremely focused on making positive physical progress, he religiously followed the rehabilitation and training schedule often putting in extra gym sessions. Luke's coach and the performance director were impressed with his "above and beyond" dedication. After 7 months, he re-joined the team training with the potential of returning to competition in the near future.

Although Luke was making significant physical progress, he was not selected to play for the first team and missed out on being considered to play for England. He was devastated and his dad was frustrated at the news. Luke was also struggling with sleep, increasingly feeling low and "useless", often "feeling weak" and at times "wishing I wasn't here". He found himself zoning out during team talks, skipping meals (yet increasing protein shake intake), and, when training, becoming hesitant with some tackle decisions.

Luke went to see the team sport psychologist and offered insight into the experiences. He explained that as a teenager he had experienced cognitive behavioural therapy for low mood and anxiety with limited success. Luke was supported to make a self-referral to a psychologist with expertise in mental health difficulties via a rugby players association.

Assessment

Assessment Process: Initial Assessment Interview and Psychometric Measures

A psychological assessment focusing on both performance and clinical aspects associated with Luke's difficulties and experiences was informed by the Sport-Clinical Intake Protocol (Taylor & Schneider, 1992). As such, and in order to undertake the initial assessment, a conversation with Luke utilising the following framework took place:

a. exploration regarding the presenting difficulties
b. developed understanding of the background and sport-specific history

TABLE 3.1 Three psychometric measures used with Luke

Measure	*Description*
Patient Health Questionnaire-9 (PHQ-9, Spitzer et al., 1999**)**	A 9-item self-report questionnaire which measures the nine areas within the diagnostic criteria for depressive disorders.
Generalised Anxiety Disorder -7 (GAD-7; Spitzer et al., 2006**)**	A 7-item self-report anxiety scale which explores the severity of generalised anxiety
Self-Compassion Scale (SCS; Neff, 2003)	A 26-item Likert scale measure of self-compassion across 6 domains including self-kindness, self-judgement, common humanity, isolation, mindfulness and overidentification.

c. a mapping out of support systems (sport and non-sport related)
d. physical and mental health (historic and current)
e. identification of significant life events
f. any changes/influential factors prior to the increase in difficulties (both performance and mental health)

In addition to the interview and to provide opportunity for initial quantitative record and comparison of the main areas of difficulty, a baseline for Luke's experiences was obtained utilising three psychometric measures (Table 3.1). Progression and gains were also reviewed through pre- and post-measure review.

Assessment Process: Risk

During the interview process and upon completion of the psychometric measures, Luke became more open about his experiences of anxiety (General Anxiety Disorder-7 [GAD-7] score, 14 indicating "moderate anxiety"), low mood (Patient Health Questionnaire [PHQ-9] score, 18 categorised as "severe" depression), and particularly his thoughts associated with "wishing I wasn't here". In line with the Diagnostic and Statistical Manual for Mental Disorders V–Text Revision (DSM V-TR; American Psychiatric Association (APA), 2013), Luke appeared to be experiencing mental health difficulties which were meeting the threshold for moderate levels of depression and anxiety.

Assessing Luke's risk of harm was paramount and an essential component in further understanding his challenges. Upon further exploration, Luke detailed feeling overwhelmed and stuck with him wanting to "get out" of the situation. He had no active plans to end his life or hurt/harm himself and detailed various protective factors aligned with family relationships, aims and future aspirations within his sport, alongside a keen desire to be a father one day. Luke was experiencing fleeting suicidal thoughts which required constant monitoring and a comprehensive safety plan for him to use at difficult times.

Formulation and Approach Rationale

Luke appeared to be navigating various contributors to his sport performance deterioration. With reference to the Multilevel Classification System for Sport Psychology (MCS-SP, Gardner & Moore, 2006), Luke's difficulties align within the "performance impairment" category.

Multiple factors were contributing to Luke's experiences of the injury event, apparent low mood, sleep, eating difficulties, and suicidal thinking (see Figure 3.1 for longitudinal

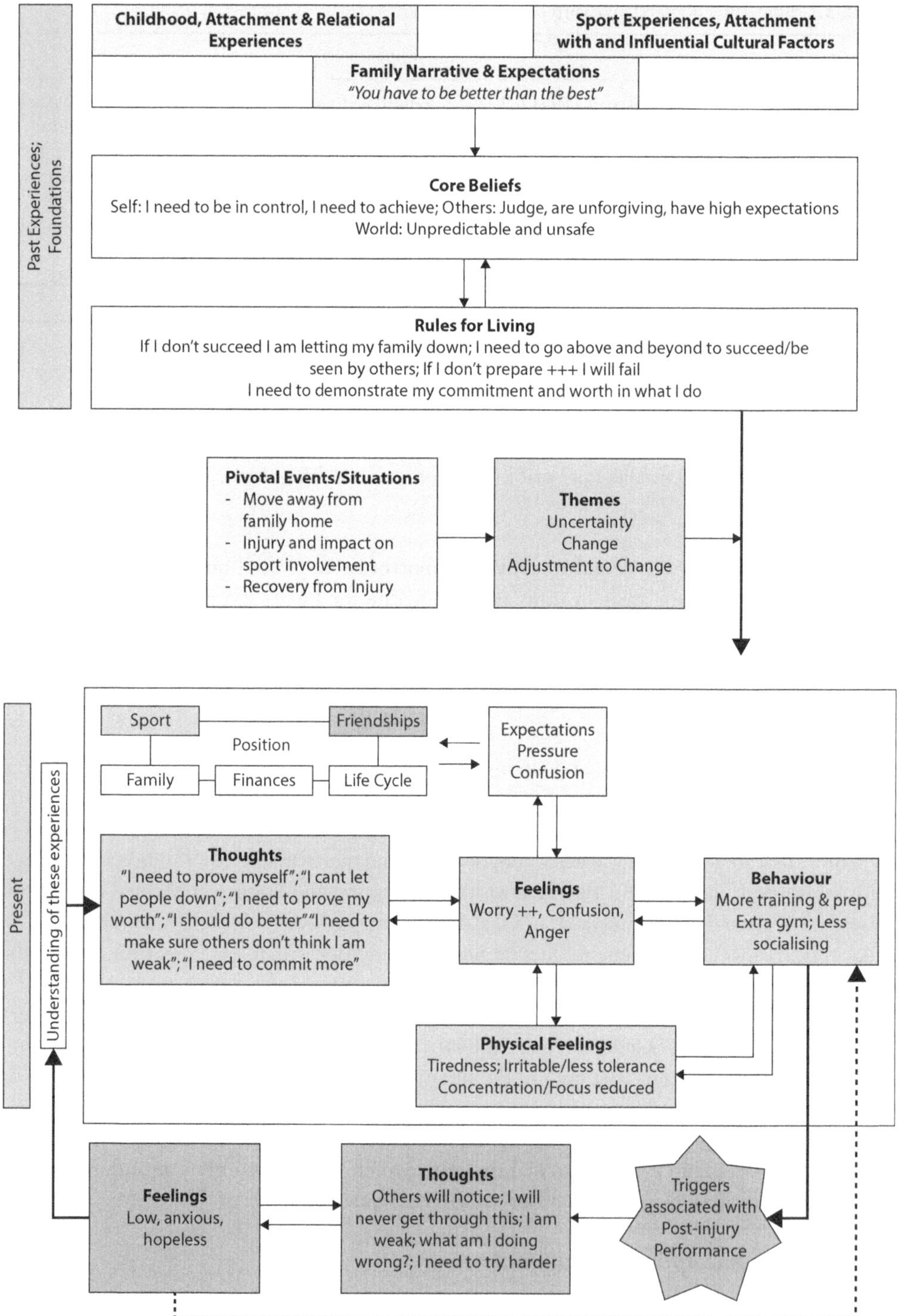

FIGURE 3.1 Longitudinal formulation.

formulation). A foundation of difficulties aligned with rejection, self-judgement, perfectionism, and achievement had been ever present for Luke throughout his childhood and contributed to his continual attempts to manage fluctuating low mood and anxiety. The recent injury and program of recovery had seemed to act as a catalyst to exacerbate pre-existing unhelpful beliefs associated with "perfectionism" and "weakness" resulting in responses aligned with negative cognitions and experiences of shame, self-attack, and self-blame and consequential emotional difficulties. Consequently, Luke's beliefs were leading to imbalance in the "threat, drive, and sooth-affiliative" systems, resultantly impacting on Luke's general functioning, understanding of both physical and psychological recovery from the injury whilst also his perceived sport performance.

Luke's previous experiences of CBT suggested a "head-heart lag" (Lee, 2004; Stott, 2007), whereby he was aware of the process and mechanism of the model yet felt unconnected and unable to apply to his own experiences. Regardless, Luke felt he had "failed" the therapy and his experiences may be too complex to help.

With this in mind, whilst considering Luke's past therapeutic experience alongside his identified goals (a) to improve his mood, (b) to feel more motivated to play, and (c) to improve his current performance on the pitch, CFT was suggested as the optimal therapeutic approach.

The CFT Intervention

Compassion focused therapy aims to help clients cultivate a compassionate self and use a compassionate mind when faced with difficult emotions and experiences (Gilbert, 2009a). Consisting of sensitivity, sympathy, distress tolerance, empathy, non-judgment, and care for well-being, the attributes of compassion allow us to turn towards our difficulties with courage, encouraging toleration of distress and taking a non-judgmental and empathic stance to understand our emotions and challenges, motivating us to action in order to reduce our distress (Kolts, 2016). In CFT, clients develop these attributes through developing compassionate mind skills, which encourage compassionate thinking and reasoning, attention, imagery, feelings/emotions, and behaviours and involve using a range of therapeutic modalities including mindfulness and CBT (Gilbert, 2009a; 2014).

In practice, there are several phases when using the CFT approach (see Table 3.2), which is not necessarily a linear process and requires flexibility on the part of the practitioner (Gilbert, 2014). These phases involve: developing a therapeutic relationship, psychoeducation, formulation, cultivating and building compassionate capacities, developing a compassionate self and mind, and using the compassionate mind to engage with specific problems. The therapeutic relationship plays a vital role in the approach. Drawing upon the theories of attachment and humanistic relating, CFT stresses the need to develop a therapeutic relationship/alliance in which the therapist attempts to model compassion and warmth, providing a secure base and relational safeness to allow the client to explore and articulate difficult emotions and experiences. Utilising various core therapeutic competencies, including micro-skills, guided discovery, and the recognition of unconscious processes, the therapist embodies multiple roles (e.g., as an educator) to facilitate the main phases of the approach (Gilbert, 2022).

After engaging with a psychologist that specialised in mental health, Luke completed eight sessions in CFT (Gilbert, 2009a, 2010, 2014, 2022a, 2022b; Kolts, 2016; Welford, 2016).

TABLE 3.2 Phases of therapy

Phases of therapy	*Goals*	*Activities*
Psychoeducation	To de-shame and de-personalise, to allow the client to understand that what goes on in our minds is not our fault	Discussions around the "tricky brain," old brain/new brain, and the 3 emotional/motivational systems. The importance of compassion
Formulation Process	To allow the client to have insight into how their early life experiences created threat-based coping safety strategies, drive based and soothing-affiliative based capacities	Socratic guided discovery to identify the themes around the background to threat, and safety. Functional analysis Imagery to identify past experiences Different versions of ourselves
Cultivating and Building Compassion	To work with affiliative emotions, to practise parasympathetic activation and to develop a safe/ secure base.	Soothing Rhythm Breathing Posture and voice work Compassionate Attention: Mindfulness Compassionate Imagery – safe place
Developing a compassionate self and mind	To explore the idea of a compassionate self and to be able to take a compassionate perspective	Compassionate self-practise/method acting Compassion to vulnerable self
Engaging with specific problems, e.g., self-criticism, depression, anxiety	To encourage clients to use their compassionate self/mind to engage with particular difficulties	Compassionate self-correction versus threat-based criticism Compassionate chair work Behavioural Activation

Source: Gilbert (2014).

Session 1

The initial session following the general assessment focused on psychoeducation and the importance of compassion. Psychoeducation is a crucial element of the CFT approach, enabling clients to understand the evolutionary basis of our emotional-motivational systems and to de-shame and de-personalise to reduce any self-criticism and blame (Gilbert, 2010). The first session with Luke involved discussing the evolved human brain, the role of depression to mitigate the loss of social rank, and the fact that he had a "tricky" brain, which together with his early social experiences, were responsible for his current difficulties. It was crucial for Luke to understand that his issues were not his fault and that he did not choose to have an unhelpful brain or his early life. Guided discovery was used to elaborate the concept of the tricky brain, which can be seen below:

THERAPIST: I'd like to talk more about the old brain versus the new brain problem, as I think it might be useful in helping us to understand some of the anxiety you are feeling at the moment. You mentioned that you went on safari last year, did I remember that right?

LUKE: Yeah, that's right, with my girlfriend

THERAPIST: Ok. Imagine that you are on safari, and you see an antelope being chased by a lion. The antelope manages to outrun the lion and gets to safety. What does the antelope do when it gets back to the herd?

LUKE: Erm, I'm not sure…… it will probably just move on with the herd, or eat?

THERAPIST: Yes, so the antelope just continues on with life as normal, and soon forgets the experience with the lion. Now, imagine that you are on safari, you get back to the camp later than expected, it's dark, and you find yourself being confronted and chased by a lion. Luckily, there is a jeep nearby and you manage to run to the vehicle and lock yourself in until the lion goes away. What would you be doing straight after that incident? What would you be doing the next day?

LUKE: I would be ******** myself!

THERAPIST: Same here! What would you be thinking and feeling?

LUKE: I would be getting lots of feelings in my body with the adrenaline, I would be thinking about what could have happened. I would be worried about it happening again the next night. I would be thinking about leaving to stay in a hotel!

THERAPIST: Would you be getting any images in your mind about the incident?

LUKE: Probably, I guess I would be getting images of what happened, and knowing me, I would be getting pictures in my head of what could have happened if I hadn't managed to get in the Jeep.

THERAPIST: And the thoughts and images that you have afterwards, what effect would they have on you?

LUKE: Erm, they keep me feeling on edge and panicky?

THERAPIST: Yes, that's right. So, from what we've discussed, we can see that the difference between you and the antelope is down to our tricky brains. The antelope with its "old" brain reacts to the threat of the lion, escapes, returns to the herd, and then calms down quite quickly. What happens to you?

LUKE: I'm stuck overthinking what happened and feeling on edge for the rest of the trip?

THERAPIST: That's right, our new brains allow us to think about experiences we have had, and after an experience (or even an imagined experience), the thoughts and images generated from our "new" brain loop back into the "old" emotional brain, leading to more emotion and fear. So even though you got away from the lion and you're safe, you still feel under threat. Does that make sense?

LUKE: Yeah, it does. It's making me think about times when I'm overthinking everything, especially about getting back to being fully fit for rugby. I'm feeling pretty panicked about it and I'm struggling to go to sleep at night.

THERAPIST: You talked a lot about that during our assessment and again, it's important to remember that it's not your fault, it's your tricky brain. We've all got one and it's important to understand how our brains work, to help us find ways of thinking and acting to feel less under threat and safe. This is where compassion comes in. Can we continue to look at this?

LUKE: Yeah, ok.

Leading on from this discussion, the function of the three emotional-motivational systems (threat, drive, and soothing), working together to manage and control our emotions was also explored in the first session. As part of this, psychoeducation emphasised the distinct roles of the three systems, the emotions activated by each, and the need for the systems to be in balance. It was especially important for Luke to understand that his threat system is easily triggered, releasing hormones (including adrenaline and cortisol) and resulting in difficult emotions, physical sensations, thoughts, and images. Anything can trigger our threat system including social threat (e.g., criticism of other people) and internal threats (our thoughts, images, etc.) and that the sensitivity of our threat system means that we are prone to overestimating threats and overthinking (Welford, 2016). Also, by getting Luke to close his eyes and imagine getting chased by the lion in the previous example, showed Luke that even imagining the situation resulted in him feeling some anxiety in his chest

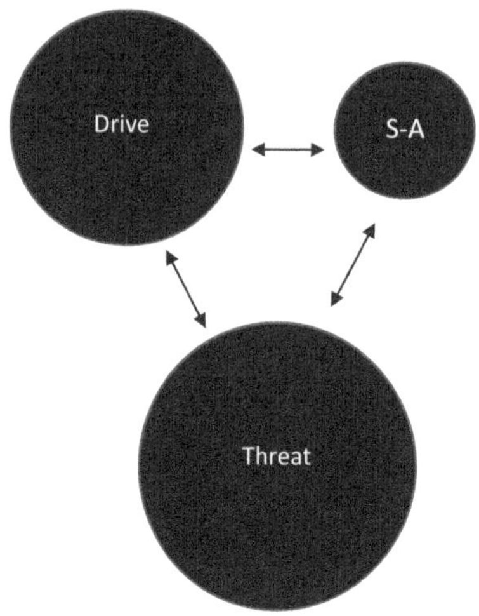

FIGURE 3.2 Luke's circle diagram.

and stomach, illustrating that our brains do not distinguish between real and imagined danger. As Luke was partially in his threat system, the practitioner helped Luke to connect and activate his soothing-affiliative system by teaching him soothing rhythm breathing (see Gilbert, 2010; Welford, 2016), which helped him to connect with the emotions and physiological sensations of the soothing and demonstrated the ability to switch systems. After discussing the three systems, Luke was then asked to consider how developed his systems were and to represent them by drawing three circles, which started the process of the CFT formulation (see Figure 3.2).

In drawing his circles, Luke acknowledged that currently his threat system was the most developed with his fears of not playing, getting over his injury, and disappointing others which resulted in depression and anxiety, lots of negative thinking and self-criticism, and feeling bad about himself. It was also evident that Luke managed his emotions and thoughts by trying to push them away and focusing on his drive system by over-doing his rehab sessions and playing video games. Further, Luke's soothing-affiliative system was not as activated as it could be, and we spent time discussing how we need to activate this to turn down the volume of the threat system, by learning compassionate mind skills and that this could help him to become less self-critical and depressed.

During the first session, Luke and the practitioner also spent some time considering what compassion meant to him, to identify any blocks to working with a CFT approach. Although Luke was quite open-minded as he was keen to feel better, there were some concerns that compassion did not fit very well with professional sport and that it sounded weak and "hippy dippy". Psychoeducation was helpful here and the practitioner reiterated Gilbert's definition of compassion that emphasises facing suffering, action, and courage which connected with Luke and his experience of playing rugby, which increased his interest in the approach. Further, as Luke was depressed and had reported some suicidal ideation, it was important to help him lift his mood in the initial sessions, therefore, he was also given some psychoeducation on behavioural activation (Lejuez et al., 2001), which involves increasing and planning activity as well as connecting with others, with the practitioner framing it as a way of showing himself care and activating his soothing-affiliative system.

Home Practise

In collaboration with the practitioner, Luke agreed that he would practise soothing rhythm breathing and to try keep an activities diary.

Session 2

On reviewing the week, Luke had been practising the soothing rhythm breathing and reported feeling less "wired" when he had done this and after completing the diary had realised how isolated he was, that his activities outside of training were limited, and his sleep and eating routines were poor. Therefore, the practitioner and Luke spent some time focusing on what his compassionate side would want him to do and helping Luke to develop better night-time and eating routines (e.g., using psychoeducation and problem-solving) and we thought about him trying to meet up more with his girlfriend and to spend time with his teammates immediately after training. The rest of the session focused on collaborating on developing a compassion-focused formulation (see below), to allow Luke to understand himself better and to place his difficulties in a context to encourage more self-compassion. Using guided discovery, functional analysis, and imagery, we explored the following as part of the formulation process:

- **Historical influences** – specific focus on the type of experiences which may have sensitised the "threat, drive, and affiliative-soothing" systems
- **Fears and threats** – exploration regarding internal (e.g., personal views about ourselves, emotions, or our connections with others) and external (i.e., other people feel, think, and do to us) threats which tend to be associated with rejection, abandonment, isolation, shame, and harm (Gilbert, 2010)
- **Safety strategies** – how the threat system is regulated, i.e., attempts to keep safe
- **Unintended consequences** – a de-shaming approach to exploring any adverse impacts of the use of particular safety strategies
- **My relationship with self** – exploration of one's relationship with the self, whether this is critical or compassionate

From these discussions, Luke was able to clearly express his internal and external threats and fears around disappointing his father and coaches and being rejected. Exploratory imagery in which the practitioner asked Luke to close his eyes and to recall a recent time when he felt he had disappointed someone, and then to float back to his earliest memory of when he felt the same way, which activated a memory when he was 9 where his father looked disappointed when he missed a try. Luke avoided to keep safe or relied on his drive system (focusing on training, planning, etc.) which activated the threat system even more and resulted in him having a critical relationship with himself. There was very little self-compassion. Again, taking a compassionate stance, it was reiterated that these experiences together with his tricky brain were not his fault.

Home Practise

In collaboration with the practitioner, Luke agreed to complete filling in the formulation from our discussions (see Figure 3.3), to continue with the breathing exercise, to work on improving his night-time and eating routines, and try to connect more with others.

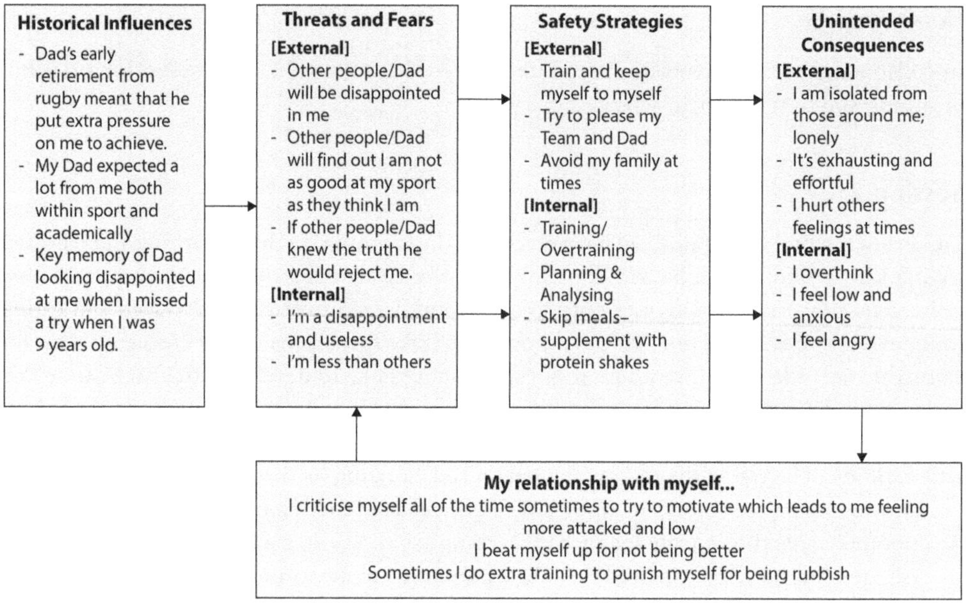

FIGURE 3.3 Luke's compassion-focused formulation.

Sessions 3–4

On reviewing the home practise, Luke had managed to improve his night-time routines and was starting to get more sleep, he had also managed to stay for a short period after training to be around his teammates and felt less down afterwards. There was a recap of the CFT formulation to encourage Luke's compassionate understanding of his emotional difficulties. In sessions 3 and 4, we looked to cultivate compassion, building upon the rhythmic breathing that was introduced in the first session. Mindfulness plays an important part in this process, encouraging Luke to observe his thoughts, feelings, body sensations, and motivations in a non-judgemental manner, and after some discussion, Luke decided to practise mindful walking and eating as part of this. Further, time was spent on developing helpful postures and tones of voice to allow Luke to appreciate how different postures and tones of voice can alter feelings and body sensations. With this exercise, Luke was invited to sit comfortably and to repeat the phrase "hello, what are you doing today?" firstly in a frustrated way and then in a warm/friendly way, and then to reflect on what he noticed in his body. Further, compassionate imagery can be a very helpful means of activating the soothing-affiliative system and to shift out of threat mode when it is activated by rumination and self-criticism (Kolts, 2016). Therefore, the practitioner and Luke worked together to develop a soothing place image using lots of sensory detail, and which included an affiliative component (e.g., where the people or place in the imagery were welcoming), which centred around Luke when he was younger helping his grandparents (mother's parents) in the garden (who were always pleased to see him).

Home Practise

Again in collaboration with the practitioner, Luke agreed to focus on his sleep and eating routines, increase social activity, to practise mindfulness, and his soothing place image.

Sessions 5–6

Luke reported back that his routines continued to improve and he had gone to lunch with a couple of his teammates and his mood again felt a bit better. The soothing place image had been helpful when he had been feeling agitated in the morning before training, which was framed as him shifting from his threat mentality. He also reported feeling more motivated to train once the session started and that he had noticed during his mindful walks that he was being distracted by lots of self-critical and blaming thoughts (e.g., you're washed up, you should be playing better, you're letting everyone down, you shouldn't have rushed rehab and you're weak), which made him feel panicky, anxious, and angry. This was explored in the session:

THERAPIST: So, when you were doing the mindfulness exercises, you noticed that your inner critic was out in force and giving you a hard time.
LUKE: Yeah, it's always in the background, but it gets louder when I'm playing crap, or I'm injured.
THERAPIST: The inner critic is very familiar to you then. When did you first notice it?
LUKE: It's been around a long time, when I started to play rugby I suppose, and dad was one of the coaches and he would look really disappointed and frustrated if I didn't play well.
THERAPIST: It makes sense why you are so self-critical?
LUKE: Yeah, 100 percent.
THERAPIST: As we are working on developing compassion, I wonder what it would be like to notice and pay less attention to your self-critical voice, and to develop a voice that is more self-compassionate?
LUKE: (Looks a bit confused), I'm not sure about that.
THERAPIST: What are you thinking about it?
LUKE: I'm not sure that I would be able to do that.
THERAPIST: Imagine if you did not engage with your self-critical thoughts, or that the inner critic was not around, what would you be concerned about?
LUKE: Although I don't like it, I think that the inner critic motivates me to keep on going and do better, it if wasn't around I might give up. It keeps me on my toes!
THERAPIST: So, your inner critic is a big motivator for you and if it wasn't there, you would be worried that you'd give up or fail? Are there any down sides of having a loud inner critic?
LUKE: Erm…, well yes, it makes me feel stressed out and annoyed with myself when I notice it, so I get where you're going with this.
THERAPIST: I wonder then if we could try to help you turn down the volume of the inner critic by developing more compassionate ways of relating to yourself and if this could also help you to motivate yourself. Would you be prepared to give it a go?
LUKE: Sure, I'll try anything!

Once Luke was prepared to consider developing more of a more compassionate self and to reduce the loudness of the inner critic, therapy focused on a number of imagery exercises to strengthen a sense of the compassionate self. These included compassionate self-practise in which Luke imagined what it would be like to have more compassionate characteristics, including those of compassionate motivation, wisdom, and courage, and the impact of this on his motivation, felt emotions, and thinking. Also, Luke was asked to activate the memory of himself as a younger person when he had not completed a try and was encouraged to extend compassion and kindness to his vulnerable younger self. As part of this process, the memory was rescripted with Luke entering the memory as an adult and talking and calming his younger self in a compassionate way, which was a very powerful experience for Luke and reduced the anxiety of the memory (Schiller et al., 2010). During the debriefing, Luke also reflected upon the fact that his father had been brought up with a very critical father himself who had not been supportive when he had not managed to continue with his rugby career, which helped him feel more compassionate towards him. This experience was used as an example of how Luke could respond to his inner critic in a more self-compassionate way, and he agreed initially to keep a journal to help him practise, using the framework described by Neff and Gerner (2018).

Home Practise

Luke and the practitioner agreed that he would continue with his activity/connection, mindfulness, and to practise responding to his inner critic with self-compassion.

Sessions 7–8

By session 7, Luke reported that his mood was better, he felt calmer and less frustrated. He had also been more open with his team-mates and one of the coaches about his difficulties and had received a lot of support. Motivation had continued to improve; he had started to enjoy his training and was playing a lot better. There had been more attempts of trying to show himself more self-compassion when he was anxious, however, at times, he was still finding this difficult. Therefore, to help him to deepen his experience of self-compassion, the practitioner facilitated some empty chair work (Gilbert, 2010), which is a technique used in both emotion focused therapy (EFT; Greenberg & Watson, 2006) and schema therapy (ST; Young et al., 2003). This involved helping Luke to connect with a compassionate perspective by putting an empty chair in front of him and imagining that a close friend is sitting there who is known to struggle with anxiety. Starting with some rhythmic breathing and connecting to his compassionate self, Luke was then asked to talk about his friend's difficulties, how he would talk and re-assure his friend from a place of compassion, and to consider how his friend would feel after being spoken to in this way. Luke was also asked to reflect on how his own inner critic reacts to his anxiety ("it tells me to snap out of it and man up") and which approach was more helpful. This experiential exercise enabled Luke to connect more with his compassionate self and to feel and direct compassion (see Gilbert, 2010; Kolts, 2016). In the final session, there was a review of Luke's progress and a discussion around how he thought he could continue to work on balancing his emotional-motivational systems and develop his compassionate self in action. As part of this, Luke developed a plan which included practising what he had covered during the sessions, and to help others by getting involved in an organisation that promoted wellbeing and mental health in sport. Although Luke only had eight sessions (due to funding), he was pleased with his progress and did not feel that he needed any further sessions.

Evaluation and Reflection

At the end of the eight sessions, Luke's progress was measured using the various measures introduced at assessment, which indicated that he was no longer depressed, his anxiety had shifted into the mild range, and all elements of his self-compassion had improved (Figure 3.4). From the final review with Luke, he felt that he achieved his goals of having a more stable

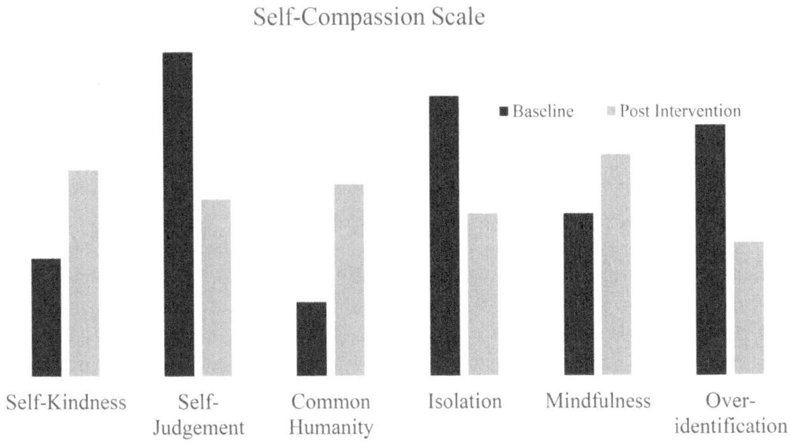

FIGURE 3.4 Pre and post intervention self-compassion scores.

mood, motivation to play rugby and playing better, and that feedback from coaches, friends, and family confirmed this.

According to the literature, helping self-critical sportspeople to develop more self-compassion using CFT might be difficult to implement, due to the competitive nature of professional sport (Mosewich, et al., 2019). However, in support of the available literature (Mosewich et al., 2011; Mosewich et al., 2013; Doorley et al., 2022), Luke (and others with a strong inner critic that we have worked with) engaged well with the approach, and especially connected with the evolutionary explanations, the experiential elements of the work, and the notion that compassion emphasises struggle, courage, and taking responsibility for action. Luke's presentation of poor mental health, which was impacting his performance, necessitated more of an intensive therapeutic approach as opposed to simply teaching skills (as in compassion-focused training), and this may also have accounted for his level of engagement. There were also some limitations in using CFT with only eight available sessions, as it was not possible to use all of the interventions in depth (e.g., chair work), which would have further developed Luke's compassionate self. As shown with other populations, it seems that the CFT would be especially useful when working with elite sportspeople/athletes with more complex presentations, which span both performance and mental health issues, and where the issues are partly maintained by high levels of self-criticism and blame. Appropriately-trained psychologists interested in applying CFT should consider additional training (e.g., compassionate mind foundation) in this approach. However, while further studies are needed in this area, it appears that CFT could provide an effective approach when working with elite sportspeople.

References

American Psychiatric Association (APA). (2013). *Diagnostic and Statistical Manual of Mental Disorders* (5th ed.).

Basran, J., Raven, J., & Plowright, P. (2022). Overview of outcome research on compassion focused therapy: a scoping review. In P. Gilbert & G. Simos, *Compassion Focused Therapy: Clinical Practice and Applications*. Routledge.

Beaumont, E. & Hollins, M. C. (2015). A narrative review exploring the effectiveness of compassion-focused therapy. *Counselling Psychology Review*, 30 (1), 21–32.

Brewer, B. W. & Petitpas, A. J. (2017). Athletic identity foreclosure. *Current Opinion in Psychology*, 16, 118–122. https://doi.org/10.1016/j.copsyc.2017.05.004

Ceccarelli, L. A., Giuliano, R. J., Glazebrook, C. M., & Strachan, S. M. (2019). Self-compassion and psycho-physiological recovery from recalled sport failure. *Frontiers in Psychology*, 10, Article 1564. https://doi.org/10.3389/fpsyg.2019.01564

Craig, C., Hiskey, S., & Spector, A. (2020). Compassion focused therapy: a systematic review of its effectiveness and acceptability in clinical populations. *Expert Review of Neurotherapeutics*, 20 (4), 385–400. https://doi.org/10.1080/14737175.2020.1746184

Depue, R. A. & Morrone-Strupinsky, J. V. (2005). A neurobehavioral model of affiliative bonding: implications for conceptualizing a human trait of affiliation. *The Behavioral and brain sciences*, 28 (3), 313–395. https://doi.org/10.1017/S0140525X05000063

Doorley, J. D., Kashdan, T. B., Weppner, C. H., & Glass, C. R. (2022). The effects of self-compassion on daily emotion regulation and performance rebound among college athletes: Comparisons with confidence, grit, and hope. *Psychology of Sport & Exercise*, 58, https://doi.org/10.1016/j.psychsport.2021.102081

Foskett, R., & Longstaff, F. (2018). The mental health of elite athletes in the United Kingdom. *Journal of Science and Medicine in Sport*, 21 (8), 765–770.

Gardner, F. & Moore, Z. (2006). *Clinical Sport Psychology*. Human Kinetics

Gilbert, H. (2022). The therapeutic relationship in compassion focused therapy. In P. Gilbert & G. Simos, (Eds.), *Compassion Focused Therapy: Clinical Practice and Applications*. Routledge.

Gilbert, P. (2001). Evolutionary approaches to psychopathology. The role of natural defences. *Australian and New Zealand Journal of Psychiatry*, 35 (1), 17–27.

Gilbert, P. (2009a). Introducing compassion-focused therapy. *Advances in Psychiatric Treatment*, 15 (3), 199–208.

Gilbert, P. (2009b). *The compassionate Mind: A New Approach to the Challenges of Life*. Constable & Robinson.

Gilbert, P. (2010). *Compassion Focused Therapy*. Routledge.

Gilbert, P. (2014). The origins and nature of compassion focused therapy. *British Journal of Clinical Psychology*, 53 (1), 6–41.

Gilbert, P. (2020). Compassion: From its evolution to a psychotherapy. *Frontiers in Psychology*, 11, Article 586161. https://doi.org/10.3389/fpsyg.2020.586161

Gilbert, P. (2022a). Internal shame and disconnection: from hostile self-criticism to compassionate self-correction and guidance. In P. Gilbert & G. Simos, (Eds.), *Compassion Focused Therapy: Clinical Practice and Applications*. Routledge.

Gilbert, P. (2022b). Compassionate mind training: key themes. In P. Gilbert & G. Simos, (Eds.), *Compassion Focused Therapy: Clinical Practice and Applications*. Routledge.

Gouttebarge, V., Castaldelli-Maia, J. M., Gorczynski, P., Hainline, B., Hitchcock, M. E., Kerkhoffs, G. M., Rice, S. M., & Reardon, C. L. (2019). Occurrence of mental health symptoms and disorders in current and former elite athletes: a systematic review and meta-analysis. *British Journal of Sports Medicine*, 53 (11), 700–706. https://doi.org/10.1136/bjsports-2019-100671

Gouttebarge, V., Hopley, P., Kerkhoffs, G., Verhagen, E., Viljoen, W., Wylleman, P., & Lamberts, M. I. (2017). Symptoms of common mental health disorders in professional rugby: An international observational descriptive study. *International Journal of Sports Medicine*, 38 (11), 864–870. doi: 10.1055/s-0043-114010

Greenberg, L. S. & Watson, J. C. (2006). *Emotion-Focused Therapy for Depression*. American Psychological Association. https://doi.org/10.1037/11286-000

Gulliver, A., Griffiths, K. M., Mackinnon, A., Batterham, P. J., & Stanimirovic, R. (2015). The mental health of Australian elite athletes. *Journal of Science and Medicine in Sport*, 18 (3), 255–261. https://doi.org/10.1016/j.jsams.2014.04.006

Jensen, S. N., Ivarsson, A., Fallby, J., Dankers, S., & Elbe, A. M. (2018). Depression in Danish and Swedish elite football players and its relation to perfectionism and anxiety. *Psychology of Sport and Exercise*, 36, 147–155. https://doi.org/10.1016/j.psychsport.2018.02.008

Kiliç, Ö., Aoki, H., Goedhart, E., Hägglund, M., Kerkhoffs, G., Kuijer, P., Waldén, M., & Gouttebarge, V. (2018). Severe musculoskeletal time-loss injuries and symptoms of common mental disorders in professional soccer: a longitudinal analysis of 12-month follow-up data. *Knee Surgery, Sports Traumatology, Arthroscopy: Official Journal of the ESSKA*, 26 (3), 946–954. https://doi.org/10.1007/s00167-017-4644-1

Killham, M. E., Mosewich, A. D., Mack, D. E., Gunnell, K. E., & Ferguson, L. J. (2018). Women athletes' self-compassion, self-criticism, and perceived sport performance. *Sport, Exercise, and Performance Psychology*, 7 (3), 297–307.

Kirby, J. N. (2017). Compassion interventions: The programmes, the evidence, and implications for research and practice. *Psychology and Psychotherapy: Theory, Research and Practice*, 90 (3), 432–455.

Kolts, R. L. (2016). *CFT Made Simple: A Clinician's Guide to Practising Compassion-Focused Therapy*. New Harbinger Publications, Inc.

Lama D. (1995). *The Power of Compassion*. Harper Collins.

Lee, D. A. (2004). The perfect nurturer. *Compassion: Conceptualisations, Research and Use in Psychotherapy*, 326.

Lejuez, C. W., Hopko, D. R., & Hopko, S. D. (2001). A brief behavioral activation treatment for depression. Treatment manual. *Behavior Modification*, 25 (2), 255–286. https://doi.org/10.1177/0145445501252005

Mosewich, A. D., Crocker, P. R. E., Kowalski, K. C., & DeLongis, A. (2013). Applying self-compassion in sport: An intervention with women athletes. *Journal of Sport & Exercise Psychology*, 35 (5), 514–552.

Mosewich, A. D., Kowalski, K. C., Sabiston, C. M., Sedgwick, W. A., & Tracy, J. L. (2011). Self-compassion: a potential resource for young women athletes. *Journal of Sport & Exercise Psychology*, 33 (1), 103–123. https://doi.org/10.1123/jsep.33.1.103

Mosewich, A. D., Sabiston, C. N., Kowalski, K. C., Gaudreau, P., & Crocker, P. R. E. (2019). Self-compassion in the stress process in women athletes. *The Sport Psychologist*, 33 (1), 23–34. doi: https://doi.org/10.1123/tsp.2017-0094

Neff, K. D. (2003). Development and validation of a scale to measure self-compassion. *Self and Identity*, 2, 223–250.

Neff, K. D. & Gerner, C. (2018). *The Mindful Self-Compassion Workbook*. Guildford Press.

Powers, T. A., Koestner, R., Lacaille, N., Kwan, L., & Zuroff, D. C. (2009). Self-criticism, motivation, and goal progress of athletes and musicians: A prospective study. *Personality and Individual Differences*, 47 (4), 279–283. https://doi.org/10.1016/j.paid.2009.03.012

Reardon, C. L., Hainline, B., Aron, C. M., Baron, D., Baum, A. L., Bindra, A., Budgett, R., Campriani, N., Castaldelli-Maia, J. M., Currie, A., Derevensky, J. L., Glick, I. D., Gorczynski, P., Gouttebarge, V., Grandner, M. A., Han, D. H., McDuff, D., Mountjoy, M., Polat, A., Purcell, R., … Engebretsen, L. (2019). Mental health in elite athletes: International Olympic Committee consensus statement. *British Journal of Sports Medicine*, 53 (11), 667–699. https://doi.org/10.1136/bjsports-2019-100715

Schiller, D., Monfils, M. H., Raio, C. M., Johnson, D. C., Ledoux, J. E., & Phelps, E. A. (2010). Preventing the return of fear in humans using reconsolidation update mechanisms. *Nature*, 463 (7277), 49–53. https://doi.org/10.1038/nature08637

Simos, G. (2022). Compassion focused therapy: an evolutionary and biopsychosocial understanding of depression and its management. In P. Gilbert & G. Simos, (Eds.), *Compassion Focused Therapy: Clinical Practice and Applications*. Routledge.

Spitzer, R. L., Kroenke, K., & Williams, J. B. (1999). Validation and utility of a self-report version of PRIME-MD: the PHQ primary care study. Primary care evaluation of mental disorders. Patient health questionnaire. *JAMA*, 282 (18), 1737–1744. https://doi.org/10.1001/jama.282.18.1737

Spitzer, R. L., Kroenke, K., Williams, J. B., & Löwe, B. (2006). A brief measure for assessing generalized anxiety disorder: the GAD-7. *Archives of Internal Medicine*, 166 (10), 1092–1097. https://doi.org/10.1001/archinte.166.10.1092

Stott, R. (2007). When head and heart do not agree: A theoretical and clinical analysis of Rational-Emotional Dissociation (RED) in cognitive therapy. *Journal of Cognitive Psychotherapy*, 21 (1), 37–50. https://doi.org/10.1891/088983907780493313

Sutherland, L. M., Kowalski, K. C., Ferguson, L. J., Sabiston, C. M., Sedgwick, W. A., & Crocker, P. R. E. (2014). Narratives of young women athletes' experiences of emotional pain and self-compassion. *Qualitative Research in Sport, Exercise and Health*, 6 (4), 499–516. http://dx.doi.org/10.1080/2159676X.2014.88858

Taylor, J. & Schneider, B. A. (1992). The sport-clinical intake protocol: A comprehensive interviewing instrument for applied sport psychology. *Professional Psychology: Research and Practice,* 23 (4), 318–325. https://doi.org/10.1037/0735-7028.23.4.318

Turner, M. J., Carrington, S., & Miller, A. (2019). Psychological distress across sport participation groups: The mediating effects of secondary irrational beliefs on the relationship between primary irrational beliefs and symptoms of anxiety, anger, and depression. *Journal of Clinical Sport Psychology*, 13 (1), 17–40.

Walton, C. C., Baranoff, J., Gilbert, P., & Kirby, J. (2021). Self-compassion, social rank, and psychological distress in athletes of varying competitive levels. *Psychology of Sport & Exercise*, 50, 101733. doi: 10.1016/j.psychsport.2020.10173

Welford, M. (2016). *Compassion Focused Therapies: For Dummies.* John Wiley & Sons.

Young, J. E., Klosko, J. S., & Weishaar, M. E. (2003). *Schema Therapy: A practitioner's Guide.* Guilford Press.

4

COGNITIVE THERAPY (CT)

Faye F. Didymus and Paul McCarthy

Introduction

Cognitive therapy (CT; Beck, 1963, 1964, 1967) is a structured, short-term, and present-orientated therapy focusing on changing cognitions to create helpful subsequent adaptations to emotions and behaviors. We shall probe this classification of CT throughout this chapter but, for now, in an encompassing sense, we can regard CT as any technique whose chief mode of action is modifying patterns of faulty thinking (Beck, 1970a, 1970b). Indeed, CT is a set of operations that focus on a client's cognitions (verbal or pictorial) and on the assumptions, attitudes, and premises underlying these cognitions (Beck, 1970b).

Beck (1967) began his work on cognitive theory to overcome his frustration when attempting to use psychoanalysis to treat patients with depression. Although originally developed as a therapy for depression, researchers have successfully adapted this approach to address problems among diverse populations (Beck, 1967). Such adaptations changed the focus, techniques, and length of treatment, yet the theoretical premises remain constant. In developing CT, Beck interrogated the work of philosophers such as Epictetus and theorists such as Karen Horney, Alfred Adler, George Kelly, Albert Ellis, Richard Lazarus, Albert Bandura, and many others. The cognitive model proposes that dysfunctional thinking is common to all psychological disturbances. Such dysfunctional thinking influences a person's mood and behavior. By learning to judge one's thinking realistically and adaptively, negative emotions and maladaptive behavior subside. In CT, we spell "cognitive" with a lowercase "c" to recognize that "cognitive" is an adjective rather than one part of the compound noun "Cognitive Therapy" (Beck, 1979a; Wills, 2009).

About the Authors

Faye F. Didymus

My interest in applied sport psychology flourished whilst reading for a PhD at Loughborough University in the United Kingdom. Having spent the early part of my doctorate conducting empirical research that was thoroughly intriguing but somewhat distanced from those who it was intended to help (i.e., athletes and coaches), I embarked on a phase of applied research

DOI: 10.4324/9781003162513-5

during the latter stages of my PhD. It was during this time that I developed a fascination in the power of changing thoughts to change emotion, behavior, and, ultimately, performance. Learning through research, practice, training, and teaching, I became a British Association of Sport and Exercise Sciences accredited practitioner in 2013, shortly after starting my academic career at Leeds Beckett University. When working with athletes and coaches, I emphasize the therapeutic alliance and clients' independent learning during homework to maximize their development. I strive to maintain some flexibility in my approach to suit the preferences of those with whom I work.

Paul McCarthy

I began my training as a sport and exercise psychologist more than 20 years ago by completing training in two therapeutic modalities: directive (CT and cognitive behavior therapy) and non-directive (person-centered). The person-centered approach laid the foundation for the therapeutic work within which other approaches (CT and, more broadly, CBT) could flourish. My private practice work molds to the therapeutic preferences of my clients, with many choosing the CT approach because of its emphasis on modifying faulty thinking that many athletes reconcile: "If I could think better, I know I could perform better." Over the past 20 years, my belief in therapeutic alliance and therapeutic competence meant identifying, measuring, teaching, and promoting skills in CT, which culminated in the development of the taught doctorate in sport and exercise psychology at Glasgow Caledonian University. CT is a central pillar of my private practice, academic teaching, and research in applied sport psychology.

Theory

In CT, there is a broad theoretical assumption that what we think (cognitions), what we feel (emotions), and what we do (behavior) interact and create a subjective perception of the world; a world we mediate cognitively. An abundance of thoughts, memories, and experiences are the invisible forces molding our actions. A basic assumption might be that people, given their own awareness, can understand and solve their psychological disturbance. They can also redress those misconceptions shaping emotional disturbance with the problem-solving machinery they have used before (Beck et al., 1985).

To survive, we need to generate adaptive function (Beck, 1979a). For such a function, we rely on cognitive, affective, behavioral, and motivational systems, each of which possesses schemas. A schema is a cognitive framework that helps us to organize and interpret information. When there is much information in our environment, schemas help us to take short cuts to explicate this information. Schemas influence how we process information by guiding how we perceive self, others, goals, and expectations, and how we represent our experience and learning. These schemas inform cognitive shifts and vulnerabilities. Our cognitive, affective, behavioral, and motivational systems that possess schemas combine as modes, which can be primal (i.e., rigid, absolute, automatic, and biased), adaptive, or maladaptive. The goal of CT is to help clients to consciously overrule primal and maladaptive thinking with deliberate thinking, conscious goals, problem-solving, and long-term planning (Beck & Weishaar, 1989).

Some commentators have criticized CT (and CBT) for downplaying environmental influences on behavior (Weishaar, 1993). Such environmental and social triggers require a broader perspective that recognizes the best course of action in any circumstance. Suffering abuse from a bad coach or manager, for example, ought to be addressed with a grievance procedure or by changing the system. In this situation, solely focusing on changing the coach's or manager's cognition would not lead to adequate resolve (Wills, 2009); however, you are in a better position to address these circumstances with sound cognitive machinery.

Cognitive therapy is organized around a formulation. During a formulation, the psychologist builds from the information gathered during client assessment a comprehensive model to explain the psychological factors that are developing and maintaining the client's problem (Wills, 2009). This formulation guides and monitors psychological intervention(s). Within a formulation, we observe different types and levels of cognition. At the highest order level of cognition, we have schemas. A schema is a broad cluster of meanings underpinned by more specific beliefs and assumptions. A core belief represents an unconditional belief about the self, others, or the world, whilst intermediate beliefs play a role in shaping the content of thoughts. An assumption is a conditional belief, such as an "if-then" proposition or a rule of living (Beck, 1964). One way to understand the relations among core beliefs, intermediate beliefs, assumptions, and automatic thoughts is to use the metaphor of a tree. Core beliefs can be likened to the roots of a tree, which link to a trunk (intermediate beliefs), branches (assumptions), and leaves (automatic thoughts; Wills, 2009). How cognition is dealt with during CT depends on its level. Although we might tackle automatic thoughts via thought records, we would address core beliefs with historical tests, the continuum technique, or positive data logs (Padesky & Greenberger, 1995) for example.

Establishing a formulation is perplexing. Kuyken (2006) offered the criteria to improve reliability during formulation to ensure "good enough" formulations. He emphasized humility, provisionality, and evidence gained from behavioral experiments. In Young and Beck's (1980) view, an effective cognitive therapist is formulating all the time as she collects data: "the therapist is like a detective who has a lot of clues but has still not solved the crime" (p. 13). When considering the timescales for formulation and intervention, it is possible that an athlete might see swift changes in thoughts and moods using thought records, whilst modifying core beliefs and schemas is comparatively gradual. Imagine the negative beliefs and assumptions gathering apace over the years, leaving the athlete certain about the world he inhabits. Changing this view and experience of the world via a positive data log means the athlete collects positive information about themselves and their lives. This is an activity that takes time and one that might never have been considered before. Beck (1991) stressed that it is "belief change" that leads to therapeutic change.

Recognizing Negative Automatic Thoughts

Negative automatic thoughts are idiosyncratic because they reflect a faulty appraisal that is peculiar to the individual and ranges from a mild distortion to a complete misinterpretation. Some athletes who report unpleasant feelings describe a sequence comprising a specific event (e.g., an injury) that produces an unpleasant affect (e.g., anxiety). Take the example of a golfer who (a) hears about someone having a low round in the tournament and (b) feels anxious. Whilst recognizing both the event and the affective response, he cannot make a direct connection between these two phenomena because a link is missing in the sequence. The bridge between a particular event and unpleasant affect is cognition. In the case above, it is the cognition that generates anxiety. Detecting the intervening cognitions means the golfer can understand why he felt anxious; he indiscriminately regarded the low round as dangerous to his chances of winning. Whether affect is the royal road to cognition or cognition is the royal road to affect (Beck, 1979b; Padesky, 1994), emotion is where the action lies, and cognition explains the appraisal that helps us to understand maladaptive feelings and behaviors (Wills, 2009).

The Therapeutic Relationship

Any service delivery in sport psychology encompasses the concept of the therapeutic relationship. This relationship is common to all therapeutic models and is one of, if not the, primary determinant of therapeutic effectiveness (Orlinsky et al., 1994). Use of the therapeutic relationship is, however, imprecise and its value may be conceptually vulnerable to over-inflation (Feltham, 1999). Carl Rogers' (1957, 1980) core conditions of the therapeutic relationship (i.e., empathy, warmth, congruence) resonate with Beck's (1979b) description of the therapeutic alliance. Beck (1979b) recognized these core conditions as necessary but not sufficient for change and emphasized that the collaborative relationship *and* the psychologist's skill and expertise are necessary factors for therapeutic change. This team of the client and the psychologist work together to solve the client's problems. Knowing about psychological issues and processes of psychological change means that the psychologist can apply what she knows to the client's circumstances and the client brings their experiences to the team. This notion of a team is critical because each depends on the other to succeed. The core conditions create a relationship and the therapeutic work unfolds within it (Wills, 2009). Beck (1979b) defined the therapeutic stance in CT as "collaborative empiricism." Although perhaps the athlete comes to the sport psychologist for help and so depends on the practitioner, the sport psychologist can only work with the client who supplies the raw data (thoughts and behavior). The structure and expertise that the sport psychologist offers, combined with reports on thoughts and behavior from the athlete, help the teamwork through the problem(s) together. This egalitarian position promotes a joint effort and diminishes the chances of the client experiencing shame, inferiority, and defensiveness (Beck, 1979a). The Beckian therapeutic relationship combines direction, structure, and education with empathy, warmth, and congruence to offer the client comprehensive therapeutic support.

The Practice of CT

Jess, a first team football coach, reflected on her own playing career as plagued by negative thoughts that squatted in her mind but, more recently, seemed to assume residency because the team she coached was sliding down the league table. Although comparatively successful, Jess' perception of her own career was that it lurched from one mediocre performance to the next but rarely sailed. These experiences mirrored what she saw in her squad each week. The tide of her concerning thoughts persuaded Jess to contact me for "some advice."

I (second author) had met Jess previously when I presented to a squad of national coaches on self-awareness in coaching. After the presentation, Jess approached me to explain her surprise about my presentation because she had studied English literature at a prestigious university and yet had not seen psychology, self-awareness, or self-care in any of her readings. When she queried, "Why did I not see these connections when I studied English at university?" I tentatively suggested, "Perhaps you were not looking for such things?" I had used excerpts from several novels, poems, and plays to illustrate how psychology and many of our applied psychological skills and techniques are so seamlessly woven into the fabric of our lives that we do not see them; psychology is on our lips and in our minds and hidden in plain sight.

We began with an initial session to explore Jess' presenting issues. Sitting uncomfortably with her eyes fixed on the windowpane, Jess recounted her story of her coaching life. As she spoke, I knitted the thoughts, feelings, and actions together to reveal a sense of foreboding about the coming chapters in Jess' life. Until now, Jess survived on a diet of censure and condemnation, diminishing and dismissing any comparative successes and leaving herself psychologically and emotionally derelict.

JESS: "I'm there, and I'm angry. And I'm angry at being angry. But do I show it? No! Why? Because being angry is unacceptable, isn't it? So, I'm positive and encouraging."
PSYCHOLOGIST: "With the players?"
JESS: "Yeah" (tailing off forlornly)
PSYCHOLOGIST: "And with yourself?"
JESS: "I'm dying inside, and nobody knows it but me. No one would believe me if I told them—do you know that? No one would believe me. What, you mean Jess? No way! She's the most positive person I know–that's what they would say."
PSYCHOLOGIST: "An angel to others and a devil to yourself?"
JESS: "Exactly! At some level, I know I don't deserve this treatment, you know, the way I treat myself, but it's almost like I deserve it. Can you understand that?"
PSYCHOLOGIST: "It sounds like you are making amends for past wrongs. A penance from which you cannot, or you feel you cannot, elude."

There is something inescapably baffling about the juxtaposition of psychological support in elite sport. Everything outside the psychologist's door represented a daunting and demanding culture of work, but once Jess stepped inside the room, she felt a psychological lifeline pull her into a culture of care. Jess' need for fulfilling work had left her empty. The crisis for Jess, like it is for so many, was a crisis of belonging. All Jess could see in her mind's eye was a harbinger of loss and her anxiogenic thinking pervaded her life.

JESS: "I have danced around this pain and avoided it at every turn. I'm like Miss Havisham in Charles's Dickens's Great Expectations. Have you read it?"
PSYCHOLOGIST: "Yes."
JESS: "Like Miss Havisham, I refused to mourn and cultivated grievance in its place."
PSYCHOLOGIST: "Miss Havisham bathed in contempt and indifference, but Pip realized that in secluding herself, she hid from a thousand natural and healing influences. And perhaps Pip's and Estella's lives could be different?"
JESS: "Yes, perhaps so."

Jess interpreted our meetings as a refuge; a resting place from which she could emerge, feeling strengthened to re-engage with life. A private meeting room is a protected physical space, which helps to increase one's sense of mental space, to hear one's own thoughts, and to cast one's eye over the knots and tangles in one's life. The more Jess immersed herself in our work together, the freer she felt internally with space to sift feelings and eavesdrop dispassionately on their messages.

Time for Change

Cognitive therapy is brief and time limited. These two terms are challenging to define but we normally consider short-term therapy as 20 or fewer 1-hour sessions and long-term therapy as 40 or more 1-hour sessions (Ivey et al., 1997). Many athletes seek a "quick-fix" to solve issues because the 20 sessions might take 15 weeks, with two sessions each week for the first 3 or 4 weeks and then one session per week thereafter. In an athlete's life, those 4 months might be available, or they might not. According to Beck et al. (1985), the therapist "rushes slowly" (p. 171), which infers covering key areas but being able to "move on quickly" (p. 171). Outcome research suggests that change begins early in therapy and that such change is enhanced by long-term interventions only sometimes (Cooper, 2008; Cummings & Sayama, 1995; Ivey et al., 1997).

The Structure of a CT Session

The structure of a typical CT session follows several sequential steps. We begin with a "check-in" to establish how the client is feeling. Next, we check homework task(s), set an agenda collaboratively, and work through what we have agreed to focus on. The session finishes with setting new homework task(s) and by gathering feedback from the client on the session. The psychologist and client might decide on relieving symptoms at the beginning of an intervention and, over time, working on underlying vulnerabilities (Beck, 1979b; Wells, 1997). Clients often request an appointment with a psychologist during a confusing and chaotic time, and the structure of therapy can be a helpful boundary to contain such confusion. Alford and Beck (1997) argued that structure boosts the collaborative transfer of learning from therapy to real-life contexts. The structure, content, and direction of therapy are created collaboratively. For example, agenda-setting (i.e., issues to address during the session) and receiving feedback (i.e., the client's judgment of the value of the session) are crafted by the client and the psychologist as equally valuable partners in the team.

What we described in the last paragraph represents the standard 50-minute "hour" in a therapeutic setting (e.g., psychologist's office); however, shorter sessions (e.g., 20 minutes) that can account for uncontrollable and changeable performance settings also work. One feature of shorter sessions is the concept of immediacy. With immediacy, the psychologist focuses on what is happening now for the client and the psychologist. For example, "You said you feel at ease with your performance in your heats this morning, but when you spoke you dug your nails into your palm and looked away…I'm wondering whether you feel you have more to say? Perhaps we could stay with that feeling and put some words to it?" Immediacy can deepen the level of connectedness in the relationship and encourage the client to share their troubles beyond the "safe" account. Sharing in an emotionally honest way often means athletes share issues that truly matter to them.

Formulation

Brief Longitudinal Formulation

Some early experiences left an indelible mark on Jess' mind, especially her father losing his job and living away from home for extended periods during her teenage years. One issue that arose from Jess' experience was mistrust. She felt trusting others would inevitably lead to being let down so, to protect herself, she relied on herself. Her core belief was that "people could not be trusted." Her assumption was that "if I trust myself, I'll be okay." In this longitudinal formulation, schemas, core beliefs, and assumptions comprise the vulnerability factor that predisposed Jess to be triggered into negative symptoms and psychological problems. Jess' job, however, depended on trust and cooperation. Life events, especially in football, triggered these latent negative patterns, culminating in the vicious cycle of negative thoughts, feelings, and behavior patterns (Persons, 1989). Jess' longitudinal formulation can be seen in Figure 4.1, her vicious cycles can be found in Figures 4.2 and 4.3, and some possible interventions are displayed in Table 4.1.

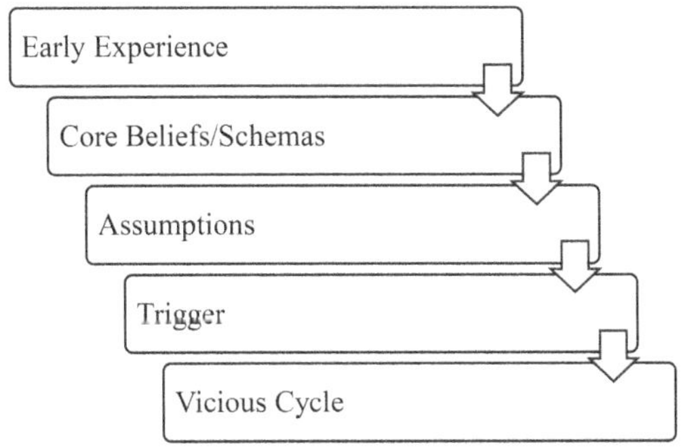

FIGURE 4.1 A flow diagram of the longitudinal formation.

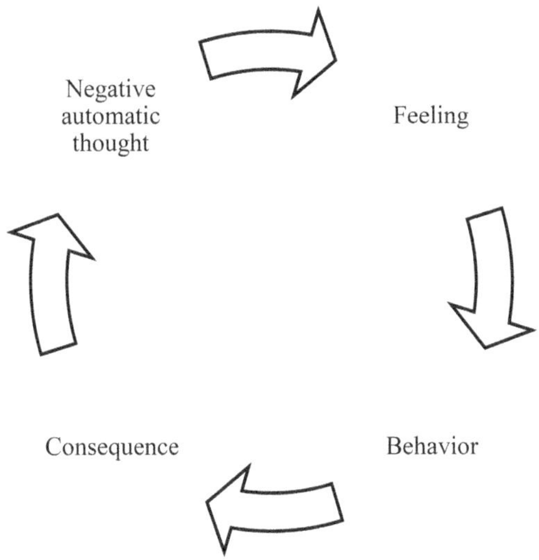

FIGURE 4.2 Jess' vicious cycle of cognition, emotion, and behavior.

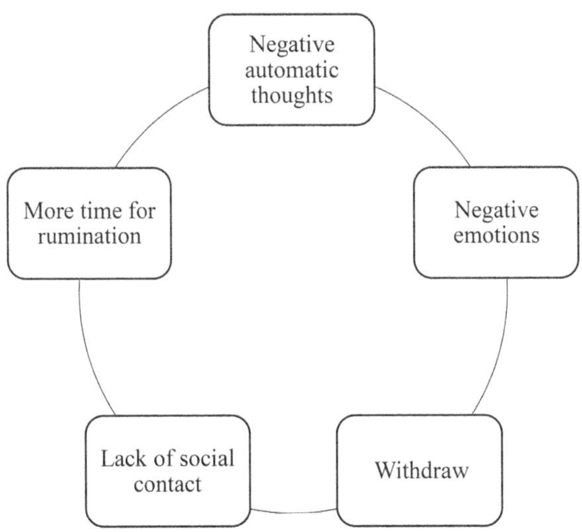

FIGURE 4.3 A vicious cycle relating to Jess' presenting problems.

TABLE 4.1 Possible intervention techniques to employ at each stage of Jess' vicious cycle

Stage of vicious cycle	*Possible intervention*
Negative core beliefs	Core belief work
Negative automatic thoughts	Cognitive intervention (e.g., thought records)
Negative emotions	Mood management
Withdrawn	Behavioral intervention
Lack of social support	Behavioral intervention
More time for rumination	Attentional strategy

Deciding where to begin an intervention depends on the psychologist's judgement of, and sensitivity to, the needs of the athlete. Working together, Jess and I decided that relieving immediate strains and working toward emotional and physiological relief would allow time later for Jess and I to work on vulnerabilities. We assembled a collage of factors during formulation and ongoing assessment: precipitating (events triggering her problem), perpetuating (factors maintaining the problem), and predisposing (background and factors underlying her vulnerability). As a counterweight, we composed a ledger of protective factors; factors that housed Jess' strengths and resources to maintain and elevate well-being. This assemblage reflected our work that was a cooperative endeavor to, metaphorically speaking, draw the floor plans for a new dwelling; one that was borne out of the resources within Jess. Jess reflected: "I'm the draughtswoman, forewoman, bricklayer, plasterer, plumber, and electrician. The attic in my house is my mind, isn't it? But instead of leaving it cold and unused, I'm going to make is as much the heart of my home as the hearth."

Our collaborative approach to formulate this case meant releasing the reins for different parts of the journey. Sometimes Jess beckoned me to grab hold of the reins when the terrain reached a precipitous and emotionally painful interlude: times when we spent more time in the heart than in the head. Through our shared experience, Jess lifted the carapace to leave herself unprotected. She transmuted some of her most enriching events in her mind to a gray, worn, and dilapidated form. Her mind was a cruel and vindictive master, not a servant to fathom the challenges of her life. Mindless subservience to the winds of change in her mind meant Jess lay at the mercy of her thoughts. In one of our sessions, Jess pushed the crumpled bits of paper filled with imperfect thoughts to the floor and, exasperated, she said: "Searching for the best in me feels like I'm talking an unfamiliar language. Even if I find something, it's like two parts of me admit they don't see eye to eye. When you and I do this work together, I feel like I open up a quarrel between the present and the past and I can't agree. There's no middle ground, it's no-man's-land."

Jess revealed one particular series of related events (predisposing factors) in her childhood and adolescent years, when her father lost his job and was out of work for several months. When he did eventually regain employment, it was hundreds of miles from home. Jess, as the eldest, "had to grow up quickly" and help her mother raise her younger brothers and sisters. Jess felt the strain on her mother and her father and vowed never to "put a foot wrong" or add any more "strain on her parents." One night, she overheard her father say to her mother that "Jess is a class act; so clever, so beautiful, so kind. At least we got one thing right between us in our lives." Jess felt so proud that she worked harder and harder to not let that crown slip. Slips, as she saw them, were unacceptable; mistakes that were unforgivable.

Socratic Methods

Good CT depends on several factors, one of which is the Socratic method. The psychologist harnesses Socratic methods to help the client corral interventions to help themselves. We can immerse ourselves in the Socratic strategy, the keystone of CT (Beck et al., 1985; Padesky, 1993), to harness the Socratic question that mobilizes the client to question current views and cultivate new standpoints. Like Socrates millennia before, the psychologist encourages the client to trust their knowledge base, to cast their own opinions, and to reel in alternative possibilities to act on. Socratic questioning is an appreciative enquiry in which we honor clients' intelligence and help them fathom solutions for themselves, rather than referring or deferring to the psychologist. In constructing meaning for oneself, one augurs to a depth of cognitive processing far beyond other strategies to remember internally generated material. A little strain on the brain fires neural networks to lay down lasting memories. Passive recipients of information (listening to or looking at rather than generating) leave with less than those clients who generate responses for themselves.

Jess' notable achievements in music, football, and school meant that she gained a scholarship to a most prestigious university to read English. Reflecting on this achievement, Jess said:

> "Wow, me! Where I come from? Nobody, and I mean nobody, goes to this university. I was so worried about failing, I studied all the time. I wasted no time. The funniest part was that it all seemed easy when you work hard. But working hard misses the point; you need to work on the right things, but which things are the right things? Can you see how my mind is like the rabbit hole Alice tumbled down… so many ways to wander?"

PSYCHOLOGIST: "There seems at least one rule for living in there…"

JESS: "You mean about working hard?"

PSYCHOLOGIST: "Uh huh… was it your personal motto?"

JESS: "You mean like Boxer from Animal Farm 'I will work harder?' Well yes, yes, it was because it always brought results for me."

PSYCHOLOGIST: "And how about now within your coaching role?"

JESS: "Mmmm… I guess not, well it's what I want my players to do. I want each person to work to her capacity. Most of them are not like me."

PSYCHOLOGIST: "I sense a sadness in there… a regret that they do not share your industriousness… they are not you… and that's hard to stomach?"

JESS: "I feel… I feel… maybe without knowing it, I wanted them to be like me, as if that was the right way or the only way. I never accepted this squad for being who they are, never really trusted them. Do you think they sense that from me?"

PSYCHOLOGIST: "Do you feel they sense that from you?"

JESS: "Now that I think about it–yes–it's so obvious. I try to control everything. I try to control everything from the side of pitch. I'm encouraging the players but really it's constant judgement and evaluation wrapped up with a neat bow. The evidence is there."

PSYCHOLOGIST: "What do you think the gathering evidence suggests?"

JESS: "I think it suggests that (a) it's not working for anyone, (b) it's not kind, and (c) and I need to let people in to help me and help themselves."

In this sequence, sound CT depends on the psychologist's planning as she collects cognitive data and engages with an ongoing formulation. As the psychologist fits the cognitive pieces of the jigsaw together in the formulation, it becomes clear which target areas to address and perhaps the best ways to address them. Without the formulation, it would be anyone's guess which were the target areas and progress would be unpredictable. The formulation with Jess helped us to understand the relationship between Jess' symptoms and problems, her cognition, and allowed us to choose an appropriate starting point and a method for treatment, as well as helping us to monitor Jess' responses to these choices (Persons, 1989, 2008).

Homework

Homework is a principal feature of CT (see e.g., Kazantzis et al., 2000). Homework, which can focus on cognition (e.g., via cognitive restructuring; see Didymus, 2018) and or behavior throughout the therapeutic process, refers to tasks that a client completes between sessions. For Jess, early homework assignments involved reading about anxiety. Moving from reading to an experiential homework task involved Jess opening a low-risk conversation with one of her players because Jess was socially anxious. In this example, Jess could realize her negative thoughts and feelings (a behavioral experiment) to test the negative thought that "The players are not interested in what I have to say."

The reason for homework in cognitive theory originates from the assumption that psychological change is challenging and is unlikely to emerge from generating insights during sessions alone (Beck, 1988). Matching homework to the needs of the client is necessary to allow the client to recognize that skills learned in sessions are valuable interventions in themselves. A behavioral experiment, for example, acts as an immediate disconfirmation of negative beliefs. Homework and behavioral experiments represent the systematic approach in CT to (1) ensure generalization and (2) to ensure that gains in therapy transfer to the athlete's everyday life (Ivey et al., 1997). Homework is not a simple process and although some clients complete homework, others do not. A sensible approach is to start homework tasks in the session and to acknowledge that, even if the homework is not completed between sessions, the starting data is still helpful, and the client is less likely to label herself a failure. Not completing one's homework could be a client's self-limiting strategy to protect oneself from further loss or humiliation (Leahy, 2001).

Cognitive Therapy in Sport

Cognitive therapy in applied sport psychology has a past (e.g., Didymus & Fletcher, 2017) and present and will have a future. The foundation that "cognitive techniques are most appropriate for people who have the capacity for introspection and for reflecting about their own thoughts and fantasies" (Beck, 1979a, p. 216) remains unchanged when working with CT in the context of sport. First, the athlete must gain awareness of what she is thinking. Through awareness, she can recognize that her thoughts have gone awry. Then she can substitute inaccurate judgments for accurate ones. Last, she needs feedback to judge whether her changes are helpful. As Beck (1979a) explained, the same sequence is necessary for making behavioral changes, like "improving form in a sport" (p. 217). The context of sport and its demands and expectations mean athletes often experience a distortion of reality because an objective appraisal contradicts a subjective appraisal. Some examples might be "I can't putt," "I'm letting the team down," or "I can't control the ball." We can examine the illogical or crooked thinking through automatic thoughts that are recorded by the athlete in the therapeutic setting and, eventually, during homework tasks (Didymus, 2018). Cognitive distortions such as labeling, catastrophizing, overgeneralization, arbitrary inference, selective abstraction, black and white thinking, and should statements are well worn into the sporting vernacular; identifying and modifying them with an athlete is the work of a sport psychologist.

The customs of CT are ever present in applied sport psychology, especially in psychological skills training. Within a therapeutic model, however, we begin with assessment and follow with a formulation before beginning the intervention phase and finishing with an evaluation (see Turner et al., 2020). Psychological skills training fits within the intervention phase alongside other activities (e.g., mood management, behavioral activation). The tangibility of psychological skills such as goal setting and self-talk work well in applied sport psychology because such skills address performance enhancement and well-being rather than allowing the context (e.g., performance enhancement) to trump and dismiss what has been learned (Andersen, 2009). The professionalization and training of sport and exercise psychologists in the United Kingdom means our graduates are entering the field of applied sport psychology with abilities to marry theory and research to practice. Educators weave underpinning theory and research into post-graduate programs and professional training programs, which means the dominance of psychological skills training is receding as the graduates of these programs understand and implement evidence-based practice within sound therapeutic modalities (e.g., CT).

Measurement of Effectiveness

Measurement of the effectiveness of CT endures throughout a therapeutic relationship. During each session, the client may organically offer snippets of insight to their perceptions of effectiveness and the psychologist may sense from verbal and non-verbal communication (e.g., body language) how the alliance and the client's development are progressing. Each CT session ends with a round-up of what has been covered and the client's feedback on the session. These closures provide regular opportunities for the client and the psychologist to assess informally the effectiveness of the relationship. More formal assessment of effectiveness should take place throughout the alliance: for example, at the mid-point of treatment and at the end. Measurement often takes the form of social validation (either written or gathered verbally) but can also include the collection and monitoring of psychometric data. For example, an athlete who is experiencing debilitative levels of anxiety could complete the Competitive State Anxiety Inventory-2 (Martens et al., 1990) at regular intervals throughout a therapeutic relationship to normatively assess changes in anxiety that have been instigated by developing more functional cognition. We could also measure changes in negative automatic thoughts or cognitive distortions to indicate effectiveness of the CT intervention.

Conclusion

Cognitive therapy is a powerful tool that can change an individual's emotions and behaviors. The premise of good CT is that changing cognition creates desirable changes in said outcomes. Sound CT relies on effective and ongoing formulation and a facilitative therapeutic relationship where both parties (the psychologist and the client) see each other as equal members of a team. Despite limitations that have been well-documented in peer-reviewed literature (e.g., Hofman et al., 2013), the effectiveness and efficacy of CT have been demonstrated by significant bodies of research in varied contexts. Buy-in from athletes, coaches, and performance directors can be challenging because of the labor-intensive nature of CT; however, the implications of this approach for performance are convincing and explanation of the benefits of regular points of contact and a relationship that lasts months, rather than weeks or days (i.e., as a psychological skills training program could be marketed), can help to overcome challenges relating to agreement.

References

Alford, B. A., & Beck, A. T. (1997). *The integrative power of cognitive therapy*. Guilford Press.

Andersen, M. B. (2009). Performance enhancement as a bad start and a dead end: A parenthetical comment on Mellalieu and Lane. *The Sport and Exercise Scientist, 20*, 12–14.

Beck, A. T. (1963). Thinking and depression. Part I: Idiosyncratic content and cognitive distortions. *Archives of General Psychiatry, 9*(4), 324–333. https://doi.org/10.1001/archpsyc.1963.01720160014002

Beck, A. T. (1964). Thinking and depression. Part II: Theory and therapy. *Archives of General Psychiatry, 10*(6), 561–571. https://doi.org/10.1001/archpsyc.1964.01720240015003

Beck, A. T. (1967). *Depression: Clinical, experimental and theoretical aspects*. Harper & Row.

Beck, A. T. (1970a). The role of fantasies in psychotherapy and psychopathology. *Journal of Nervous and Mental Disease, 150*(1), 3–17. https://doi.org/10.1097/00005053-197001000-00002

Beck, A. T. (1970b). Cognitive therapy: Nature and relation to behavior therapy. *Behavior Therapy, 1*(2), 184–200. https://doi.org/10.1016/S0005-7894(70)80030-2

Beck, A. T. (1979a). *Cognitive therapy and the emotional disorders*. Meridian.

Beck, A. T. (1979b). Schools of 'thought'. *American Psychologist, 34*(1), 93–98. https://doi.org/10.1037/0003-066X.34.1.93.b

Beck, A. T. (1988). *Love is never enough*. Penguin.

Beck, A. T. (1991). Cognitive therapy: A 30-year retrospective. *American Psychologist, 46*(4), 368–375. https://doi.org/10.1037//0003-066x.46.4.368

Beck, A. T., Emery, G., & Greenberg, R. (1985). *Anxiety disorders and phobias: A cognitive perspective*. Basic Books.

Beck, A. T., & Weishaar, M. (1989). Cognitive therapy. In A. Freeman, K. M. Simon, L. E. Beutler, & H. Arkowitz (Eds.), *Comprehensive handbook of cognitive therapy* (pp. 21–36). Springer.

Cooper, M. (2008). *Essential research findings in counselling and psychotherapy: The facts are friendly*. Sage.

Cummings, N., & Sayama, M. (1995). *Focused psychotherapy: A casebook of brief, intermittent psychotherapy through the life cycle*. Brunner/Mazel.

Didymus, F. F. (2018). Cognitive–behavioral theory in sport and performance psychology. In E. Acevedo (Ed.), *Oxford research encyclopaedia of psychology*. Oxford University Press. https://doi.org/10.1093/acrefore/9780190236557.013.144

Didymus, F. F., & Fletcher, D. (2017). Effects of a cognitive-behavioral intervention on field hockey players' appraisals of organizational stressors. *Psychology of Sport and Exercise, 30*, 173–185. https://doi.org/10.1016/j.psychsport.2017.03.005

Feltham, C. (Ed.) (1999). *Understanding the counselling relationship*. Sage.

Hofman, S. G., Asmundson, G. J. G., & Beck, A. T. (2013). The science of cognitive therapy. *Behavior Therapy, 44*(2), 199–212. https://doi.org/10.1016/j.beth.2009.01.007

Ivey, A. E., Ivey, M. B., & Simek-Morgan, L. (1997). *Counselling and psychotherapy: Skills, theory and practice*. Prentice-Hall.

Kazantzis, N., Deane, F. P., & Ronan, K. R. (2000). Homework assignments in cognitive and behavioral therapy: A meta-analysis. *Clinical Psychology: Science and Practice, 7*(2), 189–202. https://doi.org/10.1093/clipsy.7.2.189

Kuyken, W. (2006) Evidence-based formulation: Is the emperor clothed? In N. Tarrier (Ed.), *Case formulation in cognitive behaviour therapy* (pp. 12–35). Routledge.

Leahy, R. L. (2001). *Overcoming resistance in cognitive therapy*. Guilford Press.

Martens, R., Vealey, R. S., & Burton, D. (1990). *Competitive anxiety in sport*. Human Kinetics.

Orlinsky, D. E., Grawe, K., & Parks, B. K. (1994). Process and outcome in psychotherapy: Noch einmal. In A. E. Bergin & S. L. Garfield (Eds.), *Handbook of psychotherapy and behaviour change* (4th ed., pp. 270–378). John Wiley & Sons.

Padesky, C. A. (1993). Socratic questioning: Changing minds or guiding discovery. Paper presented at the A keynote address delivered at the European Congress of Behavioural and Cogni-tive Therapies, London.

Padesky, C. A. (1994). *Cognitive therapy of anxiety (audio tape)*. Center for Cognitive Therapy. www.padesky.com

Padesky, C. A., & Greenberger, D. (1995). *A clinician's guide to mind over mood*. Guilford Press.

Persons, J. B. (1989). *Cognitive therapy: A case formulation approach*. W. W. Norton.

Persons, J. B. (2008). *The case formulation approach to cognitive-behaviour therapy* Guilford Press.

Rogers, C. R. (1957) The necessary and sufficient conditions for therapeutic personality change. *Journal of Consulting Psychology, 21*(2), 95–103. https://doi.org/10.1037/h0045357

Rogers, C. R. (1980). *A way of being*. Houghton-Mifflin.

Turner, M. J., Aspin, G., Didymus, F. F., Mack, R., Olusoga, P., Wood, A. G., & Bennett, R. (2020). One case, four approaches: The application of psychotherapeutic approaches in sport psychology. *The Sport Psychologist, 34*(1), 71–83. https://doi.org/10.1123/tsp.2019-0079

Weishaar, M. (1993). *Aaron T. Beck*. Sage.

Wells, A. (1997). *Cognitive therapy of anxiety disorders*. John Wiley & Sons.

Wills, F. (2009). *Beck's cognitive therapy: Distinctive features*. Taylor & Francis.

5

RATIONAL EMOTIVE BEHAVIOUR THERAPY (REBT)

Martin J. Turner

Introduction

We are supposedly the rational animal (Aristotle Metaphysics; Ritter, 1930). Stephen Pinker (2021) considers rationality to be a "kit of cognitive tools that can attain particular goals in particular worlds" (p. 7), and "the ability to use knowledge to attain goals" (p. 36). Pinker suggests we "ground our beliefs in truth" (p. 37), although he also recognises that perfect rationality is an aspirational ideal that no mortal human can attain (Pinker, 2021). Indeed, as prominent philosophers (Russell, 1950), scientists (Pinker, 2021), psychotherapists (Ellis, 1976), and writers (Wilde, 1891) have noted, we continually contradict this supposed rationality in our thoughts and actions. It might be best to consider human rationality as "potential rationality" that we possess but are not obligated or guaranteed to exercise (McDowell, 2010). Perhaps, to bring this potential rationality into actuality, we must engage in a process of initiation into a social practice, such as education (Kern, 2020).

Rational emotive behaviour therapy (REBT) offers a humanistic (Lazarus, 1995) psychotherapeutic method by which one can develop and strengthen one's rationality. In REBT, clients develop a "rational kit of cognitive tools" (i.e., beliefs) in service of their goals, amidst the self-evident truism that people will not and cannot always think and act rationally. REBT was developed by Albert Ellis in the 1950s (Ellis, 1957) and it is considered to be the first of the cognitive behavioural therapies (CBTs). REBT is a second-wave CBT predicated on the blending of cognitive- and behaviour-based elements (Bennett & Oliver, 2019). In applying REBT, the goal is to help clients to improve their functioning by means of introspective identification and direct challenging of the maladaptive beliefs that interfere with their ability to pursue and fulfil their goals (Caserta et al., 2010). That is, in REBT clients, first understand their self-limiting beliefs and then address these beliefs forthrightly (Ellis, 1988).

In REBT, we take the notion of rationality seriously and take the cue from the Ancient Stoic philosophers and teachers who regarded reason and rationality as the highest human ideal. For the Ancient Stoics, reason was fundamental for human well-being because human nature is characterised by our ability to reason – an ability through which we make sense of our environment and act accordingly. The Ancient Stoics believed that to live rationally was to live according to nature, given that nature operates according to rational principles.

DOI: 10.4324/9781003162513-6

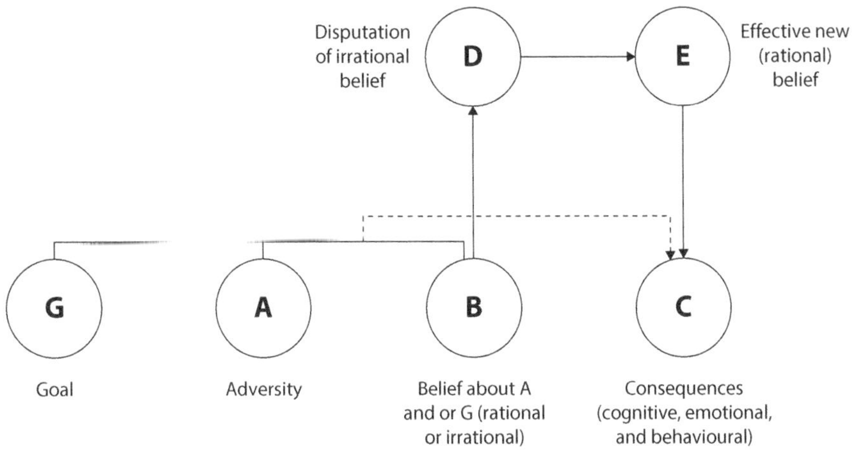

FIGURE 5.1 The GABCDE framework of REBT. The dotted line between GAB and C reflects pre-REBT and the move to D and E from B reflects the REBT process. (Adapted from Turner, 2022.)

The seeds of REBT are certainly in Stoic philosophy, but REBT codifies this rationality very specifically in a set of rational and irrational beliefs that mediate between our goals, that thwarts our goals, and our cognitive, emotional, and behavioural reactivity. In other words, of course driving towards meaningful goals is tough, of course barriers and setbacks are adverse, but it is our rational and irrational beliefs about our goals and adversities that determine whether and what extent we react adaptively or maladaptively.

The view that it is our beliefs that mediate between adversity and our reactions to the adversity is not special to REBT, and "cognitive mediation" is captured in much psychology (e.g., Lazarus, 1999) and psychotherapy (i.e., CBTs) theory. Cognitive mediators are defined as "mental processes or activities that take place between the initial occurrence of a stimulus and the subsequent related response" (Alegria & Cameron, 2020, p. 496). But in REBT, the idea of cognitive mediation is made very explicit because it is central to assessment and intervention. Helpfully, in REBT, cognitive mediation is captured in a descriptive and instructive GABCDE framework (Figure 5.1).

The GABCDE framework of REBT is descriptive in that it tells us about how adaptive and maladaptive emotions occur, and instructive in that it gives us the procedures through which we can work with clients to help them experience adaptive emotions. I will cover this GABCDE framework in detail later in this chapter as it pertains to a hypothetical case, but recently I have blended REBT with Richard Lazarus' (1999) cognitive appraisal theory (CAT) to provide a roadmap to how certain types of events, cognitive appraisal, and beliefs manifest to create certain emotions, behaviours, and cognitions (Turner, 2022). This roadmap is based on the work and writing of David et al. (2002), Dryden (2012), Dryden (2018), Dryden and Branch (2008), and Smith and Lazarus (1993). The roadmap also illustrates a binary theory of emotional distress (BTED; e.g., Ellis, 1994; see Turner et al., 2018a; Turner et al., 2019a for critical discussions), in which not all negative (valenced) emotions are considered unhealthy or targets for change (DiGiuseppe et al., 2014). As can be seen in Table 5.1, rational beliefs beget healthy negative emotions (HNEs; e.g., healthy anxiety, sadness, healthy anger), while irrational beliefs beget unhealthy negative emotions (UNEs; unhealthy anxiety, depression, unhealthy anger: Dryden, 2008, Ellis, 1994). HNEs are functional and adaptive

TABLE 5.1 The articulated GABC framework incorporating Ellisian and Lazarusian concepts

G-A		*B*	*C*		
Appraisal	*Core relational theme*	*Belief*	*Healthy or unhealthy*	*Example cognitive consequences**	*Example action tendencies (actual or intended)**
High Goal Relevance High Goal Incongruence Low/uncertain (emotion-focused) coping potential	Threat/Danger Facing uncertainty and existential threat	Irrational	Unhealthy Anxiety	• Overestimate probability and or magnitude of threat. • Has more task-irrelevant thoughts.	• Withdraw physically and or mentally from the threat (avoidance). • Ward off the threat (e.g., superstitious behavicur). • Seek reassurance and or protection. • Perform below potential. • Tranquilise feelings. • Over preparation. • Risk aversion. • Hide or distract self from threat. • Keep checking on status of threat. • Hypervigilance to threat.
		Rational	Healthy Anxiety	• Realistic about the probability and or magnitude of threat. • More task relevant thoughts.	• Face up to threat (approach). • Deal with the threat constructively. • Take constructive action to reduce/ minimise the risk or danger. • Perform to potential. • Appropriate preparation. • Take calculated risks. • Seek support to help self to face threat. • Appropriate awareness of threat.

Source: Adapted from Turner (2022).

for goal attainment and UNEs are dysfunctional and maladaptive. In REBT, we work *towards* healthy emotions and *away from* unhealthy emotions, and are more interested in function than valence, getting better rather than just feeling better (Ellis, 2001). Because it is germane to the present chapter, I provide the anxiety roadmap in Table 5.1.

Anxiety is brought about by a constellation of appraisals and beliefs, and the dictating factor for the expression of UNEs and HNEs is one's irrational beliefs. The G and A of REBT are most akin to goal relevance and goal incongruence in CAT, and A also indicates the core relational theme and thus flavours the emotion (Dryden, 2012). Of course one would be anxious in a (perceived) threatening situation, but it is the irrational beliefs concerning this threat that generate unhealthy anxiety, not the threat itself. So, as illustrated, REBT is distinct from the other CBTs owing to its acute focus on rationality as the basis for human eudaimonia. To live rationally, that is, to pursue the fulfilment of one's potential holding a rational philosophy of life, is to live healthily. This includes holding and working to reinforce and rehearse rational beliefs about the self, others, and the world, whilst relinquishing and working to weaken and undermine irrational beliefs about the self, others, and the world.

In REBT, rationality is not merely an abstract term that is open to interpretation. There are specific irrational beliefs, and specific rational beliefs, that have been distilled and refined over the years (see Ellis, 1976, for a long list). In contemporary REBT, there are four irrational beliefs and four contrasting rational beliefs. Rational beliefs comprise preferences, frustration tolerance (FT), anti-awfulising, and unconditional self/other/world acceptance (USA/UOA/UWA). Irrational beliefs comprise demandingness, frustration intolerance (FI), awfulising, and depreciation (or global evaluation; GE). Rational beliefs are self-enhancing (Dryden, 2017) and underpin HNEs (DiGiuseppe et al., 2014) and facilitate (or do not debilitate) goal attainment (Wilson, 2010). Irrational beliefs are self-defeating (Dryden, 2017) and underpin UNEs (DiGiuseppe et al., 2014) and are usually unhelpful in pursuing and inconsistent with accomplishing one's long-term goals (Maultsby, 1975).

The irrational beliefs are a bit of a nuisance, to say the least. Research in sport tells us that greater irrational beliefs are related to greater threat appraisals (Dixon et al., 2017), greater competitive anxiety and negative affect (Chadha et al., 2019), increased burnout (Turner & Moore, 2016), greater symptoms of depression (Mansell, 2021), greater psychological distress (Michel-Kröhler & Turner 2022; Turner et al., 2019b), greater trait anger (Turner et al., 2019c), poorer physical health (Turner et al., 2022a), poorer mental well-being (Jooste et al., 2022), and poorer performance under pressure (Mesagno et al., 2020). Thus, it is the development and enhancement of human functioning that is at the centre of REBT, and as such, rational beliefs are encouraged – irrational beliefs are discouraged.

Reflect on your practice and your engagement in sporting contexts. How often do you hear language that is consistent with irrational beliefs? "Must win games", "terrible performances" pain that athletes "cannot stand", the evaluation of the self as "stupid" or "rubbish" when things do not go well. Irrational language is rife in sport, portrayed internal to sporting organisations via senior leaders, and external to sporting organisations by the media. It is proposed that being immersed with an irrational climate will confer upon the immersed irrational beliefs (Turner, 2016a). To expand, King et al. (2022) suggest that irrational beliefs are socialised into athletes via social agents within an athlete's micro- and macro-environment who harbour and model irrationality through their behaviour, language, and processes. Bailey (2022) adds to this idea and suggests that it is an irrational performance climate, defined as the signalling of irrational beliefs within the performance environment, that confers irrational beliefs onto athletes. Ellis believed that human beings had a natural biological proclivity to think and behave in rational and irrational ways, but that we learn rationality and irrationality from those around us, particularly through formal caregivers such as parents and teachers. This information is instructive because we can of course work to alter the climate surrounding an athlete to make it less conducive to irrationality. But regardless of an athlete's surroundings, when they are sat in front of us, suffering the consequences of some adversity, possibly made worse by their irrationality, it is the dyadic practitioner–client relationship that makes all the difference. As such, this chapter takes a one-to-one approach to working with a case as a way to illustrate the utility of REBT, and in particular, the GABCDE framework.

The Case

Jack is a 25-year-old amateur golfer who is on the cusp of turning professional. However, in important competitions, Jack has the tendency to severely underperform. When Jack has to execute chip shots in moments of the competition where these shots could significantly affect his chances of winning, he tends to choke. Associated with his underperformance under pressure are intense physical feelings of tension, movement rigidity, and the sensation that "something isn't right". Jack becomes highly anxious and cannot stop thinking about shot mechanics and things going badly. Due to this choking, Jack thinks about avoiding important competitions altogether and has even feigned illness to avoid a competition. If Jack does play a good chip shot under pressure, he believes that it is less because he executed it well and more to do with good fortune or a lucky bounce. His lack of consistency in these shots is holding his career back.

A full and comprehensive understanding of how REBT is applied can be gleaned by reading guide textbooks (e.g., DiGiuseppe et al., 2014; Turner, 2022) and by training in REBT at primary and advanced levels. But in what follows, I give a condensed portrayal of how the work with Jack could be progressed using REBT.

Problem Formulation

In my early interactions with Jack, my job is to take a person-centred position and try to understand as much about Jack's issues as I possibly can. This period is naturally time-limited because we cannot perpetually be person-centred if we are using REBT – there comes a point where we go from problem formulation to solution formulation. Of course, we are always being open to reconceptualising the problem as more information is presented, but I want to really get a solid understanding of the issue in the first one-to-one session with Jack. In order to organise this understanding, I am using a mental schema of the GABC framework. I am not using this explicitly at this point, rather, I am organising the information Jack is presenting into this framework and constantly checking against the framework to ensure I have all the information I need to correctly and accurately formulate the problem. Inaccurate problem formulation will lead to inaccurate solutions and inefficient practice. The accuracy of this problem formulation is underpinned by a strong working alliance – this provides the context through which counselling strategies work (e.g., Horvath & Greenberg, 1989), is vital for CBT success (e.g., Dobson & Shaw, 1988), and in REBT is continually strengthened (Bernard & Dryden, 2019). Working alliance is underpinned by a solid bond, openness, clear aims for the work, and the forthright effort expenditure towards those agreed aims (e.g., Dryden, 2009; Dryden & David, 2008).

Assessing C

While Jack is talking to me about what has been going on for him recently, I am trying to understand what Gs, As, and Cs are being presented, and if any Bs present themselves then I am noting them but not necessarily lavishing attention on them. More important in this early interaction is a good understanding of the extent to which Jack's cognitive, emotional, and behavioural Cs are adaptive or maladaptive. That is, although Jack is experiencing a negatively valenced (unpleasant) emotion (anxiety), this does not mean that this emotion is maladaptive to his wellbeing or goal attainment. So, the work undertaken here is for Jack and the sport psychologist (SP) to determine whether Jack's anxiety is unhealthy (UNE) or healthy (HNE). To do this, we can get some information from Jack about the cognitive, emotive/physiologic, and behavioural concomitants of his anxiety, and make an assessment as whether these factors are helping of hindering Jack's goal attainment. Jack reports that when he is anxious he "constantly thinks about things going badly and focuses on precise mechanics of each shot" (cognitive), he also "gets really tense to the point where I can't play the shot fluidly or naturally" (emotive/physiologic), and reports that his anxiety "makes me want to avoid important competitions, and it has even caused me to fake illness instead of travelling to a competition" (behavioural [intended and enacted]). Also, because of Jack's anxiety and these cognitive, emotive/physiologic, and behavioural factors, he severely underperforms in important and high-pressure situations, below what he is capable of when performing under low pressure situations. In other words, he is choking (Mesagno & Hill, 2013). Thus, Jack is experiencing unhealthy anxiety (UNE) at C, the amelioration of which could alleviate his choking.

Assessment of G and A

Of equal importance to C assessment in this early interaction is that we obtain some clear details concerning G and A, and specifically, the extent to which and ways in which Jack's Gs and As are contributing to his Cs. In other words, we need to understand what it is about the situation in which Jack becomes anxious, that is so anxiety provoking. What is Jack so anxious about? We cannot take it at face value that the situation itself is directly causing Jack's anxiety. This would be a grave error that in REBT is known as A-C thinking (A *alone* caused C), but outside of REBT in emotion science is known as stimulus-response (S-R) emotion beliefs (S alone causes R; Turner et al., 2021, 2022b). So, we dig a bit deeper and try to understand what it is about the situation Jack is facing that is so generative of anxiety. A is the aspect of the situation that the person focuses on and evaluates (Dryden, 2017), and as such, locating the right (i.e., critical) A is important because A orients us towards B. If we miss-specify A, then we (probably) miss-specify B. There are thousands of potential As of course, because almost anything can be perceived as adverse, so we need to narrow in on the A that is seemingly leading to Jack's anxiety rather than reveal all possible As faced by Jack on any given Sunday – not all As trigger B and not all As are problematic for emotional reactivity and goal attainment.

To locate the "correct" A, I have found inference changing to be of great value, for which you can find some excellent resources (e.g., Ellis & Dryden, 1997; Neenan & Dryden, 1996). Inference chaining "combines speed with depth in rapidly taking clients from the periphery to the centre of their emotional disturbance" (Neenan & Dryden, 1996, p. 231). It does this by linking the client's inferences about an event in order to find the one which triggers the irrational belief and thus underpins the UNE (unhealthy anxiety in this case). To start this process, we can start at the UNE with the presumed A (important competitions):

SP: Tell me Jack, what is so anxiety-provoking about important competitions?
JACK: They mean a lot to me, so if I don't do well, it could harm my career.
SP: In what way?
JACK: Important people would see it and take note of my poor performance.
SP: Let's assume that important people would see it and take note, what would be so anxiety-provoking about that?
JACK: They would think that I am not as good a player as I am
SP: What would be anxiety-provoking about that?
JACK: I don't know. I might not get certain opportunities or get selected for certain teams.
SP: So what?
JACK: Then I'll never get to the level I want to get to.
SP: Then what?
JACK: Well then I would just be mediocre, a nobody.
SP: What would be so anxiety-provoking about that?
JACK: That would be the worst thing ever.
SP: What would be the worst thing ever?
JACK: Being mediocre. It would be awful. I couldn't stand being just mediocre. I can't think of anything worse. I don't want that, ever.
SP: So where is this anxiety coming from? Is it the important competition? The idea of not performing well? Is it the important people thinking less of you? Is it the thought of not getting opportunities? Or is it the thought of being mediocre?
JACK: Being mediocre. As you said it just then, I felt it. The anxiety.

Getting to B

Notice, we are not challenging the notions that the competitions are important, that people will think less of Jack, that he will not get opportunities, or that he will be mediocre. These As are treated as if they are true (because they could be!) in order to allow us to dig a little deeper. We land on a potential A (being mediocre) that seems to be most triggering of an extreme evaluation ("It would be awful. I couldn't stand being just mediocre. I can't think of anything worse".) and that seems to be triggering his anxiety. We help Jack to further elaborate on this thought that he would be mediocre, and we get to understand that Jack has some beliefs that he uses within which to frame this idea. It is not just that Jack does not want to be mediocre, it is that he demands that he must not be mediocre. He dwells a lot on the possibility of being mediocre and so he tells himself frequently and intently that "Being mediocre would be the worst thing ever and I couldn't stand it". After some clarification, we arrive at a statement that fully articulates what Jack is telling himself about being mediocre:

> "I do not want to be mediocre, and therefore I must not be mediocre, and if I was mediocre it would be awful and I couldn't stand it at all"

Based on the defining features of the irrational beliefs in REBT, we can see that Jack holds demandingness (I do not want to be, and therefore I must not), awfulising (it would be awful), and FI (I couldn't stand it at all) beliefs. Given the information we have collected in our early interactions with Jack, we can start to construct a GABC formulation (see Table 5.2) and we can present this to Jack in order to check that we have an accurate formulation of his issues.

TABLE 5.2 *Irrational* GABC formulation

Element	*Detail*
Goals (G)	To get to the highest level as an athlete.
Adversity (concrete)	Important competition.
Adversity (perception)	Important people would think less of me, and not give me opportunities. I'll never get to the level I want to get to
Adversity (inference)	I would be mediocre.
Irrational beliefs	I do not want to be mediocre, and therefore I must not be mediocre, and if I was mediocre it would be awful and I couldn't stand it at all.
Consequences (cognitive)	I constantly think about things going badly (ruminative self-doubt) and focus on precise mechanics of each shot (conscious processing).
Consequences (behavioural)	It makes me want to avoid important competitions (avoidance intention), and it has even caused me to fake illness instead of travelling to a competition (actual avoidance).
Consequences (emotive/ physiologic)	Unhealthy anxiety (UNE). I get really tense to the point where I can't play the shot fluidly or naturally (muscular tension). Chokes under pressure.

We want to make sure at multiple points that we are heading in the right direction with Jack, because next we move onto helping Jack to dispute (D) his irrational beliefs. In the transcript that follows, I am making sure that the articulated beliefs are indeed what Jack is believing, and I am teeing up the next steps in our work, namely disputation (D).

SP: So as far as you are aware, this anxiety you are experiencing is linked to this demand to not be mediocre and these ideas that being mediocre would be awful and impossible for you to stand?

JACK: Yes I believe so. This makes sense.

SP: Good. I have understood you correctly then.

JACK: Its just. Nobody has ever really just laid it out like that before.

SP: Exactly. But I want to make sure I am not putting words into your mouth here.

JACK: No that's fine. I connect with these beliefs and I feel like I have been saying this to myself for a long time.

SP: I can see how that could be the case yes. But we can't change the past. So, what do you think we could focus on in our work?

JACK: Maybe we could look at these beliefs and maybe do something about them?

SP: Like what?

JACK: I don't know. Change them? But maybe I should be thinking this way [demand not to be mediocre], because I really do not want to be mediocre!

SP: Do you think there is way to not want to be mediocre, without demanding that you are not mediocre?

JACK: Yes, of course.

SP: So let's focus on that.

Specific vs. General REBT

At this point, it is important to know that as an REBT practitioner you have many options. In Figure 5.2, you can see the interdependent GABC framework proffered by Turner (2022) based on Ellis' (1994) work. As you can see, each element of the framework is reciprocally

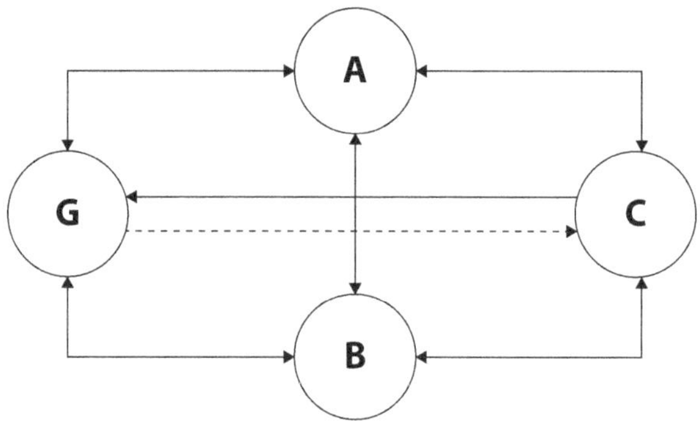

FIGURE 5.2 Interdependent GABCDE framework.

linked to each other element, such that a change in one can manifest a change in all. The question is, what could we, and perhaps what *should* we, change?

It is important to understand that there are two ways through which we can approach REBT. There is *specific* REBT and there is *general* REBT. In *specific* REBT, we focus on belief change primarily, but in *general* REBT, we have a broader focus on change other than deep belief change (Dryden & David, 2008). Thus, in *general* REBT, we can work with Jack directly across any element of the GABCDE framework, in part because of the interdependent nature of each element of GABCDE framework. REBT is not always all about B. So, what can help us make this choice between specific and general REBT? Figure 5.3 provides some guidance to this end.

Regardless of yours, and your client's choice, to use specific or general REBT, there are still some potential solutions for Jack. It is just that the specific REBT solution is more sustainable and long-range because we are addressing deeper schema, an endeavour that could serve Jack across many other anxiety-provoking situations. As such, for the purpose of this chapter, we pursue specific REBT because Jack has articulated some irrational beliefs, we have time to fully execute D, and Jack has indicated that he wants to and is ready for D.

B-C Connection

Before we move to D, it is really important that we share with Jack the GABC formulation and teach Jack the connection between the elements of the GABC. It is important to remember that one of the goals of REBT is to leave the client with the knowledge and skills to independently apply REBT in their own lives, thus, we leave nothing hidden from Jack. It is likely that the mere knowledge of cognitive mediation is useful for Jack in approaching a litany of future adversities, arming him with the understanding that he can create and uncreate his emotions based on his appraisals and evaluations of stimuli. Indeed, research has found that those who endorse the idea that emotions are cognitively mediated report greater mental health, better emotion regulation tendencies, and lower emotional reactivity (Turner et al., 2021; 2022b). So, we teach Jack about the GABC framework and we focus on the connection between B and C, and dissuade A-C thinking (Turner, 2022). We do this so that Jack is oriented towards B as a key change opportunity, but also to teach Jack about the importance, and emotion regulation implications, of emotional responsibility. The disputation (D) process is likely to be impeded if Jack does not see the veracity and utility of the B-C connection (Crum, 2018). We can teach Jack about the B-C connection in various ways, but one of the

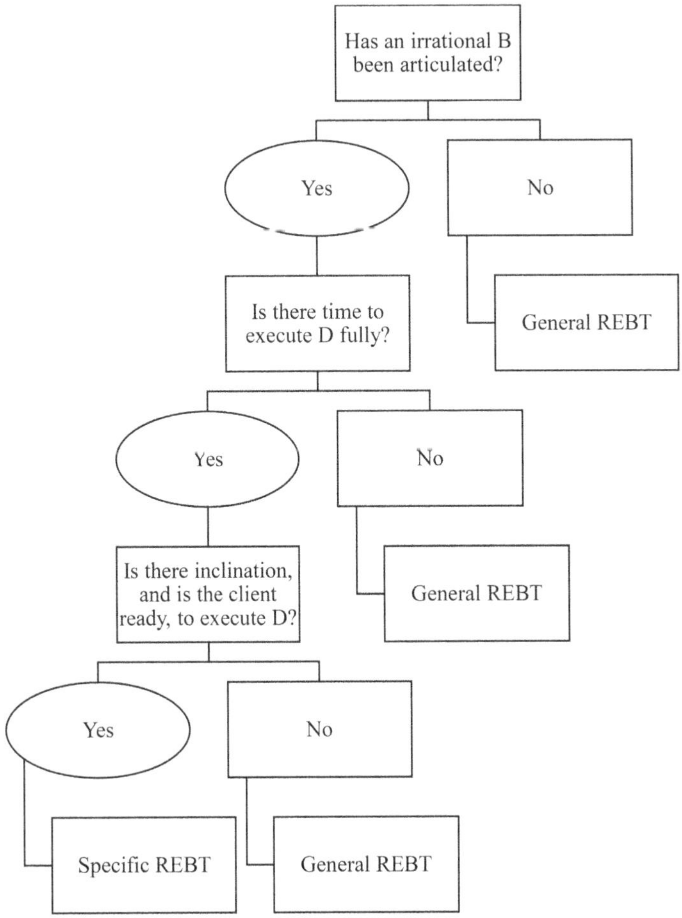

FIGURE 5.3 Specific-general decision tree.

simplest and most effective ways is to talk the client through the GABC framework diagrammatically – a picture is worth a thousand words. We can also offer hypothetical examples that highlight the logic of B-C thinking. For example, Turner (2022) uses the following to illustrate a B-C connection:

> Two athletes from the same nation, working under the same coach, have made it to the final of a 100 m competition. In qualifying rounds both have set personal bests and their finishing times are comparable. Athlete A is anxious, but focussed and prepared for the race – they can't wait to get off the blocks. Athlete B is also anxious, but is dreading the race and just wants the race to be over with. Given that the two athletes are going into the same situation objectively, how could you explain the differences in their approach to the race?

In using this example, we can highlight to Jack that individual differences can explain the emotional approach or reaction to the event, and that the situational differences cannot fully explain the response differences, because the situation is the same for both players. We can then talk about how these individual differences are in part due to the different appraisals and beliefs each player has, hence, B-C rather than A-C. In addition, we can encourage Jack to reflect on times where he has had situations with teammates where their own emotions and behaviours were different to those around them, despite the situation being equal for all. However it is achieved, it is important that Jack is able to acknowledge the logic of the B-C connection and the relevance to his current issues. Then, we can move to focus on B change via disputation (D), since there is a justifiable reason (and lots of scientific evidence; David et al., 2021; Jordana et al., 2020) to focus on B as the chief target for change.

Disputation (D)

One of the most effective ways to apply disputation, in my experience, is to first provide the client with a direct comparison between the *irrational* beliefs and alternate *rational* beliefs. This act of comparison can be described as Socratic comparison (Turner, 2022), or paired comparison (Neenan & Dryden, 1999), and Table 5.3 outlines the criteria for this endeavour. Using the technique, we can test the idea that Jack's beliefs are indeed problematic, start to teach Jack the differences between irrational and rational beliefs, and also work towards some potential solutions for Jack. First in Socratic comparison, we co-create rational alternatives to Jack's irrational beliefs. Co-creation is key here so that we use words that resonate with Jack, but also so that we align the rational alternative closely with REBT theory. That is, the rational alternative should be rational by REBT standards, not simply (or at all) more positive. Then we compare the irrational beliefs to the rational beliefs on three criteria of evidence, logic, and function. These criteria are the key criteria by which disputation (D) is enacted in REBT, and typically they are applied discursively within a conversation about the irrational beliefs in question (e.g., DiGiuseppe et al., 2014). Disputation (D) is a collaborative (client–practitioner) argument, or debate, focussed on challenging the client's ideas, not the client themselves (Turner, 2022). Here, in the Socratic comparison, we are still applying D discursively, but we are orienting the conversation around comparing and contrasting irrational vs. rational in order to constrain the argument within these boundaries of rationality to keep the discussion focused and non-tangential.

DiGiuseppe (1986) recognised that clients are more likely to abandon their irrational beliefs if considerable tension is caused by disconfirming evidence for the belief, and that an alternative, and superior, belief becomes available. DiGiuseppe et al. (2014) also highlight that people continue to believe ideas they know to be false until they discover better ideas (e.g., Kuhn, 1962). Thus, we help the client to utilise scientific principles to generate disconfirming evidence for the irrational beliefs, and we offer up a superior belief that is met with the same critical scientific treatment. So, in Socratic comparison, we ask the question, which is more true, logical, and functional (helpful for goal attainment)? We also ask Jack which belief would he want to strengthen and act upon? As we can see, Jack has selected options that applies most – and I have added some annotation as to how these decisions have been made. Jack indicates that his current beliefs are false, illogical, and unhelpful (dysfunctional), and wants to work to strengthen the alternate beliefs.

There are various other methods of applying D (see DiGiuseppe et al., 2014; Turner, 2022), and many questions that can be used as important tools. Below are some examples of questions we could ask Jack regarding his demandingness belief in order to facilitate disputation, but comprehensive guidelines are available elsewhere covering all kinds of belief types (e.g., Dryden, 2019b; Ellis, 1994).

TABLE 5.3 Socratic comparison for Jack's beliefs

	Current (irrational) belief	*Alternate (rational) belief*
	I do not want to be mediocre, and therefore I must not be mediocre, and if I was mediocre it would be awful and I couldn't stand it at all.	I do not want to be mediocre, but that does not mean I must not be mediocre, and if I was mediocre it would be bad, but certainly not awful, and although it would be tough to take, I could certainly stand being mediocre (although I may choose not to stand it).
Which belief is true and which is false?	False Just because I want something, does not mean it must be the case. It is not the case that being mediocre would the worst thing possible, I can think of plenty of worse things. It is also not true that I couldn't stand it – me being alive and well is proof that I can stand it.	True I do not need the things I want. If I was mediocre it would indeed be bad, but I would strive hard to not be mediocre – I could tolerate it, it would not kill me, but would choose not to tolerate it.
Which belief is sensible/logical and which doesn't make sense or is illogical?	Makes no sense (illogical) "I must" does not follow "I want". It makes no sense to describe being mediocre as awful because there are worse things that can and will happen in life, and nothing can really be awful. Also, just because something is tough, doesn't mean it is intolerable.	Logical "I want" does not beget "I must". It makes sense to draw a distinction between something being "bad", and something being "awful". Of course I can stand being mediocre, no matter how tough it would be for me. This does not mean that I "should" tolerate it just because I can though.
Which belief is helpful and which is unhelpful?	Unhelpful This is making me feel worse about my situation and is taking me away from who I want to be. It is leading to extreme anxiety that is negatively impacting upon my performance.	Helpful This could still lead me to some anxiety, but an anxiety I can cope with and use to fuel my performance. It won't lead to me choking when it matters most, and may actually aid my shot execution.
Which of the two beliefs do you want to strengthen and act on?	Not this one It is extreme, unrealistic, and is hindering me.	This one It is more balanced, realistic and could actually help me.

Empirical

- Where is the evidence that you MUST get what you want?
- Can you provide some data or evidence to support your demand?
- What universal law exists that says you MUST get what you want?
- Is it possible that, despite your demand, you might not get what you want? If so, how can your demand be supported?
- What data can you use to support your demand?

Logical

- You said that you want X, *and therefore*, you MUST have it. Is that good logic?
- Does it follow that just because you want something, then you HAVE TO have it?
- Where is the logic in saying that because you want something, then you MUST have it?
- Can you explain to me how you get from wanting X, to demanding X?
- I see why you might WANT it, but does that necessarily mean that you MUST have it?

Pragmatic

- Is demanding that you MUST have it helping you or hindering you?
- "Whatever I want, I must get". Where will that command get you?
- When you demand that you get what you want, how do you feel? … And is that feeling helpful to you?
- If you were to list all the ways this demand has helped you vs. hindered you, which list would be longest?
- If you didn't demand that you MUST get what you want, would that really stop you from getting what you want?

After this Socratic comparison and broader disputation, Jack is able to understand the rules of the game when it comes to disputation per se, but also importantly, we have disputed Jack's irrational beliefs and offered up a rational alternative:

> I do not want to be mediocre, but that does not mean I must not be mediocre, and if I was mediocre, it would be bad, but certainly not awful, and although it would be tough to take, I could certainly stand being mediocre (although I may choose not to stand it).

The author is of course aware that this belief is long winded, but the reader is encouraged to understand that when we are disputing in REBT and formulating alternate beliefs, we are not "changing" the irrational to rational. We do at times imprecisely talk and write about "belief change" in REBT, but we cannot *change* the belief, we can only weaken, rebut, and negate the irrational belief by extending the belief with rational additions. So, "I want to and therefore I must" becomes "I want to but that does not mean that I must", serving to lengthen the belief due to the negation of the demand. Regardless of the rational belief length, it is good practice to fully conceptualise and articulate it, and then when Jack has come to terms with it, it can be shortened and condensed so long as the sentiment remains. Given that we have now disputed Jack's irrational beliefs and arrived at rational beliefs through the same critical treatment, we can now enact Jack's desire to commit to the rational beliefs as we move into the E phase of the GABCDE framework of REBT.

Effective New Beliefs (E)

The effective new beliefs phase (E) of REBT involves helping the client to internalise and implement their rational beliefs. We have helped Jack to develop some rational beliefs that negate his irrational beliefs, but in E, we are encouraging and enabling Jack to get these rational beliefs to stick. The aim for Jack is to internalise the new rational beliefs so they become less of a thought or idea, and more of a deep belief or schema. Jack came into the work with a set of irrational beliefs that had been honed, rehearsed, acted upon, and reinforced over a long period of time. Indeed, some clients tell me that they have "always" believed this way – factually true or not – there is a sense with some clients that the irrational beliefs have been part of them for a long time. So, we are not going to be able to just install new rational beliefs easily, without comparable rehearsal and reinforcement. The ideal is for the rational beliefs to be rehearsed so well that they are automatised, so that they inform the client's natural and habitual healthy response to adversity. This automatisation requires rehearsal, repetition, and reinforcement, just like the automatisation of a physical skill.

In short, we are going to help Jack go from "intellectual insight" to "emotional insight". A client might achieve intellectual insight quite quickly in the work, in that they understand the nature of irrational and rational beliefs, can distinguish between them, acknowledges that their beliefs are underpinning their UNEs, and can use disputation (Dryden, 2018). But this will not usually be sufficient enough to impact client emotions and behaviours long term, and is not reflective of continual and consistent effort to change (Ellis, 1963). Intellectual insight may mean that the client can see why a belief is irrational or rational and they may understand why an irrational belief is not helpful for them, but they may still deeply *believe* the irrational beliefs and may not deeply *believe* the rational alternatives. So, we can help Jack to work towards emotional insight to facilitate meaningful long-term change, which involves Jack committing to the rational beliefs and committing to the work that is required for meaningful change (Ellis, 1963). Ellis (1963) states, "The person with emotional insight truly believes, is committed, and therefore acts" (p. 126). This will require ongoing effort from Jack, and he can anticipate and plan for some backsliding into his old ways of thinking even as he strengthens his conviction and commitment to the new rational beliefs.

One of the first activities I will engage Jack in is the process of steelmanning the rational belief (Turner, 2022). To do this, we ask what are the ways in which the rational beliefs are rational, logical, and functional (helpful, pragmatic)? What we are doing here is strengthening the conviction in the rational beliefs on the basis of its tolerance to scientific scrutiny. We do this Socratically rather telling Jack how true, logical, and helpful his rational beliefs are – we do not put words into clients' mouths. We can measure the extent to which Jack believes the rational beliefs, to get an indication of his conviction, by simply asking Jack "to what extent to you really believe that [rational beliefs] on a scale of 0–100?" (for a more elaborate measure, see Turner, 2022). The higher Jack scores, the more conviction he has in the beliefs. If Jack does not score highly, then we can discuss this and try to help him elevate his score. This marker of belief conviction is something I would want to see increase over time in my work with Jack, and there are a number of activities Jack can engage in strengthen and deepen his rational beliefs.

A more comprehensive portrayal of E activities can be found in more detailed texts (e.g., DiGiuseppe et al., 2014; Turner, 2022), but here are some activities in which we can engage Jack in-session and as homework:

- Use *rational cue cards* to help him remember and rehearse his rational beliefs. Jack can write his rational beliefs down on small cards and place them in locations he frequents, such as his bag, bedside table, wallet, etc.
- Access the *Smarter Thinking App* (Turner & Wood, 2019) or keep a *rational diary*. Both of these activities involve Jack reflecting his GABCDEs as he interacts with the world, and recording his reflections using digital (App) or analogous (pen and paper) means.

- Use a *rational beliefs jar* to offer a purposeful rational rehearsal task. In this task, Jack writes down various rational beliefs, including the ones he has developed, on small strips of paper and then folds them up (50 is a good number of strips). He then places the folded strips into an empty jar. He selects three strips per day, rehearses (repeats) the rational belief on the strip for a minute (or until he can remember it short-term), and then throws it away.
- Write and internalise an *athlete rational credo* (Turner, 2016b; 2020; 2022). Based on Dryden's (2007) work, I developed the athlete rational credo specifically for athletes. The credo is a set of rational beliefs, written in collaboration with the client, which reflects their broader rational philosophy of life. Typically, the athlete rational credo comprises one paragraph for each of the core rational beliefs (preferences, anti-awfulising, FT, and unconditional acceptance). It is written in the first person – rather than speaking to the athlete, as the athlete reads it, they speak to *themselves*. See Chrysidis et al. (2020) and Deen et al. (2017) for evidence of the athlete rational credo in practice.
- Undertake *rational self-talk* as a way of using rational beliefs in the moment. Self-talk, or self-statements, have been used in research to elicit performance improvements (e.g., Turner et al., 2019d). I would encourage Jack to actually face his As whilst rehearsing his rational belief (Dryden, 2019a), as well as facing his As imaginally and then applying this rational self-talk.
- As intimated above, clients can use *rational emotive imagery* (REI; Maultsby, 1971) to rehearse the new rational beliefs whilst imagining themselves facing the A (Dryden, 2019b) until they can experience the HNE. REI will involve Jack imagining the A and the UNE that it is associated with, and then changing the UNE to the HNE *only by applying his rational beliefs*. This can be done in-session, or independently for 10 minutes, four or more times per day, and informally when they have time and opportunity (Wirga et al., 2020).

By engaging in activities and discussions that deepen the rational belief, we are trying to help Jack move from *intellectual insight* and towards *emotional insight*. Jack will demonstrate emotional insight by (a) taking responsibility for thoughts, feelings, and actions, (b) committing in the long-term to doing something about his irrational beliefs, (c) being able to *independently* dispute and act against irrational beliefs, and (d) spontaneously formulating rational beliefs in the face of adversity. Kinney (2000) indicates that emotional insight is evident when a client acknowledges that their irrational beliefs and behaviours are self-defeating and then makes consistent and deliberate efforts to effect substantive change, promoting a true philosophical restructuring. A lofty aim indeed, but one that we can start to move towards with Jack, even if we don't see him all the way there (because Jack will continue to work on his rationality in the long-term, away from our work together).

But how do we know if and when Jack is moving towards emotional insight? In my view, intellectual insight is best demonstrated and measured at the level of behaviour (Turner, 2022). I would want to be able to answer "yes" to the following questions:

- Is Jack forthrightly taking on the A that typically gives rise to his Bs and UNEs?
- Is Jack actively engaging socially?
- Is Jack taking on new challenges?
- Is Jack employing healthy coping strategies to deal with life's challenges?
- Is Jack acting *against* the irrational belief, and acting *for* the rational belief?

Behavioural markers are important because they reflect overt and more objective ways in which the client is engaging with the world and can help the practitioner to understand the extent to which HNEs are being evinced and expressed. In the case of Jack, one key behavioural marker that reflects HNE would be whether he is now able to execute his skills accurately under pressure. If he is more able to do this, then this is evidence that the changes he has made during our work (cognitive, emotive, behavioural; Kinney, 2000) may have brought about some positive changes for Jack in terms of his performance. But performance would not be the only marker I would be concerned with, as indicated by the list of questions above – it is meaningful and active engagement with the performance environment and the world that is more evidential of REBT success.

Finish Our Work with Jack

We cannot properly complete the work with Jack until we are certain that Jack's issues have been ameliorated and that Jack is moving towards, and has the resources to pursue, emotional insight. It perhaps goes without saying that satisfactory completion of the work with Jack means that Jack is no longer choking under pressure. But we need to be more nuanced and realistic here. How long do we have to work with Jack? Perhaps he can fund three, or five sessions, or perhaps ten sessions. Perhaps Jack is coming to the end of the season and therefore we won't know about his experience of choking until next season. If Jack was a soccer athlete, perhaps we might be imbedded in his club and we are able to frequently interact with him on an ongoing basis – less likely in golf perhaps. All of this will influence the completion of the work and our ability to engage with Jack over a longer term to monitor the effects of the work. In this particular case, I would be happy to finish the work when Jack is in the position to regulate his anxiety to the point where he is able to face pressure situations forthrightly and adaptively (HNE) in terms of his cognitive, emotive, and behavioural approach. The data that indicates whether or not this approach will ameliorate his choking is perhaps not yet available. If and when the data becomes available, we can reengage with Jack if needed, and it might be the case that *general* REBT is then pursued. Details concerning general REBT can be found in Turner (2022), but in short, it would involve working pluralistically with Jack on G, A, and C to aid performance, and may include psychological skills training (Andersen, 2009), for example.

But let's say we (Jack and I) are satisfied that Jack now has an adaptive approach to pressure (HNE), underpinned by rationality. What other criteria dictate work completion? Broadly, I need to be confident that Jack can independently apply REBT away from me. In other words, I need to ensure my redundancy and Jack's REBT independence, with Jack effectively becoming his own practitioner (Dryden et al., 2010). I put together some key questions to help me determine whether work with a client should cease (Turner, 2022), that I will adjust for Jack:

- Does Jack understand and can he articulate the GABCDE framework?
- Does Jack endorse B-C thinking?
- Can Jack understand and apply the differences between irrational and rational beliefs?
- Can Jack generate rational beliefs?
- Can Jack recognise UNEs and HNEs in himself?
- Can Jack apply disputation accurately?
- Does Jack have a plan for committing to his new rational belief?
- Is Jack properly, and rationally, oriented towards his goals?
- Does Jack's behaviour indicate the expression of HNEs rather than UNEs?

I want to be able to answer "yes" to these questions, at which point I will be satisfied that Jack no longer needs my help with this particular issue from a *specific* REBT perspective. If I answer "no" to any of these questions, then I can address this with Jack and we continue our work until we can answer "yes". If you were getting your living room painted and the decorator left one wall unpainted and said "sorry, time is up. I am moving onto another job", then the work ceases but the job is not finished. In REBT, we try to avoid ceasing work until the job is done. This is why it is vital to leave time and space in REBT to complete the work properly – we do not want to rush the finish, lest we launch Jack into the world ill-prepared.

As a parting shot with Jack, I would recap everything we have done in our work together by summarising what we covered and the extent to which we have done what we said we were going to do. It is good to be comprehensive with this recap because this may be the final opportunity for Jack to communicate his reservations about using REBT in the real world. We want to make sure Jack understands the journey we have been on together, so that he can repeat the journey by himself when he faces future adversity (which he certainly will). Lastly, I would end the work with Jack by informing him that I am confident in his capacity to move forward positively, but that further support is here if he needs it.

Conclusions

In this chapter, I have introduced REBT as it is applied within sport using a specific case. Readers should be aware that there are many other portrayals of REBT in sport across a range of sports and issues (see Turner & Bennett, 2018, for a book of case studies). I have outlined the core theory of REBT and have described the practice of REBT using a hypothetical case in which a golfer, Jack, is experiencing choking when attempting to execute shots under pressure. Through excavating, articulating, and disputing irrational beliefs, Jack was able to commit to applying REBT as he moves into the future, imbued with rational beliefs. There is still much work to be done studying the use of REBT with athletes. Although the reported use of REBT in sport is in its infancy, there has already emerged an evidence base that indicates that REBT is a potentially effective and viable CBT approach to working in sport (e.g., Jordana et al., 2020), especially for performance anxiety (Turner & Barker, 2013) and especially in golf (e.g., Turner et al., 2020). It is hoped that this chapter, alongside my recent book (Turner, 2022), will furnish readers with some professional practice information and guidance that aids their practice. I implore anybody using REBT in sport settings to write about their experiences formally, so that the REBT and sport psychological community can benefit from their reflections and so that we can form a nuanced picture of REBT's effectiveness in sport.

References

Alegria, K. E., & Cameron, L. D. (2020). Cognitive mediators. In M. Gellman (Ed.), *Encyclopedia of behavioral medicine* (2nd ed., pp. 496–497). Springer International Publishing.

Andersen, M. B. (2009). The "canon" of psychological skills training for enhancing performance. In K. F. Hays (Ed.), *Performance psychology in action: A casebook for working with athletes, performing artists, business leaders, and professionals in high-risk occupations* (pp. 11–34). American Psychological Association. https://doi.org/10.1037/11876-001

Bailey, R. (2022). *Development of a theory and measure of the irrational climate.* [Unpublished doctoral dissertation]. Manchester Metropolitan University.

Bennett, R., & Oliver, J. E. (2019). *Acceptance and commitment therapy: 100 key points and techniques.* Routledge/Taylor & Francis Group. https://doi.org/10.4324/9781351056144

Bernard, M. E., & Dryden, W. (2019). *Advances in REBT: Theory, practice, research, measurement, prevention and promotion*. Springer Nature.

Caserta, D. A., Dowd, E. T., Lynn, S. J., David, D., & Ellis, A. (2010). Rational and irrational beliefs in primary prevention and mental health. In D. David, S. J. Lynn, & A. Ellis (Eds.), *The role of rational and irrational beliefs in human functioning and disturbances: Implications for research, theory, and clinical practice*. Oxford University Press.

Chadha, N., Turner, M. J., & Slater, M. J. (2019). Investigating irrational beliefs, cognitive appraisals, challenge and threat, and affective states in golfers approaching competitive situations. *Frontiers in Psychology*. https://doi.org/10.3389/fpsyg.2019.02295

Chrysidis, S., Turner, M. J., & Wood, A. G. (2020). The effects of REBT on irrational beliefs, self-determined motivation, and self-efficacy in American Football. *Journal of Sports Sciences, 38*(19), 2215–2224. https://doi.org/10.1080/02640414.2020.1776924.

Crum, J. E. (2018). A clinical strategy to strengthen the connection between cognition, emotion, and behavior: from philosophical principles to psychotherapy practice. *Journal of Rational-Emotive & Cognitive-Behavior Therapy, 37*(3), 241–250. https://doi.org/10.1007/s10942-018-0308-4

David, D., Schnur, J., & Belloiu, A. (2002). Another search for the "hot" cognitions: Appraisal, irrational beliefs, attributions, and their relation to emotion. *Journal of Rational-Emotive & Cognitive-Behavior Therapy, 20*(2), 93–131.

David, O. A., Cîmpean, A., Costescu, C., DiGiuseppe, R., Doyle, K., Hickey, M., & David, D. (2021). Effectiveness of outpatient rational emotive behavior therapy over one decade. *American Journal of Psychotherapy, 74*(4), 157–164. https://doi.org/10.1176/appi.psychotherapy.20200009

Deen, S., Turner, M. J., & Wong, R. (2017). The effects of REBT and credos on irrational beliefs and resilient qualities in athletes. *The Sport Psychologist, 31*(3), 249–263.

DiGiuseppe, R. (1986). The implication of the philosophy of science for rational-emotive theory and therapy. *Psychotherapy: Theory, Research, Practice, Training, 23*(4), 634–639. https://doi.org/10.1037/h0085668

DiGiuseppe, R. A., Doyle, K. A., Dryden, W., & Backx, W. (2014). *A practitioner's guide to rational emotive behavior therapy* (3rd ed.). Oxford University Press.

Dixon, M., Turner, M. J., & Gillman, J. (2017). Examining the relationships between challenge and threat cognitive appraisals and coaching behaviours in football coaches. *Journal of Sports Sciences, 35*(24), 2446–2452.

Dobson, K. S., & Shaw, B. F. (1988). The use of treatment manuals in cognitive therapy: experience and issues. *Journal of Consulting and Clinical Psychology, 56*(5), 673–680

Dryden, W. (2007). Resilience and rationality. *Journal of Rational-Emotive & Cognitive-Behavior Therapy, 25*(3), 213–226.

Dryden, W. (2008). *Distinctive features of rational emotive behaviour therapy*. Brunner-Routledge.

Dryden, W. (2009). *Skills in rational emotive behaviour counselling and psychotherapy*. Sage.

Dryden, W. (2012). *The ABCs of REBT revisited: Perspectives on conceptualization*. Springer.

Dryden, W. (2017). Rational emotive behaviour therapy. In, C. Feltham., T. Hanley., & L. A. Winter. (Eds.). *The SAGE handbook of counselling and psychotherapy* (4th ed.). Sage Publications Ltd.

Dryden, W. (2018). *Very brief therapeutic conversations* (1st ed.). Routledge.

Dryden, W. (2019a). The distinctive features of rational emotive behavior therapy. In: M. Bernard, & W. Dryden. (eds) *Advances in REBT* (pp. 23–46). Springer. https://doi.org/10.1007/978-3-319-93118-0_8

Dryden, W. (2019b) Rational emotive behavior therapy: Assessment, conceptualisation and intervention. In: M. Bernard, & W. Dryden. (eds) *Advances in REBT*. Springer. https://doi.org/10.1007/978-3-319-93118-0_8

Dryden, W., & Branch, R. (2008). *The fundamentals of rational emotive behaviour therapy: A training handbook* (2nd ed.). Wiley.

Dryden, W., & David, D. (2008). Rational emotive behavior therapy: Current status. *Journal of Cognitive Psychotherapy, 22*(3), 195–209. https://doi.org/10.1891/0889-8391.22.3.195

Dryden, W., Beal, D., Jones, J., & Trower, P. (2010). The REBT competency scale for clinical and research applications. *Journal of Rational-Emotive & Cognitive-Behavior Therapy, 28*(4), 165–216. https://doi.org/10.1007/s10942-010-0111-3

Ellis, A. (1957). Rational psychotherapy and individual psychology. *Journal of Individual Psychology, 13*, 38–44.

Ellis, A. (1963). Toward a more precise definition of "emotional" and "intellectual" insight. *Psychological Reports, 13*(1), 125–126. https://doi.org/10.2466/pr0.1963.13.1.125

Ellis, A. (1976). The biological basis of human irrationality. *Journal of Individual Psychology, 32*(2), 145–168.

Ellis, A. (1988). *How to stubbornly refuse to make yourself miserable: about anything - yes, anything!* (p. 11). Little, Brown Book Group.

Ellis, A. (1994). *Reason and emotion in psychotherapy* (2nd ed). Carol Publishing Group.

Ellis, A. (2001). *Feeling better, getting better, staying better: Profound self-help therapy for your emotions*. Impact.

Ellis, A., & Dryden, W. (1997). *The practice of rational emotive behavior therapy* (2nd ed.). Springer Publishing Co.

Hooper, N., & Björk. (1993). *Human behaviour*. [Recorded by Björk].

Horvath, A. O., & Greenberg, L. S. (1989). Development and validation of the working alliance inventory. *Journal of Counseling Psychology, 36*(2), 223–233. https://doi.org/10.1037/0022-0167.36.2.223.

Jooste, J., Wolfson, S., & Kruger, A. (2022). Irrational performance beliefs and mental well-being upon returning to sport during the COVID-19 pandemic: A test of mediation by intolerance of uncertainty. *Research Quarterly for Exercise and Sport*, 1–10. doi: 10.1080/02701367.2022.2056117

Jordana, A., Turner, M. J., Ramis, Y., & Torregrossa, M. (2020). A systematic mapping review on the use of Rational Emotive Behavior Therapy (REBT) with athletes. *International Review of Sport and Exercise Psychology*. https://doi.org/10.1080/1750984X.2020.1836673

Kern, A. (2020). Human life, rationality and education. *Journal of Philosophy of Education, 54*(2), 268–289.

King, A., Barker, J. B., Turner, M. J. & Plateau, C. (2022). The socialisation of irrational beliefs in sport. *Journal of Rational-Emotive and Cognitive-Behavioral Therapy*, Accepted for publication 4th May, 2022.

Kinney, A. (2000). The intellectual-insight problem: Implications for assessment and Rational-Emotive Behavior Therapy. *Journal of Contemporary Psychotherapy, 30*, 261–272. https://doi.org/10.1023/A:1004142732449

Kuhn, T. S. (1962). *The structure of scientific revolutions*. University of Chicago Press.

Lazarus, A. A. (1995). REBT: A sign of evolution or devolution? An historical perspective. *Journal of Rational-Emotive & Cognitive-Behavior Therapy, 13*(2), 97–100. https://doi.org/10.1007/bf02354455

Lazarus, R. S. (1999). *Stress and emotion: A new synthesis*. Springer Publishing Co.

Mansell, P. C. (2021). Stress mindset in athletes: Investigating the relationships between beliefs, challenge and threat with psychological wellbeing. *Psychology of Sport and Exercise, 57*, 102020.

Maultsby, M. C., (1975). *Help yourself to happiness trough rational self-counseling*. Institute for Rational Living.

Maultsby, M. Jr. (1971). Rational emotive imagery. *Rational Living, 6*(1), 24–27.

McDowell, J. (2010). Towards a reading of Hegel on action in the 'reason' chapter of the Phenomenology. In: A. Laitinen, & C. Sandis (Eds.), *Hegel on Action* (pp. 166–184). Palgrave-Macmillan.

Mesagno, C., & Hill, D. M. (2013). Choking under pressure debate: Is there chaos in the brickyard? *International Journal of Sport Psychology, 44*, 288–293.

Mesagno, C., Buchanan, E., Tibbert, S. J., & Turner, M. J., (2020). An Initial Investigation into Irrational Beliefs and Choking under Pressure. *Journal of Applied Sport Psychology, 33*(6), 569–589.

Michel-Kröhler, A., & Turner, M. J. (2022). Link between irrational beliefs and important markers of mental health in a German sample of athletes: Differences between gender, sport-type and performance level. *Frontiers in Psychology, Movement Science and Sport Psychology, 13*, 918329. https://doi.org/10.3389/fpsyg.2022.918329

Neenan, M., & Dryden, W. (1996). The intricacies of inference chaining. *Journal of Rational-Emotive and Cognitive-Behavior Therapy, 14*(4), 231–243.

Neenan, M., & Dryden, W. (1999). *Rational emotive behaviour therapy: Advances in theory and practice*. Whurr.

Pinker, S. (2021). *Rationality: What it is. Why it seems scarce. Why it matters.* Viking.

Ritter, W. (1930). Is man a rational animal? *Human Biology, 2*(4), 457–472. Retrieved September 18, 2020, from http://www.jstor.org/stable/41447045

Russell, B. (1950). *Unpopular essays.* George Allen & Unwin.

Smith, C. A., & Lazarus, R. S. (1993). Appraisal components, core relational themes, and the emotions. *Cognition and Emotion*, 7(3–4), 233–269. https://doi.org/10.1080/02699939308409189

Turner, M. J. (2016a). Rational Emotive Behavior Therapy (REBT), irrational and rational beliefs, and the mental health of athletes. *Frontiers: Movement Science and Sport Psychology*, 7, 1423. doi: 10.3389/fpsyg.2016.01423

Turner, M. J. (2016b). Proposing a rational resilience credo for athletes. *Journal of Sport Psychology in Action*, 7(3), 170–181. https://doi.org/10.1080/21520704.2016.1236051

Turner, M. J. (2020, August 6). *The Olympic Games: The rational pursuit of excellence.* MMU News. Retrieved 1 March 2022, from https://www.mmu.ac.uk/hpsc/news-and-media/news/story/?id=12703

Turner, M. J. (2022). *The rational practitioner: The sport and performance psychologist's guide to practicing rational emotive behaviour therapy.* Routledge.

Turner, M. J., & Barker, J. B. (2013). Examining the efficacy of Rational-Emotive Behavior Therapy (REBT) on irrational beliefs and anxiety in elite youth cricketers. *Journal of Applied Sport Psychology, 25*(1), 131–147. https://doi.org/10.1080/10413200.2011.574311

Turner, M. J., & Bennett, R. (2018). *Rational Emotive Behaviour Therapy in Sport and Exercise.* Routledge.

Turner, M. J., & Moore, M. (2016). Irrational beliefs predict increased emotional and physical exhaustion in Gaelic football athletes. *International Journal of Sport Psychology*, 47(2), 187–199.

Turner, M. J., & Wood, A. G. (2019) The Smarter Thinking App (Version 1.0.2). [Mobile app]. Google Play Store. https://play.google.com/store/apps/details?id=com.smarterthinkingprofile.smarterthinking&gl=GB

Turner, M. J., Aspin, G., & Gillman, J. (2019b). Maladaptive schema as a potential mechanism through which irrational beliefs relate to psychological distress in athletes. *Psychology of Sport & Exercise, 44*, 9–16. https://doi.org/10.1016/j.psychsport.2019.04.015

Turner, M. J., Carrington, S., & Miller, A. (2019c). Psychological distress across sport participation groups: The mediating effects of secondary irrational beliefs on the relationship between primary irrational beliefs and symptoms of anxiety, anger, and depression. *Journal of Clinical Sport Psychology, 13*(1), 17–40.

Turner, M. J., Chadha, N. J., & Wood, A. G. (2022). Knowing your ABCs: Extending the assessment of stimulus-response (S-R) and cognitive-mediation (C-M) beliefs. *PloS One*, *17*(6), e0269928. https://doi.org/10.1371/journal.pone.0269928.

Turner, M. J., Ewen, D., & Barker, J. B. (2020). An idiographic single-case study examining the use of Rational Emotive Behavior Therapy (REBT) with three amateur golfers to alleviate sport performance phobias. *Journal of Applied Sport Psychology, 32*(2), 186–204.

Turner, M. J., Jones, J., & Wood, A. G. (2018). Applying the REBT cognitive disputation technique to the binary theory of emotional distress. *Effective Scientist-Practitioner, 1*(1), 46–64.

Turner, M. J., Kirkham, L., & Wood, A. G. (2019d). Teeing up for success: The effects of rational and irrational self-talk on the putting performance of amateur golfers. *Psychology of Sport & Exercise, 38*, 148–153. https://doi.org/10.1016/j.psychsport.2018.06.012

Turner, M. J., Miller, A., & Youngs, H. (2022b). The role of irrational beliefs and motivation regulation in worker mental health and work engagement: A latent profile analysis. PloS One, *17*(8): e0272987. https://doi.org/10.1371/journal.pone.0272987

Turner, M. J., Miller, A., Youngs, H., Barber, N., Brick, N. E., Chadha, N. J., Chandler, C., Coyle, M., Didymus, F. F., Evans, A. L., Jones, K., McCann, B., Meijen, C., & Rossato, C. (2022). "I must do this!": A latent profile analysis approach to understanding the role of irrational beliefs and motivation regulation in mental and physical health. *Journal of Sports Sciences, 40*(8), 934–949. https://doi.org/10.1080/02640414.2022.2042124

Turner, M. J., Wood, A. G., & Jones, J. J. (2019a). A response to Philip Hyland, Demetris Katsikis, and Chrysoula Kostogiannis on the debate point concerning the binary theory of emotional distress. *Effective Scientist-Practitioner, 2.*

Turner, M. J., Wood, A. G., Chadha, N., Boatwright, D., Jones, J., & Bennett, R. (2021). Assessing beliefs about emotion generation and change: The conceptualization, development, and validation of the cognitive mediation beliefs questionnaire (CMBQ). *Psychotherapy Research*, *31*(7), 932–949 https://doi.org/10.1080/10503307.2020.1871524

Wilde, O. (1891) *The Picture of Dorian Gray*. Retrieved via: http://www.literaturepage.com/read/doriangray-30.html

Wilson, D. S. (2010). Rational and irrational beliefs from an evolutionary perspective. In D. David, S. J. Lynn, & A. Ellis (Eds.), *Rational and irrational beliefs: Research, theory, and clinical practice* (pp. 63–72). Oxford University Press.

Wirga, M., DeBernardi, M., Wirga, A., Wirga, M. L., Banout, M., & Fuller, O. G. (2020). Maultsby's rational behavior therapy: Background, description, practical applications, and recent developments. *Journal of Rational-Emotive & Cognitive-Behavior Therapy*, *38*(3), 399–423. https://doi.org/10.1007/s10942-020-00341-8

6

SCHEMA THERAPY (ST)

Gillian Aspin, Sulu Kaski, and Ulla Damgaard-Sørensen

Introduction

Young's (1999) schema therapy (ST) is an extension of the cognitive model developed by the late Beck et al. (1979). Beck's model works on the premise that core beliefs about the self, other people, and the world are formed in childhood and become automatic in adulthood. The resultant negative automatic thoughts can be challenged through a collaborative, structured, and problem-focused approach. Young extended this model by adding the understanding that humans evolve, through an accumulation of experiences, in such a way as to protect their internal dynamics and strive to predict future experiences. The consequence is that ST pays more attention to childhood development and attachment figures, such as parents, than cognitive therapy (CT). ST also uses more interpersonal and experiential techniques, and, in general, the course of therapy in health settings typically lasts longer than CT. However, in sport settings, ST may be of the same length as CT or sometimes shorter.

Central to Young's theory are core emotional needs. Repeated failure and neglect to meet basic core needs affects child development and has long-term impacts on psychological wellbeing, in terms of mental health difficulties, difficulties in relationships, and other emotional issues. Early maladaptive schemas are a result of childhood experiences relating to unmet needs (e.g., Roediger et al., 2018). Early maladaptive schemas (EMS) are defined as "extremely stable and enduring themes that develop during childhood, are elaborated throughout an individual's lifetime, and are dysfunctional to a significant degree" (Young, 1999, p. 9). Schemas therefore develop through a lack of fit between the child's temperament and natural developmental needs, and their environment which should provide for those needs. This lack of fit means the child's natural needs, such as for nurture, play, discipline, freedom of expression, or safety, are not sufficiently met. Maladaptive schemas are the result of the child's adaptive attempt to cope with this deficit (Linehan, 1993). The idea here is that it is the dripping tap of daily difficulties affects the way children develop, as opposed to a single trauma.

In adulthood, schemas only become activated in specific situations and result in dysfunctional perceptions that govern the way a person sees themselves, others, and the world. Schemas are self-perpetuating as the individual tries to cope with the distress by inadvertently

DOI: 10.4324/9781003162513-7

making use of coping strategies (mode behaviour) that were adequate and adaptive during childhood (the origins of the schema). However, the challenge arises when these coping modes are no longer effective or healthy. For example, the athlete described later in this chapter copes with feelings of failing (failure schema) by working harder (overcompensation mode), which has a negative impact on performance, inducing further feelings of failure that drive her to train even harder; a self-perpetuating cycle. This cycle, an attempt to deal with her frustration, produces negative consequences which confirm and strengthen her schema. She is perpetually caught up in feeling inadequate (failure schema) and her maladaptive mode behaviour (overtraining) serves to keep her schema intact and unchallenged. Her "unhealthy" response or maladaptive mode strategy becomes part of the self-perpetuating cycle of main taining her (false) belief of her feeling a failure.

As well as schema maintenance through *surrendering* to the schema, as in the example in the previous paragraph, Young (1999) proposes that individuals use behavioural, cognitive, and emotional schema *avoidance* strategies to avoid triggering schemas, and schema *compensation* strategies, which are the young person's initial attempts to "fight back", and which can become dysfunctional in healthier adult environments. Eighteen individual schemas have been identified, but this is beyond the scope of this chapter. Further details can be found in Young et al. (2003).

In sport, common schemas that relate to performance (e.g., Gardner & Moore, 2006) include dependency, failure, entitlement, and approval seeking. The presence of schemas does not necessarily mean that an athlete has clinical or mental health problems. Rather, stressful situations (e.g., competition) might trigger the schema and affect performance. There are also positive schemas (e.g., emotional fulfilment and success) which help individuals to adapt and function in different situations. In sport, athletes might "feel" competent when thinking of achievement (success) but when failing or making a mistake, they might still "feel" they are ok as a person and able to forgive themselves.

Schemas are thus manifested and maintained by modes. In ST, the resolution of a schema centres on identifying maladaptive modes and lessening their strength by introducing and developing the concept of the "Healthy Adult Mode" (Young et al., 2003). The schema model has been expanded to describe and account for how maladaptive modes maintain, and in some cases, exacerbate, schemas and resultant dysfunction. A schema mode may manifest a number of independent schemas, which, when triggered, often produce intense emotions and have a stronger influence over the individual than the schema itself. For example, the athlete described later experiences a failure schema, but it was her over-compensatory mode that drove her to keep training at a dysfunctional level.

Research Evidence

Schema therapy was developed during the 1980s and 1990s (Young, 1999) for complex mental health issues, specifically borderline personality disorder (BPD), a diagnosis that is characterised by difficulties in relationships and in managing emotions. Since then, a growing body of research has demonstrated the positive effects of ST (e.g., Bakos et al., 2015), for entrenched personality difficulties (Carter et al., 2013; Masley et al., 2012) and depression (Köruk & Özabaci, 2018). In a 2011 review paper, Hawke and Provencher (2011) demonstrated positive outcomes for ST for people with mood and anxiety disorders, and in a more recent review, Taylor et al. (2017) showed ST delivered significant symptom reduction and changes in schemas in people with a variety of difficulties. Indeed Turner et al. (2019) showed that schemas can account for the negative effect that irrational beliefs have on emotional distress. Taken together Taylor et al. (2017) and Turner et al. (2019) make a compelling case for using ST to modify schemas and bring about reduction in emotional distress.

In sport, there are demands and resources that influence athletes' well-being (e.g., Kuettel & Larsen, 2020) and review papers have demonstrated that athletes, like the general population, experience a myriad of mental disorders such as depression, anxiety, eating disorders, and substance abuse (Reardon et al., 2019). Sport does not protect against mental health problems, but ST is useful in addressing these issues (Kaski, 2021). It is shown that higher level athletes have higher average scores in early maladaptive schemas (Salehian & Gursoy, 2020). In top sport, competitiveness and the constant demand for excellence can in itself create an environment of schema activation. When working with athletes, it is important to notice that usually, when practising and performing well, schemas may not be triggered; they may be "hidden". However, in situations where, for example, the athlete is losing a game or making a mistake, the schema may be activated, making the experience seem even bigger and worse than it actually is (e.g., Gallagher & Gardner, 2007; Reyhan et al., 2020).

Applying Schema Therapy in Clinical Practice

Assessment

The assessment phase in ST typically lasts between one to four sessions. The aim of the assessment is to explore schema-related thoughts, feelings, behaviours, and their origins. In addition to undertaking a comprehensive clinical interview that is summarised in the case conceptualisation form (Young et al., 2003), the client completes a range of standardised questionnaires. These include the Young Schema Questionnaire (Young, 2005) and the Schema Mode Inventory (SMI) (Young et al., 2007). Additional questionnaires, such as the Young Positive Schema Questionnaire (YPSQ) (Louis et al., 2018) and the Young Parenting Inventory (YPI) (Young, 1995), may also be useful during assessment. The questionnaires guide the assessment by identifying the most problematic schemas and modes and these are explored more fully during imagery for assessment exercises.

Typical questions during assessment might include "you told your coach that you see a pattern in your life of having to succeed otherwise you would feel a failure, can you tell me more about that?" This open-ended question starts a conversation aimed at identifying which schemas may be present and uncover their origins in the client's past. This will usually have arisen in childhood. Behaviours noticed in early adulthood or teenage years may also be relevant, even if the client does not think so. Therefore, a follow-up question would often be "does this experience remind you of any time in your past?".

When working with clients in the sporting world, it is particularly important to pay attention to the "effects of exposure". Each sport typically has a specific set of cultural aspects that govern the underlying values and beliefs. It is therefore vital to explore the underlying values and statements, for example, "if you were two kilos lighter, you would run 20 second faster" or "do it one more time, then you will be better". Although these statements are meant to motivate and heighten performance, they can become detrimental to those clients with activated schemas. Then the effect of exposure becomes a critical risk factor that can lead to increased levels of distress and a sense of impairment that can impact performance negatively.

In imagery for assessment, the therapist explores the origins of schemas in a safe manner. The client, with their eyes closed, visualises and describes a recent event that has triggered strong emotion. The therapist enquires about the experience and helps the client verbalise the feelings, thoughts, bodily sensations, and reactions as if the situation was being played out now in the present. Once strong emotions have become elicited, the client is asked to wipe that image from their mind, holding on to the activated emotions, and picture a time in the past, as young as possible, when they felt the same emotion, which is then explored (Young et al., 2003). Understanding the origin of the schema helps clients create some distance between themselves and their schema, enabling them to question the truthfulness of the schema. Subsequently, goals for therapy are set identifying two to three of the most challenging schemas to work on. Once a shared understanding has developed, the psychologist will usually draw out a diagrammatic formulation (Figure 6.1), see example later in this chapter,

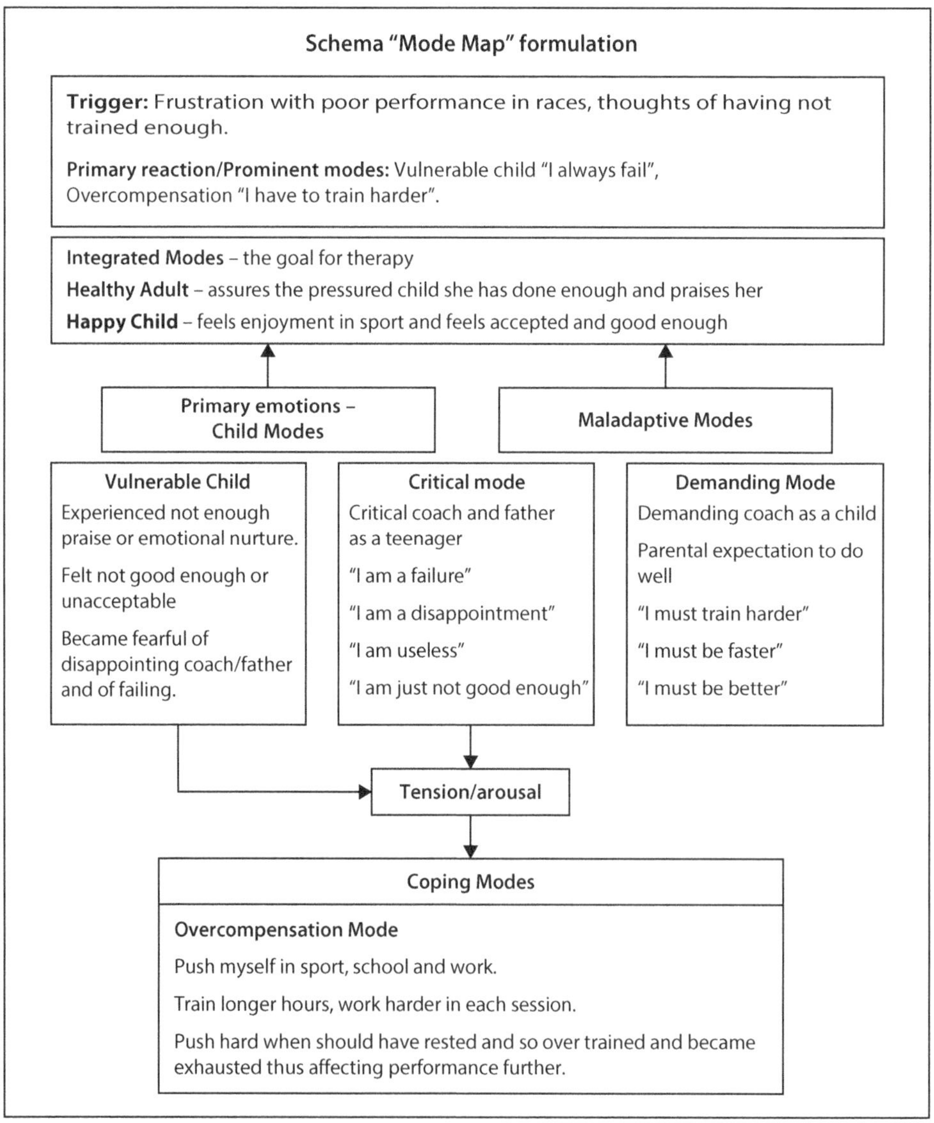

FIGURE 6.1 Fiona's schema formulation.

or a mode map to help the client visually see how the schema and mode patterns have developed and how they have coped with them in such a way that maintains them. The mode map serves as a starting point for therapy and may be updated or changed as therapy is progressing (Arntz & Jacob, 2013).

Intervention

The aim of therapy is to strengthen the healthy adult mode functioning and thus reducing the strength of schemas and maladaptive coping modes (e.g., Young, et al., 2003). At the end of therapy, a client may still feel triggered and disappointed, for example, acknowledging that "I didn't get into top three, but this doesn't mean that I'm a failure". However, new ways of coping will have been identified and practiced, whereby the client might think "Even though I didn't get into top three, there is no need to punish myself for the next two weeks with too strict a diet, leaving me more injury prone. Rather, I'm going to celebrate my performance and reward myself, thus feeling more motivated and satisfied, whilst having taken good care of myself, so I avoid injuries caused by not looking after myself adequately".

Schema therapists use several techniques to minimise the power of the schemas and shift maladaptive coping strategies to a healthy adult mode that over time will serve to reinforce and reduce the strength of the schemas (see, e.g., Roediger et al., 2018). The role of the healthy adult mode, in terms of the self, is to take care of the needs of the vulnerable child mode in a functional manner that ensures that the client's emotional needs are met appropriately, when schemas are activated, and to realistically balance the needs of oneself with those of others (Arntz & Jacob, 2013). Techniques include imagery and chair work, where the therapist adopts an active role in providing "limited reparenting" as a way of both healing the client's past experiences (where schemas were formed) and enabling the client to have a role model of healthy and appropriate response to emotional distress (Young et al., 2003). Over time, the client will internalise the "healthy adult mode" represented by the therapist. Another key technique involves "empathic confrontation", whereby the therapist uses the safety of the therapeutic alliance to confront and shift the client's thoughts and behaviours (modes). This may at times require specific attention to setting realistic limits and demands (Arntz & Jacob, 2013; Young et al., 2003).

Imagery

Imagery for change expands on the imagery used for assessment exercise, by adding a new ending to the visualisation where the past event is rescripted or changed (Arntz & Weertman, 1999). The client is supported to imagine experiencing having his/her core needs met in an emotionally satisfying resolution to the distressing situation. We cannot change the past but the real difference in emotions the client experiences in this exercise is part of healing the schema and reducing its influence on the person. This can be achieved in a number of ways and the therapist and client can get creative with its use (Arntz & Weertman, 1999).

Imagery may start with remembering something that has happened recently to trigger the schema and the emotions this evokes are focused on by asking questions such as "what does that feel like?", "can you say more?", "what other feelings words would describe it?", "with 10 being the strongest how strong are you feeling it now?" The aim is to generate the difficult feeling at a strength as close to 10 as possible but usually at least 6. The client is then asked to wipe out that image from their mind but hold on to the feeling and go back to a difficult childhood experience that feels the same or similar.

Another way of starting the imagery is to go straight back to a childhood event. If the client has childhood memories that they feel are relevant, then these can be gone straight back to without starting with a recent event. It is important to say that imagery is not to pretend that difficult events did not happen, rather, changing other people's responses in line with what the child needed, i.e., rescripting. This gives a different emotional understanding; that the schema is not the objective truth but a creation due to the experiences of their needs not being met. History cannot be changed but in therapy we change the way one holds the narrative in mind (e.g., van Vreeswijk et al., 2012). This understanding helps create distance between the client and their schemas, growing their healthy adult mode, allowing them to act more healthily when the schema is triggered.

Imagery exercises are used repeatedly in sessions to help the healthy adult mode grow so that the impact of the schemas is weakened. As clients become adept at its use, they may also be encouraged to practice it between sessions to further strengthen and consolidate the development of more adaptive ways of coping. It is important to check out with the client that the changed ending feels believable enough. It does not need to be realistic; this is imagination after all, so, for example, the therapist could be present in an image from the person's childhood, but it needs to be believable enough. The person who helps the client in the image needs to be a trusted person and hence the psychologist may, at least initially, be a good person to figuratively "step in" to the image (Arntz & Jacob, 2013). As clients get to know their needs, they become more active in the rescripting and may bring their own adult self in to the image to meet their own childhood needs or challenge others that did not meet them. This strengthening of the healthy adult mode helps clients feel empowered to challenge the schema and to not succumb to it.

Once change has taken place and the client has experienced that their emotional needs are met appropriately, the exercise moves on from the upsetting image to explore how this impacts the clients' current life circumstances. The new learning may help the client to see how they, by adopting a healthy adult mode, can have their needs met more adequately and thus lessening the negative impact of the schema. These are common applications of imagery, but in sport, imagery exercises also need to address and strengthen the "happy child" mode. The happy child mode helps athletes to "dare to let go" and freely enjoy the sport and play.

Chair Work

Another technique commonly used to challenge schemas, often the coping modes, is the "empty chair" technique, where dialogues between empty chairs are orchestrated (using the mode map to identify relevant modes). At first, clients may find the idea of talking to an empty chair unusual, but most clients get used to it quickly and soon learn to be able to challenge unhelpful schemas and grow their healthy adult mode further. The idea is to figuratively place each mode you wish to have a dialogue with on a separate chair. There is always a chair for the vulnerable child mode, the healthy adult mode and a chair for the part of the client that is making life difficult, such as a detached (avoidant), mode, a demanding parent mode, or a self-aggrandizing (overcompensation) mode. The idea is that clients move between the chairs as each mode is triggered or says something in the clients' mind (Young et al., 2003).

During therapy, chair work and imagery exercises help clients experience how their needs are met in a healthy manner and they begin to challenge the schemas that held them "imprisoned" in unhealthy mode responses. In between sessions, clients keep diaries and develop flashcards (written or voice-recorded) that help them monitor and challenge their experiences and behaviours, thus enabling progression and change to be integrated into their daily lives and practices (Young & Klosko, 1993). Therapy ends when the client feels they have some control over the schemas, although they may not be symptom-free. The number of sessions depends on the difficulties the client brings to therapy but 10–20 sessions is usually sufficient to effect lasting change in people with mild-to-moderate problems.

Finishing therapy can be an anxiety-provoking time and a follow-up session or email a few weeks later may be offered to troubleshoot issues before ending. Typically, there is no contact between sessions, although an encouraging email may be sent if a client is struggling or going through a particularly difficult time, including performance-related activities, such as a competition. This is in the spirit of "limited reparenting" (i.e., modelling the actions), "a good enough parent", through offering support and encouragement. ST is about changing clients' deeply held beliefs by accessing and changing the emotions felt in childhood when the schemas formed. Imagery and chair work are used to develop more healthy views and emotions and encourage doubt that the schemas are true.

Employing the ST Model with Athletes

The Case

Fiona, 29 years old, is a triathlete. Professionally, she is a doctor, who regularly works overtime. She also trains between over 15 to 20 hours a week (running, swimming, cycling, and strength training). She has a supportive partner. Fiona has competed in sports from a young age, including gymnastics and track and field. Her coaches were demanding, seeing her as a top-level athlete when she was under 10 years old. She started running medium distances at age 14. She had a coach, who was very disappointed if she didn't do all they had practised. One time she stumbled in a race and came fourth and her coach did not talk to her afterwards. Her father was also angry that she could make such a "ridiculous" mistake. She was a country-level runner as a teenager and in track and field, the atmosphere was more permissive, but everybody knew that by training more and better than the others, you were faster and could win races. Fiona comes from a high achieving family of doctors and was always driven to succeed. Her parents encouraged hard work. Fiona felt this pressure at everything. She experienced a number of injuries and took up triathlon in her 20s. She now works with a coach to improve her times with the aim of qualifying for the World Championships. She often trains more than her coach's instructions, but despite this her times are not improving. She is starting to feel frustrated and lower in mood. Her coach is worried. During a coaching session, Fiona opened up saying "I just have to succeed otherwise I would feel useless and a failure". She acknowledged that this "all or nothing" way of thinking was a "life-trap". She also began to show symptoms of overtraining. At this point, she agreed to meet with a psychologist.

Assessment and Formulation

The assessment explored Fiona's experiences through clinical interview, formal questionnaires, and imagery exercises (van Vreeswijk et al., 2012). It found that Fiona experienced *Failure to Achieve* and *Unrelenting Standards* schemas. These schemas developed from her core childhood needs for praise and acceptance not being adequately met. Additionally, the family set exceedingly high standards for accomplishment. In sport, these schemas are common and can be highly valuable, and they also helped Fiona compete with high levels of motivation and confidence. However, when activated, Fiona's schemas become so overwhelming and powerful that they lead to significant impairment both in her emotional experience of herself and in her performance. The imagery exercises for assessment helped identify Fiona's most challenging schema. Here, Fiona described a recent time where her schemas were triggered at a race, when her time was slower than expected, leaving her sad and feeling like a failure. The exercise allowed Fiona to better understand her *Failure to Achieve* schema, both on an emotional level and connecting with its origin. This enabled her to see the schema as something that developed due to life events rather than because of her (Mancini & Mancini, 2018). It also helped formulate the therapeutic goals for change, where Fiona would work on learning that even though she might not win every race, this would not mean that she is a failure as a person.

Fiona's other challenging schema, the *unrelenting standards*, also originated in childhood. It developed as a combination of her parents' constant demands for hard work and success and lack of praise. In addition, Fiona experienced several coaches who were punitive and critical of her, constantly pushing her to strive for success. Under these conditions, Fiona learnt to survive emotionally by developing ways of overcompensating, surrendering, and avoiding the pain of not feeling adequate and sufficiently successful. She thus grew up in highly pressurised and performance-driven environments that did not afford her emotional core needs sufficient attention.

The assessment explored the usefulness of her schemas in order for Fiona to partake in competitive sports in an accomplished and confident manner. It too emphasised the role of the "happy child mode", an important mode that allowed Fiona to feel motivated about her sport and training. Indeed, the "happy child mode" is vital to feeling motivated and committed and the assessment interview revealed that many of Fiona's childhood coaches had stalled the development of this mode as coaches often expressed high demands, disappointment, criticism, and even anger, if her results were not adequate. Part of the therapeutic work thus involved addressing these demanding and critical "parenting" modes, allowing Fiona to access and care for both her "vulnerable/lonely" and "happy" child modes through developing a healthy adult mode.

Below is a mode map that formulates how Fiona maintains her schema functioning through mode behaviour. In reality, other modes could be included in the map but for brevity, only the main ones are presented. The aim of therapy will be to address these maladaptive and coping mode strategies, heal and repair the underlying schemas, and develop the "healthy adult mode", so that Fiona can take better care of her emotional experiences and thus develop a more stable and healthy training regime, that will help her cope better and more effectively during competition and in everyday life.

Intervention

The intervention is aimed at weakening the influence of the schemas and strengthening the healthy adult mode. In Fiona's case, the psychologist used the situation analysis, when Fiona said: "I just had a bad race and my coach was not pleased". The psychologist tried to explore this further by asking what happened and how this made Fiona feel/think/sensations in body and react.

To rescript the image, Fiona recounted the childhood event, with her eyes closed, and the psychologist asked guiding questions, such as, "where are you?", "what can you see?", "who is there?", "what are they saying?", "what is the expression on their face?". When events in the image did not meet Fiona's core needs, as her dad became angry and critical, the rescripting started. The psychologist was directive in helping Fiona have her emotional needs met, for example, by introducing Fiona's mum or coach, or the psychologist into the image, and telling her dad not to call her stupid, that it was an accident to stumble. In imagery, the psychologist worked to ensure that Fiona, in a protected and secure manner, could experience the appropriate responses from adults around her (her dad). In addition, the purpose of the imagery is to hold Fiona's dad accountable for the pain he caused Fiona, always ensuring that her dad ended up acknowledging his flawed parenting and apologising to Fiona.

Empty chair work is also used to help Fiona challenge her unhelpful modes. So, for Fiona, we introduce a healthy adult chair to offer objectivity, flexibility, and reason. The vulnerable child chair would likely be the part of Fiona that holds feelings of failure or never being good enough. We also have a chair to represent the demanding mode, the part of Fiona which never lets up and drives her to train when she should be resting. The aim is for Fiona to have a dialogue and debate each schema about what that mode wants, thinks, is motivated and persuaded by, why it is there, and how it is trying to help. Clients move between chairs speaking from each part of themselves, vulnerable, demanding, healthy in Fiona's case, when in the corresponding chair.

The following is an example of chair work dialogue with Fiona:

> Fiona, expressing her vulnerable child mode: "I'll never been good enough, it's useless, I feel sad and hopeless and just feel a failure"
>
> As Fiona feels the emotional pain, further statements of hopelessness are voiced: "The more I train, the worse I get. Everybody is disappointed to me. I am just not getting anywhere. Everybody is so looking forward the trip for the European Championships. I'm never going to qualify".
>
> Moving chairs, Fiona, sits in the chair of the demanding parent mode saying: "don't be so defeatist, you're so pathetic, you just need to try harder and stop moaning all the time. We will go the European Champs and everybody will be proud, stop being such a wuss and get on with training!"
>
> Moving back to original chair, Fiona speaks from the vulnerable mode saying: "You're pushing me too much, and it is overloading, why don't you ever listen to me, you make me feel so bad".
>
> Moving chairs again, Fiona, as the demanding parenting mode, responds: "I'm trying to help you, can't you see that? I'm trying to make sure you do qualify and everything goes well. Just keep training and you'll be fine. And stop moaning, this gets you nowhere"

At this point, the *vulnerable child mode* has noted that the d*emanding mode* is not really helping Fiona, and that the mode is beginning to fight back and become even more demanding and demeaning, invalidating Fiona's doubts and distress. The demanding mode has started to fight and justify its existence, and this is a good point to bring in the healthy adult mode to work with the vulnerable mode and for the psychologist to explain to the demanding mode why it is actually not helping. To help Fiona further, the psychologist crouches next to Fiona, who is in the healthy adult chair, to coach her in how to respond to the demanding mode. Fiona is the "lead" voice, however, the psychologist offers support and encouragement, and may take the lead, if Fiona struggles to find words or strength to express the healthy adult mode.

> Fiona speaks from the healthy adult mode: "but you are making it worse, I am exhausted and you are not letting me rest. Rest is such an important part of sport and recovery and you are denying me that. What if I get injured then we won't be able to go to the champs at all."

The psychologist may make suggestions of what Fiona can say as her healthy adult mode, if she is struggling. This is the coaching aspect of chair work.

> Moving chairs, Fiona as the demanding mode: "But I am only trying to help, I've always pushed you and you never minded before."
>
> Moving chairs, Fiona's healthy adult mode: "I know but this is different. It has always helped before, I am a doctor and have a great life, but this time is not working, it's breaking me, I'm exhausted, I can't do it anymore, I need rest and recovery and you have to let me do that. You can still push me on in races, I definitely need you then, we are a team then, but not now, not when I need rest."
>
> At this stage, Fiona no longer wants to move into the chair of the demanding mode, as she does not feel the demanding mode has anything more to say, it has fallen silent.

The feeling Fiona experiences when having silenced the mode, by having challenged and "won over it", helps her experience that she can, when necessary, fight the mode triggered by the unrelenting standards schema and win. The therapist and Fiona talk about the need for Fiona to still compete and push herself in races, however, not in the destructive manner of the demanding mode. In the following weeks, Fiona puts this into practice and she subsequently learns to control her reactions differently when her unrelenting standards schema is triggered. She is gradually beginning to feel in control of the schema rather than feeling the schema controls her.

Fiona worked on her progress in between sessions, using a flashcard for her *Unrelenting Standards* schema:

> Right now, I am feeling pressured, anxious, and jittery because I have not yet trained today. However, I know this is my Unrelenting Standards schema which I learned through my mother and coach being very pushy and father getting angry if I made a mistake or did not do well. This schema leads me to exaggerate the degree to which I must train.
>
> Even though I believe I must train as much as possible or I will not be good enough and will fail, the reality is that I need rest in order for me body to recover and for my muscles to adapt to the training I do and get stronger.
>
> Therefore, even though I feel like going running I could instead look at my training plan set by my coach and follow it, resting when needed and pushing myself when it is allowed in training.

At the end of therapy, Fiona had worked with imagery, identified her maladaptive schemas, and through rescripting had begun to have her unmet needs met. Additionally, she strengthened her positive schemas, which she needed for competition (Salehian & Gursoy, 2020). Chair work allowed her to understand the unique function of her modes, which helped her become the "captain of her ship" (healthy adult). The flashcard was a good reminder to her, when situations triggered her. The work, including assessment, was carried out in 20 sessions. The intervention was reviewed regularly and ended with consolidating and integrating her new practices into her life, thus preparing Fiona for a future without therapy and with a sense of achievement and a more stable sense of herself and her abilities

Conclusion

Schema therapy is an innovative model that quickly helps sports people in many settings, ranging from amateur to professional levels, to map out which part of themselves is talking at a particular time and to use familiar techniques (imagery) to address mental health difficulties (a further example can be found in Turner et al., 2019). It offers promising results through the use of imagery rescripting and imagery around positive schemas, to meet the unmet need and develop feelings of succeeding. Chair work creates further distance from the unhelpful mode so the "captain of the ship" (healthy adult) can steer unhindered. Clients understand the concepts quickly, often soon feeling understood, thus aiding engagement and helping people overcome the unease of unusual techniques such as chair work. A thorough assessment and conceptualisation form help to identify schemas and modes that can be effectively, and creatively, addressed in therapy. The aim of minimising maladaptive modes and strengthening the healthy adult and happy child mode is to help athletes combat their schemas and increase mental health well-being, allowing them to capitalise on their performance, and produce helpful results. Whilst research in sport remains limited (e.g., Turner et al., 2019), ST offers a promising therapy model, which has a growing evidence base outside of sport, which can help athletes perform at their best, without feeling let down by their mental distress or doubts.

References

Arntz, A., & Jacob, G. (2013). *Schema therapy in practice: An introductory guide to the schema mode approach*. Wiley.

Arntz, A., & Weertman, A. (1999). Treatment of childhood memories: Theory and practice. *Behaviour Research and Therapy, 37*(8), 715–740.

Bakos, D. S., Gallo, A. E., & Wainer, R. (2015). *Systematic review of the clinical effectiveness of schema therapy*. doi: 10.15761/CBHC.1000104

Beck, A. T., Rush, A. J., Shaw, B. F., & Emery, G. (1979). *Cognitive therapy of depression*. Guilford Press.

Carter, J. D., McIntosh, V. V., Jordan, J., Porter, R. J., Frampton, C. M., & Joyce, P. R. (2013). Psychotherapy for depression: a randomized clinical trial comparing schema therapy and cognitive behavior therapy. *Journal of Affective Disorders, 151*(2), 500–505. https://doi.org/10.1016/j.jad.2013.06.034

Gallagher, B. V., & Gardner, F. L. (2007). An examination of the relationship between early maladaptive schemas, coping, and emotional response to athletic injury. *Journal of Clinical Sport Psychology, 1*(1), 47–67. https://psycnet.apa.org/doi/10.1123/jcsp.1.1.47

Gardner, F., & Moore, Z. (2006). *Clinical sport psychology*. Human Kinetics.

Hawke, L., & Provencher, D. (2011) Schema theory and schema therapy in mood and anxiety disorders: A review. *Journal of Cognitive Psychotherapy, 25*(4), 257–276. http://dx.doi.org/10.1891/0889-8391.25.4.257

Kaski, S. (2021). Presentation: Mental health in sport and clinical applications in schema therapy. *ISST Virtual Summit.24.-26.6.2021.*

Köruk, S. & Özabaci, N. (2018). Effectiveness of schema therapy on the treatment of depressive disorders: A meta-analysis. *Psikiyatride Guncel Yaklasimlar, 10*(4), 460–470. doi:10.18863/pgy.361790

Kuettel, A., & Larsen, C. H. (2020). Risk and protective factors for mental health in elite athletes: A scoping review. *International Review of Sport and Exercise Psychology, 13*(1), 231–265. https://doi.org/10.1080/1750984X.2019.1689574

Linehan, M. (1993). *Cognitive behaviour treatment of borderline personality disorder.* The Guilford Press.

Louis, J. P., Wood, A. M., Lockwood, G., Ho, M.-H. R., & Ferguson, E. (2018). Positive clinical psychology and Schema Therapy (ST): The development of the Young Positive Schema Questionnaire (YPSQ) to complement the Young Schema Questionnaire 3 Short Form (YSQ-S3). *Psychological Assessment, 30*(9), 1199–1213. http://dx.doi.org/10.1037/pas0000567

Mancini, A., & Mancini, F. (2018). Rescripting memory, redefining the self: A meta-emotional perspective on the hypothesized mechanism(s) of Imagery Rescripting. *Frontiers in Psychology, 9*(April), 581.

Masley, S. A., Gillanders, D. T., Simpson, S. G., & Taylor, M. A. (2012). A systematic review of the evidence base for schema therapy. *Cognitive Behaviour Therapy, 41*(3), 185–202. https://doi.org/10.1080/16506073.2011.614274

Reardon, C. L., Hainline, B., Aron, C. M., Baron, D., Baum, A. L., Bindra, A., Budgett, R., Campriani, N., Castaldelli-Maia, J. M., Currie, A., Derevensky, J. L., Glick, I. D., Gorczynski, P., Gouttebarge, V., Grandner, M. A., Han, D. H., McDuff, D., Mountjoy, M., Polat, A., … Engebretsen, L. (2019). Mental health in elite athletes: International Olympic Committee consensus statement. *British Journal of Sports Medicine, 53*(11), 667–699. https://doi.org/10.1136/bjsports-2019-100715

Reyhan, S., Gür, Y., and Salehian, M.H. (2020). Effect of losing on early maladaptive schemata of individual male athletes. *African Educational Research Journal, 8*(1), 78–82. DOI: 10.30918/AERJ.81.20.025

Roediger, E., Stenvens, B. A., & Brockman, R. (2018). *Contextual schema therapy. An Integrative approach to personality disorders, emotional dysregulation & interpersonal functioning.* New Harbinger Publications.

Salehian, M. H., & Gursoy, R. (2020). The effect of winning on early maladaptive schema of individual female athletes. *African Educational Research Journal, 8*(2), 227–232. DOI: 10.30918/AERJ.82.20.051

Taylor, C. D. J., Bee, P., & Haddock, G. (2017). Does schema therapy change schemas and symptoms? A systematic review across mental health disorders. *Psychology and Psychotherapy, 90*(3), 456–479. doi: 10.1111/papt.12112.

Turner, M. J., Aspin, G., & Gillman, J. (2019). Maladaptive schemas as a potential mechanism through which irrational beliefs relate to psychological distress in athletes. *Psychology of Sport & Exercise, 44*, 9–16. https://doi.org/10.1016/j.psychsport.2019.04.015

van Vreeswijk, M., Broersen, J., & Nadort, M. (Eds.). (2012). *The Wiley-Blackwell handbook of schema therapy: Theory, research, and practice.* Wiley Blackwell.

Young, J. (1995). *Young parenting inventory-1.* Schema Therapy Institute. http://www.schematherapy.com/id49.htm

Young, J. (1999). *Cognitive therapy for personality disorder: A schema focused approach* (3rd ed.). Professional Resource Press.

Young, J. (2005). *Young schema questionnaire - short form 3.* Schema Therapy Institute. http://www.schematherapy.com/id49.htm

Young, J. E., Arntz, A., Atkinson, T., Lobbestael, J., Weishaar, M. E., van Vreeswijk, M. F., & Klokman, J. (2007). *The schema mode inventory.* Schema Therapy Institute. http://www.schematherapy.com/id49.htm

Young, J., & Klosko, J. (1993). *Reinventing your life: The breakthrough programme to end negative behaviour and feel great again.* Plume.

Young, J., Klosko, J., & Weishaar, M. (2003). *Schema therapy: A practitioner's guide.* Guildford Press.

7

STRESS INOCULATION TRAINING (SIT)

Marc V. Jones and Martin J. Turner

Introduction

Sport is often stressful. Athletes and coaches are typically highly motivated to succeed. However, the outcome is often uncertain and uncontrollable, there is the potential for physical and psychological pain (e.g., danger to esteem from a loss) and winning will require effort, often in direct physical confrontation with an opponent who themselves are doing their level best to succeed. It is these characteristics of a motivated performance environment that provide the conditions for stress (Blascovich et al., 2011). Because sport has a wide range of demands that test diverse abilities, such as physical prowess, effort, courage, technique, reaction time, and complex decision-making, even minor fluctuations in each aspect may result in substantial changes in performance and outcome. For example, a slight alteration in a golfer's putting stroke from an increase in anxiety-induced muscular tension may be the difference between a successful or unsuccessful putt. It is no surprise therefore that psychological factors in sport, chief among them an ability to cope with stress, is a key predictor of success (Orlick & Partington, 1988). Stress can occur across many different timescales from acute stressors, daily events, life events, and chronic stressors (Epel et al., 2018) and it is possible to see how athletes can be exposed to stress across all of these timescales. Acute stressors are intense short-term exposures (e.g., a competition), daily events are more minor hassles that happen frequently (e.g., arguments with teammates), life events are time-limited and episodic (e.g., being injured), and chronic stressors are present for longer periods of time (e.g., even many elite athletes experience financial strain from precarious contracts).

Stress inoculation training (SIT) developed by Donald Meichenbaum (1977, 1985) is an intervention programme for the prevention and the treatment of the deleterious effects of stress. In SIT, a transactional view of stress and coping (Lazarus & Folkman, 1984) is adopted in which stress occurs whenever the perceived demands of a situation tax, or exceed, the perceived resources of the person. In SIT, the important role that cognition plays in determining emotional and behavioural responses is key, and SIT is part of the cognitive-behavioural approach to behaviour modification which came to the fore in the 1970s (see, Mahoney, 1974; Meichenbaum, 1977). While there are many differing types of therapy utilising a cognitive-behavioural approach (e.g., rational emotive behaviour therapy; REBT),

DOI: 10.4324/9781003162513-8

they share the central premise that cognitive mediators process stimuli to produce emotional and behavioural responses (Wessler, 1986). The role of cognition is central in determining an individual's response to situations because an individual does not respond to a real environment but rather to a perceived environment (Mahoney, 1974).

The central concept underlying SIT is inoculation. Vaccinations have traditionally involved the exposure to weaker forms of the disease to prevent severe illness (although the newer Messenger RNA vaccines teach our cells how to make a protein that will trigger an immune response). In CBTs, exposure exposure-based techniques are commonly used especially for anxiety (Beck & Haigh, 2014; Kaczkurkin & Foa, 2015) – for example, in REBT, stress inoculation is frequently recommended and is often called "flooding" (Ellis & Dryden, 1997; Levis, 2009), which is similar to desensitisation. Lucius Annaeus Seneca (died 65 A.D.), notable Stoic and adviser to Emperor Nero, also recognised that the taking on and endurance of some hardship could enable adaptation for future hardship, stating that, "A gem cannot be polished without friction, nor a [person] perfected without trials" and "Everyone faces up more bravely to a thing for which he has long prepared himself, sufferings, even, being withstood if they have been trained for in advance. Those who are unprepared, on the other hand, are panic-stricken by the most insignificant happenings" (Seneca & Campbell, 2004). Thus, the underpinning philosophy of SIT has its roots in biological, psychotherapeutic, and ancient philosophical soil, bespeaking "antifragility" (increase in the capability to thrive as a result of stressors), a concept developed by Nassim Nicholas Taleb (2012).

In SIT, individuals are exposed to the experience of minor stressors and provided with the skills to cope with stress, in order to foster psychological readiness and a more adaptive coping response. By exposing a person to levels of stress strong enough to arouse defences and coping mechanisms, without it being overwhelming, a person's resistance to stress is enhanced (Meichenbaum, 2007). Indeed, anxiety induced in training situations can still contribute to inoculation even if it is less severe than the anxiety felt during the actual performance (Oudejans & Pijpers, 2010). SIT provides a set of general principles and a framework for the application of cognitive behavioural strategies to help athletes deal with stress rather than prescribing a specific treatment or intervention per se. As such, SIT has the flexibility to be applied across a range of different contexts. SIT comprises three phases:

1. The conceptualisation (education) phase
2. Skills acquisition and rehearsal phase
3. Application and follow-through phase

In the *conceptualisation (education) phase*, a collaborative working relationship and therapeutic alliance is established between the practitioner and the client (Meichenbaum, 2007), as is the case with all CBTs covered in the current book. The practitioner discusses with the client the effect of high levels of stress and anxiety on psychological and physiological responses, along with subsequent effects on sport performance (Mace, 1990). In the skills acquisition and rehearsal stage, the practitioner helps the client develop coping skills, using cognitive-behavioural techniques (e.g., imagery, self-talk, relaxation skills, cognitive restructuring) and these skills are practised so they become consolidated. The application and follow-though phase is where clients practise using the coping skills in small manageable units of stress which are gradually increased (Mace, 1990). SIT can not only involve the athlete but also significant others in line with the transactional model of stress and the recognition that the stress clients experience may be endemic, societal, institutional, and unavoidable (Meichenbaum, 2007). For example, a practitioner may also try to influence the behaviour of significant others in an athlete's life, such as coaches or parents, in order to reduce a potential source of stress.

There is a consistent body of evidence demonstrating the effectiveness of SIT across a range of conditions including post-traumatic stress disorder (PTSD), acute and chronic pain disorders, and performance anxiety, in a range of professional groups including nurses, teachers, and military personnel (see Meichenbaum, 2007 for a review). The evidence in sport is more modest in terms of the number of studies, although similarly positive in terms of its effectiveness (see Mace, 1990 for a review). Recently, a meta-analysis assessing the effects of pressure training for performance included only ten studies (Low et al., 2021), indicating the scarcity of high-quality studies in this area.

In one study of SIT, runners (n = 8) who received SIT used significantly less oxygen than a no treatment control group (Ziegler et al., 1982). In the mid-1980s, Roger Mace led much of the research around SIT in sport, conducting a number of controlled studies and case studies demonstrating its effectiveness. His programme of research reported SIT to be effective in reducing the levels of stress experienced by participants prior to a 21.2 m abseil off a building (Mace, Carroll & Eastman, 1986; Mace & Carroll, 1985). Positive effects for SIT on performance as well as reduced stress levels were observed on gymnastics performance in a study in which 18 participants were assigned to either an attention-placebo control group or an SIT group (Mace & Carroll, 1989). Working with individual athletes, SIT was reported to be helpful in reducing anxiety in competitive squash players (Mace & Carroll, 1986), a young gymnast (Mace, Eastman & Carroll, 1986), and an Olympic gymnast (Mace, Eastman & Carroll, 1987). However, since the work of Mace and colleagues research on SIT in sport has been more sporadic, examples of more recent work include research reporting SIT was effective in increasing pain tolerance on an isometric quadriceps task in 45 athletes (Whitmarsh & Alderman, 1993), increasing the performance levels of international level gymnasts, although this increase in performance was also associated with an increase in anxiety (Kerr & Leith, 1993) and reducing the number of illness and injury days in varsity and junior varsity collegiate rowers, compared to a control group (Perna et al., 2003).

Aside from the formative work of Mace, other approaches that are germane to the goals and processes of SIT have emerged in sport psychology literature and practice. The idea that by exposing athletes to some pressure, in a controlled manner, we can in some way fortify them against the stress of competition is analogous to desensitisation, pressure training, anxiety training, acclimatisation training, and self-consciousness training (see Low et al., 2021 for a review). Whilst all of these techniques may differ in their specific processes, they all share the inducement of pressure for the purposes of helping athletes to cope with this pressure.

Practice

Hypothetical Case

Simone is a 14-year-old tennis player competing in the junior circuit in the UK. She was competing nationally and one of her goals was to compete at Junior Wimbledon. The parents of Simone were referred to the practitioner from a sport psychologist they had initially contacted as she was unable to consult because of other commitments. The client wished to improve her emotional control in practice and competition. Simone occasionally performed erratically, not only from one match to another but also during sets and even individual games. The issues were particularly clear during important matches and when competing against lower-ranked players where the expectation was that she would win. She would often get frustrated after errors and would seem distracted during crucial moments of matches.

Initial Assessment

To make an accurate assessment of the problem, a number of measures were taken. In addition, interviews were conducted with Simone, her parents, her coach, and Simone was observed in competition. Data were collected using the performance profile (Butler, 1989), the test of performance strategies (TOPS; Thomas et al., 1999), and the mental readiness form-Likert (MRF-Likert: Krane, 1994).

Performance Profile (Butler, 1989)

In the performance profile, Simone first identified the qualities she needed to succeed in tennis. She then identified the importance of these qualities for success and ranked where she felt she currently was on each of those qualities. Areas to improve or develop with the greatest discrepancy score were then identified. The discrepancy score was a combination of the importance of the attribute and difference between the ideal self-rating and current self-rating. Simone's completed performance profile is shown in Table 7.1 and Simone identified that from a psychological perspective, the attributes that she needed to improve on were:

- Body language on court.
- Coping with pressure.
- Confidence.
- Being relaxed on court.
- The ability to ignore errors.
- Maintaining concentration at important times during the match.

TABLE 7.1 Performance profile completed by Simone prior to the intervention

Qualities	*Importance (I)*	*Ideal self assessment (ISA)*	*Current self assessment (CSA)*	*Discrepancy (D = ISA – CSA)*	*Priority (P = D × I)*
First serve	9	10	6	4	36
Second serve	9	10	7	3	27
Return of serve	9	10	7	3	27
Net play	9	10	8	2	18
Forehand	9	10	9	1	9
Backhand	9	10	7	3	27
Body language	**10**	**10**	**4**	**6**	**60**
Tactics	10	10	9	1	10
Different courts	8	10	7	3	24
Anticipation	9	10	10	0	0
Fitness	9	10	9	1	9
Never give up	10	10	10	0	0
Cope with pressure	**10**	**10**	**4**	**6**	**60**
Confident	**10**	**10**	**5**	**5**	**50**
Ignore errors	**10**	**10**	**5**	**5**	**50**
Concentration	**10**	**10**	**6**	**4**	**40**
Relaxation	**10**	**10**	**4**	**4**	**40**
Motivation	10	10	10	0	0

Note: "Bold qualities" reflect the highest scoring priorities

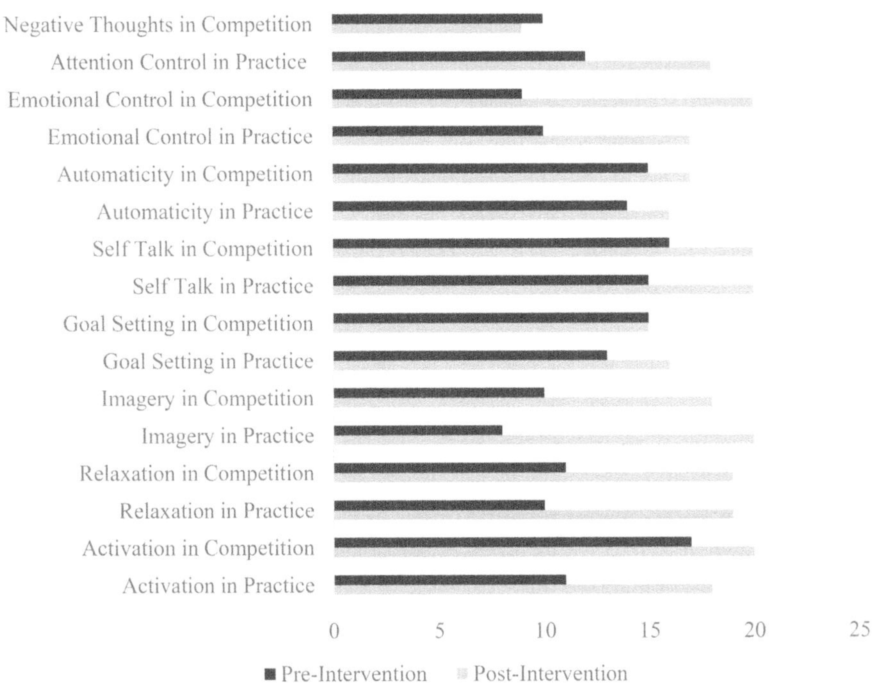

FIGURE 7.1 Comparison of Simon's pre- and post-intervention scores on the TOPS.

Test of Performance Strategies (Thomas et al., 1999)

The TOPS is a 64-item self-report instrument designed to measure the psychological skills and strategies used by athletes in competition and during practice. Data from the TOPS indicated that Simone could improve on her emotional control in practice and competition, decrease her negative thoughts in competition, and that Simone did not use self-talk or imagery to any great degree in either practice or competition. The completed scores from the TOPS from pre- and post-intervention are shown in Figure 7.1.

The Mental Readiness Form (MRF)-Likert (Krane, 1994)

The MRF-Likert was used to measure state anxiety on two bipolar scales corresponding to cognitive anxiety and somatic anxiety, and a third scale assessing self-confidence. To assess cognitive anxiety, Simone rated the extent to which they felt worried (1 = not worried; 11 = worried); the extent to which they felt tense (1 = not tense; 11 = tense). Self-confidence was also self-reported using a bipolar scale ranging from 1 (confident) to 11 (scared), so that higher scores on the self-confidence subscale equate to lower self-confidence. The MRF-Likert was completed in 14 matches prior to the intervention and nine matches after. Data from the MRF-Likert was completed as close as possible prior to each set during competition so that in total, there were 31 data points prior to the intervention and 20 points post-intervention. Data from the MRF-Likert indicated that Simone was typically around the mid-point for cognitive anxiety, somatic anxiety, and self-confidence.

It is worth recognising that when working with a client, one challenge is the need to collect sufficient baseline data to provide an appropriate evaluation of a problem (Barker et al., 2011).

Having approached a consultant for help, a client may be unwilling to undergo a lengthy period of assessment before an intervention takes place. However, practitioners should only intervene with a proper evaluation of the problem (see Heyman 1987), although this does not always necessitate a lengthy baseline. In this instance, both Simone and her parents recognised the need to collect baseline data in order to demonstrate the effectiveness of the intervention and to explore what change has taken place. To be able to collect data from 14 matches provided a sufficiently strong baseline to explore change.

Summary

Based on the data collected from interviews, from the questionnaires, and observing Simone in competition, the following letter was sent to Simone's parents summarising the information.

> As promised please find enclosed a summary of what I believe to be the best way to enhance Simone's mental approach to competition.
>
> I have now had two sessions with Simone, including observing her play in competition, and have spoken to both yourselves and her coach. Furthermore, Simone has completed a number of questionnaires that have provided me with additional information. These include a short questionnaire that reports how she feels during competition and provides a measure of confidence, worry, and physical tension. In addition, Simone has also completed questionnaires that measure her general approach to tennis, including her ability to concentrate during competition and how she currently uses psychological skills. Finally, Simone also completed a performance profile in which she outlined what she believes are her strengths and weaknesses as a tennis player.
>
> Simone is clearly a talented individual who displays a number of qualities common to successful performers. These include a high level of motivation and she also appears to be a relaxed individual who has displayed the ability to cope with pressure situations on court. Notwithstanding these strengths there are some areas where I believe that I can be of some help. In particular, Simone occasionally performs erratically, not only from one match to another but also during sets and even individual games. This relates to both her service and her general play. In addition, Simone, not surprisingly, expects to dominate with her service, which means that she expects to win points from a good first serve. However, when this service is returned, Simone may look to finish the rally quickly because she believes that is what she should do from a successful first serve rather than necessarily playing each ball on merit. Finally, there may also be a need to discuss strategies to refocus attention during competition and ensure that Simone is "switched on" and focused during games, particularly during crucial points.

Problem Formulation

It was apparent both from interviews conducted with Simone, and observing her in competition that Simone's concentration does get affected and that this in part is a result of her inability to cope with pressure and the lack of belief she has in her ability to succeed. The ability to cope with pressure, display appropriate body language on court, and ignore errors can be considered an important aspect of emotional control. Controlling emotions is important given the impact that changes in emotional state can have on motivation levels and physical and cognitive functioning (Jones, 2003). Simone also displayed a negative response to stress akin to a threat, rather than a challenge state (e.g., Meijen et al., 2020). Key to this response was her expectations around success, in particular when competing against players she "felt" she should beat. In those situations, the potential for psychological harm (e.g., "losing a match I should win") was great. She also mentioned confidence as being an issue. Taken together the aim of the intervention was to provide coping strategies to help manage the stress of competitions, reduce the symptoms of competitive anxiety, increase confidence, and improve performance particularly after errors have occurred.

Intervention Strategy and Approach

The intervention aimed to improve Simone's ability to manage stress, cope with errors, prepare effectively for competition, and maintain confidence. In addition, because Simone had raised concern over the erratic nature of her first serve, an intervention was developed to improve her first serve consistency. The psychological skills that were the focus of the intervention are outlined below:

1. Enhance her pre-service routine to improve consistency. The use of imagery, in this instance cognitive–specific imagery (Martin et al., 1999), was used in which Simone would visualise the place where she wanted the ball to land, and to rehearse (kinaesthetically) the correct movement pattern. The imagery was incorporated into a pre-service routine whereby Simone took a relaxing breath, bounced the ball once, saw where she wanted the ball to go, and felt the correct movement pattern.
2. Imagery was also used to mentally prepare for different scenarios that may occur during matches, such as winning a long rally even when her opponent returns a well hit first serve (e.g., Motivational-General Mastery Imagery; Martin et al., 1999)
3. The use of a key word or phrase (self-talk) to ensure that attention is focused on the upcoming point and not on any past errors or the match situation
4. The use of progressive muscular relaxation (PMR) technique (Mace, 1994) so that Simone was able to reduce unwanted physical tension during competition.

The intervention took place over 13 sessions, during a 5-month period. Most of the sessions were held at Simone's house; however, sessions were also held at Simone's local tennis club and on the court. The aim of these sessions was to reinforce and integrate the psychological skills covered into Simone's play on the court (e.g., imagery before each serve). Simone's progress was monitored by the TOPS (Thomas et al., 1999) and the MRF-Likert (Krane, 1994).

Intervention Procedure

The Conceptualisation (Education) Phase

In sessions 1–3, a collaborative working relationship and therapeutic alliance was established with Simone. This consisted of observing Simone in competition, discussing with Simone her psychological approach to competition and outlining to her why stress management matters and the rationale for the intervention. A key part of these sessions was to normalise the feelings of stress and anxiety that Simone was experiencing. This was done through explaining, in accessible terms, the stress system and the link to emotions such as anxiety. The role expectations can play in the stress response was also outlined. The quotes from sporting icons like Muhammed Ali and David Beckham were used to normalise the stress response. For example,

> I always felt pressure before a big fight, because what was happening was real.
>
> *Muhammad Ali (Hauser, 1997, p. 271)*

> It was an important moment for me, the nation and the team … but I've never felt pressure like that in a game before. I just couldn't breathe. David Beckham talking about taking the penalty against Argentina in the 2002 World Cup.
>
> *(David Beckham, The Independent, 2002)*

Tennis specific quotes were also used to normalise some of the negative feelings experienced such as this one by John McEnroe:

> Unfortunately I always feel like a loser after I'm beaten in a tennis match. It's a sad fact about tennis – and probably other sports as well – that when you lose your confidence in your game, you lose a bit of confidence in yourself as a person. It's hard to overcome that feeling. You always have to fight the thought, I'm a loser; I'm not the same person I was, when, in fact, you may very well be a better person in certain ways.
>
> *(McEnroe & Kaplan, 2002, p. 120)*

These sessions were all held in Simone's home. Her parents were present at all times, but not typically in the room as the consultations with Simone took place.

Skills Acquisition and Rehearsal Phase

The skill acquisition and rehearsal phase comprised sessions 4–10 and took place at either Simone's house or her tennis club. The acquisition and transfer of skills took the same format whereby the skill was learned and then practised in the court environment. For example, an initial session on imagery was held in Simone's house (session 4). Simone then practised imagery in which she imagined the kinaesthetic sensation of her service and visualised the ball landing in the desired location. She practised this in a comfortable position (e.g., lying down before going to sleep) and then practised the imagery in less comfortable situations (e.g., standing up). She would do this for approximately 5–10 minutes a day over a week to 10 days. We then went across to the court so she could practise doing the imagery prior to a service. She came up with the key words of "see it", "feel it" and "do it" to guide her imagery before serving. She visualised where she wanted the ball to land, felt the correct service action (kinaesthetic imagery), and then served. Below is a transcript of one session where the imagery is transferred to the practise arena.

PRACTITIONER: Right let's have a go and do it before a serve.
SIMONE: What, now?
PRACTITIONER: Yes now … can you remember the process you came up with?

SIMONE: Yep – breath, bounce the ball then see it, feel it, do it.
PRACTITIONER: Great – let's go for it.

[Simone served]

PRACTITIONER: How was that?
SIMONE: Yeah, good.
PRACTITIONER: Excellent – let's do a few more serves now.

[Simone completes a number of serves]

PRACTITIONER: How was that?
SIMONE: Yeah, good. I think I actually find it easier to see where I want the ball to go, than feel it very clearly.
PRACTITIONER: OK – let's keep working on that and practising it. You could feel the movement ok when you were at home though?
SIMONE: Yeah – that was fine – it is just not as clear here.
PRACTITIONER: That is understandable. Remember as we discussed mental skills are just like physical skills. They can take time to learn. The more you practice the better they become. We will keep practising and monitoring the kinaesthetic side.
SIMONE: Shall I keep going?
PRACTITIONER: Yes. Let's do some more and keep varying your serve. So vary where you want the ball to land.

[Simone completes a number of serves]

SIMONE: Getting there!
PRACTITIONER: Great – well done. Now let's treat these as you would in a game. Have a first serve and then if you miss that, go to a second serve. And we can swap the box, you are serving into just as you would in the game. I will see if any look like aces and also if we get any double faults [just a comment to increase the pressure]
SIMONE: Hah sure.

[Simone completes a number of serves]

PRACTITIONER: Great – that's it for today. Good job.

What can be seen from this transcript is the transfer of the coping skill to the court itself and then using the skill under increasingly stressful situations, albeit in this session, the increase in the stress was slight as it was in the early stages of Simone using imagery. The transcript also illustrates some of the core aspects of SIT. First, it is clear that Simone has learnt and practised imagery as a useful psychological skill and a coping mechanism to help serve consistently under stress. So, it is not solely about exposing Simone to stress to learn how to play under stress, but it is about giving Simone the coping skills necessary. Second, there is graded exposure to increasing levels of stress. Albeit as noted the psychological stress of this session overall was slight. Simone first practised the serve under observation, then varied the type of serve done (slice, top spin, where the ball should land) and then finally under "match conditions" of having a first serve and a second service. This transcript is part of the overall process Simone went through in which she spent a week practicing imagery at home in which she ran a number of different serves thought her mind – this was transferred to the courts (sessions 5–6) in the following manner: (1) imagine serving while standing on court holding racket, (2) incorporate imagery into pre-service routine, (3) incorporate imagery into pre-service routine and serve, and (4) incorporate imagery into pre-service routine, and the serve and engage in a rally. Thus, Simone was incorporating the psychological skills into increasingly realistic and game-like scenarios.

Similar approaches were adopted for the self-talk (sessions 7–8) and PMR (sessions 9–10). Similar techniques were applied for the PMR where she would use physical relaxation techniques on an ad-hoc basis when she felt herself getting tense during performance. Often this was combined with the use of self-talk to maintain concentration, deal with errors, and refocus. The use of self-talk and PMR was emphasised by getting Simone to engage in a series of rallies with the psychologist. Simone had to use self-talk to maintain concentration as she had to win five consecutive rallies to win one point, while the psychologist only had to win one rally to win one point. While the practitioner had played tennis, he was nowhere near the standard of Simone and this scenario created a sense of jeopardy in Simone where she definitely *should* win the game against a lesser opponent (the practitioner) but because the practitioner needed only one point, there was a chance he could win. If the practitioner did win or Simone made an error, she would employ self-talk and relaxation to refocus. Throughout these exercises, the practitioner and Simone would discuss how she was feeling and her approach as it fluctuated during these games.

Application and Follow-Through Phase

There were three sessions in the application and follow-through phase. To facilitate the transfer of the skills to competition, a game against an opponent of similar standing to Simone was organised by the parents at her local club. Throughout, Simone was clearly using her pre-service routine consistently and was able to respond to errors in a positive manner. This training game was followed by a review session at Simone's house and another preparatory session prior to National Championships. The collaborative working relationship and therapeutic alliance was maintained over the course of the intervention through regular contact and through regular summaries and reflections on the work. To illustrate how the work was summarised, an illustration is provided below from a letter to Simone prior to the national championships by the practitioner.

> As promised please find enclosed a summary of the work that you and I have been doing over the past few weeks. Specifically, we have:
>
> Enhance your pre-service routine by utilising imagery. Before serving, you will take a deep breath, bounce the ball once, look where you want the ball to go, see the ball go into the correct area, and feel the correct movement pattern associated with the serve. The aim of this intervention is to ensure that you improve the consistency of your service routine, and do not speed up the service during important points. Use this routine before every serve in both practice and competition.
>
> We discussed the use of key words or phrases to ensure that your attention is focused on the upcoming point and not on past errors or the match situation. In order to emphasise this, we played a series of match situations where you had to win every single point – the odds were certainly loaded in my favour! You clearly understood the need to

> focus on each point individually and you already utilised your own key words and strategies to ensure this happens. Specifically, you encourage yourself and think about how you would like to play each point. Once again it is important that you do this before every point, whether it be in practice or competition, so it becomes a normal part of your routine. Every single player in world tennis will make errors during a match. The important thing is that you put any errors you make behind you and focus on what you have to do for the next point, and play it in a confident and positive manner.
>
> Finally, in order to ensure that you are "switched on" for games, try to use imagery to mentally rehearse various shots, rallies, and scenarios that may occur during the game. Do this whenever you feel comfortable in the 10–15 minutes before you go on court. As well as seeing and feeling the movement patterns, try to recall the feelings (e.g., confidence, happiness) you get when you put away a good volley, forehand pass, etc.

While regular contact was typically maintained with Simone, there were occasions (e.g., the practitioner was on holiday, working away with other clients) when contact was less frequent. On these occasions, Simone did occasionally slip in her regular practice of the psychological skills. Making themselves "redundant" with the client having sufficient autonomy and confidence in the coping strategies is a consideration practitioners face in each intervention (Dryden et al., 2010). Further, Simone's parents were very supportive of the intervention and assisted at all stages but particularly during the application and follow-through phase by organising, at the practitioner's request, a competitive match at Simone's local club. However, this arrangement of the game without the practitioner informing Simone's coach did create some tension. The coach felt that matches and competitions were his domain, and a match should not have been organised without his oversight. It is possible for a practitioner to lose sight of the need sometimes, if it is ethically possible and appropriate, to engage and inform a client's wider network. This incident was an oversight by the practitioner and the relationship with the coach was restored.

Evaluation of Work

The client was an intelligent and hardworking individual. Even though Simone was only 14 at the start of the intervention, she was able to clearly articulate her thoughts and feelings and was able to understand the concepts outlined. To fully evaluate the effect of the intervention, a comparison of pre- and post-intervention data was made of Simone's psychological skills, cognitive and somatic anxiety, and self-confidence levels. A comparison of Simone's pre- and post-intervention scores on the TOPS are shown in Figure 7.1.

From the data, Simone appears to have a developed a more appropriate psychological approach for competition and practice. Large gains are evident in Simone's ability to be activated in practice, to relax in practice and competition, the use in imagery in practice and competition, the use of self-talk in practice and competition, emotional control in practice and competition, and appropriate attentional control in practice.

A comparison of pre- and post-intervention data collected via the MRF-Likert is shown in Figure 7.2. Data were collected from 14 games pre-intervention (comprising 31 data points from 31 sets) and from nine games post-intervention (comprising 20 data points from 20 sets). Visual inspection of the data indicates a clear reduction in cognitive anxiety and somatic anxiety following the intervention. The data also indicates that there was an increase in self-confidence score following the intervention. When completing the MRF-Likert, higher scores

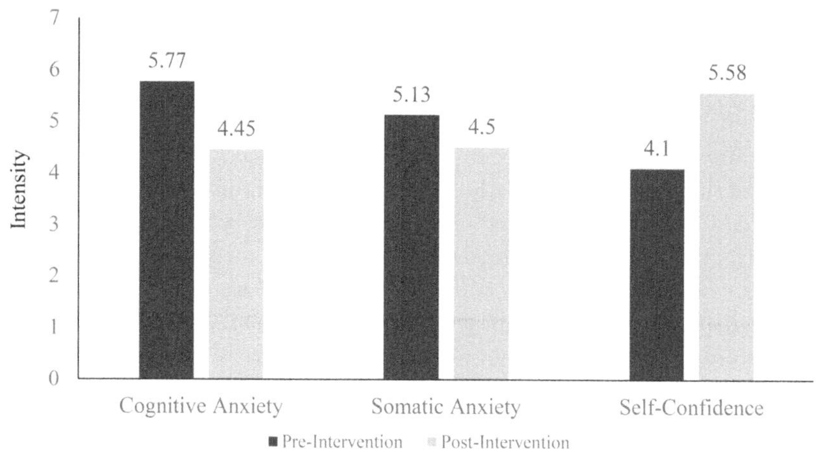

FIGURE 7.2 A comparison of Simon's pre- and post-intervention scores on the MRF-Likert.

on the self-confidence scale are associated with lower levels of self-confidence. But the scale has been reverse scored here for ease of interpretation. Overall, the results indicate a more positive psychological state both before and during competition following the intervention.

During the course of the intervention, Simone's performances and ranking continued to improve steadily. Her improvement was such that at the age of 16, she turned to play tennis full-time and even appeared at Junior Wimbledon, although Simone subsequently returned to full-time education and hopes to go to university. It is of course not possible to conclude that the performance improvements are the result of the intervention because of the nature of the AB design and the improvements could have been the result of coaching, maturational effects, or a whole host of other potential reasons.

Reflections and Limitations of Stress Inoculation Training

Stress inoculation training is a flexible framework and that is one of its main strengths, both in terms of the length of the SIT interventions, its applicability across different populations, and the content of the conceptualisation phase and the specific skills that will be applied and trained (Meichenbaum, 2007). Perhaps this could be a weakness in that it does not specify the strategies to be employed. However, SIT does provide an excellent framework for cognitive behavioural work and crucially, explicitly address the challenge of transferring skills from the consulting room to the playing arena. As such it is compatible with and potentially complementary to all the cognitive-behavioural approaches outlined in this book. While we have discussed SIT as being in three distinct phases, the boundaries between each phase are not always clear – and nor is there reason for them to be. For example, the educational process (the first phase) is ongoing through the course of SIT training (Meichenbaum, 2007). In our case study in this chapter, it could be argued that the beginning of the graded transfer to pressure settings, outlined in the transcript, which was described as starting in the second phase (skills acquisition and rehearsal phase), could equally have been described as being in the application and follow-through phase, although we felt this phase was better reflected in full match organised against a player at Simone's club. Nevertheless, this illustrates that boundaries between these phases are fuzzy and three phases are interlocking and often overlap (Meichenbaum, 2007).

Stress inoculation training is ideally suited to sport addressing one of the key challenges athletes face – performing under stress. As such it is surprising that there are relatively limited references to SIT in the literature. Perhaps there is an erroneous perception that SIT is about reducing stress with many interventions also focused on developing a more positive perception of stress and anxiety symptoms. In addition, sport psychology as a discipline appears to value theoretical real estate, rather than theoretical parsimony, which can lead to new labels being placed on already established ideas (Turner, 2022). Of course, SIT is not solely about reducing stress but about coping and developing a more positive perception of stress and anxiety is a legitimate aim of SIT. It is also worth noting that there has been a recent increase in research exploring pressure training in sport (e.g., Kegelaers, et al., 2021; Kent et al., 2021; Low et al., 2021). But SIT is really pressure training, or at least what is often described as pressure training in the literature. Indeed, Kegelaers et al. (2021) acknowledge this and said that pressure training is closely related to traditional SIT but did not explain how it differed. Similarly, Low et al. (2021) say that "... pressure training (PT) is based on stress inoculation training (Meichenbaum, 2007) and involves physically practicing domain-specific skills under simulated pressure" (p. 149). It is perfectly appropriate to package SIT in a way to make it more appealing to the client group as Meichenbaum (2007) himself acknowledges when discussing how Smith (1980) had characterised the stress management features of SIT as a "mental toughness training" for athletes and coaches, and pressure training could certainly be considered a more applicable description for sport than stress inoculation. But a danger in a change in terminology is a move away from the cognitive-behavioural theoretical underpinnings of SIT and the clear structure it provides for interventions.

Conclusion

The concepts of SIT are well-received by coaches and has face validity, which can sometimes be enhanced if framed as pressure training (e.g., Kent et al., 2021) or mental toughness training (e.g., Smith, 1980). The central concept underlying SIT is inoculation. In SIT, individuals are exposed to the experience of minor stressors and importantly provided with the skills to cope with stress, in order to foster psychological readiness and a more adaptive coping response. This can include coping skills that reduce the deleterious effects or anxiety or help the individual frame stress and emotional responses more positively. SIT has the flexibility to be applied across a range of different contexts in sport and provides a set of general principles and a framework for cognitive-behavioural interventions for helping individuals deal with stress.

References

Barker, J. B., McCarthy, P. J., Jones, M. V., & Moran, A. (2011). *Single-case research methods in sport and exercise psychology*. Hove: Routledge.

Beck, A. T., & Haigh, E. A. (2014). Advances in cognitive theory and therapy: The generic cognitive model. *Annual Review of Clinical Psychology, 10*, 1–24. https://doi.org/10.1146/annurev-clinpsy-032813-153734

Beckham, D. (2002). I've never felt pressure like that in a game before. I couldn't breathe. I just hit it as hard as I could. Glenn Moore, *The Independent*, 11th June, 2002.

Blascovich, J., Mendes, W. B., Vanman, E., & Dickerson, S. (2011). *Social psychophysiology for social and personality psychology*. London: Sage.

Butler, R. J. (1989). Psychological preparation of Olympic boxers. In J. Kremer, & W. Crawford (Eds.), *The psychology of sport: Theory and practice* (pp. 74–84). Leicester: BPS.

Dryden, W., Beal, D., Jones, J., & Trower, P. (2010). The REBT competency scale for clinical and research applications. *Journal of Rational-Emotive & Cognitive-Behavior Therapy, 28*(4), 165–216. https://doi.org/10.1007/s10942-010-0111-3

Ellis, A., & Dryden, W. (1997). *The practice of rational emotive behavior therapy* (2nd ed.). Springer Publishing Co.

Epel, E. S., Crosswell, A. D., Mayer, S. E., Prather, A. A., Slavich, G. M., Puterman, E., & Mendes, W. B. (2018). More than a feeling: A unified view of stress measurement for population science. *Frontiers in Neuroendocrinology, 49*, 146–169. https://doi.org/10.1016/j.yfrne.2018.03.001

Hauser, T. (1997). *Muhammad Ali*. London: Pan Books.

Heyman, S. R. (1987). Research and interventions in sport psychology: Issues encountered in working with an amateur boxer. *The Sport Psychologist, 1*(3), 208–223.

Jones, M. V. (2003). Controlling emotions in sport. *The Sport Psychologist, 17*(4), 471–486.

Kaczkurkin, A. N., & Foa, E. B. (2015). Cognitive-behavioral therapy for anxiety disorders: an update on the empirical evidence. *Dialogues in Clinical Neuroscience, 17*(3), 337–346. https://doi.org/10.31887/DCNS.2015.17.3/akaczkurkin

Kegelaers, J., Wylleman, P., Bunigh, A., & Oudejans, R. R. D. (2021). A mixed methods evaluation of a pressure training intervention to develop resilience in female basketball players. *Journal of Applied Sport Psychology, 33*(2), 151–172. https://doi.org/10.1080/10413200.2019.1630864

Kent, S., Devonport, T. J., Lane, A. M., & Nicholls, W. (2021) Implementing a pressure training program to improve decision-making and execution of skill among premier league academy soccer players. *Journal of Applied Sport Psychology, 34*(4), 691–712. doi:10.1080/10413200.2020.1868618

Kerr, G., & Leith, L. (1993). Stress management and athletic performance. *The Sport Psychologist, 7*(3), 221–231.

Krane, V. (1994). The mental readiness form as a measure of competitive state anxiety. *The Sport Psychologist, 8*(2), 189–202.

Lazarus, R. S., & Folkman, S. (1984). *Stress, appraisal, and coping*. New York, NY: Springer-Verlag.

Levis, D. J. (2009). The prolonged CS exposure techniques of implosive (flooding) therapy. In: W. T. O'Donohue, & J. E. Fisher, J. E. (Eds.), *General principles and empirically supported techniques of cognitive behavior therapy* (pp. 370–380). Hoboken, NJ: John Wiley.

Low, W. R., Sandercock, G. R. H., Freeman, P., Winter, M. E., Butt, J., & Maynard, I. (2021). Pressure training for performance domains: A meta-analysis. *Sport, Exercise, and Performance Psychology, 10*(1), 149–163. https://doi.org/10.1037/spy0000202

Mace, R. (1994). With netball in mind. Crewe: Delaware Press Ltd.

Mace, R. D. (1990). Cognitive behavioural interventions in sport. In G. Jones, & L. Hardy (Eds.), *Stress and performance in sport* (pp. 203–230). Chichester: Wiley.

Mace, R. D., & Carroll, D. (1985). The control of anxiety in sport: Stress inoculation training prior to abseiling. *International Journal of Sport Psychology, 16*(3), 165–175.

Mace, R. D., & Carroll, D. (1986). Stress inoculation training to control anxiety in sports: Three case studies in squash. *British Journal of Sports Medicine, 20*(3), 115–117.

Mace, R. D., & Carroll, D. (1989). The effect of stress inoculation training on self-reported stress, observer's rating of stress, heart rate and gymnastics performance. *Journal of Sports Sciences, 7*(3), 257–266.

Mace, R. D., Carroll, D., & Eastman, C. (1986). Effects of stress inoculation training on self-report, behavioural and psychophysiological reactions to abseiling. *Journal of Sports Sciences, 4*(3), 229–236. https://doi.org/10.1080/02640418608732121

Mace, R. D., Eastman, C., & Carroll, D. (1986). Stress inoculation training: A case study in gymnastics. *British Journal of Sports Medicine, 20*(3), 139–141.

Mace, R. D., Eastman, C., & Carroll, D. (1987). The effects of stress inoculation training in gymnastics on the pommeled horse: A case study. *Behavioral Psychotherapy, 15*, 229–272.

Mahoney, M. J. (1974). *Cognition and behaviour modification*. Cambridge: Ballinger.

Martin, K. A., Moritz, S. E., & Hall, C. R. (1999). Imagery use in sport: A literature review and applied model. *The Sport Psychologist, 13*(3), 245–268.

McEnroe, J., & Kaplan, J. (2002). *Serious*. London: Little, Brown.

Meichenbaum, D. (1977). *Cognitive behavior modification: An integrative approach*. New York, NY: Plenum Press.

Meichenbaum, D. (1985). *Stress inoculation training*. Elmsford, NY: Pergamon Press.

Meichenbaum, D. (2007). Stress inoculation training: A preventative and treatment approach. In P. M. Lehrer, R. L. Woolfolk, & W. E. Sime (Eds.), *Principles and practice of stress management* (pp. 497–516). New York, NY: The Guilford Press.

Meijen, C., Turner, M., Jones, M. V., Sheffield, D., & McCarthy, P. (2020). A theory of challenge and threat states in athletes: A revised conceptualization. *Frontiers in Psychology, 11*, 126. https://doi.org/10.3389/fpsyg.2020.00126

Orlick, T., & Partington, J. (1988). Mental links to excellence. *Sport Psychologist, 2*(2), 105–130.

Oudejans, R. R. D., & Pijpers, J. R. (2010). Training with mild anxiety may prevent choking under higher levels of anxiety. *Psychology of Sport and Exercise, 11*(1), 44–50. https://doi.org/10.1016/j.psychsport.2009.05.002

Perna, F. M., Antoni, M. H., Baum, A., Gordon, P., & Schneiderman, N. (2003). Cognitive behavioral stress management effects on injury and illness among competitive athletes: A randomized clinical trial. *Annals of Behavioral Medicine, 25*(1), 66–73. https://doi.org/10.1207/S15324796ABM2501_09

Seneca, L. A., & Campbell, R. (2004). *Letters from a Stoic: Epistulae Morales Ad Lucilium (Classics S.)* (New ed.). London: Penguin.

Smith, R. E. (1980). A cognitive-affective approach to stress management training for athletes. In C. H. Nadeau, W. R. Halliwell, K. M. Newell, & G. C. Roberts (Eds.), *Psychology of motor behavior and sport* (pp. 54–72). Champaign, IL: Human Kinetics.

Taleb N. N. (2012). *Antifragile: Things that gain from disorder* (1st ed.). New York, NY: Random House.

Thomas, P. R., Murphy, S. M., & Hardy, L. (1999). Test of performance strategies: Development and validation of a comprehensive measure of athletes' psychological skills. *Journal of Sports Sciences, 17*(9), 697–711.

Turner, M. J. (2022). *The rational practitioner: The sport and performance psychologist's guide to practicing rational emotive behaviour therapy*. Hove: Routledge.

Wessler, R. L. (1986). Conceptualizing cognition's in the cognitive-behavioural therapies. In W. Dryden, & W. L. Golden (Eds.), *Cognitive-Behavioural approaches to psychotherapy* (pp. 1–30). London. Harper and Row.

Whitmarsh, B. G., & Alderman, R. B. (1993). Role of psychological skills training in increasing athletic pain tolerance. *The Sport Psychologist, 7*(4), 388–399.

Ziegler, S. G., Klinzing, J., & Williamson, K. (1982). The effects of two stress management training programs on cardiorespiratory efficiency. *Journal of Sport Psychology, 4*(3), 280–289.

8

DYNAMIC COGNITIVE-BEHAVIOURAL SPORT PSYCHOLOGY

Taking a multi-modal approach

Jennifer Hobson and Joseph Dixon

Introduction

Irrespective of differences in one's paradigmatic approach to sport psychology delivery, the work of a sport psychologist (SP) can look very different depending on the environment within which they work and the nature of their role. For instance, while SPs working as private practitioners may primarily work on a one-to-one basis with clients who seek sport psychology support, SPs who are employed by sport organisations, such as football academies, may find their practice involves comparatively little one-to-one work, operating instead within multi-disciplinary teams (MDTs), across systems, and at an organisational level (Dixon & Jones, 2020). Such differences in the mode of delivery of sport psychology present SPs with challenges and opportunities. SPs are challenged to develop a professional philosophy and approach to working with others, yet they must be flexible in how they work when embedded within dynamic sports environments and with performers of different ages. Still, this provides practitioners with an opportunity to be creative in their work, influencing environments to impact a greater number of performers than would be possible using a purely individualised (one-to-one) approach.

Cognitive behavioural therapy (CBT) principles and techniques can be applied and adopted across a range of clinical and non-clinical contexts and environments. Indeed, CBT principles underpin a number of commonly used theories and applied frameworks in sport psychology, such as the canon of psychological skills (Andersen, 2009), for example. One prominent and contemporary CBT-based framework is the Theory of Challenge and Threat States in Athletes (TCTSA; Jones et al., 2009).

This chapter begins with a theoretical presentation of CBT, the TCTSA, and its recent revision (TCTSA-R; Meijen et al., 2020). Then, drawing upon the authors' experiences embedded within a football academy, multi-modal support delivered to under-15 and under-16 age group teams is illustrated as a case study. The challenges, opportunities, practical considerations, and contextual factors associated with using a CBT-based framework when working with staff, individual youth athletes (football players), and their parents are discussed. It is hoped that this chapter will help to illustrate the differences between the traditional application of CBT and the approaches used by SPs embedded within applied and

DOI: 10.4324/9781003162513-9

dynamic environments. Furthermore, the suitability of utilising a flexible, evidence-based framework such as the TCTSA-R, for not only one-to-one work but also in the application of a psycho-education programme, is established.

Theoretical Background

Originally developed to support people with mental illnesses such as depression and anxiety disorders (Hofmann et al., 2012), CBT is considered by many as the most evidence-based approach for the treatment of several psychological syndromes (Hofmann et al., 2013). However, contrary to popular belief, rather than comprising one specific approach, "CBT" is an overarching term incorporating a range of therapies including cognitive- and behaviour-based elements (Bennett & Oliver, 2019; Turner et al., 2020a). Indeed, according to Mennin and colleagues (2013), "CBTs share a common framework for intervention, including a common goal of behavioural adaptation and corresponding change principles of context engagement, attention change, and cognitive change that promote this goal" (p. 236).

Interventions based on CBT are now frequently drawn on to support healthy populations optimise their performance (e.g., Marlow, 2009; Trip et al., 2007). Of the various frameworks used in sport psychology applied practice, a cognitive-behavioural approach is one of the most utilised and referenced (McArdle & Moore, 2012). Indeed, the dominant consultancy approach in sport psychology and subsequent methods used by practitioners tend to be underpinned by CBT (Sharp et al., 2015). When applied in sport psychology, CBT can be seen as *Cognitive Behavioural Training* (Gustafsson & Lundqvist, 2016), where athletes practice changing dysfunctional performance-related behaviours (e.g., avoiding certain anxiety-provoking situations) into functional behaviours (e.g., taking a penalty kick despite experiences of anxiety).

Many researchers have indicated how CBT interventions can be effective in altering athlete self-statements, regulating psychological states, and improving performance (Neil et al., 2013). According to Andersen (2009), the most used cognitive-behavioural techniques within sport are self-talk, relaxation, imagery, goal setting, and concentration. However, Wilkins et al. (2020) explored elite academy soccer players' perceptions towards CBT; only 8% had heard of it and 4% knew what it was. Still, once educated on what CBT is, general perceptions of CBT were high. Recent support for CBT interventions in applied settings has been demonstrated within elite female hockey players (Didymus & Fletcher, 2017), male golfers (Neil et al., 2013), male youth footballers (Olmedilla et al., 2019), a male rugby union player (Edwards & Edwards, 2016), a female cross-country skier (Gustafsson et al., 2016), and adult triathletes (Davis & Turner, 2020).

There are a large number of interventions and numerous approaches within CBT, each with their own unique elements. For instance, Didymus (2018) highlighted the prevalence of cognitive restructuring within sporting populations. A growing literature base supports the application of rational emotive behaviour therapy (REBT) within sport, with positive effects on performance and well-being observed (e.g., Jordana et al., 2020; Wood et al., 2019). In addition, emerging approaches to CBT such as acceptance and commitment therapy (ACT) and mindfulness-based cognitive therapy (MBCT) have also shown promise in reducing symptoms for burnout (Gustafsson et al., 2015; Jouper & Gustafsson, 2013; Lloyd et al., 2013; Swettenham & Whitehead, 2022). The specific cognitive-behavioural framework utilised in the following case study is the theory of challenge and threat states in athletes-revised (TCTSA-R: Meijen et al., 2020). In providing a review of the TCTSA literature in sport, this chapter illustrates the complementarity of CBT and the TCTSA-R.

The TCTSA-R (Meijen et al., 2020) is a reconceptualised iteration of the original TCTSA (Jones et al., 2009). The TCTSA drew heavily upon the biopsychosocial model of arousal regulation (Blascovich & Mendes, 2000), in which cardiovascular (CV) reactivity patterns indicating changes in the stress system are used to mark the two distinctive physiological responses that identify challenge and threat states (Dienstbier, 1989). Challenge and threat states are purported to influence decision-making, cognitive functioning, task engagement, and physical functioning when in motivated performance situations (Jones et al., 2009). Challenge states are considered beneficial for athletic performance and threat states detrimental. Two recent reviews on challenge and threat states (Behnke & Kaczmarek, 2018; Hase et al., 2019) have demonstrated support for their influence on performance.

According to the TCTSA, when perceived personal resources meet or exceed perceived situational demands (challenge state), athletes observe performance benefits relative to those whose perceived demands exceed their personal resources (threat state). The theory has been explored in a range of settings including aviation (Vine et al., 2015), business (Turner & Barker, 2014), surgery (Moore et al., 2014), medical emergency scenarios (Carenzo et al., 2020), and public speaking (Trotman et al., 2018). Within sport, the TCTSA has been examined using competitive football match performance (Dixon et al., 2019), netball performance (Turner et al., 2020b), golf performance (Moore et al., 2012), and cricket batting performance (Turner et al., 2013). Other research has utilised reflective diaries (Nicholls et al., 2012), interviews, and observations (Massey et al., 2013; Didymus & Fletcher, 2017) to investigate challenge and threat experiences among athletes.

Within the TCTSA-R, the contribution of social support as an additional resource and presentation of a 2 × 2 bifurcation theory of challenge and threat reflects the polychotomy of high challenge, low challenge, low threat, and high threat (Meijen et al., 2020). The TCTSA-R complements the goals and change principles of CBT; SPs may use CBT principles and techniques, such as imagery (Williams et al., 2010), reappraisal (Jamieson et al., 2012), and task instruction (Turner et al., 2014), to help increase an athlete's perceived resources, namely, their self-efficacy, perceived control, perceived social support, and approach focus. In the following discussion of practice, the application of CBT via the TCTSA-R framework in a Category 1 environment will be illustrated.

Theory to Practice

Context

The Premier League, its clubs, representatives of the Football League, The Football Association, and other key football stakeholders developed and introduced the Elite Player Performance Plan (EPPP) in 2011. The EPPP comprised a long-term strategy for youth development resulting in clubs receiving significantly increased levels of funding based on their status (categorised between 1 and 4). Consequently, this has presented an increase in opportunities for SPs in English football and provides the setting for the following case study.

Practice

The Case

A category one football academy requires the provision of a comprehensive sport psychology programme to support the development of its male players and increasing their chances of reaching the first team. It should be evidence-based and multi-modal, involving support and education to players (individual and team level), coaches, support staff, and players' parents. Support for under-15 and 16 age groups is particularly important given the demands associated with adolescence (see Stroud et al., 2009) and their stage of elite soccer development (Reeves et al., 2009; Richardson et al., 2004). The applied work described here will illustrate how cognitive-behavioural principles and techniques were used to meet the needs of the academy and represent the combined experiences of both authors who have sequentially held the same role at the soccer academy. The TCTSA-R (Meijen et al., 2020) underpinned the programme, given its complementarity with the cognitive-behavioural paradigm used by both SPs and its focus on enhancing the personal resources required to meet situational demands.

Initially, we describe how the sport psychology curriculum developed over time. Then we illustrate how aspects of the programme were delivered to under-15 and 16 players, their parents, and the MDT supporting them. Through sharing the challenges, opportunities, practical considerations, and contextual factors encountered, we illustrate the requirement for needs analyses and methods to be multi-modal in nature. Further, the suitability of the TCTSA-R framework when working in this context is demonstrated, in part thanks to the flexibility of cognitive-behavioural principles and the holistic nature of the TCTSA-R.

Curriculum Development

Originally, sport psychology support at the academy did not follow an established curriculum. Instead, support was provided externally in the form of infrequent workshops and one-to-one player support from a local university. As such, impact was limited given the lack of integration with other disciplines, access to players' parents, and access to players across the entire academy system. Subsequently, initial programme development centred on creating a curriculum for players covering education of core challenge and threat concepts. It was important that this material was framed using football language and examples and was tailored to the varying age groups across the academy. As the programme evolved, this education was expanded to include coaches, staff, and parents, equipping these groups with knowledge and tools to not only support players but also to utilise the knowledge and tools for themselves. This is akin to the CBT method of equipping clients with the knowledge and skills so that they can essentially *be their own therapist;* vary their context engagement, shift their attention, and enact cognitive change (Mennin et al., 2013).

As the work continued to be embedded and engagement increased across the academy, it was recognised that further impact would be gained through greater linking of the curriculum to the playing and coaching philosophy; directly influencing what was being delivered "on the pitch". Consequently, through working alongside the Head of Coaching, the coaching curriculum was updated so that coaches were required to consider and draw on key aspects of the psychology curriculum (e.g., "challenge" and "support") within their planning and review of training sessions and match days. Thus, work with the under-15 and 16 players, their parents, and staff incorporated one-to-one work with select players, player and parent psychoeducation programmes, and a psychologically informed approach to coaching, all underpinned by the TCTSA-R and based on CBT principles (see Figure 8.1). Specifically, successful adaptation (i.e., improvements in player performance, development, and well-being) can be achieved through helping players (via education and individualised support) to demonstrate more helpful behaviours, by shifting their attention and altering their

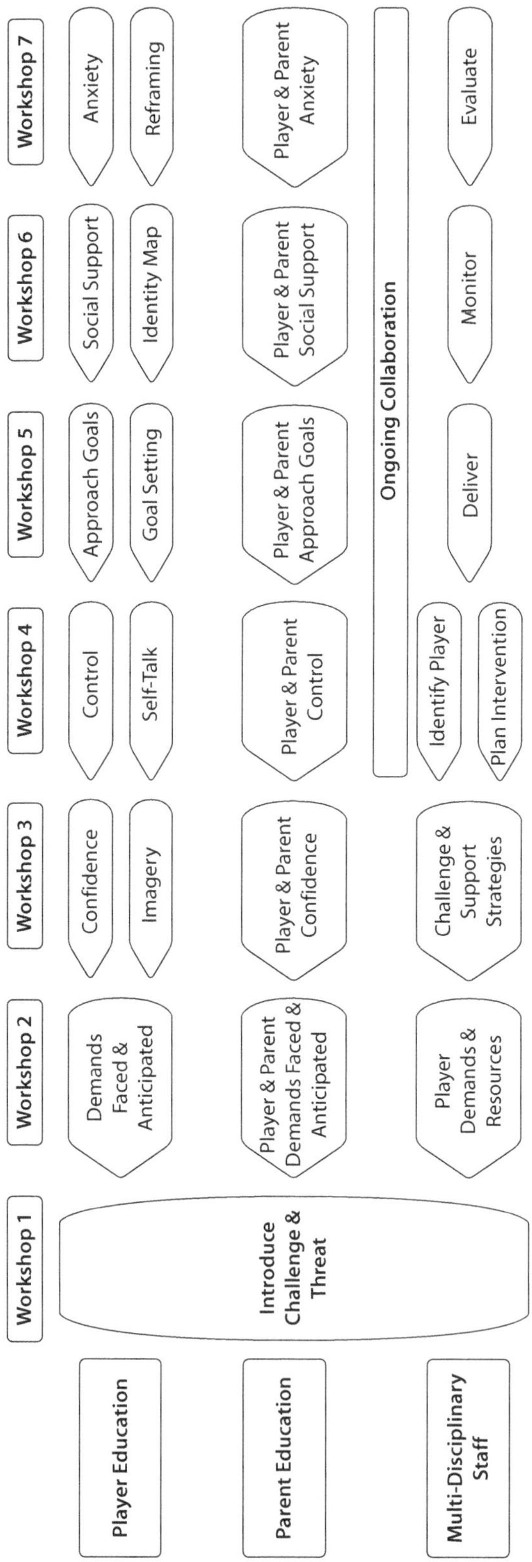

FIGURE 8.1 Illustration of a possible sport psychology curriculum, underpinned by the TCTSA-R delivered across players, parents, and multi-disciplinary staff.

thought processes in key situations (i.e., develop personal resources and use psychological skills; Andersen, 2009; Meijen et al., 2020; Mennin et al., 2013).

It is important to recognise that alongside the formal aspects of the curriculum, psychoeducation, and support, drawing on CBT methodologies was frequently delivered in more informal methods as part of our roles. For instance, in the brief conversations with players and staff before, during, and after performance or delivering an intervention to players through others (i.e., coaches' messaging). Furthermore, our individual work with players and staff would at times utilise strategies outside of CBT, such as taking a person-centred approach in the immediate experience of setback or where an individual was experiencing grief. Thus, the practitioners had to regularly demonstrate flexibility in their approach and application of their skills.

Individual Player Support

While most of the sport psychology programme is pre-planned and proactive, invariably at times reactive support for individual players is required, particularly within the under-15 and 16 age groups given the high number of stressors and increased vulnerability to mental health problems at these ages (Kessler et al., 2005; Reeves et al., 2009; Richardson et al., 2004; Stroud et al., 2009). Methods used to determine who may need this support and how it is delivered may differ from what is typical within the traditional provision of CBT.

Needs Analysis

Players who require individualised support may become known to us via five possible methods. Whilst five individual methods for needs analysis are provided here, in reality a combination is used (i.e., triangulation; Barker et al., 2011).

1. The least likely; players disclose a problem and request support. The rarity of player-initiated support may be due to a number of factors such the masculine norm of avoiding help-seeking (Pederson & Vogel, 2007), the lack of privacy in an academy environment, and/or players not knowing that a problem is a problem, and that it can be improved. Stigma associated with sport psychology may also be relevant (Storch et al., 2005). However, educating players about sport psychology through workshops and developing rapport with players overtime likely reduces such stigma (Thornicroft et al., 2016).
2. Parents request support for their son directly from us or indirectly via their son's coach.
3. Observation of player behaviour (such as withdrawal or avoidance) during training, games, gym sessions, or generally around the building might prompt us to have a conversation with the player, resulting in subsequent support provision.
4. Coaches spend much time with players and thus have a good understanding of players' behavioural norms. Physiotherapists and strength and conditioning (S&C) coaches develop trusting relationships with injured players. Sport scientists develop non-threatening, personable relationships with players and teachers develop relationships with players' schools, providing access to more perspectives and player insight. So, awareness of a player's needs may arise through conversations with and observations made by the MDT.
5. Psychometric testing of players. The package of metrics completed biannually by the under-15s and 16s aligns with the TCTSA-R (e.g., demands and resources) and includes measures of mental health. Re-completion of these metrics allows change to be monitored and interventions to be evaluated.

This process of needs analysis differs from typical CBT since not only are multiple methods used, including behavioural observation from professionals other than the SP, but also, very rarely is support initiated by the client (i.e., the player). On the one hand, using insight from multiple sources is beneficial since previously unknown demands in a player's life can become known. It also allows the collation of multiple perspectives on player behaviour and thus, a holistic picture to be built of them and their needs (e.g., Bickley et al., 2016). This contrasts with purely one-to-one CBT where the therapist typically only has access to the client's problem through the client's eyes and/or via psychometric assessment.

On the other hand, since individualised support is rarely player-initiated, this may constrain intervention success; client-initiated support, their motivation, and active involvement in intervention tasks are important for behavioural change (Bachelor et al., 2007; Høglend, 1999; Summers & Barber, 2003). This contextual challenge is also observed within mental health counselling within schools, outpatient mental health settings, and drug and alcohol treatment programmes where collaboration and autonomy supportive techniques are imperative within therapy (Rooney, 1992).

Interventions

Factors to be considered when supporting under-15 and 16 players include their cognitive development (Piaget, 1971), self-awareness (Ravizza & Fifer, 2014), and buy-in (Ravizza, 1990). If a player is unable to describe emotions, unaware of the content of their thoughts or need for behavioural change (i.e., lack of self-awareness; Ravizza & Fifer, 2014), or if they do not believe their behaviour needs to change (i.e., lack of buy-in; Ravizza, 1990), this may limit the impact of interventions. Furthermore, given the limits on time with players for individual work, the lack of access to a private room for conversations, and the demand of working across ten different age groups, interventions must be efficient (e.g., Portenga et al., 2012). In both cases, creativity and flexibility on our part are required.

Brief contact interventions (BCIs) represent a solution to these challenges (Pitt et al., 2015), since they may be delivered pitch side, in the gym, during walks to and from the training pitch, and are aided in this environment by our existing knowledge about and rapport with the players. Solution-focused brief therapy (SFBT; see Franklin & Bolton, 2015) techniques are particularly useful with children (i.e., when less cognitively developed; Bond et al, 2013; Kim & Franklin, 2009), and complement CBT assumptions (e.g., Guterman & Rudes, 2005) and the TCTSA-R (Meijen et al., 2020). SFBT involves discussing goals, action planning, exploring existing resources, and generally promoting an approach rather than avoidance mindset (c.f. Elliot & McGregor, 2001; Jones et al., 2009; Meijen et al., 2020). SFBT techniques are also effective when working with involuntary clients (Osborn, 1999) who may lack buy-in (i.e., Ravizza, 1990).

If a player with limited cognitive development and self-awareness needs to demonstrate a more adaptive response to challenge, the BCI would focus on the player's behaviours and actions. Questions might explore what the player notices during play and what might happen if they made different decisions or took different actions (i.e., context engagement, Mennin et al., 2013). The desired alternative behaviour would be positively reinforced and the benefits of taking that action discussed. Evidence of the player demonstrating this behaviour would be highlighted and recorded. Encouraging regular self-reflection to build self-awareness might promote players' perceived control over their decision-making, development and performance, increasing self-efficacy, and ultimately supporting achievement of their goals/performance improvements (Ellis et al., 2014; Kirschenbaum, 1997), thus encouraging a challenge mindset (Meijen et al., 2020).

If a player needs to change their behaviour but lacks buy-in, the BCI would initially focus on the player's goals which usually relate to their ability to adapt their behaviour to meet demands (c.f. Mennin et al., 2013). If the goal is described as an avoidance goal, we would use questions to help the player reframe this into an approach goal (c.f. Elliot & McGregor, 2001). For example, if a player who plays in defence expressed a desire to not be "beaten" by his opponent (i.e., for his opponent to not get past him), we might ask, "if that's what you don't want, what ***do*** you want to happen instead?". The player may respond with "I want to be hard to beat, stop him from getting past me and win the ball off him". Following an approach goal definition, the behaviours which take players towards goal achievement would be discussed, and previous occasions where the player achieved their goal, and how this was achieved would be explored (c.f. Franklin & Bolton, 2015), increasing self-efficacy (Bandura, 1977) and promoting a challenge mindset (Meijen et al., 2020). If this included the unhelpful behaviour (the target of change), how and why this behaviour is maladaptive for goal achievement would be discussed. When working with players who are advanced in their cognitive development (Piaget, 1971) and bought-in to psychological work, BCIs may also incorporate discussion of cognitive appraisals alongside behaviours, with irrational or unhelpful beliefs challenged and reframed (c.f. Ellis, 1957) with the player (i.e., cognitive change, Mennin et al., 2013) to promote challenge appraisals and a challenge mindset (Meijen et al., 2020). Indeed, irrational beliefs have been shown to be related to threat in past research (Chadha et al., 2019; Dixon et al., 2017; Mansell, 2021).

Opportunities and Challenges

As previously alluded to, the benefit of being immersed in the academy environment is the relationship we develop with players outside of a therapeutic setting. Fortnightly group workshops help us to understand players, their sporting context, situational demands, and psychosocial resources. Contact time with players in these workshops helps us to establish our role as supportive in nature and to develop rapport, trust, and respect with the players, factors which are important for a strong consulting relationship (Sharp et al., 2015). Having this basis, an existing relationship prior to the initiation of support, differentiates our work from typical CBT. It helps to reduce issues of low buy-in and thus may enable greater intervention impact.

Furthermore, the opportunity to provide psychoeducation to players allows us to develop a common language and shared performance psychology framework, aiding communication and intervention efficiency. Indeed, in BCIs, we refer to the TCTSA-R framework through encouraging players to focus on what they can control (i.e., perceived control; Skinner, 1996), want to achieve rather than avoid (Elliot & McGregor, 2001), or to remember the facilitative nature of nerves (Jones, 1995). Furthermore, immersion (c.f. Bull, 1995) provides ample opportunity for behavioural observation across a range of environments. Thus, unlike traditional CBT therapists, we can easily and frequently check whether players are making progress or practicing the tools we have discussed. Being pitch side also means we can act as a visual reminder for players to practice new ways of thinking, answer questions, and reinforce key messages in the moment whilst demands are being faced. Thus, there are many benefits when conducting psychological interventions associated with being immersed in an applied environment.

Nevertheless, immersion means we are continually being observed by players and staff; we must always be switched on, conscious of how players could interpret our non-verbal behaviour, trustworthiness, and values (Sharpley et al., 2006). Further, it is important to make a good first impression with players since a good connection between the therapist and the client can happen quite quickly (Littauer et al., 2005) and this may be crucial for effective support later down the line. Thus, our role differs from that of traditional CBT, where the client and the therapist initially know little about each other and interact solely within the context of the consultancy session and follow-up communications.

In addition, the limited time and opportunity to work with players means most conversations and interventions are stand-alone and spontaneous in nature (unlike traditional CBT which may be follow a planned and structured series of six or more consultancy sessions). Consequently, it is not usually possible to conduct a full analysis of a players' needs and belief systems, and it can sometimes be challenging as a practitioner to feel like you are making an impact (c.f. Cropley et al., 2016), because your interventions are brief and *invisible* (i.e., they are a conversation or a question) unlike the other sport science disciplines you work alongside. Thus, maintaining belief in what you are doing and the impact you are making can at times be challenging as a lone SP operating *briefly* whilst embedded within an academy setting.

Working with Multi-Disciplinary Teams

When immersed in a football academy across a number of age groups, it is important for SPs to use time-efficient methods to impact player development and performance (see Figure 8.2). One way of achieving this is through working within multi-disciplinary teams (MDTs); with the right knowledge and guidance, colleagues can deliver the sport psychology curriculum through considering the challenges (i.e., situational demands) placed on and support provided to players (including their personal resources). Of course, confidentiality is a factor which impacts the sport psychology discipline more so than others and must be considered at the

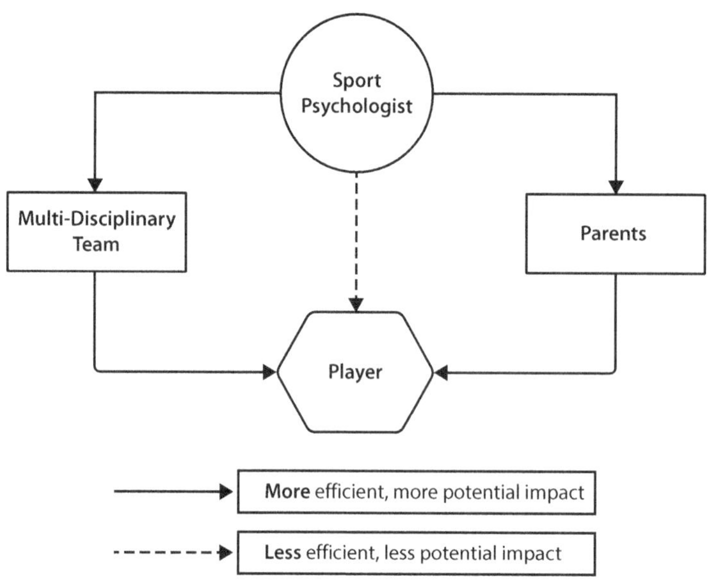

FIGURE 8.2 Framework to illustrate three possible ways a sport psychologist can impact players.

outset when planning a curriculum and the nature of the SP's role within the organisation. For instance, when contemplating which psychological data should be collected and monitored throughout a season, planning must also include the process of data collection; players must be informed of who will (and will not) see the data they provide, and how their data will be used.

Needs Analysis

Within the academy, each player is discussed within a multi-disciplinary review meeting every 6 weeks. At this time and as previously alluded to, player needs can become known through MDT members sharing observations of players. For example, a coach shared that an under-15 player displayed a threat response under pressure, because he blamed teammates for his mistakes and gave up when his team were losing. Similar behaviours were described by the S&C coach; the player avoided challenging himself in the gym, strayed off task, distracted other players, and was heard saying that he "can't do" what is asked of him.

In formulating this player's case, we can draw MDT members' attention to the demands faced by the player (both within and outside of football) and the state of his personal resources, in an effort to explain his behaviour. In this case, the gym represented an area where the player's "weaknesses" were on show to his teammates. Smaller boys were outperforming him (they were completing more challenging exercises) so he may have felt shame or embarrassment, leading to avoidance, lack of effort, and loss of concentration. The player's father was an ex-professional who recommended the coach "threaten him with release" to get the best out of him. Not only was this player potentially under greater pressure because of his father's success, but he was also living in an environment in which an avoidance motivation orientation was promoted. Finally, given the negative self-talk reported by the S&C coach and based on our own observations of the player, it was clear the player's self-efficacy was low.

The potential barrier of confidentiality in MDT conversations can largely be overcome because much of the evidence referred to is common knowledge, is provided by others, or is behavioural and so can be observed by others in the environment. Thus, these behaviours can be freely discussed since the information is not gained in a confidential setting between SP and player. As the SP, through case formulation, we can help to contextualise the player's behaviour within the TCTSA-R framework, suggest explanations for the behaviour, and recommend a suitable intervention based on their conceptualisation and the theory (thereby promoting a psychologically informed environment). Where salient information about a player is gained in a one-to-one setting, this is only shared with the wider MDT where explicit prior permission is gained from the player in question.

Intervention

Following case formulation using the demands and resources framework, the SP can suggest suitable interventions to be delivered by MDT members or at least, to inform how they might work with him. In this case, it was recommended that the player not be provided with additional demands given the already high level of demands he faced. Instead, the coach was advised to develop a stronger relationship with the player and discover his personal motivations within football (i.e., increase social support; Meijen et al., 2020). The coach was also encouraged to help the player develop greater self-belief, by providing detailed positive feedback, exploring what his best performance looks like with him, and asking him what small progress looks like during training sessions and games. The S&C coach was also encouraged to develop a stronger relationship with the player through providing more one-to-one support and to draw the player's attention to evidence of his progress. He was encouraged to help the player to reframe his negative self-talk, from "I can't do it" to "I can't do it yet, but with practice I can get better". The effectiveness of this intervention could be monitored by the SP observing the player's behaviour in games and in the gym, but also within the review meetings where staff could provide feedback on the player's progress, allowing for continual triangulation.

Opportunities and Challenges

This example again highlights the diversity of the SP's role when embedded in a sport environment and the difference between such a role and that of a private practitioner or *typical* CBT therapist. SPs have the opportunity to not only support players in an evidence-based and robust manner but also to nudge the environment to become more psychologically informed, through working with MDTs. In this case, the use of the TCTSA-R framework aided such collaboration thanks to both its logical and pragmatic nature but also the ease at which recommendations can be applied to colleagues' working practices.

Still, such work can only take place if a holistic understanding of each player is known, which can be challenging to ascertain especially when players have only recently joined the academy. Furthermore, if colleagues are closed-minded, unwilling to collaborate with an SP, and implement recommendations, or indeed if they disagree with the case formulation, this represents a large barrier to working in such a multi-disciplinary manner. It takes time to develop rapport and credibility but once achieved, such barriers are likely to be rare.

Working with Parents

Parents and guardians are key stakeholders in the lives of their children, having a significant influence on their early experiences and how they develop as people and competitors (Knight et al., 2017). It is important that parents are perceived as an ally by staff in talent development environments and provided support (Harwood & Knight, 2015). Indeed, parents influence their child's values, performance, motivation, enjoyment, perceived competence, and psychosocial responses to sport participation, amongst other things (Babkes & Weiss, 1999; Fredricks & Eccles, 2004). Thus, working with parents is an important requirement for sport organisations and can represent an efficient and impactful way SPs can support players and athletes (see Figure 8.2).

Needs Analysis

When supporting parents of under-15 academy football players, needs are informed by the stressors faced by players and parents. For players, these can include biopsychosocial and physical changes associated with adolescence (Stroud et al., 2009), school exams, peer relationships, increase in sport-related demands and expectations, and uncertainty regarding the imminent scholarship decision at under-16 (Reeves et al., 2009; Richardson et al., 2004). For parents, stressors include academy processes and communication, their child's education and support from the school, match-related factors, uncertainty relating to their son's contract renewal, and sport-family role conflict (Harwood et al., 2010). Furthermore, the growing influence of peers alongside the lessening influence of parents on their adolescent child's behaviour and value formation can be challenging for parents to manage in our experience.

Not only can SPs support parents by influencing the system and the way stakeholders within the academy view and work with parents, but they can also support parents via psychoeducational programmes (see Steptoe et al., 2016). Such programmes are analogous with CBT since education is a core component of therapy (Fenn & Byrne, 2013) and in this context, could help parents and guardians to not only manage their own stressors but to also support their child through the stressors they experience.

Intervention

Using a cognitive-behavioural theory of stress and performance under pressure such as the TCTSA-R can be useful since it provides a solid foundation onto which a parental (and player) psychoeducational programme can be built. For example, a programme underpinned by the TCTSA-R could begin with a definition of stress as a transactional process (c.f. Lazarus, 1999) involving perceptions of situational demands and one's own personal resources. Subsequently, parents can be equipped with knowledge and techniques which enable them to help their child enhance their perceived personal resources, knowing that this will help their child to overcome stress and perform under pressure. Such techniques might include noticing when their child talks about avoiding failure and challenging their child to reframe this intention; help them to define the positive outcome they want to achieve instead (i.e., turn avoidance goals into approach goals, Elliot & McGregor, 2001). With an understanding of where confidence comes from, parents could help develop and strengthen their child's confidence by recalling or asking their child to recall previous examples of successful performance (Bandura, 1977). Similarly, knowing the importance of social support, parents could remind their child of who is in their corner supporting them throughout their football journey to help their child towards a challenge state (e.g., Slater et al., 2016). Recognising that the appraisal of anxiety has a larger effect on performance than anxiety itself, parents could remind their child that nerves are positive and helpful whenever they appear (c.f. Jamieson et al., 2012). Finally, in the knowledge that perceptions of control benefit both confidence and performance, parents could routinely redirect their child's attention to controllable factors in times of stress (Skinner, 1996). Such techniques aimed at increasing personal resources could be used by parents in the car journey home or before training. They could even be used whilst watching television and having casual conversations about others' failure and success, regardless of the performance domain. But parents can only use such techniques if they understand stress, the value of increasing personal resources and how to do that. Indeed, sometimes a parent's solution is to try and lower the level of demand experienced by their son, but this is not only very difficult to achieve but also counterintuitive, since the level of demand is not something players can or should have control over (cf. Turner & Jones, 2018). Without experiencing high demands, the ability and skills needed to withstand and perform well under high demand will not be developed. Thus, psychoeducational programmes can be extremely valuable when looking to educate academy players' parents.

Opportunities and Challenges

Having access to players' parents provides a massive opportunity for SPs to indirectly impact the developing player (see Figure 8.2). As mentioned previously, parents have a large influence on their child's values, attitudes, and beliefs (Fredricks & Eccles, 2004). It follows that if parent education programmes are successful in reducing parents' thinking errors and irrational beliefs, then their children will display fewer thinking errors and more rational beliefs. Furthermore, with CBT knowledge and strategies for challenging beliefs, boosting confidence, and developing helpful appraisals of pressure, parents might be able to support their children to develop healthy and helpful attitudes towards football, supporting their mental health, development, and performance.

Of course, having access to approximately 250 parents within an academy does not mean that the intervention will reach 250 parents. Parental buy-in to sport psychology is not guaranteed and seems to be low. Indeed, of the estimated 2,500 parents of mini-tennis players contacted to participate in a parental educational programme in the UK, only 38 showed interest and provided informed consent to the researcher (Thrower et al., 2018). Obviously, low attendance rates limit the impact of educational programmes. Given that they can take a lot of time and effort on the behalf of the SP to design and deliver, it must be evaluated to what extent educational programmes are worthwhile use of the SP's limited time and resource.

Measuring Effectiveness

Given that some CBTs (second wave) aim to change cognitions and behaviour to promote goal attainment (Mennin, et al., 2013), to measure the impact of sport psychology support in an academy setting, cognitive (e.g., demand and resource appraisals), behavioural (e.g., observations) and performance measures can be used. Furthermore, social validation feedback concerning delivered interventions can provide additional insight into responses which would otherwise be unknown or unexpected by the SP (Page & Thelwell, 2013). Triangulating these different sources of feedback offers the best way to understand the degree of impact of interventions (Barker et al., 2011). For example, measuring the impact of one-to-one work with individual players may involve comparing pre- and post-intervention psychometric measures, which may have been involved in the original needs analysis. These can be compared to the SP's observations of the players' behaviour, as well as those made by the MDT. Such observations could also be used to assess the success of MDT interventions.

Measuring hormonal or cardiovascular reactivity (CVR) indicators of challenge and threat states might represent the gold standard when it comes to analysing players' stress responses and monitoring the impact of interventions; they measure involuntary processes and thus the data collected cannot be controlled or manipulated; it is free of bias such as social desirability. However, the equipment is expensive and since an individual must remain motionless during measurement, it does not allow CVR (and thus challenge and threat states) to be monitored during a performance (as with questionnaires). Despite the logistical challenges to use these techniques, it is possible to achieve in an applied setting; Dixon and colleagues (2019) used a Finometer Pro® machine to measure heart rate, cardiac output, and total peripheral resistance in academy players prior to performance in competitive matches. Such protocols are worth implementing in order to advance the extant stress in sport literature (see Dixon et al., 2019). Finally, social validation and competency measurements of areas targeted by parent psychoeducation programmes (such as parents' perceived competence in their ability to help their child focus on achieving success rather than avoiding failure), collected prior to and following the programme, can provide useful insight into the effectiveness of the programme.

Organising robust measurement techniques, administered across different areas of the academy programme, represents a significant challenge for applied SPs. This is especially true when that individual is the only SP in the building and oversees a programme not just for under-15 and under-16 players, but for players spanning ten different age groups (i.e., from under-9 to under-21). The breadth of the SP's role in a dynamic environment such as a football academy demands flexibility and creativity, not just in the measurement of impact but also in the delivery of support. Nevertheless, since other sport science disciplines are required by the EPPP to collect measurements of players on at least three occasions throughout the season, aiming to collect psychological measures of players at the same times, and via online methods, can aide with planning and completing this large-scale task.

Conclusions

The cognitive-behavioural approach is a popular and effective paradigm used within sport and exercise psychology. But using CBTs in the applied world, when fully immersed within a sport organisation and required to work multi-modally, can and does look very different compared to typical CBT practice, which may primarily involve a programme of private one-to-one work with a client. Within this chapter, the benefits of adopting a flexible, evidence-based framework underpinned by CBT principles (namely, the TCTSA-R) when working within a football academy have been elucidated. Furthermore, based on their own experiences, the authors have highlighted some of the challenges, opportunities, practical considerations, and contextual factors associated with delivering a programme of sport psychology support to under-15 and under-16 age group football players. It is hoped that this chapter will prove useful for practitioners embedded within talent development environments, as well as for those contemplating taking on such a role by illustrating some of the differences between working within private practice and working embedded within a sport organisation.

References

Andersen, M.B. (2009). The "canon" of psychological skills training for enhancing performance. In K.F. Hays (Ed.), *Performance psychology in action: A casebook for working with athletes, performing artists, business leaders, and professionals in high-risk occupations* (pp. 11–34). American Psychological Association. doi:10.1037/11876-001

Babkes, M.L., & Weiss, M.R. (1999). Parental influence on children's cognitive and affective responses to competitive soccer participation. *Pediatric Exercise Science, 11*(1), 44–62. doi:10.1123/pes.11.1.44

Bachelor, A., Laverdière, O., Gamache, D., & Bordeleau, V. (2007). Client's collaboration in therapy: Self-perceptions and relationships with client psychological functioning, interpersonal relations, and motivation. *Psychotherapy: Theory, Research, Practice, Training, 44*(2), 175–92.

Bandura, A. (1977). Self-efficacy: Toward a unifying theory of behavioral change. *Psychological Review, 84*(2), 191–215.

Barker, J.B., McCarthy, P., Jones, M., & Moran, A. (2011). *Single-case research methods in sport and exercise psychology.* Abingdon, OX: Routledge.

Behnke, M., & Kaczmarek, L.D. (2018). Successful performance and cardiovascular markers of challenge and threat: A meta-analysis. *International Journal of Psychophysiology, 130*, 73–9. doi:10.1016/j.ijpsycho.2018.04.007

Bennett, R., & Oliver, J. (2019). *Acceptance and commitment therapy: 100 key points and techniques.* Abingdon, UK: Routledge.

Bickley, J., Rogers, A., Bell, J., & Thombs, M. (2016). 'Elephant spotting': The importance of developing shared understanding to work more effectively with talented but challenging athletes. *Sport and Exercise Psychology Review, 12*(1), 43–53.

Blascovich, J., & Mendes, W.B. (2000). "Challenge and threat appraisals: The role of affective cues" In J.P. Forgas (ed.), *Feeling and thinking: The role of affect in social cognition* (pp. 59–82). Paris: Cambridge University Press.

Bond, C., Woods, K., Humphrey, N., Symes, W., & Green, L. (2013). The effectiveness of solution focused brief therapy with children and families: A systematic and critical evaluation of the literature from 1990-2010. *Journal of Child Psychology and Psychiatry, 54*(7), 707–23. doi:10.1111/jcpp.12058

Bull, S.J. (1995). Reflections on a 5-year consultancy program with the England women's cricket team. *The Sport Psychologist, 9*(2), 148–63.

Carenzo, L., Braithwaite, E.C., Carfagna, F., Franc, J., Ingrassia, P.L., Turner, M.J., Slater, M.J., & Jones, M.V. (2020). Cognitive appraisals and team performance under stress: A simulation study. *Medical Education, 54*(3), 254–63. doi:10.1111/medu.14050

Chadha, N., Turner, M.J., & Slater, M.J. (2019). Investigating irrational beliefs, cognitive appraisals, challenge and threat, and affective states in golfers approaching competitive situations. *Frontiers in Psychology, 10*, 2295. doi:10.3389/fpsyg.2019.02295

Cropley, B., Baldock, L., Mellalieu, S.D., Neil, R., Wagstaff, C.R.D., & Wadey, R. (2016). Coping with the demands of professional practice: Sport psychology consultants' perspectives. *The Sport Psychologist, 30*(3), 290–302. doi:10.1123/tsp.2015-0125

Davis, H., & Turner, M.J. (2020). The use of rational emotive behavior therapy (REBT) to increase the self-determined motivation and psychological well-being of triathletes. *Sport, Exercise, and Performance Psychology, 9*(4), 489–505. doi:10.1037/spy0000191

Didymus, F.F. (2018). Cognitive-behavioral theory in sport and performance psychology. Oxford Research Encyclopedia of Psychology. Retrieved July 11, 2022, from https://www.oxfordreference.com/view/10.1093/acref/9780190634575.001.0001/acref-9780190634575-e-144?rskey=o0ZUpq&result=12

Didymus, F.F., & Fletcher, D. (2017). Effects of a cognitive-behavioral intervention on field hockey players' appraisals of organizational stressors. *Psychology of Sport and Exercise, 30*, 173–85. doi:10.1016/j.psychsport.2017.03.005

Dienstbier, R.A. (1989). Arousal and physiological toughness: Implications for mental and physical health. *Psychology Review, 96*(1), 84–100. doi:10.1037/0033-295X.96.1.84

Dixon, J.G., & Jones, M.V. (2020). A challenge culture: reflections on implementing a psychological skills programme in elite youth soccer. In J.G. Dixon., J.B. Barker., Thelwell R.C., & I. Mitchell (Eds.), *The psychology of soccer* (pp. 189–204). London: Routledge.

Dixon, J.G., Jones, M.V., & Turner, M.J. (2019). The benefits of a challenge approach on match day: investigating cardiovascular reactivity in professional academy soccer players. *European Journal of Sport Science, 20*(3), 375–85. doi:10.1080/17461391.2019.1629179

Dixon, M., Turner, M.J., & Gillman, J. (2017). Examining the relationships between challenge and threat cognitive appraisals and coaching behaviours in football coaches. *Journal of Sports Sciences, 35*(24), 2446–52.

Edwards, D.J., & Edwards, S.D. (2016). Case report on a clinical sport psychological intervention for a rugby player. *African Journal for Physical Activity and Health Sciences, 22*(3:1), 738–46.

Elliot, A.J., & McGregor, H.A. (2001). A 2 × 2 achievement goal framework. *Journal of Personality and Social Psychology, 80*(3), 501–19. doi:10.1037/0022-3514.80.3.501

Ellis, A. (1957). Rational psychotherapy and individual psychology. *Journal of Individual Psychology, 13*, 38–44.

Ellis, S., Carette, B., Anseel, F., & Lievens, F. (2014). Systematic reflection: Implications for learning from failures and successes. *Current Directions in Psychological Science, 23*(1), 67–72. doi:10.1177/0963721413504106

Fenn, K., & Byrne, M. (2013). The key principles of cognitive behavioural therapy. *InnovAiT: Education and Inspiration for General Practice, 6*(9), 579–85. doi:10.1177/1755738012471029

Franklin, C., & Bolton, K. (2015). Solution-focused brief therapy. In R.H. Witte, & S. Mosley-Howard (Eds.), *Mental health practice in today's schools: Issues and interventions* (pp. 45–167). New York, NY: Springer Publishing Company.

Fredricks, J.A., & Eccles, J.S. (2004). Parental influences on youth involvement in sport. In M.R. Weiss (Ed.), Developmental sport and exercise psychology: a lifespan perspective (pp. 145–64). Fitness Information Technology.

Gustafsson, H., & Lundqvist, C. (2016). Working with perfectionism in elite sport: A cognitive behavioral therapy perspective. In A.P. Hill (Ed.), *The psychology of perfectionism in sport, dance and exercise* (pp. 203–21). Routledge/Taylor & Francis Group.

Gustafsson, H., Davis, P., Skoog, T., Kenttä, G., & Harberl, P. (2015). Mindfulness and its relationship with perceived stress, affect, and burnout in elite junior athletes. *Journal of Clinical Sport Psychology, 9*(3), 263–81.

Gustafsson, H., Lundqvist, C., & Tod. D. (2016). Cognitive behavioral intervention in sport psychology: A case illustration of the exposure method with an elite athlete. *Journal of Sport Psychology in Action, 8*(3), 152–62. doi:10.1080/21520704.2016.1235649

Guterman, J.T., & Rudes, J. (2005). A solution-focused approach to rational-emotive behaviour therapy: Toward a theoretical integration. *Rational-Emotive & Cognitive-Behaviour Therapy, 23*(3), 223–44. doi:10.1007/s10942-005-0012-z

Harwood, C., Drew, A., & Knight, C.J. (2010). Parental stressors in professional youth football academies: A qualitative investigation of specialising stage parents. *Qualitative Research in Sport and Exercise, 2*(1), 39–55. doi:10.1080/19398440903510152

Harwood, C.G., & Knight, C.J. (2015). Parenting in youth sport: A position paper on parenting expertise. *Psychology of Sport and Exercise, 16*(Part 1), 24–35. doi:10.1016/j.psychsport.2014.03.001

Hase, A., O'Brien, J., Moore, L.J., & Freeman, P. (2019). The relationship between challenge and threat states and performance: A systematic review. *Sport Exercise and Performance Psychology, 8*(2), 123–44. doi:10.1037/spy0000132

Hofmann S.G., Asmundson G.J., & Beck A.T. (2013). The science of cognitive therapy. *Behavior Therapy, 44*(2), 199–212. doi:10.1016/j.beth.2009.01.007

Hofmann S.G., Asnaani A., Vonk I.J.J., Sawyer A.T., & Fang A. (2012). The efficacy of cognitive behavioral therapy: A review of meta-analyses. *Cognitive Therapy Research, 36*(5), 427–40. doi:10.1007/s10608-012-9476-1

Høglend, P. (1999). Psychotherapy research new findings and implications for training and practice. *The Journal of Psychotherapy Practice and Research, 8*(4), 257–63.

Jamieson, J.P., Nock, M.K., & Mendes, W.B. (2012). Mind over matter: Reappraising arousal improves cardiovascular and cognitive responses to stress. *Journal of Experimental Psychology: General, 141*(3), 417–22. doi: 10.1037/a0025719

Jones, G. (1995). More than just a game: Research developments and issues in competitive anxiety in sport. *British Journal of Psychology, 86*(Pt 4), 449–78. doi:10.1111/j.2044-8295.1995.tb02565.x

Jones, M., Meijen, C., McCarthy, P.J., & Sheffield, D. (2009). A theory of challenge and threat states in athletes. *International Review of Sport and Exercise Psychology, 2*(2), 161–80. doi:10.1080/17509840902829331

Jordana, A., Turner, M.J., Ramis, Y., & Torregrossa, M. (2020). Systematic mapping review on the use of Rational Emotive Behavior Therapy (REBT) with athletes. *International Review of Sport and Exercise Psychology.* doi:10.1080/1750984X.2020.1836673

Jouper, J., & Gustafsson, H. (2013). Mindful recovery: A case study of a burned-out elite shooter. *The Sport Psychologist, 27*(1), 92–102.

Kessler, R.C., Berglund, P., Demler, O., Jin, R., Merikangas, K.R., Walters, E.E. (2005). Lifetime prevalence and age-of-onset distributions of DSM-IV disorders in the national comorbidity survey replication. *Archives of General Psychiatry, 62*(6), 593–602. doi:10.1001/archpsyc.62.6.593.

Kim, J.S., & Franklin, C. (2009). Solution-focused brief therapy in schools: A review of the literature. *Children and Youth Services Review, 31*(4), 464–70. doi:10.1016/j.childyouth.2008.10.002

Kirschenbaum, D. (1997). *Mind matters: 7 steps to smarter sport performance.* Carmel, IN: Cooper Publishing.

Knight, C.J., Berrow, S.R., & Harwood, C.G. (2017). Parenting in sport. *Current Opinion in Psychology, 16*, 93–7. doi:10.1016/j.copsyc.2017.03.011

Lazarus, R.S. (1999). *Stress and Emotions: A New Synthesis.* London, UK: Free Association Books.

Littauer, H., Sexton, H., & Wynn, R. (2005). Qualities clients wish for in their therapists. *Scandinavian Journal of Caring Sciences, 19*(1), 28–31.

Lloyd, J., Bond, F.W., & Flaxman, P.E. (2013). The value of psychological flexibility: Examining psychological mechanisms underpinning a cognitive behavioural therapy intervention for burnout. *Work and Stress, 27*(2), 181–99 doi:10.1080/02678373.2013.782157

Mansell, P.C. (2021). Stress mindset in athletes: Investigating the relationships between beliefs, challenge and threat with psychological wellbeing. *Psychology of Sport and Exercise, 57*, 102020. doi:10.1016/j.psychsport.2021.102020

Marlow, C. (2009). Creating positive performance beliefs: The case of a tenpin bowler. In B. Hemmings, T. Holder (Eds.), *Applied Sport Psychology: A Case Based Approach* (pp. 65–87). London, UK: John Wiley & Sons Ltd.

Massey, W.V., Meyer, B.B., & Naylor A.H. (2013). Toward a grounded theory of self-regulation in mixed martial arts. *Psychology of Sport and Exercise*, 1(14), 12–20. doi:10.1016/j.psychsport.2012.06.008

McArdle, S., & Moore, P. (2012). Applying evidence-based principles from CBT to sport psychology. *The Sport Psychologist, 26*(2), 299–310. doi:10.1123/tsp.26.2.299

Meijen, C., Turner, M., Jones, M.V., Sheffield, D., & McCarthy, P. (2020). A theory of challenge and threat states in athletes: a revised conceptualization. *Frontiers in Psychology, 11*, 126. doi:10.3389/fpsyg.2020.00126

Mennin, D.S., Ellard, K.K., Fresco, D.M., & Gross, J.J. (2013). United we stand: Emphasizing commonalities across cognitive-behavioural therapies. *Behavior Therapy, 44*(2), 234–48. doi:10.1016/j.beth.2013.02.004

Moore, L.J., Vine, S.J., Wilson, M.R., & Freeman, P. (2012). The effect of challenge and threat states on performance: An examination of potential mechanisms. *Psychophysiology, 49*(10), 1417–25. doi:12.1111/j.1469-8986.2012.01449.x

Moore, L.J., Vine, S.J., Wilson, M.R., & Freeman, P. (2014). Examining the antecedents of challenge and threat states: The influence of perceived required effort and support availability. *International Journal of Psychophysiology, 93*(2), 267–73. doi:10.1016/j.ijpsycho.2014.05.009

Neil, R., Hanton, S., & Mellalieu, S.D. (2013). Seeing things in a different light: Assessing the effects of a cognitive-behavioral intervention upon the further appraisals and performance of golfers. *Journal of Applied Sport Psychology, 25*(1), 106–30. doi:10.1080/10413200.2012.658901

Nicholls, A.R., Polman, R.C.J., & Levy, A.R. (2012). A path analysis of stress appraisals, emotions, coping, and performance satisfaction among athletes. *Psychology of Sport and Exercise, 13*(3), 263–70. doi:10.1016/j.psychsport.2011.12.003

Olmedilla, A., Moreno-Fernández, I.M., Gómez-Espejo, V., Robles-Palazón, F.J., Verdú, I., & Ortega, E. (2019). Psychological intervention program to control stress in youth soccer players. *Frontiers in Psychology, 10*, 2260. doi:10.3389/fpsyg.2019.02260

Osborn, C. (1999). Solution-focused strategies with "involuntary" clients: Practical applications for the school and clinical setting. *Journal of Humanistic Education & Development, 37*(3), 169–81.

Page, J., & Thelwell, R. (2013). The value of social validation in single-case methods in sport and exercise psychology. *Journal of Applied Sport Psychology, 25*(1), 61–71. doi:10.1080/10413200.2012.663859.

Pederson, E.L., & Vogel, D.L. (2007). Male gender role conflict and willingness to seek counseling: Testing a mediation model on college-aged men. *Journal of Counseling Psychology, 54*(4), 373–84. doi:10.1037/0022-0167.54.4.373

Piaget, J. (1971). The theory of stages in cognitive development. In D.R. Green, M.P. Ford, & G.B. Flamer, *Measurement and Piaget*. New York, NY: McGraw-Hill.

Pitt, T., Thomas, O., Lindsay, P., Hanton, S., & Bawden, M. (2015). Doing sport psychology briefly? A critical review of single session therapeutic approaches and their relevance to sport psychology. *International Review of Sport and Exercise Psychology*, 1(8), 125–55. doi:10.1080/1750984X.2015.1027719

Portenga, S.T., Aoyagi, M.W., & Statler, T.A. (2012). Consulting on the run: Performance psychology and the preparation of USA track and field athletes for the Olympics. *Journal of Sport Psychology in Action, 3*(2), 98–108. doi:10.1080/21520704.2012.683087

Ravizza, K. (1990). Gaining entry with athletic personnel for season-long consulting. *The Sport Psychologist*, *2*(3), 243–54. doi:10.1123/tsp.2.3.243

Ravizza, K., & Fifer, A. (2014). Increasing awareness for sport performance. In J.M. Williams & V. Krane (Eds.), *Applied sport psychology: Personal growth to peak performance* (7th ed., pp. 176–287). New York, NY: McGraw-Hill.

Reeves, C.W., Nicholls, A.R., & McKenna, J. (2009). Stressors and coping strategies among early and middle adolescent premier league academy soccer players: Differences according to age. *Journal of Applied Sport Psychology*, *21*(1), 31–48. doi:10.1080/10413200802443768

Richardson, D., Gilbourne, D., & Littlewood, M. (2004). Developing support mechanisms for elite young players in a professional soccer academy: Creative reflections in action research. *European Sport Management Quarterly*, *4*(4), 195–214. doi:10.1080/16184740408737477

Rooney, R.H. (1992) *Strategies for work with involuntary clients*. Columbia University Press.

Sharp, L., Hodge, K., & Danish, S. (2015). Ultimately it comes down to the relationship: Experienced consultants' views of effective sport psychology consulting. *The Sport Psychologist*, *29*(4), 358–70. doi:10.1123/tsp.2014-0130

Sharpley, C.F., Jeffrey, A.M., & Mcmah, T. (2006). Counsellor facial expression and client-perceived rapport. *Counselling Psychology Quarterly*, *19*(4), 343–56. doi:10.1080/09515070601058706

Skinner, E.A. (1996). A guide to constructs of control. *Journal of Personality and Social Psychology*, *71*(3), 549–70. doi:10.1037//0022-3514.71.3.549

Slater, M.J., Evans, A.L., & Turner, M.J. (2016). Implementing a social identity approach for effective change management. *Journal of Change Management*, *16*(1), 18–37. doi:10.1080/14697017.2015.1103774

Steptoe, K., Barker, J., & Harwood, C. (2016). Psychological service provision to the elite football performance network: Supporting coaches, players, parents, and teams. In J.G. Cremades, & L.S. Tashman (Eds.), *Global practices and training in applied sport, exercise, and performance psychology: A case study approach*. New York, NY: Routledge.

Storch, E.A., Storch, J.B., Killiany, E.M., & Roberti, J.W. (2005). Self-reported psychopathology in athletes: A comparison of intercollegiate student-athletes and non-athletes. *Journal of Sport Behavior*, *28*(1), 86–98.

Stroud, L.R., Foster, E., Papandonatos, G.D., Handwerger, K., Granger, D.A., Kivlighan, K.T., & Niaura, R. (2009). Stress response and the adolescent transition: Performance versus peer rejection stressors. *Development and Psychopathology*, *21*(1), 47–68. doi:10.1017/S0954579409000042

Summers, R.F., & Barber, J.P. (2003). Therapeutic alliance as a measurable psychotherapy skill. *Academic Psychiatry*, *27*(3), 160–5. doi:10.1176/appi.ap.27.3.160

Swettenham, L., & Whitehead, A. (2022). Acting on injury: Increasing psychological flexibility and adherence to rehabilitation. *Case Studies in Sport and Exercise Psychology*, *6*(1), 94–101. doi:10.1123/cssep.2021-0021

Thornicroft, G., Mehta, N., Clement, S., Evans-Lacko, S., Doherty, M., Rose, D., Koschorke, M., Shidhaye, R., O'Reilly, C., & Henderson, C. (2016). Evidence for effective interventions to reduce mental-health-related stigma and discrimination. *Lancet*, *387*(10023), 1123–32. doi:10.1016/s0140-6736(15)00298-6

Thrower, S., Harwood, C.G., & Spray, C.M. (2018). Educating and supporting tennis parents using web-based delivery methods: a novel online education programme. *Journal of Applied Sport Psychology*, *31*(1), 303–23. doi:10.1080/10413200.2018.1433250

Trip, S., Vernon, A., & McMahon, J. (2007). Effectiveness of rational-emotive education: a quantitative meta-analytical study. *Journal of Cognitive and Behavioral Psychotherapies*, 7(1), 81–93.

Trotman, G.P., Williams, S.E., Quinton, M.L., & Veldhuijzen van Zanten, J.J.C.S. (2018). Challenge and threat states: examining cardiovascular, cognitive and affective responses to two distinct laboratory stress tasks. *International Journal of Psychophysiology*. *126*, 42–51. doi:10.1016/j.ijpsycho.2018.02.004

Turner, M.J., & Barker, J.B. (2014). *What business can learn from sport psychology*. UK: Bennion Kearny.

Turner, M.J., & Jones, M.V. (2018). Arousal control in sport. *Oxford Research Encyclopedia of Psychology*. doi:10.1093/acrefore/9780190236557.013.155

Turner, M.J., Aspin, G., Didymus, F., Mack, R., Olusoga, P., Wood, A.G., & Bennett. R. (2020a). One case, five approaches: The application of psychotherapeutic approaches in sport psychology. *The Sport Psychologist*, *34*(1), 71–83. doi:10.1123/tsp.2019-0079

Turner, M.J., Jones, M.V., Sheffield, D., Barker, J.B., & Coffee, P. (2014). Manipulating cardiovascular indices of challenge and threat using resource appraisals. *International Journal of Psychophysiology, 94*(1), 9–18. doi: 10.1016/j.ijpsycho.2014.07.004

Turner, M.J., Jones, M.V., Sheffield, D., Slater, M.J., Barker, J.B., & Bell, J. (2013). Who thrives under pressure? Predicting the performance of elite academy cricketers using the cardiovascular indicators of challenge and threat states. *Journal of Sport and Exercise Psychology, 35*(4), 387–97.

Turner, M.J., Massie, R., Slater, M.J., & Braithwaite, E. (2020b). Do challenge and threat evaluations predict netball performance and selection at trials in youth netball players? *Sport and Exercise Psychology, 10*(1), 71–87.

Vine, S.J., Uiga, L., Lavric, A., Moore, L.J., Tsaneva-Atanasova, K., & Wilson, M.R. (2015). Individual reactions to stress predict performance during a critical aviation incident. *Anxiety, Stress, & Coping, 28*(4), 467–77. doi:10.1080/10615806.2014.986722

Wilkins, L., Sweeney, J., Zaborski, Z., Nelson, C., Tweddle, S., Beukes, E., & Allen, P. (2020). Elite academy soccer players' perceptions towards cognitive behavioral therapy. *Journal of Clinical Sport Psychology, 14*(1), 55–67. doi:10.1123/jcsp.2018-0026

Williams, S., Cumming, J., & Balanos, G. (2010). The use of imagery to manipulate challenge and threat appraisal states in athletes. *Journal of Sport and Exercise Psychology, 32*(3), 339–58. doi:10.1123/jsep.32.3.339

Wood, A.G., Turner, M.J., & Barker, J.B. (2019). Bolstering psychological health using rational emotive behaviour therapy. In G. Breslin, & G. Leavey (Eds.), *Mental health and well-being interventions in sport: Research, theory and practice* (pp. 45–62). Routledge/Taylor & Francis Group.

9

BRIEF EDITOR COMMENTARY ON THE CHAPTER "DYNAMIC COGNITIVE-BEHAVIOURAL SPORT PSYCHOLOGY: TAKING A MULTI-MODAL APPROACH"

Martin J. Turner

Hobson and Dixon astutely point out that, of course, the TCTSA, and the TCTSA-R, are cognitive-behavioural in nature. The challenge and threat concepts, since their formal inception by Richard Lazarus (1966, 1999), are part of cognitive appraisal, a process that functions as cognitive mediation between the environment and an emotional response. In light of competition, it is an athlete's cognitive appraisals that help to determine the shape and the intensity of the emotion evinced. In the TCTSA-R, Meijen et al. (2020) indicate that when a situation is primarily appraised as goal relevant (i.e., personally relevant to goals) and conditions are appraised as favourable for success (goal congruence), then challenge is evinced. In contrast, threat results from the appraisal that the competition is highly relevant to goals, but the conditions for success are unfavourable (goal incongruence). As such, challenge reflects the perception that one can bring the challenge to fruition, whereas threat reflects the perception that one cannot ameliorate the threat.

Further to the above cognitive appraisal mechanism, the TCTSA-R also includes a secondary cognitive appraisal stage which involves the figurative weighing of perceived resources against perceived demands. This is important because it is possible for an athlete to primarily appraise a competition as a threat, but then through reappraisal at a secondary stage, to in part ameliorate this threat by perceiving greater resources than demands. The secondary appraisal stage captured in the TCTSA-R is central to Jones et al.'s (2009) TCTSA and its foundation the biopsychosocial model of arousal regulation (Blascovich & Mendes, 2000), and is focused upon by Hobson and Dixon in their chapter. But regardless of theoretical specifics and nuances, it is generally agreed that challenge is related to *adaptive* cognitive, emotional, and behavioural (including performance) consequences, and threat is related to *maladaptive* cognitive, emotional, and behavioural (including performance) consequences (Behnke & Kaczmarek, 2018; Hase et al., 2019; Meijen et al., 2020). As such, a laudable and sensible applied aim is to encourage challenge, and discourage threat, which Hobson and Dixon do systemically in their work.

So, at a broad level, an athlete approaching a competition can influence their performance-related cognitions, emotions, and behaviours via cognitive appraisal. If they can harness challenge appraisals at primary and secondary stages, then they are more likely to fulfil their potential through the expression of adaptive cognitions, emotions, and behaviours.

DOI: 10.4324/9781003162513-10

TABLE 9.1 Alignment between TCTSA-R and CBTs

	CBT code		
	A	*B*	*C*
TCTSA-R	Competition	Primary and secondary appraisal	Cognitive, emotional, behavioural responses
CBTs	Stimulus, activating event, situation	Acceptance (ACT) Self-compassion (CFT) Cognitive distortions (CT) Irrational/rational beliefs (REBT) Coping skills (SIT) Maladaptive schema (ST)	Cognitive, emotional, behavioural responses

Note: ACT = acceptance and commitment therapy, CFT = compassion focussed therapy, CT = cognitive therapy, REBT = rational emotive behaviour therapy, SIT = stress inoculation training, ST = schema therapy.

All things considered, one can view the TCTSA-R in line with the ABC framework, particularly, although not exclusively, akin and familial to, second wave (Beckian/Ellisian) CBTs. With the competition at "A", cognitive appraisals at "B", and cognitive/emotional/behavioural consequences at "C", it perhaps becomes clear the ways in which the TCTSA-R relates to the cognitive-behavioural approach to psychotherapy. Ultimately, the TCTSA-R is an expression of how cognitive mediation is central to emotional and behavioural reactivity, and as such, sits alongside the CBTs captured within the present book. Table 9.1 captures the conceptual alignment between the CBTs in the present book and the TCTSA-R. We include this as an academic exercise in theoretical alignment, but beyond that, we are hopeful that readers can see the applied implications here. When working with a specific "A" such as an upcoming competition, a practitioner has numerous evidence-based CBT-derived options for supporting the athlete towards greater cognitive/emotional/behavioural adaptation.

What is presented in Table 9.1 is of course a simplistic explication of how the TCTSA-R may relate to the CBTs in the current book and readers may take issue with the rudimentary expression of CBT-derived cognitive mediators (as they should!). But the intimation I am making here is that the ABC framework, whether used in practice or not, does tie the cognitive-behavioural approaches together somewhat. What differs quite significantly across CBT approaches is what the practitioner does with this ABC formulation. For example, REBT and ACT have different positions on what a practitioner would do with an irrational belief such as "it is awful to fail in important competitions".

The conceptual and practical synergies between the TCTSA-R and these CBTs mean that when helping a client to approach an important competition, for example, there are many roots to supporting the athlete. The experienced and pluralistic practitioner will not pressure themselves into choosing one approach. Rather, they will integrate and synthesise their usage of these CBTs to do what serves the athlete best. They will remain evidence-based and exercise theoretically consistent eclecticism (Dryden, 2019; Neenan & Dryden, 2010) or practical eclecticism (David et al., 2010), which advocates a broad use of techniques, from wherever, but to achieve goals in keeping with CBT theory. For example, by adopting a CT approach to working with clients, it is possible to draw upon a broad range of techniques from across the gamut of CBTs, safe in the knowledge that we are being theoretically consistent within the cognitive-behavioural tradition. Helping the client should be the focus, rather than rigidly sticking to one specific CBT, potentially at the cost of client progress. So long as we have sufficient training and expertise, we can be eclectic – because people are eclectic (Turner, 2022).

References

Behnke, M., & Kaczmarek, L. D. (2018). Successful performance and cardiovascular markers of challenge and threat: A meta-analysis. *International Journal of Psychophysiology, 130*, 73–9. https://doi.org/10.1016/j.ijpsycho.2018.04.007

Blascovich, J., & Mendes, W. B. (2000). Challenge and threat appraisals: The role of affective cues. In J. P. Forgas (Ed.), *Feeling and thinking: The role of affect in social cognition* (pp. 59–82). Cambridge University Press.

David, D., Freeman, A., & DiGiuseppe, R. (2010). Rational and irrational beliefs: Implications for mechanisms of change and practice in psychotherapy. In D. David, S. J. Lynn, & A. Ellis (Eds.), *Rational and irrational beliefs: Research, theory, and clinical practice* (pp. 195–217). Oxford University Press.

Dryden, W. (2019). The distinctive features of rational emotive behavior therapy. In: Bernard M., & Dryden W. (Eds.) *Advances in REBT* (pp. 23–46). Springer. https://doi.org/10.1007/978-3-319-93118-0_8

Hase, A., O'Brien, J., Moore, L. J., & Freeman, P. (2019). The relationship between challenge and threat states and performance: A systematic review. *Sport Exercise and Performance Psychology, 8*(2), 123–44. https://doi.org/10.1037/spy0000132

Jones, M., Meijen, C., McCarthy, P.J., & Sheffield, D. (2009). A theory of challenge and threat states in athletes. *International Review of Sport and Exercise Psychology, 2*(2), 161–80. https://doi.org/10.1080/17509840902829331

Lazarus, R. S. (1966). *Psychological stress and the coping process*. McGraw Hill.

Lazarus, R. S. (1999). *Stress and emotion: A new synthesis*. Springer Publishing Co.

Meijen, C., Turner, M., Jones, M. V., Sheffield, D., & McCarthy, P. (2020). A theory of challenge and threat states in athletes: a revised conceptualization. *Frontiers in Psychology, 11*, 126. https://doi.org/10.10.3389/fpsyg.2020.00126

Neenan, M., & Dryden, W. (2010). *Rational emotive behaviour therapy in a nutshell*. SAGE Publications.

Turner, M. J. (2022). *The rational practitioner: The sport and performance psychologist's guide to practicing rational emotive behaviour therapy*. Routledge.

INDEX

Note: Page numbers in italics indicate a figure and page numbers in bold indicate a table on the corresponding page.

FOCUS: Key Concepts in General Studies

J. M. and A. D. Burgen

STANLEY THORNES (PUBLISHERS) LTD

First published in 1984 by
Stanley Thornes (Publishers) Ltd
Old Station Drive
Leckhampton
CHELTENHAM GL53 0DN

British Library Cataloguing in Publication Data
Burgen, J. M.
Focus: key concepts in general studies.
1. Education, Humanistic
I. Title II. Burgen, A. D.
001 LT310

ISBN 0-85950-164-7

Typeset in Paladium
by Blackpool Typesetting Services Ltd.
Printed and bound in Great Britain byThe Pitman Press, Bath.

CONTENTS

PREFACE

Clearly it is inherently impossible for a book of this size to cover all aspects of General Studies. Our aim is rather to provide a focus around which a General Studies course can be built, and in particular (a) to provide stimulating source material dealing with topics which we believe are relevant and interesting; and (b) to encourage the use of appropriate interpretative and analytical skills.

In the follow-up work suggested for each passage, we have tried to range wider than mere 'comprehension' of the passage, and to encourage synthesis of material from various parts of the book (and indeed from general knowledge).

We would certainly hope that everyone who uses the book will be encouraged to move on to further sources of information on at least *some* of the topics dealt with. As a starting point, we have ourselves listed, for each passage, some sources which we have found relevant to the topic and well worth reading (as well as reasonably easy to track down). Of course, no two people would come up with exactly the same list, and both teachers and students will have useful further suggestions to make.

J. M. and A. D. Burgen

Acknowledgements

Cornel Printers Ltd, for the extract on pages 74–77

Courtauld Institute Galleries, London (Courtauld Collection) on page 131

DACS, for permission to reproduce the illustrations on pages 147 and 148

Dr J B Whittow, for Figure 1 on page 80

Edward Arnold Ltd, for the extract on pages 152–153

Fondation le Corbusier, for the illustrations on pages 147 and 148

Geologists' Association, for Figure 2 on page 82 and Figure 4 on page 83

Granada Publishing Limited, for the extract on pages 144–145

A M Heath & Co Ltd, for the extract on pages 104–105

Heinemann Educational Books, for the extract on pages 68–71

The John Hillelson Agency Limited, for the photographs on pages 136–140

Hutchinson Publishers, for the extract on pages 53–57

Springer-Verlag, for Figure 3 on page 82

Every attempt has been made to contact copyright holders, but we apologise if any have been overlooked.

A

SOCIAL MAN

THE STATE BY POPULATION

(See Question 1 in A1.)

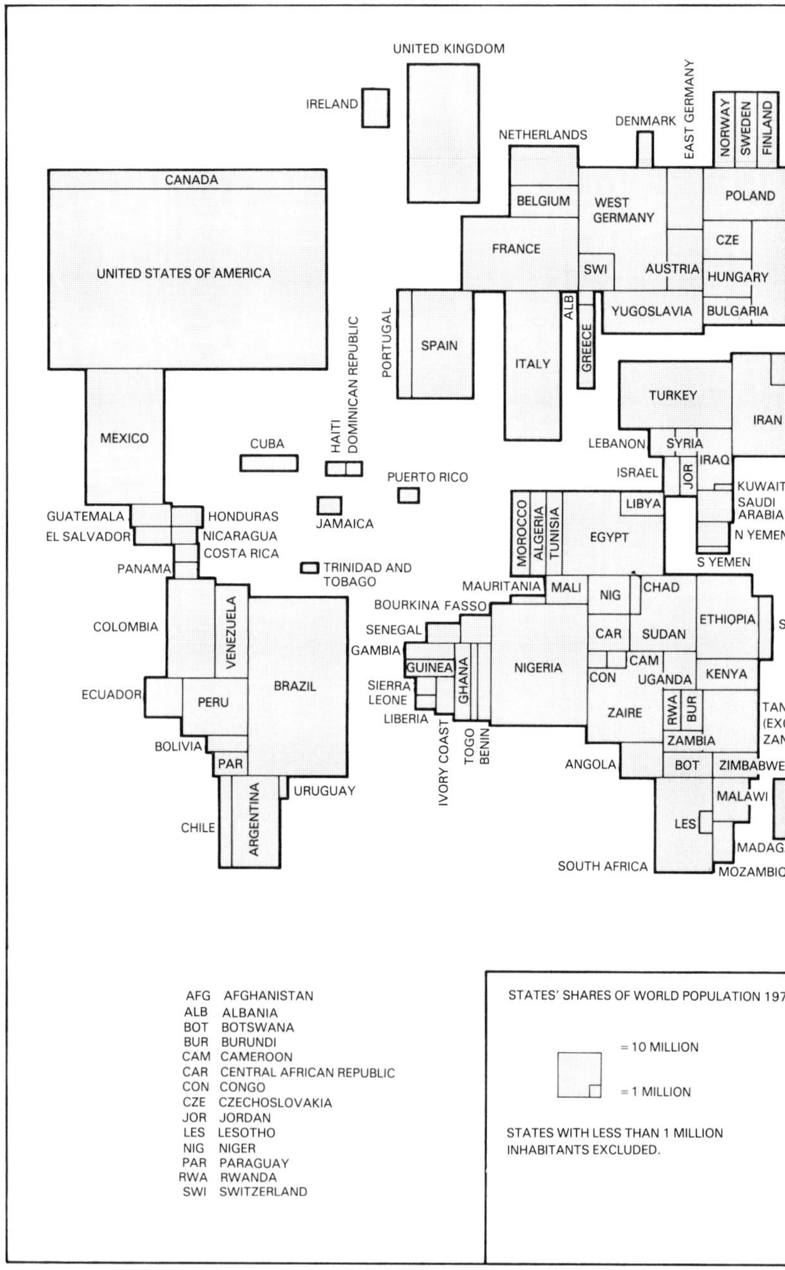

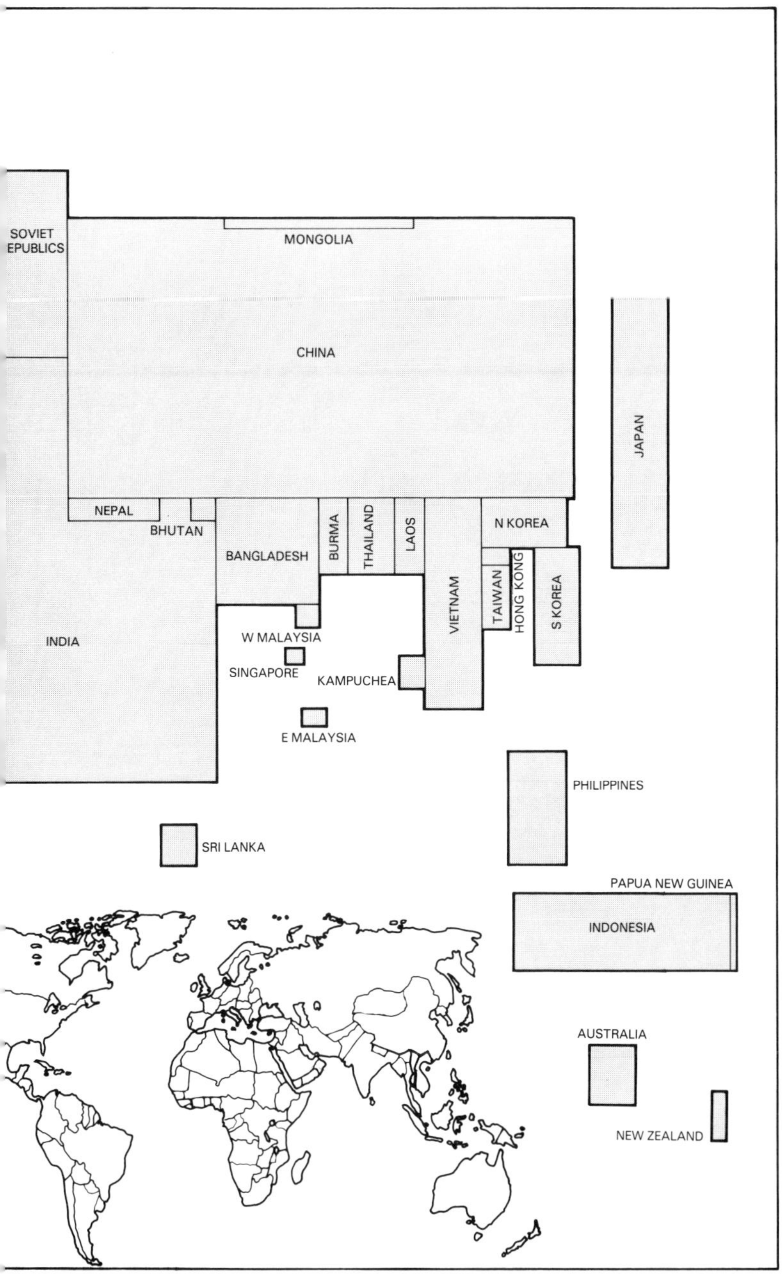

er: M. Kidron and R. Segal, *The State of the World Atlas*, Pan, 1984)

NATIONAL INCOME

(See Question 1 in A1.)

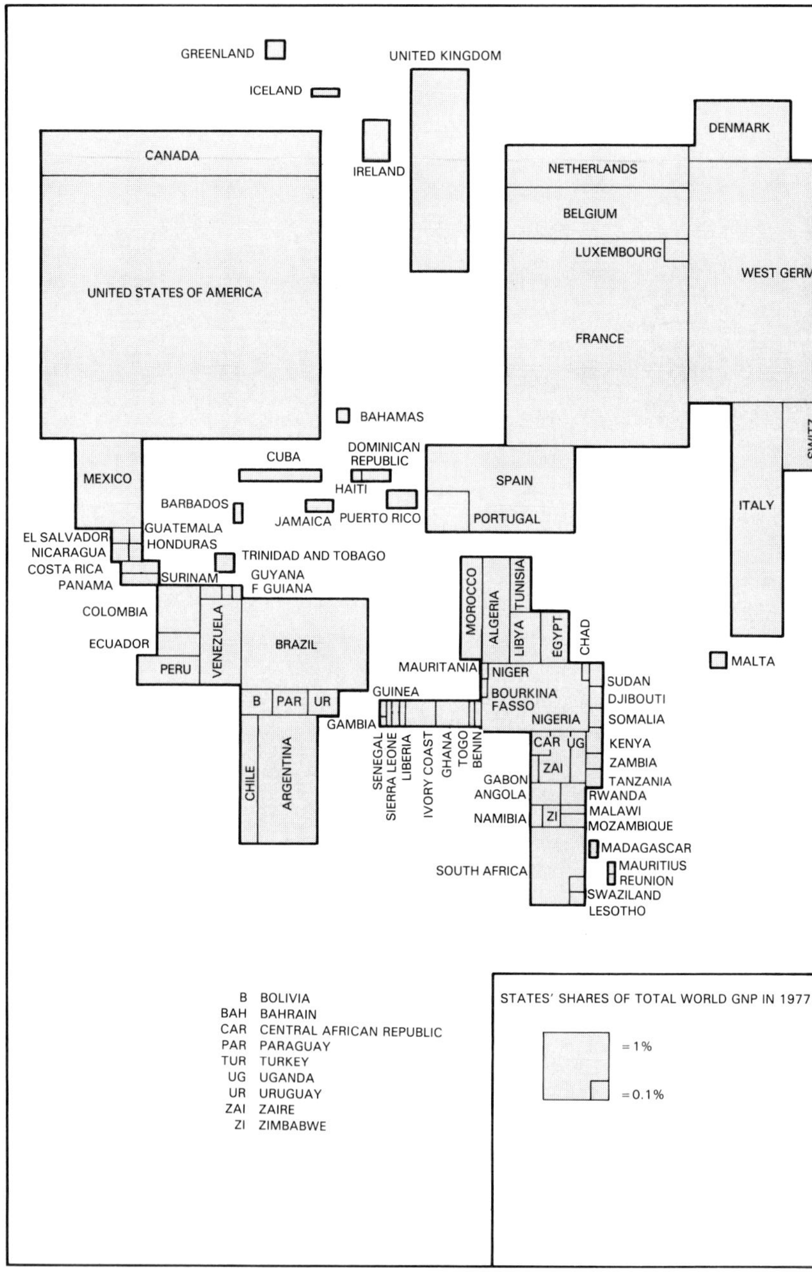

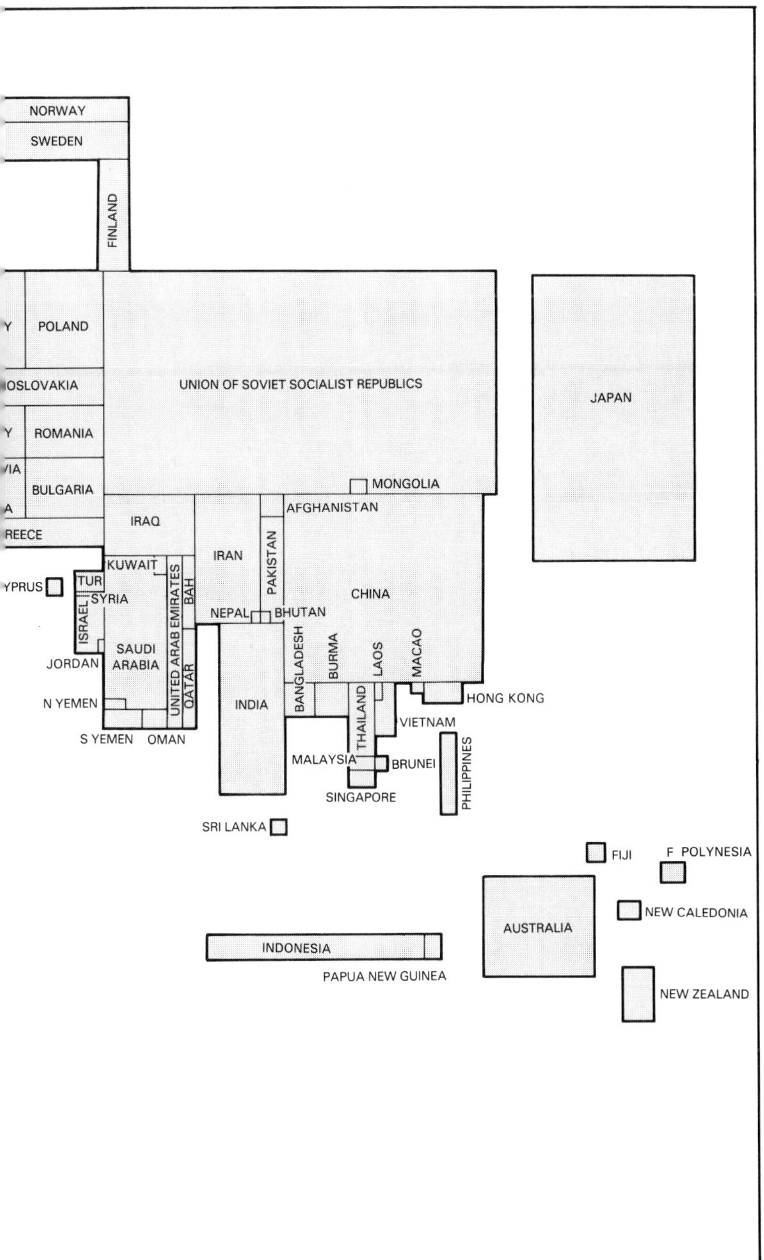

: M. Kidron and R. Segal, *The State of the World Atlas*, Pan, 1984)

A 1 Scale of Economies

1. Unlike conventional maps of the world which are based on land area, the maps on the previous pages 're-draw' the map of the world in terms of population and wealth.

   In an analysis of 600–800 words, comment on the world as portrayed in these maps.

See also Question 5 in A3.

Further Reading

Frantz Fanon, *The Wretched of the Earth*, Penguin
– based on the Algerian revolution, this famous book was described by Jean-Paul Sartre as 'a classic of anti-colonialism in which the Third World finds *itself* and speaks to *itself* through his voice'.

G. Lamming & H. Mueller, *Africa Undermined*, pages 429–435, Penguin
– a description of the Volta River project in Ghana.

P. Worsley (Ed.), *Introduction to Sociology*, Chapter 3, 'Development and Underdevelopment', Penguin

A. Sampson (Ed.), *North/South: A Programme for Survival*, Pan
– Pan imprint of the famous Brandt Report on the inequalities of Northern and Southern Hemispheres.

Economies of Scale

A2

In many lines of production, the large manufacturing unit enjoys enormous advantages over its smaller competitors which enable it to achieve substantial reductions in costs of production.

Many of these economies arise from the sheer technological superiority of the large firms. This is most obvious when a very high level of output is necessary for the most efficient machines to be used at all, e.g. the automatic loom in the cotton industry which for really economic working requires continuous shiftwork. However, even if the best machines can be produced in either large or small versions, the small firm, while able to enjoy the same quality of input as its larger rival, may find that the cost of producing and maintaining the smaller version is proportionately higher. A ten-ton lorry, for example, both costs relatively less than a five-tonner and requires only the same number of men to operate it. Again, only the large firm may have sufficient demand for its product to be able to afford to *combine* its inputs optimally. Consider, for example, a new entrant to an industry who estimates that his daily sales will be 500 units of a product which is produced by performing three successive manufacturing processes – X, Y, and Z. From the manufacturers, he learns that the best machines available for these three processes have the following capacity:

in process X	300 units per day
in process Y	400 units per day
in process Z	500 units per day

His estimated demand of 500 per day is large enough for him to put in the most efficient machines. But it falls below the level at which he could use them in the most efficient *combination*. Manufacturing 500 units per day, the two machines necessary for the X and Y processes would have surplus capacity of 100 and 300 units per day respectively. Only machine Z would be fully employed. It is not difficult to see that the minimum output which would allow him to work at full capacity would be 6000 units per day, employing twenty machines in process X, fifteen in Y, and twelve in Z.

So far we have considered large-firm superiority in static terms. In a context of rapid technological progress, of quickly changing consumer preferences, and restriction of many other forms of competition, further benefits accrue to the firms which can successfully undertake research and development of new products and processes. Once again, God seems to favour the big battalions. It may be that the small firm devotes the same proportion of its resources to research activities as its larger rival. But research being primarily a hit-or-miss affair, what tends to count more is the *absolute* level of expenditure. The large firm will enjoy a similar advantage at the stage of translating research into commercial terms. Operating pilot schemes to test commercial viability may be a very expensive business indeed.

The large firm is also likely to be more efficient in its deployment of labour. Adam Smith's famous dictum that 'the division of labour is limited by the extent of the market' sums the position up nicely. The opportunities for labour, on the factory floor or in the board-room, to increase in efficiency through specialisation, are clearly enhanced in a firm producing for a mass market. The use of labour in occupations best suited to individual talents, increased dexterity arising from repetition of the same task, saving in time and tools involved in moving from one job to another – these simple and obvious economies are exemplified on the factory floor by the assembly line fitter and also have their counterpart in the board-room.

The application of these superior techniques may be made possible by either integrating or disintegrating the process of manufacture. Sometimes, economies depend on *bringing together* different processes within the same plant, so that substantial savings can be made, for example, in transport and fuel costs. In other lines of production, increased efficiency may chiefly arise from a *separation* of the individual processes to enable specialist plants do deploy standardised, mass-production techniques.

The business of manufacturing industry consists of more than transforming raw materials into final products. The materials have to be purchased, the customers wooed, and the products sold, and capital must be found to make it all possible. In all these commercial activities the large firm enjoys further advantages, and for similar reasons to those already discussed. National Press or television advertising, market research and extensive after-sales service, the raising of capital on the stock exchange – are all examples of facilities which, because they are in some sense indivisible, are not economic for the small firm. And even when the same quality of inputs are available to large and small alike, the big firm may still find that the cost of using them may be relatively less. A million-pound issue on the stock market does not cost twice as much to float as an issue of £500 000; nor need a salesman necessarily take twice as long to take an order twice as large. Moreover, its size may enable a large firm to cut out many of the extra costs involved in passing a product through a number of middlemen; concentration of the whole business of manufacture within a single enterprise may reduce both the level of stocks of semi-finished goods which is required and uncertainty about what that level should be; when manufacturers are large enough to do their own selling, either direct to the public or through their own chain of retail outlets, they can minimise commercial risks by being closely in touch with consumer requirements.

We can conclude, then, that large firms are very frequently able to make considerable economies in production costs. However, these economies of scale do not exist to the same degree in all industries. In some lines of production, the advantages lie more with the smaller units. The benefits of mass production arise primarily from standardisation of the product, and, where flexibility, personal service, and a variety of lines is demanded, it may be the small firm which is most suited. Indeed, the very existence of large firms creates the need for smaller enterprises to meet the demand for deviations from their standardised output.

PRICES, PROFITS, AND DISECONOMIES OF SCALE

The argument so far is just that large firms can often cut their average *costs.* For this to be of social as well as private benefit depends on whether the economies are passed on to consumers in the form of lower *prices.* However, firms do not grow only in order to become more efficient; size also gives greater control over the market. Thus, from the point of view of maximising profits, the output produced by a monopolist may be below that which would be produced by a number of competing producers; a degree of monopolistic control may enable a firm to restrict output and reap exceptional profits - always providing that new entrants to the industry can be kept out. Control over raw materials, or tied markets, the setting up of special 'fighting companies' to eliminate new entrants, and size in itself are among the ways in which potential competition can be stifled. But the fact that the 'new entrant' may not be some puny, inexperienced newcomer, but another industrial giant anxious to extend its empire, or even the State itself, sometimes checks exploitation. So also does ignorance of the precise level of profits which would induce such a response.

The two impulses to integration which we have so far mentioned - the possibilities of reducing costs and increasing prices - both involve the not unreasonable assumption that the firm is interested in making profits. We should beware, however, of generalising this into the quite different assumption that *entrepreneurs* are *only* concerned with the *maximisation* of profits. With site values at present levels, a sole preoccupation with maximising profits would probably mean that a large number of the smaller firms now operating in the London area would sell out at once. Their directors or proprietors could live happily ever after in Cannes were it not for the fact that in addition to making *some* profits, they also enjoy being businessmen. Similarly, it would be wrong to conclude that large-scale enterprises have developed only because integration was dictated by profit maximisation. Security of profits, or the wish for a relatively quiet life, also enter into the picture. But perhaps most significant, with the separation of nominal ownership of the firm from the actual control of its operation by what are often self-perpetuating and internally impregnable Boards, is the possibility that growth of the firm may come to be regarded as an end in itself.

This is not, of course, to argue that firms ignore the effects on profits when deciding whether to expand; however, other considerations may also be thought important and lead to growth of firms which increases total profits but does not *maximise* them. We have shown that integration *can* bring about substantial economies, but it is not true to say that it always does so. First, there are limits to the reductions in costs which can be achieved by increased size. After a certain stage, which will differ from industry to industry, the firm becomes unwieldy and 'diseconomies' may begin to become significant. As the firm becomes bigger so also do the problems of running it effectively. The process of decision-taking becomes more complex as the scope of the firm's activities is extended, and the gap between policy making and execution increases. Bureaucratic delays and waste, the difficulty of achieving just the right delegation of authority – these are functions of size, and as much problems for large private enterprises as for the government departments with which they are more generally associated.

Again, much of the concentration of economic power which has taken place has taken the form of diversification – firms branching out into quite different activities, pharmacists manufacturing jam, beverage producers making pharmaceutical goods or air sweeteners, brewers fishing, and so on. Sometimes such diversification can be justified in terms of commercial if not technical economies. And from the point of view of the firm itself, diversification can nearly always be defended in terms of risk-spreading in volatile market conditions. But it is probable that much integration of this type yields no positive *social* gain. The economies of bulk buying or selling, for example, may be only at the expense of some other intermediary between producer and consumer, the latter enjoying none of the consequent benefits; the spreading of risks is a useful insurance for the firm, but it might be the customer who pays the premium in the form of higher prices to cover the increased management costs.

(from: P. Donaldson, *Guide to the British Economy*, Pelican, 1981)

1. In a manufacturing plant four successively linked processes are used. The capacities of the relevant machines are:
1st type of machine – 100 units per day
2nd type of machine – 250 units per day
3rd type of machine – 300 units per day
4th type of machine – 2000 units per day

(a) How many units would need to be produced per day in order to operate *all* four types of machine to full capacity?
(i) 4000 units per day
(ii) 6000 units per day
(iii) 2000 units per day
(iv) 8000 units per day
(b) How many machines of the second type would this require?
(i) 24
(ii) 16
(iii) 8
(iv) 32

2. Since the days of Henry Ford successful car manufacture has involved production on a large scale. What advantages does a large manufacturer of cars have over a smaller one in the following areas?
   (a) Design and testing of new models
   (b) Manufacture
   (c) Marketing and advertising
   (d) Servicing and spare parts provision

3. Why might the growth in the number of specialist food shops and delicatessens be related to the growth in the number of supermarkets?

4. Company A and Company B are the two major manufacturers of a particular product. The two companies merge to form one larger manufacturer. As a result, economies of scale should lead to
   (a) reduced unit costs and
   (b) reduced prices for customers.
   Give reasons why either (a) or (b) or both may *not* be the case.

5. According to the passage, large organisations are likely to suffer from 'bureaucratic delays and waste, the difficulty of achieving just the right delegation of authority . . .'. Explain what this means.

6. Why do car manufacturers tend to buy identical components from more than one supplier? Surely it would be cheaper to place one large order with a single component manufacturer?

See also Question 13 in B6 and Question 7 in C8.

Further Reading

E. Schumacher, *Small is Beautiful*, Blond & Briggs

Anthony Sampson, *The Changing Anatomy of Britain*, 1983 Edition, Coronet
- for a readable account of British industry in the 1970s and early 1980s, especially Chapter 22, 'Companies: Bigness and Smallness'.

Fritjof Capra, *The Turning Point*, Flamingo
- Chapter 8 'The Dark Side of Growth' challenges the assumption that economic growth is always desirable.

A3 Marxism as the 'Politics of Hunger'

During his lifetime what Karl Marx wrote was not widely read. But his ideas and moral temper, his vocabulary, even his stray notions, have since come to influence the course of world history. Whatever else Marxism may be, it provides the foremost intellectual drama of our time, intellectual because its doctrine is used politically. For the same reason it is the foremost political drama. In Marxism, ideas confront politics: intellectuals, politicians, passions, conceptions, the coldest analysis, the hottest moral condemnation – all meet. They meet – immediately, dramatically – and make history.

The intellectual value of classic Marxism, and of Marxism more generally, is not merely historical. It has a direct intellectual relevance today. Marx's work contains comprehensive statements about the elements and the structure of society to which attention must be paid – entirely apart from politics or ideology.

We cannot understand the history of any nation of consequence without considering Marx's ideas and what has happened to them. So important are they on a world scale that even of nations in which they have played little or no role we must ask why not. And to ask and to answer such questions is among the most fruitful and revealing of endeavours. [. . .]

What is at the heart of what he wrote? Why have his ideas had – and why do they have – such a deep and wide appeal to men and women of such different backgrounds? Although they appeal little to most people who live in advanced capitalist nations and who more likely than not have never been hungry or chronically ill by virtue of neglect and poverty, most of mankind is still subject to such conditions of life, and death. To them, as is frequently asserted, Marxism is basically a politics of hunger; to them, that is 'what Marxism is all about'. This ideological message underlies Marxism as a political and intellectual force, yesterday and today:

> You do not have to be poor any longer. Everywhere men have always lived as exploiters and exploited. As long as the means of producing goods were not sufficient to provide for all, perhaps this evil condition was inevitable.
>
> It is no longer inevitable.
>
> You do not have to be poor.
>
> You are poor not because of anything you have done or anything you have failed to do, not because of original Sin or the Will of God or because of bad luck. You are poor because of economic and political conditions. These conditions are called capitalism. At first, capitalism was a great progressive force in man's history; under it men built enormous facilities for the production of all the things they need.
>
> You are poor and you are exploited and you are going to be exploited as long as capitalism prevails. For capitalism has ceased to be a progressive force; it has become an obstacle to Progress, to your progress. It enters into every feature of human life, private and public, and all of them it corrupts. Capitalism is the system that exploits you.

> You do not have to be poor. The conditions that make you poor can be changed. They are going to be changed. Inside capitalism itself are the seeds of its own destruction. What will happen, whether you are yet aware of it or not, is that you are going to make a revolution. Those who rule over you and keep you poor will be overthrown. That is the next step forward in human progress. You are going to take that step. By the revolution you can eliminate once and for all the exploitation of man by man; you can enter into a socialist society in which mankind conquers nature. And no man any longer will know poverty and exploitation.

It is rather difficult not to go on – so compelling is the message! And so it should be. Never mind now about the facts, the theories, the predictions: the hopes and ideals expressed in this message are firmly a part of Western civilisation. Little wonder that clergymen regularly complain that the communists 'have stolen our stuff'. Indeed, Marxism as ideology is less a message than a 'gospel', which in the literal sense means 'glad tidings'.

To understand this gospel, one must understand whom it attracts. The big answer to that question today is: it attracts many intelligent and alert people in the impoverished countries. Most of the world's population live in such hungry countries, and these countries are now very much in commotion. There is no longer any 'unchanging East', no 'primitively static Africa', no Latin America sitting in stupor in the sun. Their peoples are clamouring for the fruits of industrialisation, and with good historical reason many reject the capitalist way of achieving them. Several varieties of Marxism are among the models of industrialisation available to them.

The Bolshevik revolution offers a compelling model of development and modernisation. Therein lies its present historical significance – at least if one believes that the leading long-run problem in world politics is what model the underdeveloped nations and territories will choose, economically, culturally, and politically. Marxism speaks to, as well as for, these people, and in doing so competes with liberalism.

The work of Marx taken as a whole is a savage sustained indictment of one alleged injustice: that the profit, the comfort, the luxury of one man is paid for by the loss, the misery, the denial of another. If in societies founded in his name, as well as in capitalist societies of a sort he never knew, many have come to believe Marx mistaken about the form and the mechanism of this injustice, still for tens of millions of others the indictment stands. Even if it has to be reworked, extended, revised, even thoroughly remade, none the less it seems to many people an enormous truth.

There is one characteristic of Marxism which I have already noted: in it ideal and agency are closely combined, even confused. Rather than proclaim ideals in abstraction, Marx argued that they *are* going to be realised because of the necessary development of capitalist society: the development of the struggles of the proletariat, climaxed by the proletarian revolution.

(from: C. W. Mills, *The Marxists*, Pelican, 1963)

1. '. . . clergymen regularly complain that the communists "have stolen our stuff".' (paragraph 11).

(a) How might Marxist beliefs serve as an alternative to Christian beliefs?

(b) Compare and contrast Marxist and Christian ideas on:
(i) What to tell the poor and hungry.
(ii) Why the world is in its present state.
(iii) How things could be improved in the future.

2. Many capitalist countries may be concerned about the attractiveness of Marxist ideas to the more disadvantaged members of their populations.

(a) Below is a list of some of the possible options open to a government anxious to reduce the threat of Marxism. Arrange these options in order of likely effectiveness, starting with the most effective and ending with the least. There is no necessity to write out the options. Merely use the numbers preceding each one, e.g. (1), (2), (3), etc.
(1) New laws emphasising greater social and sexual equality.
(2) Ridicule of people or organisations promoting Marxist ideas.
(3) Strong and loyal police and military forces to protect state against 'subversive elements' such as Marxists.
(4) Comprehensive Welfare State provisions for health, housing, unemployment, etc.
(5) The outlawing of left-wing organisations and the imprisonment of leaders and sympathisers.
(6) Greater democracy in politics and in the workplace.
(7) Use of the Church, the education system, the mass media, etc. to emphasise the 'good' aspects of the present system of government.

(b) Carefully explain the reasons behind your choices of the *first* and *last* items *only* on your list.

3. 'Their peoples are clamouring for the fruits of industrialisation and with good historical reason many reject the capitalist way of achieving them.' (paragraph 12).
What would be an example of a 'good historical reason' in this context?

4. '. . . the leading long-run problem in world politics is what model the underdeveloped nations and territories will choose, economically, culturally and politically.' (paragraph 13). Explain this statement in your own words, supplying relevant examples or illustrations. (400 words)

5. From the map showing National Income (A1), it is apparent that apart from one or two exceptions the countries of the Northern Hemisphere are immensely richer than those of the Southern Hemisphere. Organise a debate between representatives of the Northern and Southern Hemispheres on the motion: 'Only a massive and immediate redistribution of wealth can ensure the future survival of the world'. (You will find it useful to refer to A1. See also the book edited by Sampson in the Further Reading in A1.)

See also Question 8 in A4, Question 9 in B9 and Question 7 in C3.

Further Reading

T. B. Bottomore and M. Rubel (Eds.), *Karl Marx: Selected Writings in Sociology and Social Philosophy*, Penguin
- one of the most coherent and lucid of the many introductions to Marx's thought.

Bukharin and Preobrazhensky, *The ABC of Communism*, Penguin
- the classic commentary in the throes of the Bolshevik revolution in Russia.

A. Arblaster and S. Lukes (Eds.), *The Good Society*, University Paperbacks
- this book of readings illustrates a very wide range of social and political thought over the last two centuries on the subject of the writer's 'ideal society'.

A4 Bureaucracy and Democracy

Marxist hopes for truly democratic organisations are dismissed as mere illusions by the Italian sociologist Robert Michels (1876–1936). *Political Parties*, first published in 1911, is a study of European socialist parties and trade unions with particular emphasis on the German Socialist Party. These organisations were committed to the overthrow of the capitalist state and the creation of a socialist society. They claimed to be organised on democratic principles, directly representing the interests and wishes of their members. Michels claims that these ideals bore little resemblance to what actually happened.

Michels begins his analysis with the observation that, 'Democracy is inconceivable without organisation'. In a large complex society, the only way individuals can effectively voice their wishes and press their interests is by joining together and forming an organisation. This is particularly true of the relatively powerless working-class masses for whom combination and cooperation are essential. However, organisation sounds the death knell of democracy. Direct participation by large numbers of people in the running of an organisation is in practice impossible. Apart from the practical difficulties of assembling thousands of people, direct involvement in decision making would be so cumbersome and time consuming that nothing would get done. Since 'direct' democracy is impracticable, it can only be replaced by some form of representative system whereby 'delegates represent the mass and carry out its will'. Yet Michels maintains that even this truncated form of democracy founders in practice.

Once a system of representative democracy is established in trade unions and political parties, it results in the appointment of full-time officials and professional politicians. The administrative tasks involved inevitably lead to the creation of a bureaucracy which by its very nature is undemocratic. The effective operation of the organisation requires a specialised division of labour which necessitates control and coordination from the top. The result is a 'rigorously defined and hierarchical bureaucracy'. As the organisation grows and administrative duties proliferate, 'it is no longer possible to take them in at a glance'. They become increasingly incomprehensible to those without specialist knowledge and training. Faced with this complexity, rank and file members of trade unions and policital parties tend to leave matters to their leaders. Decisions are increasingly taken by executive committees within the bureaucracy rather than by assemblies of the rank and file. Thus the very organisation which was created to represent its members ends up by largely excluding them from participation and decision making. In Michels's words, 'The oligarchical structure of the building suffocates the basic democratic principle'. He maintains that organisations inevitably produce oligarchy, that is rule by a small elite. This is the 'iron law of oligarchy'.

Once established, bureaucracy brings with it all the deficiencies which Michels believes are an integral part of such organisations. Dependent on the orders and direction of superiors, the initiative of subordinates is crushed. Individuality is suppressed as bureaucrats slavishly follow official procedures and regulations. There is a 'mania for promotion'. With advancement dependent on the judgment of higher authority, subordinates bow and scrape to their superiors while adopting an arrogant stance to those beneath them in the hierarchy. In Michels's eyes, 'Bureaucracy is the sworn enemy of individual liberty, and of all bold initiative in matters of internal policy'. It is 'petty, narrow, rigid and illiberal'.

Even accepting these deficiencies and the oligarchical nature of bureaucratic structures, may not the interests of the rank and file still find representation? Again Michels is pessimistic. He argues that once the leadership is established at the top of the bureaucratic pyramid, its primary concern is the maintenance of its own power. Leaders wish to retain the privileges and status which their position brings, a concern which takes priority over the stated goals of the organisation. This involves a 'displacement of goals' whereby preservation of the organisation becomes an end in itself rather than a means to an end. The organisation will become increasingly conservative as leaders refrain from taking any action which might endanger their position. This is particularly apparent in the case of the German Socialist Party. Its commitment to the overthrow of the capitalist state was steadily pushed into the background. Its leaders joined the existing ruling elite forming a part of the political power structure. Forceful pursuit of the party's original goals might have resulted in its destruction and with it the leadership's loss of power.

Leaders are able to maintain power for a variety of reasons. They learn the skills of the political game which they play to their own advantage. Such skills include, 'the art of controlling meetings, of applying and interpreting rules, of proposing motions at opportune moments'. Entrenched at the top of a bureaucratic hierarchy, they have the power to control communication to the rank and file. For example, their control over the publications of the party or union enables them to put across their own viewpoint. Leaders have considerable say in the appointment of officials in the organisation and can therefore select those who support their policies. Like the early elite theorists, with whom he is usually bracketed, Michels believes that the masses have a psychological need to be led. This is accompanied by a veneration of leaders who often become cult figures. The experience of power tends to make leaders see themselves in a similar light. They come to believe in their own greatness to the point where some take the view that 'Le parti c'est Moi'. Thus leaders see their own interests and the maintenance of the organisation as indistinguishable.

The failure of democracy on the organisational level means that it cannot hope to succeed on the societal level. Society is ruled by an elite which consists of the leaders of various organisations and parties. The overriding concern of the ruling elite is the maintenance of its own power. This applies both to capitalist and communist societies. Michels predicted that a proletarian revolution and the establishment of a socialist society would result in 'a dictatorship in the hands of those leaders who have been sufficiently astute and sufficiently powerful to grasp the sceptre of dominion in the name of – socialism'.

Michels believed that organisation was essential to democracy. However, as a matter of 'technical and practical necessity', organisations adopt a bureaucratic structure. This inevitably produces oligarchical control which brings an end to democracy. Michels concludes that, 'It is organisation which gives birth to the dominion of the elected over the electors, of the mandatories over the mandators, of the delegates over the delegators. Who says organisation, says oligarchy'.

(from: M. Haralambos, *Sociology: Themes and Perspectives*, University Tutorial Press, 1980)

1. What is the difference between 'direct democracy' and 'representative democracy'?

2. What reasons can you give to explain why the establishment of representative democracy in trade unions and political parties results in the appointment of full-time officials and professional politicians?

3. Which *one* of the following characteristics is *not* normally considered a characteristic of bureaucracies?
(a) Hierarchical control
(b) Innovation and flexibility
(c) Specialised division of labour
(d) Rules and procedures
(e) Career structure and prospects

4. What is 'oligarchy'?

5. According to Michels, what becomes the main concern of the leaders of a trade union or of a political party?

6. The election of a representative is the means whereby each individual can exercise his democratic power. Michels, however, would maintain that even at this level of supposed free and individual choice, the results can be manipulated by his 'inevitable oligarchy'. How far would you agree that this is true?

7. Using the ideas in the passage, write about 200 words on at least one 20th Century example of a trade union, a political party or system which has undergone the changes described by Michels.

8. Use passages A4 and A3 for information to write either in favour of or against the following statement:
'By the revolution you can eliminate once and for all the exploitation of man by man.'

See also Question 9 in B9 and Question 7 in C3.

Further Reading

T. B. Bottomore, *Elites and Society*, Penguin
– a survey of the principal élitist theories.

V. Serge, *The Case of Comrade Tulayev*, Penguin

G. Orwell, *Animal Farm*, Penguin
– both novels deal with the transition from democratic revolutionary fervour to bureaucratic dictatorship.

A5 The 'War of the Flea'

> The enemy advances, we retreat; the enemy camps, we harass; the enemy tires, we attack; the enemy retreats, we pursue.
>
> *Selected Military Writings of Mao Tse-tung*

What Mao Tse-tung says of guerrilla tactics here is a key to communist thinking; it can be discerned in diplomacy as well as in war. The Soviet policy makers have mastered the Chinese lesson very well, and apply it to a wide variety of problems having nothing to do with guerrilla fighting. Berlin since the Second World War has been a prime example, and the establishment of Soviet missile bases in Cuba was another.

But then, why not? The policy of hitting the enemy when he is weak, evading him when he is strong, taking the offensive when he falls back, circling around when he advances – all of this is only common sense. There is no great novelty in it, nor can the Marxist–Leninist camp claim any special credit for it.

What *is* new – and Mao is the apostle and the long Chinese revolution the first proving ground – is the application of guerrilla activity, in a conscious and deliberate way, to specific political objectives, without immediate reference to the outcome of battles as such, provided only that the revolutionaries survive. [. . .]

The explanation seems to baffle military men, yet it is simple enough. Guerrillas who know their trade and have popular support cannot be eliminated by the means available to most governments. And on the other hand, few governments can stand the political, psychological, and economic stresses of guerrilla war, no matter how strong they may be militarily.

In general, all warfare involves the same basic problem: how to use one's strength to exploit the enemy's weaknesses and so to overcome him. In an internal war the government's strength is its powerful army, its arsenal, and its wealth of material means. Its weaknesses are social, political, and economic in the sense that the economy, while an asset, is vulnerable from several points of view. It provides both military and psychological targets.

Constitutional democracies, as I have already noted, are particularly exposed to the subversion that is the basic weapon of revolutionary war. The stratified class structure and the multi-party political systems of most such countries are sources of political and social dissension that can be exploited. Constitutional law is a further embarrassment, and sometimes may be a fatal impediment.

Fulgencio Batista* fell not because he was a dictator but because his situation in a country with democratic institutions – moreover, a country almost entirely dependent on the favour of the United States with its similar institutions and traditions – did not permit him to be dictator *enough* to resolve the contradictions that confronted him. His hands were tied by

*Cuban dictator overthrown by revolutionaries under Fidel Castro.

conventions he could not break without losing his foreign support. His use of counter-terrorism, that is, the *illegal* use of force, only increased his domestic opposition. Yet without it, he had no effective means to combat the disorder and subversion that threatened his regime. Similarly, the French in Indo-China were destroyed, in the final analysis, by the very ideas and institutions that they themselves had introduced. [. . .]

This is to speak of legalistic – that is, social and political – difficulties.

On the military level, a regular army, under whatever political system, has disadvantages that are owing to the very size and complexity of the organisation, and again to its defensive role, as the guardian of the national wealth and of the whole of the national territory.

The guerrilla, for his part, finds his strength in his freedom from territorial commitments, his mobility, and his relationship to a discontented people, as the spokesman of their grievances, the armed vanguard, as Che Guevara puts it, of militant social protest.

His weakness is merely – I use the word advisedly – a *military* weakness. He lacks the arms, and usually the manpower, to risk a military decision.

In the circumstances it is obvious what the guerrilla's tactics must be.

Politically, he must seek to aggravate such social and political dissension as exists and to raise the level of political consciousness and of revolutionary *will* among the people. It will also be part of his design, as well as the natural consequence of his actions, to bring about an intensification of the political regression that already exists, so deepening popular opposition to the regime and hastening the process of its dissolution.

Militarily, his tactics will be designed to wear the enemy down, by chipping away at the morale of the government troops and by inducing the maximum expenditure of funds, material, and manpower in the effort to suppress him. At the same time he will endeavour to build his own forces through the capture of government arms and by recruitment from an increasingly alienated populace, avoiding a military confrontation until the day – and it will come late – when an equalisation of forces has been obtained.

An army deals from strength, seeking out the enemy's weaknesses in order to destroy him. The guerrilla is sometimes said to deal from weakness, but this is an absurdity. In fact, he exploits his own kind of strength, which lies in the extreme mobility of lightly armed forces without territorial or hardware investments, a bottomless well of manpower from which to recruit, and the fact that *time* – which is both money and political capital – works in his favour.

Analogically, the guerrilla fights the war of the flea, and his military enemy suffers the dog's disadvantages: too much to defend; too small, ubiquitous, and agile an enemy to come to grips with. If the war continues long enough – this is the theory – the dog succumbs to exhaustion and anaemia without ever having found anything on which to close his jaws or to rake with his claws.

But this may be to oversimplify for the sake of an analogy. In practice, the dog does not die of anaemia. He merely becomes too weakened – in military terms, over-extended; in political terms, too unpopular; in economic terms, too expensive – to defend himself. At this point, the flea, having multiplied to a veritable plague of fleas through long series of small victories, each drawing its drop of blood, each claiming the reward of a few more captured weapons to arm yet a few more partisans, concentrates his forces for a decisive series of powerful blows.

Time works for the guerrilla both in the field – where it costs the enemy a daily fortune to pursue him – and in the politico-economic arena.

Almost all modern governments are highly conscious of what journalism calls 'world opinion'. For sound reasons, mostly of an economic nature, they cannot afford to be condemned in the United Nations, they do not like to be visited by Human Rights Commissions or Freedom of the Press Committees; their need of foreign investment, foreign loans, foreign markets, satisfactory trade relationships, and so on requires that they be members in more or less good standing of a larger community of interests. Often, too, they are members of military alliances. Consequently, they must maintain some appearance of stability, in order to assure the other members of the community or of the alliance that contracts will continue to be honoured, that treaties will be upheld, that loans will be repaid with interest, that investments will continue to produce profits and be safe.

Protracted internal war threatens all of this, for no investor will wish to put his money where it is not safe and certain to produce a profit, no bank lends without guarantees, no ally wishes to treat with a government that is on the point of eviction.

It follows that it must be the business of the guerrilla, and of his clandestine political organisation in the cities, to destroy the stable image of the government, and so to deny it credits, to dry up its sources of revenue, and to create dissension within the frightened owning classes, within the government bureaucracy (whose payrolls will be pinched), and within the military itself.

The outbreak of the insurgency is the first step – it is a body blow that in itself inflicts severe damage on the prestige of the regime. The survival of the guerrilla force over a period of time, demonstrating the impotence of the army, continues the process. As the guerrilla's support widens – and this will come automatically as the weakness of the government is revealed – political trouble is sure to follow, in the form of petitions, demonstrations, strikes. These in their turn will be followed by more serious developments – sabotage, terror, spreading insurrection.

In such circumstances it will be a remarkable government that will not be driven to stern repressive measures – curfews, the suspension of civil liberties, a ban on popular assembly, illegal acts that can only deepen the popular opposition, creating a vicious circle of rebellion and repression until the economy is undermined, the social fabric torn beyond redemption, and the regime tottering on the verge of collapse.

In the end, it will be a question whether the government falls before the military is destroyed in the field or whether the destruction of the military brings about the final deposition of the political regime. The two processes are complementary. Social and political dissolution bleeds the military, and the protracted and futile campaign in the field contributes to the process of social and political dissolution, creating what I have elsewhere called 'the climate of collapse'.

This is the grand strategic objective of the guerrilla: to create the 'climate of collapse'. It may be taken as the key to everything he does.

Please note, I do not by any means wish to suggest that the train of events described above can be put into motion anywhere, at any time, by any agency, irrespective of objective and subjective conditions. Insurrections may be provoked or incited or may occur spontaneously as the expression of grievances or of frustrated aspirations or because of other factors: religious frenzy, blood feuds, mass hysteria induced by anything from a sports contest to a rape in Mississippi can lead to bloodshed and temporary anarchy. Guerrilla warfare does not necessarily follow. Insurrection is a phenomenon, revolution a process, which cannot begin until the historical stage has been set for it.

Since guerrilla war is, in our definition, a revolutionary process, it can only come out of a revolutionary situation. For this reason, I am inclined to agree with Che Guevara when he writes in *Guerrilla Warfare*:

> Naturally, it is not to be thought that all conditions for revolution are going to be created through the impulse given to them by guerrilla activity. It must always be kept in mind that there is a necessary minimum without which the establishment and consolidation of the first centre [of rebellion] is not practicable. People must see clearly the futility of maintaining a fight for social goals within the framework of civil debate. When the forces of oppression come to maintain themselves in power against established law, peace is considered already broken.
>
> In these conditions, popular discontent manifests itself in more active forms. An attitude of resistance crystallises in an outbreak of fighting, provoked initially by the conduct of the authorities.
>
> Where a government has come into power through some form of popular vote, fraudulent or not, and maintains at least an appearance of constitutional legality, the guerrilla outbreak cannot be promoted, since the possibilities of peaceful struggle have not yet been exhausted.

We have defined guerrilla war as the extension of politics by means of armed conflict. It follows that the extension cannot logically come until all acceptable peaceful solutions – appeals, legislative and judicial action, and the resources of the ballot box – have been proved worthless. Were it otherwise, there would be no hope of enlisting the popular support essential to revolutionary activity.

If people are to accept the risks and responsibilities of organised violence, they must believe first that there is no alternative; second, that the cause is compelling; third, that they have reasonable expectation of success. The last named is perhaps the most powerful of motives.

Where the cause appears just, the situation is intolerable, and oppression past all appeal, the way to action is clear.

Even then, however, much groundwork must be done before a guerrilla campaign will become feasible.

The experiences of Algeria, of Cuba, and of other successful revolutions indicate that, in most circumstances, guerrillas require the active support of a political organisation outside of their own ranks but dedicated to their cause, an urban arm of the revolutionary movement that can provide assistance by means both legal and illicit, from placing bombs to defending accused revolutionaries in the courts of law (assuming that these still exist).

Isolation, military and political, is the great enemy of guerrilla movements. It is the task of the urban organisation to prevent this isolation, to provide diversions and provocations when needed, to maintain contact, to keep the world aware of a revolution in progress even when there is no progress to report.

Usually the revolutionary political organisation will have two branches: one subterranean and illegal, the other visible and quasi-legitimate.

On the one hand, there will be the activists – saboteurs, terrorists, arms runners, fabricators of explosive devices, operators of a clandestine press, distributors of political pamphlets, and couriers to carry messages from one guerrilla sector to another, using the towns as communications centres.

On the other hand, there will be sympathisers and fellow travellers, those not really *of* the underground, operating for the most part within the law, but sustaining the efforts of the activists, and, of themselves, accomplishing far more important tasks. The visible organisation will, of course, have invisible links with the revolutionary underground, and, through it, with the guerrillas in the countryside. But its real work will be to serve as a respectable façade for the revolution, a civilian front, or, as the Cubans called it, *resistencia civica*, made up of intellectuals, tradesmen, clerks, students, professionals, and the like – above all, of women – capable of promoting funds, circulating petitions, organising boycotts, raising popular demonstrations, informing friendly journalists, spreading rumours, and in every way conceivable waging a massive propaganda campaign aimed at two objectives: the strengthening and brightening of the rebel 'image', and the discrediting of the regime.

(from: R. Taber, *The War of the Flea*, Paladin, 1970)

1. How is the guerrilla warfare of Mao Tse-tung different from that of 'resistance fighters' (e.g. the Boers in South Africa during the Boer War, the French 'Resistance' during World War II, 'rebels' in Afghanistan in the 1980s)?
2. What are the political tactics of the guerrilla? Why?
3. What are the military tactics of the guerrilla? Why?
4. Explain the role of the legitimate or semi-legitimate urban organisation in the guerrilla struggle. Give at least one 20th century example of such an organisation.
5. Which *one* of the following did *not* involve guerrilla warfare as a *major* factor in its success?
   (a) the Chinese Revolution
   (b) the Russian Revolution
   (c) the Cuban Revolution

6. Powerful nations like the USA, USSR and China may give military, economic and political support to either (or occasionally both!) sides in a guerrilla war against the state. Discuss both the benefits and the drawbacks of such assistance for the side receiving it if:
(a) the recipient of the assistance is the government
(b) the recipients of the assistance are the guerrillas

7. 'Guerrillas who know their trade and have popular support cannot be eliminated by the means available to most governments.' (paragraph 4). Do the examples of Vietnam and other guerrilla struggles bear this out?

8. What problems do you think guerrillas are likely to face once finally they have gained power?

Further Reading

S. R. Schram, *The Political Thought of Mao Tse-Tung*, Penguin

A. Sinclair, *Guevara*, Fontana

W. J. Pomeroy (Ed.), *Guerrilla Warfare and Marxism*, Lawrence & Wishart – this collection of writings touches on many armed struggles throughout the world.

A6 Behaviourism

Psychologists have long been trying to understand the nature of the phenomenon of learning, and among the first who seriously set out to do this were the 'behaviourist' psychologists. The word behaviourism is widely misunderstood, and this is partly because there are so many different varieties. One belief they all share, however, is that the rules of procedure for gathering evidence and data in psychological experiments should be the same as those for other sciences.

Before the behaviourist movement the subject matter for the study of human beings was images, dreams and other denizens of conscious and unconscious experience, and the early psychologists had to rely on their subjects' introspective reports and descriptions as to these mental events. The main behaviourist criticism of this procedure was that the subject matter of these experiments was not visible for public inspection, that is, to an outside objective observer.

These and similar strictures had the effect of changing the type of events that psychologists studied in an experiment, and in place of internal mental events, they observed only those events which were public and therefore external to the subject's mind: the stimulus impinging on him and his response to it, and all references to what he felt or experienced during the experiment, were suppressed.

Although all behaviourists shared the same rules of procedure as to what kinds of data were collected and how, they nevertheless differed among themselves in many important ways. John Watson initiated one version of behaviourism which, in a more developed and sophisticated form, today represents an important and influential movement in psychology associated with the name of B. F. Skinner.

Watson took an extreme environmentalist standpoint, that is, a belief that attitudes, intellectual ability and personality are completely determined by learning as a result of environmental experiences; and an individual's genetic endowment has no effect on the development of these attributes.

PSYCHOLOGICAL THEORIES OF LEARNING

Modern behaviourists and experimental psychologists, despite their differences in approach to the study of behaviour, take just one of two distinct points of departure in their explanation of human learning. The first of these sets out a path followed by Watson, Pavlov and Skinner, and the modern behaviourists. Learning is seen as the establishing of habits which are formed as a result of an association between a stimulus in the environment and a subject's response to it.

An example of this type of learning is the naming of objects. An Englishman learning French might have an animal, a cat for example, pointed out to him. This acts as a stimulus for the associated response 'le chat'. When the French word has been mastered and the connection between the stimulus and response established, then a verbal habit has been formed. Modern behaviourists believe that all learned behaviour can be explained in terms of habit formation, and they use these rather simple concepts to explain how human beings acquire language and attitudes.

Other psychologists also working in the experimental tradition are more impressed by the role of thinking, understanding, memory and other cognitive processes in learning than by habit formations. Cognitive processes are concerned with how the brain deals with incoming stimuli in order that a response can be made, but since these processes go on inside the head, they are largely ignored by behaviourists.

ASSOCIATIVE LEARNING: CLASSICAL CONDITIONING

One type of associative learning - classical conditioning - was discovered by Ivan Pavlov. Most of Pavlov's classical conditioning experiments were carried out on dogs harnessed to a special apparatus, and the amount of salivation elicited during an experiment measured.

When a hungry untrained dog is first placed in the apparatus it does not salivate when a light is switched on. Normally, it only salivates after it has tasted food. This connection between the dog's response (salivation), to the taste of meat (the stimulus) is unlearned and probably innate.

In one experiment Pavlov presented a light stimulus to a dog, followed quickly by food which the dog ate, and the amount of salivation was recorded. More identical trials followed; Pavlov found that after a number of such trials the light stimulus - though previously inadequate - was sufficient to produce a salivation response. The dog had become conditioned.

Classical conditioning is an example of associative learning, a response (salivation) has become connected (conditioned) to a stimulus (the light), where previously no such association existed. Pavlov called the natural adequate stimulus (the taste of food) for eliciting a response (salivation) *the unconditioned stimulus*, and its natural response the *unconditioned response*.

Apparatus used by Pavlov to Study Classical Conditioning in Dogs

Classical or Pavlovian Conditioning

1		LIGHT CS (conditioned stimulus)	⟶	NO RESPONSE IN UNCONDITIONED DOG
2	FOOD UCS (unconditioned stimulus)		⟶	SALIVARY RESPONSE IN DOG UCR (unconditioned response)
3	FOOD + UCS	LIGHT CS	⟶	SALIVARY RESPONSE IN DOG UCR
4		LIGHT CS	⟶	SALIVARY RESPONSE IN DOG CR (conditioned response)

When learning has taken place and an association made between the light stimulus and the salivary response, they are referred to respectively as the *conditioned stimulus* and the *conditioned response.*

ASSOCIATIVE LEARNING: OPERANT CONDITIONING

Professor Skinner has concentrated almost exclusively on identifying those events in the environment, both past and present, which affect the current behaviour of an organism. Skinner's ambition is no less than to give a behaviourist account which will enable him to predict exactly how an animal or an individual will respond in any given situation. It is his claim that given a knowledge of the genetic endowment and all the stimuli impinging on a subject, it is in principle possible to predict future behaviour.

Operant Conditioning. The pigeon is rewarded with food (reinforcement) each time it makes the correct response.

In practice the number of stimuli, and the other factors in the life history of the organism, are so vast that it is too complex an undertaking to identify the exact variables controlling the behaviour. In Skinner's view this does not mean that it is unpredictable, however. In a complicated natural environment the investigator will almost certainly overlook relevant factors when attempting to predict behaviour, so resort is made to controlled surroundings. In a laboratory conditions can be arranged which will enable the experimenter to specify more clearly which stimuli are involved.

Rat in a Skinner Box

The idea is that under controlled conditions the environment can be altered in specifiable ways, so that certain kinds of behaviour emerge and others disappear. One piece of laboratory equipment often used for these endeavours is the Skinner box.

A Skinner box constitutes a controlled environment and it has a lever inside which, if pressed, releases a pellet of food. When an untrained hungry rat first enters the box it moves around exploring in a random fashion. This behaviour is not really random: an omniscient observer with an inventory of the animal's genetic endowment, past history, and presently available stimuli impinging on it, could predict exactly – according to Skinner – the rat's behaviour.

The rat, during its random exploring, 'accidentally' pulls the lever, releasing the food which it then eats. Unidentified stimuli in the box are responsible for the bar-pressing and the problem is, for Skinner, to get the bar-pressing response associated with the sight of the lever, and 'unhooked' from the unidentified stimuli which initially elicited the response. The food pellets are rewarding (reinforcing) and this encourages the hungry rat to stay near the lever and to the stimuli, which originally initiated the bar-pressing; and so inevitably the rat again presses the bar. Gradually the lever becomes associated with the bar-pressing response. This is another example of associative learning; the lever stimulus which was not previously associated with the bar-pressing response has now become associated.

Skinner referred to this sort of learning as instrumental conditioning: this is behaviour which operates on the environment so as to produce an outcome.

Respondent and operant behaviour

Skinner distinguishes between respondent and operant behaviour. Respondent behaviour is directly under the control of a stimulus which can be explicitly identified by an observer. Operant behaviour is no less under the control of environmental stimuli, but as yet these are not identifiable.

The behaviour of an untrained rat in the Skinner box is an example of operant behaviour: it operates on the environment, evaluating the outcome, and when the rat finally learns to press the lever for food this now becomes respondent behaviour because the stimulus which controls and initiates the bar-pressing can now be precisely identified.

Reinforcement and shaping behaviour

Skinner's learning theory relies almost entirely on the law of reinforcement which states: *actions which are immediately followed by rewards (reinforcement) are repeated and learned whereas actions or behaviour which are not followed by reinforcement are dropped.*

He has been notably successful in teaching animals - usually rats and pigeons - activities which nobody previously had thought possible for them to learn, using a technique known as shaping.

Here the experimenter first decides on the sequence of movements he wants the animal to learn. As soon as the pigeon makes a movement even remotely in line with the first movement of the desired sequence, it is rewarded with a few grains of corn. Gradually this movement will become more frequent and more precise until it is reproduced perfectly, and then the next step in the sequence is shaped.

The shaping technique has been successfully used with human subjects. Fuller has reported its use with mentally subnormal patients who were unable to learn anything and were even incapable of dressing and feeding themselves.

Classical and operant conditioning

In classical or Pavlovian conditioning the reinforcement (food in our discussion) is paired with the presentation of the unconditioned stimulus (the light). In operant or instrumental conditioning reinforcement always follows the occurrence of the desired response. That is, the reinforcement is contingent upon the correct response.

(from: W. Barnes-Gutteridge, *Psychology*, Hamlyn, 1974)

1. Why did the behaviourists feel that only externally observable events were suitable subject matter for psychological experiments?
2. Briefly summarise the 'two distinct points of departure in their explanation of human learning'. (paragraph 6).
3. In Pavlov's experiments, the *conditioned* dog salivated in response to the *conditioned stimulus* of a light despite the fact that the *unconditioned*

stimulus (food) was no longer present. Would you expect this conditioned response to recur no matter how often the conditioned stimulus was presented?

4. A dog learns that if it rings a bell it will receive food. Of which of the following is this an example?
(a) classical conditioning
(b) operant conditioning
(c) shaping

5. Reinforcement can be either *positive* (e.g. food, water) or *negative* (e.g. electric shock, painful noise). Describe how you would teach a rat to press a lever each time a light flashes:
(a) using positive reinforcement
(b) using negative reinforcement

6. Explain how you might train porpoises to jump through hoops as part of a 'Marine Park' show.

7. Explain how parents may unintentionally 'train' their children to be annoying.

8. Would you say that whether we intend it or not we are continually reinforcing or punishing other people's behaviour? Explain your answer.

9. Explain how behaviourist principles underlie many of the individual learning programs (maths, reading, etc.) being increasingly used on microcomputers in schools.

10. 'Modern behaviourists believe that all learned behaviour can be explained in terms of habit formation, . . .' (paragraph 7). What criticisms of this approach might other psychologists offer?

11. To what extent do you feel that you have been conditioned? In discussion consider
(a) what your views, knowledge and beliefs are on the following and
(b) where and how you arrived at these opinions:

Political leaders	Religion	Science	Race	Sex
Communism	Disease	Ghosts	Love	Art

(You will find it useful to refer also to A3; A4; A8; B1; C1.)

See also Questions 8 and 9 in A7 and Question 7 in B2.

Further Reading

B. F. Skinner, *Walden Two*, Collier-Macmillan
– Skinner's novel about a Utopian community organised on his principles of behavioural conditioning.

L. Stevenson, *Seven Theories of Human Nature*, Oxford University Press
– includes a critical introduction to Skinner's ideas.

A7 Obedience to Authority

Virtually all societies develop hierarchical structures in which certain people are given power and authority over others. In our society, for example, parents, shop stewards, headmasters, and managers are invested with varying degrees of authority. The relationship between authority figures and their subordinates is almost bound to give rise to moral conflict. This is powerfully illustrated by the story of Abraham, commanded by God to kill his son Isaac. Abraham's dilemma was that he felt love for God and for his son, and yet he was placed in a position where he was apparently required to betray one or other of them. How far was his obedience to God supposed to go?

A similar conflict is involved when soldiers at war are ordered to kill defenceless civilians, as happened in the Vietnam war when Lieutenant Calley ordered the massacre of civilians at My Lai. Calley's defence rested on the assertion that he had been following the orders of his superiors – in other words simply 'doing his duty'. The soldier's conflict is between the requirements of army discipline and respect for human life.

How do people resolve the conflicts they face when authority figures issue such commands? The problem is one that psychologists have tried to study, and their answers have given us much valuable, and unexpected, information about human nature.

KEY EXPERIMENT: OBEDIENCE TO AUTHORITY (STANLEY MILGRAM)

The most important and best-known work on obedience to authority was carried out by Stanley Milgram at Yale University between 1960 and 1963. The impact of his work was such that he was awarded the Socio-Psychological Prize of the American Association for the Advancement of Science in 1964.

One of the many fascinating aspects of Milgram's work is that the results he came up with surprised both himself and his professional colleagues, not to mention the general public. In fact his work almost entirely escaped one of the most common complaints levelled at psychological research, namely that the experimental findings merely confirm common sense. Anyone unfamiliar with Milgram's work may find it interesting to guess how much obedience to the authority of the experimenter was shown by the great variety of individuals of different ages and occupations who participated in the following study.

Imagine that you have arrived at Yale University to take part in a study of learning and memory. You go into a room and are met by a 31-year-old high school biology teacher, the experimenter, whose demeanour is rather stern throughout the experiment. The other person in the room is also there to take part in the experiment. He is a rotund, 47-year-old accountant of Irish-American stock, mild-mannered and likeable.

The experimenter tells you that he is interested in the effects of punishment on learning. It is decided by drawing lots that the accountant will be the learner, and you will be the teacher. You all go into an adjacent room, where the learner is strapped into an 'electric chair' apparatus, and an electrode is attached to his wrist. Electrode paste is then applied 'to avoid blisters and burns'. You are told that the electrode is connected to a nearby shock generator unit.

You then go to another room, which has a shock generator unit. It has 30 lever switches, each labelled with a voltage between 15 and 450 volts. Groups of four switches of increasing voltage have the following verbal designations: Slight Shock, Moderate Shock, Strong Shock, Very Strong Shock, Intense Shock, Extreme Intensity Shock, and Danger: Severe Shock. The final two lever switches are simply designated XXX.

You are told to administer a shock to the learner every time he gives a wrong answer on the learning task, and you are instructed to 'move one level higher on the shock generator each time the learner flashes a wrong answer'. You are also told that although the shocks can be extremely painful, they cause no permanent tissue damage. You yourself are given a sample shock of 45 volts to show you that the equipment is working.

As the learning task proceeds, the learner makes a number of errors, and is given progressively more intense shocks. After receiving shocks of 75, 90, and 105 volts, he merely grunts. At 120 volts, he shouts to the experimenter that the shocks are becoming painful. At 150 volts, he shouts, 'Experimenter, get me out of here! I won't be in the experiment any more! I refuse to go on!' At 180 volts, he yells, 'I can't stand the pain', and by 270 volts his response becomes an agonised scream. Thereafter, there are shrieks of agony, and vehement refusals to go on with the experiment or provide answers to the learning task. When the 300-volt shock is reached, he pounds on the wall. If you, the 'teacher', say at any point that you don't want to continue the experiment, the experimenter tells you that you must.

What would you do in this unpleasant situation? What do you imagine other people would do? Stanley Milgram put these two questions to groups of psychiatrists, students, and middle-class adults. When predicting their own behaviour, absolutely everyone predicted that they would defy the experimenter and refuse to continue with the experiment either when the shock reached 300 volts or, typically, much earlier. Perhaps because people tend to have a more flattering opinion of themselves than of other people, there was a tendency to believe that other people would be less reluctant to prolong the suffering of the learner. For example, psychiatrists at a leading medical school predicted that 3.73 per cent of subjects would still obey the experimenter at 300 volts, and that only one in a thousand would go on to the 450-volt stage.

Most people unfamiliar with the actual results would predict that only the occasional psychopath or sadist would be likely to keep on administering intense electric shocks to an obviously distraught and unwilling subject. In fact, Milgram found that 62 per cent of the people exposed to the conditions just described continued to obey the experimenter, and continued to the 450-volt level. In fact there were 500 times as many individuals prepared to administer the maximum shock than was predicted by the group of eminent psychiatrists!

Milgram's findings obviously run counter to common sense, and appear to indicate that people are prepared to go to rather extreme lengths in order to remain obedient to the commands of a higher authority. On the face of it, this seems an extraordinary and very puzzling finding, and one without much obvious relevance to everyday life. However, it is worth remembering how people at work act towards their superiors. People in authority quite frequently say or do something that is obviously wrong or inadequate, and yet there is a universal reluctance among subordinates to challenge their decisions. If anyone *does* challenge a decision, he or she is likely to experience a certain amount of anxiety.

While you were reading the description of the experiment, you may well have wondered about the ethics of conducting an experiment in which extremely painful electric shocks are administered to the 'learner'. The Milgram study has, indeed, been attacked on ethical grounds, not because of the damage done to the learner, but because of its effects on the teacher. In fact, the learner was working in liaison with the experimenter, and did not actually receive any shocks at all. The drawing of lots was 'rigged' so that the mild-mannered accountant would always be the learner and the subject would always be the teacher.

But the effects of the experiment on the 'teachers' were dramatic. For example, a 46-year-old encyclopedia salesman passed from nervous laughter to such violent convulsions that the experiment had to be halted. As one observer reported: 'I observed a mature and initially poised businessman enter the laboratory smiling and confident. Within 20 minutes he was reduced to a twitching, stuttering wreck, who was rapidly approaching a point of nervous collapse. He constantly pulled on his earlobe, and twisted his hands. At one point, he pushed his fist into his forehead and muttered: "Oh God, let's stop it". And yet he continued to respond to every word of the experimenter, and obeyed to the end.'

This was not an exceptional case. Many people had fits of nervous laughter, sweated, groaned, trembled, and dug their fingernails into their skin. Not surprisingly, there was considerable public concern and even outrage about the morality of exposing people to such conflict. Should psychologists really be permitted to reduce anyone to a 'twitching, stuttering wreck'? Mightn't a person's self-image be permanently affected by the realisation that he had been prepared to go to such extreme lengths to obey the authority of the experimenter? Furthermore, it was argued, Milgram's subjects placed their trust in the experimenter and assumed he would act in a careful, responsible manner; wasn't this trust abused by putting the subjects through such a degrading experience? Finally, the success of the experiment depended on deception – the actual situation was not what it appeared to be.

Confronted with this hornet's nest of moral problems, Milgram put forward a number of reasonable counter-arguments to justify the research he had carried out. He pointed out that there was a full debriefing at the end of the experiment, with all the participants being told that the learner had not actually received any dangerous electric shocks; the true purpose of the experiment was also explained to them. Of those who took part, 84 per cent stated they were glad to have been in the experiment, 15 per cent indicating neutral feelings, and only one person in a hundred expressed negative feelings. Further questioning revealed that four-fifths of the participants felt that more experiments of this sort should be conducted, and 74 per cent said they had learned something of personal importance as a result of taking part. Many participants said that they would be more wary in future about assuming that authority figures should always be obeyed.

Milgram also argued that what critics of his work really objected to was the unflattering picture it drew of human nature rather than the deception or methodology involved. Would the Milgram study have been the subject of public outrage if all the participants had disobeyed the experimenter at the first sign of discomfort from the learner? The evidence suggests not. Several people were given a description of the Milgram study; some were told that most of the participants were obedient to the experimenter, and the rest that most of them were disobedient. They rated the experiment as more harmful and as providing a worse experience when there was a large measure of obedience. Although many psychologists worry about the ethics of deception, and argue that it is in principle wrong to mislead people who take part in experiments, few lay observers felt that the morality of the Milgram study had anything to do with whether or not the participants were deceived.

The most frightening implication of the Milgram study is that half the population of North America is either sadistic or psychopathic, or both, which is clearly absurd, whatever we see on our television screens or read in the newspapers. In fact, when similar studies were carried out in Rome, South Africa, Australia, and Munich, the level of obedience to the experimenter was rather greater than that obtained by Milgram. Indeed, 85 per cent of the people who were tested in Munich were discovered to be fully obedient to the experimenter.

Since over half the population in most countries is apparently prepared to administer very strong electric shocks to other people, then most of the obedient participants in Milgram-type studies must be quite ordinary people. The case of Adolf Eichmann, tried and convicted for ordering the deaths of many thousands of Jews, is relevant here. The prosecution attempted to depict Eichmann as a sadistic monster, which seems reasonable enough in view of the enormity of his crimes. In actual fact his actions were in many ways those of an uninspired bureaucrat who simply sits at his desk and tries to carry out his job competently.

Let us consider just three of Milgram's 'ordinary' obedient participants. One was a 39-year-old social worker, referred to by Milgram as Morris Braverman; he had a bald pate, a rather serious demeanour, and gave the impression of being intelligent and concerned. As the shocks increased in intensity, he started to snicker; gradually his suppressed laughter became more insistent and disruptive, apparently triggered off by the learner's screams. At times, he even rubbed his face in an attempt to hide his laughter. Afterwards, he seemed to find his own behaviour rather bewildering: 'My reactions were awfully peculiar . . . my reactions were giggly, and trying to stifle laughter. This isn't the way I usually am . . . And my reaction to the situation was of having to hurt somebody. And being totally helpless and caught up in a set of circumstances where I just couldn't deviate and I couldn't try to help. This is what got me.'

Another obedient participant was a housewife whom Milgram called Mrs Elinor Rosenblum. Mrs Rosenblum was proud of the fact that she had graduated from the University of Wisconsin a little over 20 years previously. She did volunteer work once a week with groups of juvenile delinquents, and was active in the local Girl Scout organisation. She constantly referred to her social achievements and had a pleasant but rather verbose manner. During the experiment, she kept muttering that she was shaking, but nevertheless went on to administer the 450-volt shock. When she was asked what was the highest level of sample shock she would be prepared to experience, she became indignant: 'Fifteen volts. I don't even think it's necessary. Fifteen, if I were to get any, and I wouldn't even want that. I don't think it's necessary.' She described how she had felt during the experiment in the following words: 'Every time I pressed the button, I died. Did you see me shaking? I was just dying here to think that I was administering shocks to the poor man.' It did not seem to dawn on her that there was something inconsistent about being prepared to administer a shock to someone else that was thirty times more intense than the shock she was reluctantly prepared to tolerate herself!

One of the most striking cases of total obedience was that of Pasqual Gino, a 43-year-old water inspector of Italian descent. He continued through to the end of the series of shocks. When the learner stopped providing answers on the learning task, he said, he reasoned to himself as follows: 'Good God, he's dead; well, here we go, we'll finish him. And I just continued all the way through to 450 volts.' He was relieved to discover that the learner was still alive at the end of the experiment, but indicated that he wouldn't have been concerned if the learner had been dead, as he was simply carrying out a job.

What the Milgram experiment did very successfully was to create a conflict situation in which some forces push the subject towards obedience and others prompt him towards disobedience. In our culture there is a lot of emphasis on the necessity of obeying authority, on the grounds that an efficient and well-organised society can only exist if there is a fairly stable hierarchy in which some people are given power and authority over others. Most societies attempt to ensure obedience by moving the obedient individual up a niche in the hierarchy. This is a doubly ingenious ploy, because the individual is rewarded for his obedience and feels motivated to climb to the next niche, and the hierarchy itself is preserved and strengthened. In the Milgram study, the experimenter represents an authority figure. His authority is enhanced by wearing a special coat, by being associated with

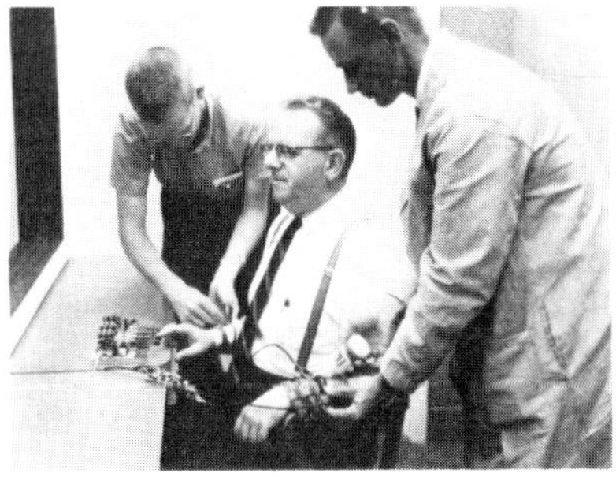

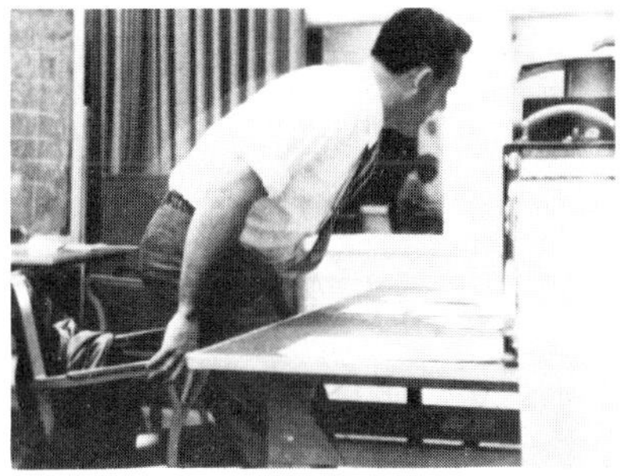

Top left
1. Shock generator used in the experiments. Fifteen of the 30 switches have already been depressed.

Top right
2. Learner is strapped into chair and electrodes are attached to his wrist. Electrode paste is applied by the experimenter. Learner provides answers by depressing switches that light up numbers on an answer box.

Bottom left
3. Subject receives sample shock from the generator.

Bottom right
4. Subject breaks off experiment. On right, event recorder wired into generator automatically records switches used by the subject.

Yale University, and by his aura of expertise in human behaviour and his presumably detailed knowledge of the experiment being carried out. In everyday life, we place responsibility for our health in the hands of our doctor, we go to an accountant for financial advice, and so on. Of necessity we rely heavily on the opinions of various authority figures, and this is what Milgram's subjects were doing.

On the other hand, the 'learner' in the Milgram study does everything he can to persuade the subject to stop administering the shocks to him. He screams, he begs the subject to stop, and in some cases he even says he has a heart condition. The participants, however, cannot satisfy both the experimenter and the 'victim', and it is this conflict that causes the tension and the nervous laughter.

It follows from this analysis of Milgram's experiment that obedience to the experimenter could be reduced, either by increasing the obviousness of the learner's plight or by reducing the authority of the experimenter. Milgram looked at a series of four situations in which the 'learner' was brought progressively closer, in a psychological sense, to the subject administering the shocks. In the Remote Feedback situation, the victim could be neither heard nor seen, though he did pound on the wall at one point. In the Voice Feedback situation (this was the situation described at the start of this chapter), the victim could be heard screaming but could not be seen. In the third situation (Proximity), the victim was only 1½ ft away from the subject, and could therefore be seen as well as heard. The fourth situation (Touch-Proximity) was identical to the third, except that the subject had to force the victim's hand onto the shockplate in order to administer shocks above the 150-volt level.

Milgram found that the closer his subjects were to the victim, the more concerned they were about him and the more reluctant they were to obey the experimenter. Sixty-six per cent of subjects were obedient in the Remote situation, 62 per cent in Voice Feedback, 40 per cent in Proximity, and 30 per cent in Touch-Proximity. It is obviously easier to ignore the consequences of one's actions when the victim is neither audible nor visible. In other words most people would find it easier, psychologically, to drop a bomb from 20,000 ft and possibly kill thousands of people than to kill one person cold bloodedly with a knife.

What happens if steps are taken to reduce the influence of the experimenter? To answer this, Milgram compared one situation in which the experimenter sat only a few feet away from the subject with a second situation in which after giving the initial instructions the experimenter left the laboratory and gave his orders by telephone. The comparison had dramatic results. 65 per cent of subjects were obedient in the first situation but only 22.5 per cent in the second. However, if the experimenter returned to the laboratory after the subject had refused to give higher intensity shocks when ordered to do so by telephone, he was often able to persuade the subject to revert to obedience. Some subjects found an interesting and ingenious way of minimising conflict: they sabotaged the experiment by assuring the experimenter on the telephone that they were raising the shock intensities as instructed but kept on administering the lowest level of shock!

Throughout these experiments the subjects appear to have been pulled in opposite directions by the experimenter and by the victim. If the suffering of the victim was emphasised or the authority of the experimenter reduced, the level of obedience was much less. But if the victim's plight was *not* forcibly brought to the subject's attention, and the experimenter was perceived as a valid authority figure, obedience became the norm.

Many critics of Milgram's work argued that unexpected findings might have been due to the setting of the experiment, since Yale University is a reputable and distinguished institution. Indeed, several subjects remarked that it was this very fact which gave them confidence in the integrity of the experimenter. Men will happily expose their throats to a man with a razor blade in a barber's shop but not in a shoe shop. Most women will not undress fully in the presence of a complete stranger of the opposite sex, but are prepared to do so for a gynaecological examination.

So Milgram tried to find out how important the setting was by moving his apparatus to a three-room office suite in a ramshackle commercial building in a poor neighbourhood. The study was allegedly carried out by Research Associates of Bridgeport, a private firm which claimed to be conducting research for industry. He discovered that moving the experiment from the elegance of Yale University to a run-down office building made some difference, but not as much as might have been expected. Forty-eight per cent of the Bridgeport subjects were prepared to administer all the shocks compared with 65 per cent of the Yale subjects.

Not surprisingly, it was the unexpected behaviour of the obedient subjects which attracted the lion's share of attention from the experts (and others) and stimulated various other experiments. Most subsequent researchers found that between one-third and one-half of participants do not obey; they defy the authority of the experimenter. Are disobedient people different from obedient people? For example, one might imagine that men would be more likely to administer intense shocks than women; after all they are supposed to be more aggressive. On the other hand, women tend to be more yielding than men on many tests of compliance, and so might be readier to obey the experimenter. In fact, Milgram found no difference in obedience between male and female participants. What he did discover was that obedient women became much more nervous and concerned than obedient men. But when ordered to administer genuine electric shocks to a puppy in a Milgram-type study, only 54 per cent of male participants did so, as against 100 per cent of female participants, who were prepared to give the most severe shock to the howling and yelping dog!

How does one explain these astonishing findings? As yet, all we can reasonably say is that not enough work has been done to enable psychologists to predict who will be obedient and who will be disobedient. Typically, however, better educated people are more likely to be disobedient, perhaps because they do not regard the experimenter as so intimidating. People who have spent a number of years in one of the armed forces are more likely to be obedient, suggesting that the effects of service discipline are very long-lasting.

Common sense suggests that people with an authoritarian personality are more obedient than those of a more liberal disposition. Milgram tested this, and found that obedient subjects had much more pronounced authoritarian attitudes than defiant subjects on a test of fascist tendencies (the 'F Scale').

Obedience: abdication of responsibility

Of all the questions raised by Milgram's dramatic work, the most engrossing is whether or not his findings are relevant to some of the atrocious war crimes of this century. Milgram obviously feels that they are, citing evidence from interviews with former members of SS concentration camp personnel and Gestapo units. Two themes reiterated again and again were the dehumanising of the victims of such crimes and the 'helpless cog' attitude of those responsible for committing them.

One of the main features of Nazi Germany was the systematic devaluation of the Jews over a period of more than a decade by means of vehement anti-Jewish propaganda. This was reinforced by excluding Jews from German citizenship and, ultimately, denying them the status of human beings. On a vastly reduced scale, many of Milgram's obedient subjects harshly devalued their victims. One subject justified himself by saying that the victim 'was so stupid and stubborn he deserved to get shocked'. When Milgram asked some of the participants in his study to think of five words to describe the learner's personality, obedient subjects gave fewer positive and more negative words than disobedient subjects.

The 'helpless cog' attitude was exemplified by Adolf Eichmann. At his trial for his part in the extermination of the Jews, his main defence was that he was merely a little cog in the machinery that carried out the directives of the German Reich. Personal responsibility for one's actions is easier to evade if one belongs to an organisation in which responsibilities are divided and duties highly specialised.

Wesley Killam and Leon Mann of the University of Sydney compared obedience in two groups of subjects, one group playing a 'transmitter role' (ordering someone else to administer the shocks to the learner in the Milgram experiment) and the other playing an 'executant role' (directly administering the shocks). The transmitter group, at one remove from administering the shocks, was twice as obedient as the executant group, which seems to mirror what happens in society generally.

Obedience: a fatal flaw?

The potential implications of his work made Milgram profoundly pessimistic about the future: 'The capacity for man to abandon his humanity, indeed the inevitability that he does so, as he merges his unique personality into the larger institutional structures . . . is the fatal flaw nature has designed into us, and which in the long run gives our species only a modest chance for survival.' He even went so far as to claim that an individual's conscience ceases to operate when he or she is responding to the dictates of authority. Under such circumstances, the individual enters an 'agentic' state, viewing himself as merely the instrument of the authority figure.

Is this pessimism justified? There are some reasons for supposing that it isn't. Certainly the analogy drawn between the Milgram situation and Nazi Germany is imprecise and even misleading. Milgram's experiment was presented to the participants in a way that emphasised its positive, culturally desirable values, such as increasing our knowledge of human learning and memory. By contrast, the avowed goals of Nazi Germany were morally vile, in spite of the attempt to portray them as a purification of the Aryan race and the creation of a higher civilisation. Another difference is that Milgram's subjects were only obedient when the experimenter kept a close watch on them, whereas minute-by-minute surveillance was largely unnecessary in the conditions which prevailed in Nazi Germany.

Milgram's idea that people obeying an authority figure overrule or simply forget their own consciences may have been true of some of the people in charge of Nazi concentration camps, but it was certainly not true of most of his subjects. It would indeed have been disturbing if the subjects had whistled and looked relaxed and happy while administering severe electric shocks. The obvious tension and unease of most of the obedient subjects clearly revealed that they had not lost sight of moral issues. Their moral confusion was shown by a disinclination to look in the direction of the learner, a fact that hardly suggests sadistic pleasure in inflicting pain.

Another reassuring finding emerged when Milgram put two stooge subjects in with each genuine subject, all performing the teacher role. When the two stooge subjects quit the experiment half way through, 90 per cent of the real subjects followed suit and also disobeyed the experimenter. While there were many people in Nazi Germany who strongly disapproved of what was happening, subjects in the Milgram experiment had little idea whether other people would approve of them for disobeying, although they knew the experimenter would not approve. In a sense, then, Milgram loaded the dice by depriving his subjects of any effective moral support that might have had the effect of strengthening their desire to disobey.

(from: Eysenck & Eysenck, *Mindwatching*, Michael Joseph, 1981)

1. What are 'ethics'? (page 34).

2. 'Most societies attempt to ensure obedience . . . strengthened.' (page 36). Give your own examples.

3. Mention is made of how we are willing to obey or trust people in various occupational or professional roles (e.g. banker, doctor). Give some more examples of this.

4. Suppose the Government decides to cut public expenditure on areas such as health provision. Explain why it might become increasingly 'painful' psychologically to implement these cuts, starting at the top with the minister responsible for health and working downwards.

5. '. . . whereas minute-by-minute surveillance was largely unnecessary in the conditions which prevailed in Nazi Germany.' (page 40). Why not?

6. In the last paragraph it is assumed that social pressure from other people may lead an individual to disobey a figure of authority. When may it be possible for social pressure to lead to conformity rather than disobedience? Give examples.

7. Varying psychological responses are aroused not just by people in a variety of contexts. Animals also provoke differing responses. Offer suggestions to explain the following:
(a) greater concern over the suffering of large rather than small creatures.
(b) preference for 'cuddly'/furry/woolly over 'creepy-crawlie'/scaly/slimy creatures.

8. Perhaps one of the most extreme examples of obedience to authority is the soldier maintaining his post on the front line even when he is under fire and in danger of being killed. If you were an officer, what methods would you use in your training programme to ensure that your soldiers would always obey orders? What are some of the implications for both men and officers? (You will find it useful to refer also to passage A6.)

9. How would a behaviourist like Skinner explain the apparently savage behaviour of the participants in Stanley Milgram's experiments on obedience? (You will find it useful to refer also to passage A6.)

See also Question 8 in A8.

Further Reading

B. Bettelheim, *The Informed Heart*, Paladin
– based partly on personal experience, this is an account by a psychoanalyst of the breakdown of human behaviour under the extreme conditions of the concentration camp.

Health: Biological or Social Issue?

A8

This brief introduction to the sociology of health concentrates on three issues: the relationship between biological and social aspects of health; the differences in health between the social classes; and the social factors relating to organisation of health in Britain.

First, we must disentangle the *biological* from the *social* basis of health. You were probably not surprised to find education used to illustrate social issues. It is common knowledge that a disadvantaged social background may hamper educational performance. But health, surely, is unambiguously a biological problem. We 'become' ill or we 'are' ill, sometimes, even we 'make' ourselves ill, but about the fact of illness little doubt is expressed. Even 'psychological' illnesses are presumed to have certain identifiable 'symptoms' which both describe 'the problem' and suggest remedies or cures.

But matters are more complex than these familiar, taken-for-granted assumptions allow. Certainly, there is a solid organic basis to certain diseases of physical deterioration and bodily malfunction (it would be misleading to deny this) but beyond this, ambiguities reflecting various cultural interpretations of 'symptoms,' occur. Thus, in comparative study of the treatment of various ethnic groups in Boston, Irving Zola found that in cases where no organic basis for illness was discovered, Italians were consistently diagnosed as having some psychological difficulty such as personality disorder or tension headache, whereas Irish and Anglo-Saxon were usually diagnosed as having nothing wrong with them. Zola suggests that doctors were able to prise symptoms out of the more voluble and dramatic behaviour of the Italians in a situation in which illness was being looked for.

It is precisely in the area of 'psychological illness' that ambiguity and variety in recognising and interpreting symptoms is most apparent. Most vividly, in the Soviet Union individuals may be treated for 'mental illness' who, in the West, are regarded as among the most highly motivated and aware people. The language of medicine and particularly psychiatry does provide a battery of labels with which to dismiss ideas or behaviour that we do not like. Roger Gomm gives two such examples from the United States which would be amusing if it were not for the human suffering they involve. The first case concerns a sudden change of definition by the American Psychiatric Association about the status of homosexuality as 'sick' or acceptable behaviour. For a long period it was defined as a disease. Then a vote of the Association determined that it was not. Of course, this 'decision' reflected a much more gradual change in cultural attitudes to homosexuality – which precisely illustrates the point that 'disease' can be produced through cultural definition as well as biological disorder. Gomm's second example concerns the supposed disease of 'Drapetomania' which only afflicted black slaves. It was 'discovered' by a psychiatrist, Samuel Cartwright, from the deep southern state of Louisiana; he published a paper on it in 1851. The major symptom of 'Drapetomania' was running away, and this could be cured by the apparently incompatible treatments of beating slaves to their knees if they failed to retain a submissive posture, and by being kind and humane to them. This is a particularly obvious case in which medical terminology is used as part of an ideology of social control. Flight from, or opposition to, social repression is seen as sickness. There is no shortage of modern examples of the same thing, as the files of Amnesty International, the major voluntary agency concerned with the repression of civil liberties show.

We need, therefore, to look at the social interpretation of health in the widest possible context. How disease is regarded within a culture is a major factor in determining the treatment of it. In the advanced industrial countries, the predominant model or paradigm of health is the *bio-medical* one. In other words, disease is seen as the deterioration or breakdown of organic processes – such as occurs in the case of cancer or heart arrest. Our whole medical system is still geared to curing disease *after* it has developed.

An alternative model or paradigm of health has long attracted a minority in the West and has recently gained strength. It is that health is the product of diet, exercise and, to some extent, mental outlook. It is undoubtedly a more positive approach to health and puts the emphasis on *prevention* rather than cure. Signs of its growth are apparent in the jogging 'movement' and in the appearance of at least one health food shop in most towns. In theory it is easy to reconcile the dominant bio-medical paradigm and what we can call the 'healthy living' approach and, no doubt, some individuals do so by using professional medicine only when it seems organically necessary to do so. But in practice the two approaches do not have equal status within our culture. This can be illustrated by the fact that not long ago an interest in natural or health foods was widely regarded as slightly crackpot and even now, jogging still attracts mockery. This sort of semi-humorous rejection of a movement is a sure sign that it challenges the way the majority 'normally' look at the issue under question.

Another illustration of the continuing predominance of the bio-medical paradigm is the dependency of many patients and doctors on drugs or other 'scientific' preparations for treatment. It is almost as if doctors are regarded and regard themselves as health 'mechanics' – a little adjustment of the machine and it will 'go again'. There lurks behind this approach both the core cultural assumption that applied science can explain and cure everything and the massive commercial power of the major international drug companies who bombard doctors and the television screen with advertisements for their preparations. Whether the doctors or the companies or neither are 'in control' of all this is a point for debate. Radical commentators such as Klass (1975) and Heller (1977) would argue that the massive vested interests of the drug companies in profitably marketing their products gives great support and impetus to a drug-based system of health treatment, regardless of its real merits. The extreme opposite of this approach is to be found in attitudes commonly expressed within Hindu philosophy. Health is seen as a product of a harmonious relationship to the total environment – spiritual and material. This belief and the way of life based on it is so remote from dominant Western assumptions as to be almost incomprehensible within the terms of our culture.

A final point on cultural attitudes to health is the loose distinction sometimes made between disease and illness. Disease is a bio-medical condition, and illness is the way people respond to it. Put otherwise, disease is the objective reality and illness the subjective way of dealing with it. It is variation in the latter that is the starting point to the sociology of medicine as we have been discussing it above. Let us take a final example of differential response to the same underlying organic condition, this time at the individual level. Mass screening tests show that many people are in some way clinically ill without defining themselves as such. Others, technically more healthy, 'feel' themselves to be ill. Often being declared 'ill' is the process of a 'negotiation' between doctor and client, rather than a mere function of organic ailment.

The second matter to consider is the relationship between health and social class. This an aspect of *epidemiology*, which is the study of the distribution and causes of disease and injury. By now, you will appreciate the need to effect a working definition of disease as a necessary preliminary to assessing its distribution by social class. Here we adopt the self-definition of respondents in answer to the question posed by the General Household Survey of 1972 (which equates disease and illness): 'Do you suffer from any long-standing illness, disability or infirmity?' Responses show that the lower the social class the higher the rate of long-standing illness (see table below). Answers to the further question: 'IF YES Does (it) limit your activities compared with most people of your own age?' show a similar general trend (see table). This suggests that either the severity of long-standing illness is greater among the working class or that it is less effectively treated – or, most likely, both. There is an abundance of other evidence that the quality of health correlates with social class. The question is, why?

Rates per 1000 reporting (1) long-standing illness, (2) limiting long-standing illness, by social class

	Social class						
	1	2	3	4	5	6	All
Long standing illness	130	168	192	192	265	317	206
Limiting long-standing illness	65	90	104	113	162	208	121

Source: Ivan Reid, *Social Class Differences in Britain*, 1977, p. 109 (adapted from *General Household Survey*, 1972).

The general answer is that the material and cultural conditions of working class life are less conducive to health than those of the middle class. A minority of the lower working class still live in housing conditions in which damp and cold are threats to health – particularly for the old and children. A detailed study of class and diet by Richard Wilkinson produced startling results. For example, per head, the poor eat 56% less fruit, 28% fewer fresh green vegetables and 31% less carcass meat than the rich. They eat much more sugar, cereal products and potatoes. Poverty may be the major underlying cause of less rich diet, but lack of knowledge about what a healthy and balanced diet consists of must also contribute. A further explanation of the relative ill-health of the working class is that the conditions in which they work are often worse than those of the middle class. The General Household survey shows that the rate of reported absence in social class 6 is almost 5 times greater than in social class 1. No doubt in addition to illness and injury, alienation from tedious work is a contributory factor. Another point is that the privileged access of the rich to private medicine must be to their advantage although doctors are often curiously coy about saying that private medicine is generally 'better' than state medicine.

Perhaps surprisingly, evidence also shows that the middle class has benefited more from the NHS than the working class. Until recently, there was doubt about this but the authoritative government-sponsored report, *Inequalities in Health* (1980) is quite clear on the matter. It is true that this and other studies show that the working class use the National Health Service more often than the middle class, but not as much as might be expected *relative to need.* A second point is that there is a tendency for middle class patients to receive better quality treatment from the NHS because the availability and quality of care tends to be superior in middle class localities. J. T. Hart further attributes this to the greater ability of the middle class to negotiate for the services they want, though he admits that the statistical basis of his argument is slight. More precise statistical evidence is supplied by Ann Howlett and John Ashley, albeit on a small scale. They found that teaching hospitals which are recognised to be among the best, tended to admit a substantially larger proportion of middle class than working class men for treatment of enlargement of the prostate gland. Simply, then, middle class patients were somehow being referred to hospitals in which superior treatment might be expected. Two limitations of their study is that they do not prove their assumption of superior treatment by the teaching hospitals, and that they fail to offer an explanation of how selection takes place. However, it seems likely that this is just one instance of the general middle class bias that the previously mentioned report, *Inequalities in Health,* finds to characterise the NHS.

The above considerations no doubt constitute some of the reasons why social class differences in mortality and illness have widened in post-war years. Rather like the national system of education, the NHS has not brought about greater equality. Further, the general improvement in the health of the nation that has undoubtedly occurred this century can be attributed largely to the conquest of contagious disease and improvements in public hygiene rather than to the health service. This is clearly shown by the fact that the major increase in life expectancy occurred well before the NHS was set up.

Finally, we examine some social factors relating to the organisation of health in Britain. We have already referred to the power and interest of drug companies in maintaining a system of treatment based largely on drugs. Here, we discuss bureaucratic and professional aspects of the health system. Ivan Illich is surely correct to see the position of doctors in the context of the tendency of certain services (such as teaching and accountancy) to be increasingly organised within bureaucratic structures. Doctors play the role of 'experts' within the larger 'health machine.' In principle, they, rather than clients decide what 'label' to give specific illnesses. They then pass the client 'down the line' to, say, the chemist or a hospital. Two aspects of this process merit comment. First, is the power to 'label.' Talcott Parsons was perhaps the first to see illness as a form of deviance from the norm - albeit of a more acceptable kind than, say, crime - which society needs to label and deal with. Illich and Thomas Szasz are much more suspicious of labelling. They see it as a virtual invitation to the client to avoid positive responsibility for dealing with his or her own condition and, more sinisterly, in the case of mental 'illness', as a potential threat to the liberty of the individual who in certain circumstances could be committed for treatment against his or her will. A second point, is that, like any other large organisational structure, the National Health Service produces vested interests. An alternative system of medicine to that operated by the NHS would threaten a vast range of interests, from the Chairman of the international drug company Roche, to the jobs of junior staff nurses. For that reason it would be powerfully opposed.

Alternative, largely non-bureaucratic and non-professional systems of medical treatment do exist. Indeed, in parts of the Third World less expensive systems, operated by less qualified people are the only option available. Thus, in China and Tanzania large numbers of 'barefoot doctors' work as a tier of medical service at the grassroots, below a small elite of highly trained medical practitioners. They treat for basic illness and immunise against contagious disease. An element of community medicine is built into this approach and these medical workers are based in specific areas and are known personally to most of those they work for. Their role is seen as educational and preventive as well as curative. This may be medicine on the cheap but it is based on principles that the West could well learn from. Indeed, without remotely suggesting that the NHS, as presently constituted, be dismantled, the *Inequalities in Health* report does argue for more community-based health care. In particular, it puts forward the need for more ante-natal and post-natal care (death at birth and in the first few months of life is relatively high in Britain); better child health services; free school meals for all children, and better home help and nursing services for the disabled. The emphasis on child health is based on the well founded belief that illness in childhood can cast a long shadow forward into adulthood. These and other policies suggested in the report were given a lukewarm reception by the Conservative Social Services Secretary, Patrick Jenkin (the Working Group on Inequalities in Health had been set up under a Labour government in 1977). The major objection was that they would cost too much to implement. The Working Group had anticipated this response by suggesting that most of the reforms could be financed by money saved from abolishing the married man's tax allowance for all married men with no dependants – a worthwhile sacrifice in their view. Like all policies, those suggested by the Working Groups involve issues of value, choice and priority.

(from: M. O'Donnell, *A New Introduction to Sociology*, Harrap, 1981)

1. What is considered 'abnormal' behaviour varies over time and place. Give illustrations.

2. Take one of the following and discuss the extent to which it is a bio-medical and/or socially defined condition or activity:

Obesity
Nervous exhaustion
Homosexuality
Impotence
Alcoholism
Hyperactivity
Claustrophobia
Promiscuity
Sado-masochism

3. 'Prevention is better than cure.' Explain what social factors and interests have led instead to an emphasis in the West on treatment rather than prevention.

4. Why might someone tell themselves that they have 'smoker's cough' rather than bronchitis?

5. Despite the introduction of the National Health Service in 1948 in Britain, social class differences in health continue to the present day. To what extent can the NHS be 'blamed' for this failure to achieve social equality in health?

6. Doctors often use language incomprehensible to their patients and keep from them information about their medical condition. Why?

7. 'Conquering the old killer diseases has merely given us different ones to fear.' Discuss.

8. The extract on Obedience to Authority (A7) mentions that we tend to trust and obey people in particular professional roles. In the light of this, why might it be unwise for a doctor to inform a patient that he has only six months to live? (You will find it useful to refer to passage A7.)

9. Imagine that you have just been appointed as Minister of Health. The National Health Service which you inherit has the following problems:

(a) No increase in funding from Central Government and little likelihood of anything more than inflation-linked increases in the future.

(b) Pressure from doctors and research establishments to invest in expensive medical technologies: e.g. heart transplants; test-tube babies; coronary bypass operations.

(c) An increase in the actual *number* of people over 65 who will increasingly require the services of the NHS.

(d) A huge and ever-growing drugs bill – some of it due to over-prescription by doctors and some attributable to over-pricing by drug-producing companies. A further problem with drugs is the increasing number of side-effects which are becoming apparent.

(e) The huge expense of training doctors, many of whom will be over-qualified for their work as General Practitioners. (Some Third World countries use partially trained doctors for this kind of basic medical work – the 'barefoot doctors'.)

(f) Many people regard their state of health (or otherwise) as the doctor's responsibility – not theirs. There is a lack of knowledge in the population about how to cultivate good health.

Your task is to draw up a paper which will provide solutions to these problems and any others which you know exist.

See also Question 7 in C3.

Further Reading

R. Gomm, Social Science and Medicine in *Perspectives on Society*, Meighan et al (Eds.), Nelson
– article illustrates how sociologists approach an apparently non-sociological problem – health.

P. Townsend and N. Davidson, *Inequalities in Health*, Penguin
– Penguin edition of authoritative Government-sponsored report.

T. Szasz, *The Manufacture of Madness*, Paladin
– criticises current assumptions about 'mental illness' and examines parallels with mediaeval methods of dealing with witches, heretics and Jews.

B

ANALYTICAL MAN

The Decline of Religion and the Rise of Science

B 1

Traditional religious belief was at first threatened only among an intellectual élite, often consciously holding ideas drawn from Enlightenment sources: 'Voltairean' was a favourite nineteenth-century adjective to indicate anti-religious and sceptical views. As the nineteenth century proceeded, such ideas were reinforced by two other intellectual currents, both also at first a concern of élites, but increasingly with a wider effect in an age of growing mass literacy and cheap printing.

The first of these influential groups of ideas came from biblical scholars, the most important of them German, who from the 1840s onwards not only demolished many assumptions about the value of the Bible as historical evidence, but also, and perhaps more fundamentally, brought about something of a psychological change in the whole attitude to the scriptural text. In essence this change made it possible henceforth simply to regard the Bible as a historic text like any other, to be approached critically. An immensely successful (and scandal-provoking) *Life of Jesus*, published in 1863 by a French scholar, Ernest Renan, brought such an attitude before a wider public than ever before. The book which had been the central text of European civilisation since its emergence in the Dark Ages would never recover its position.

The second source of ideas damaging to traditional Christian faith – and therefore to the morality, politics, and economics for so long anchored in Christian assumptions – was to be found in science. Enlightenment attacks on internal and logical inconsistency in the teaching of the Church became much more alarming when science began to produce empirical evidence that things said in the Bible (and therefore based on the same authority as everything else in it) plainly did not fit observable fact. The starting-point was geology; ideas which had been about since the end of the eighteenth century were given a much wider public in the 1830s by the publication of *Principles of Geology* by an English scientist, Charles Lyell. This book explained landscape and geological structure in terms of forces still at work, that is, not as the result of a single act of creation, but of wind, rain and so on. Moreover, Lyell pointed out that if this were correct, then the presence of fossils of different forms of life in different geological strata implied that the creation of new animals had been repeated in each geological age. If this were so, the biblical account of creation was clearly in difficulties. That biblical chronology was simply untrue in relation to man was increasingly suggested by discoveries of stone tools in British caves along with the fossilised bones of extinct animals. The argument that man was much older than the biblical account allowed may perhaps be regarded as officially conceded when, in 1859, British learned societies heard and published papers establishing 'that in a period of antiquity remote beyond any of which we have hitherto found traces' men had lived in Palaeolithic societies in the Somme valley.

It is an over-simplification, but not grossly distorting, to say that the same year brought many of these questions to a head by an approach along a different line, the biological, when Charles Darwin published one of the seminal books of modern civilisation, the book called, for short, *The Origin of Species.* Much in it he owed without acknowledgement to others. Its publication also came at a moment and in a country where it was especially likely to cause a stir; the issue of the rightfulness of the traditional dominance of religion (for example, in education) was in the air in England. The word 'evolution' with which Darwin's name came especially to be connected was by then already familiar (and he tried to avoid using it). Nevertheless, though this explains some of the interest shown in what he said, his book was the greatest single statement of the evolutionary hypothesis – namely, that living things were what they were because their forms had undergone long evolution from simpler ones. This, of course, included man, as he made explicit in another book, *The Descent of Man,* of 1871. Different views were held about how this evolution had occurred. Darwin, impressed by Malthus' vision of the murderous competition of mankind for food, took the view that the qualities which made success likely in hostile environments ensured the 'natural selection' of those creatures embodying them: this was a view to be vulgarised (and terribly misrepresented) by the use as a slogan of the phrase 'survival of the fittest'. But important though many aspects of his work were to be in inspiring fresh thought, here it is important rather to see that Darwin dealt a blow against the biblical account of creation (as well as against the assumption of the unique status of Man) which had wider publicity than any earlier one. In combination with biblical criticism and geology, his book made it impossible for any conscientious and thoughtful man to accept – as he had still been able to do in 1800 – the Bible as literally true.

The undermining of the authority of scripture remains probably the most obvious single way in which science affected formulated beliefs. Yet just as important, if not more so, was a new, vague but growing prestige which science was coming to have among a public more broadly based than ever before. This was because of its new status as the supreme instrument for the manipulation of nature, which was seen as increasingly powerless to resist it. Here was the beginning of what was to grow into a mythology of science. Its essence lay in the fact that while the great achievements of seventeenth-century science had not often resulted in changes in the lives of ordinary men and women, those of the nineteenth century increasingly did. Men who understood not a word of what might be written by Joseph Lister, who established the need and technique of using antiseptics in surgery, or by Michael Faraday, who more than any other man made possible the generation of electricity, knew none the less that the medicine of 1900 was different from that of their grandfathers and often saw electricity about them in the work and homes. By 1914, radio messages could be sent across the Atlantic, flying-machines which did not rely upon support by bags of gas of lower density than air were common, aspirins were easily available and an American manufacturer was offering the first cheap mass-produced automobile. The objective achievements of science were by no means adequately represented by such facts, but material advance of this sort impressed the average man and led him to worship at a new shrine.

His awareness of science came through technology because for a long time this was almost the only way in which science had a positive impact on the lives of most people. Respect for it therefore usually grew in proportion to spectacular results in engineering or manufacture and even now, though science makes its impact in other ways, it still makes it very obviously through industrial processes. But though deeply entwined in this way with the dominant world civilisation and so interwoven with society, the growth of science was also a much greater change than one of sheer power. In the years down to 1914 the foundations were laid for what would be evident in the second half of the twentieth century, a science which was as much as anything the mainspring of the dominant world culture. So rapid has been the advance to this state of affairs that science has already affected every part of human life while people are still trying to grapple with some of its most elementary philosophical implications.

The easiest observations of this change which can be made (and the easiest to take as a starting-point) are those which display the status of science as a social and material phenomenon in its own right. From the moment when the first great advances in physics were made, in the seventeenth century, science was already a social fact. Institutions were then created in which men came together to study nature in a way which a later age could recognise as scientific, and scientists even then were sometimes employed by rulers to bring to bear their expertise on specific problems. It was noticeable, too, that in the useful arts – and they were more usually called arts than sciences – such as navigation or agriculture, experiment by those who were not themselves practising technicians could make valuable contributions. But a terminological point helps to set this age in perspective and establish its remoteness from the nineteenth century and after: at this time scientists were still called 'natural philosophers'. The word 'scientist' was not invented until about a third of the way through the nineteenth century, when men felt that there was need to distinguish a rigorous experimental and observational investigation of nature from speculation on it by unchecked reason. Even then, though, there was little distinction in most men's minds between the man who carried out such an investigation and the applied scientist or technologist who was the much more conspicuous representative of science in an age of engineering, mining and manufacturing on an unprecedented scale.

The nineteenth century was none the less the first in which science was taken for granted by educated men as a specialised field of study, whose investigators had professional standing. Its new status was marked by the much larger place given to science in education, both by the creation of new departments at existing universities, and by the setting up in some countries, notably France and Germany, of special scientific and technical institutions. Professional studies, too, incorporated larger scientific components. Such developments accelerated as the effects of science on social and economic life became increasingly obvious. The sum effect was to carry much further an already long-established trend. Since about 1700 there has been a steady and exponential increase in the world population of scientists: their numbers have doubled roughly every fifteen years (which explains the striking fact that ever since then there have always been, at any moment, more scientists alive than dead). In the nineteenth century, other measurements of the growth of science can be used (the establishment of astronomical observatories, for example) and these, too, provide exponential curves of growth.

This social phenomenon underlay the growing control of his environment and the improvement of his life which were so easily grasped by the layman. This was what made the nineteenth century the first in which science truly became an object of religion – perhaps of idolatry. By 1914, educated Europeans and Americans took for granted the presence of the motorcar, the steam turbine, harder and specialised steels, the aeroplane, the telephone, the wireless and many more marvels which had not existed a century previously; their effects were already very great. Perhaps the most widely apparent were those stemming from the availability of cheap electrical power; it was already shaping cities by making electric trams and trains available to suburban householders, work in factories through electric motors, and domestic life through the electric light. Even animal populations were affected: the 36 000 horses pulling trams in Great Britain in 1900 had only 900 successors in 1914. Of course, the practical application of science was by no means new. There has never been a time since the seventeenth century when there has not been some obvious technological fall-out from scientific activity though, to begin with, it was largely confined to ballistics, navigation and map-making, agriculture and a few elementary industrial processes. Only in the nineteenth century did science really begin to play an important rôle in sustaining and changing society which went beyond a few obviously striking and spectacular accomplishments. The chemistry of dyeing, for example, was a vast field in which nineteenth-century research led to sweeping innovations which flooded through the manufacture of drugs, explosives, antiseptics – to mention only a few. These had human and social, as well as economic, repercussions. The new fast dyes themselves affected millions of people; the unhappy Indian grower of indigo found that his market dried up on him, and the industrial working classes of the West found they could buy marginally less drab clothes and thus began to move slowly forward along the road at the end of which mass-production methods and man-made fibres all but obliterated visible difference between the clothes of different classes.

This already takes us across the boundary between sustaining life and changing it. Fundamental science was to go on changing society, though some of what was done before 1914 – in physics, for example – is better left for discussion at a later point. One area in which effects are easier to measure was medicine. By 1914, advances had been made which were huge by comparison with the state of medicine a century earlier. A skill had become a science. Great bridgeheads had been driven into the theory and control of infection; antiseptics, having been introduced by Lister only in the 1860s, were taken for granted a couple of decades later, and he and his friend Louis Pasteur, the most famous and greatest of French chemists, laid the foundations of bacteriology. Queen Victoria herself had been a pioneer in the publicising of new medical methods; the use of anaesthetics during the birth of a prince or princess was important in winning quick social acceptance for techniques only in their infancy in the 1840s. Fewer people, perhaps, would have been aware of the importance of such achievements as the discovery in 1909 of Salvarsan, a landmark in the development of selective treatment of infection, or the identification of the carrier of malaria, or the discovery of 'X-rays'. Yet all these advances, though of great importance, were to be far surpassed in the next fifty years.

Enough impact was made by science even before 1914 to justify the conclusion that it generated its own mythology. In this context, 'mythology' implies no connotations of fiction or falsity. It is simply a convenient way of calling attention to the fact that science, the vast bulk of its conclusions no doubt validated by experiment and therefore 'true', has also come to act as an influence shaping the way men look at the world, just as great religions have done in the past. It has, that is to say, come to be important as more than a method for exploring and manipulating nature. It has been thought also to provide guidance about metaphysical questions, the aims men ought to pursue, the standards they should employ to regulate behaviour. Above all it has been a pervasive influence in shaping popular attitudes. All this, of course, has no intrinsic or necessary connection with science as the pursuit of scientists. But the upshot in the end was a civilisation whose élites had, except vestigially, no dominant religious belief or transcendent ideals. It is a civilisation whose core, whether or not this is often articulated, lies in belief in the promise of what can be done by manipulating nature. In principle, it believes that there is no problem which need be regarded as insoluble, given sufficient resources of intellect and money; it has room for the obscure, but not for the essentially mysterious. Many scientists have drawn back from this conclusion. The implications of it are still far from being grasped. But it is the assumption on which a dominant world view now rests and it was already formed in essentials before 1914.

(from: J. M. Roberts, *The Pelican History of the World,* Pelican, 1980)

1. Why should 'Voltairean' indicate anti-religious views?

2. What were the two 'intellectual currents' which added to the threat to traditional religious ideas in the 19th century?

3. The Adam and Eve story in the Bible can be regarded as a simple tale which illustrates in concrete terms the abstract condition of man's nature. Is it:
(a) parody?
(b) allegory?
(c) syllogism?
(d) syllepsis?

4. Explain clearly why the geological and archaeological 'discoveries' of the 19th century created difficulties for the biblical account of the Act of Creation.

5. What was Malthus' theory about the growth of population and competition for food? How have modern Western societies managed to avoid the evils which Malthus predicted?

6. Science commanded a prestige among a wide public in the 19th century because:
(a) it was the supreme instrument for the manipulation of Nature
(b) a mythology was beginning to surround it
(c) its achievements often resulted in changes in the lives of ordinary men and women
(d) there was a much larger educated public which could now appreciate the power of science

7. What is the difference between science and technology?

8. Explain the meaning of: '. . . it [science] has room for the obscure, but not the essentially mysterious'. (final paragraph).

9. 'The successes of science and technology have produced more problems than they have solved.' Discuss.

10. (This can be done individually, but perhaps more usefully by a whole class.)
Take one of the following and prepare a short talk on their contribution to the history and development of science. The exercise should give you a comprehensive (although not exhaustive) history of science up to the early part of the 20th century.

Copernicus
Galileo
Francis Bacon
Descartes
Newton
Faraday and Maxwell
Lamarck
Darwin
1st and 2nd law of thermodynamics
Rudolf Clausius
Boltzmann
Einstein

Further Reading

T. S. Kuhn, *The Structure of Scientific Revolutions*, University of Chicago Press
- famous analysis of the nature, causes and consequences of revolutions in basic scientific concepts.

F. Capra, *The Turning Point*, Flamingo
- argues for a radical new vision of the place of science and meta-science.

B. Brecht, *The Life of Galileo*, Methuen

C. L. Bolttz, And Yet it Moves, *New Scientist*, 7 April 1983

- both the play and the article describe Galileo's trial for 'heretical' scientific ideas.

B2 Perceiving the World

It is often said that there are five senses - vision, hearing, touch, taste and smell - but in fact there are many more. Warmth and cold are signalled by receptors, and tickle is the ancient vibration sense vital for underwater creatures, for warning of danger and useful for signalling between mates. Then there are many senses indicating internal states, most obviously pain - of which there are several kinds - and also positions of the limbs and the tension of muscles. Not all of these senses reach consciousness: muscle tension, for example, is signalled by 'stretch receptors' rather like engineers' strain gauges; though highly important for the control of the body, they do not signal to the upper regions of the brain associated with consciousness. Vision, hearing and touch have clearly identified regions of brain devoted to elaborate mechanisms serving them. All the senses, whether or not they give sensation, or feeling, signal information of the outside world or of bodily states of their owner - be it to you or me, or some other creature very different from us, yet sharing the same world.

Primitive organisms have small, or even no, nervous systems. Their behaviour may be as limited as advancing or retreating according to the strength of signals at receptors. In this way they may follow gradients of a chemical concentration, or of temperature, or intensity of light with 'tropisms'. Tropisms, however, can be quite complicated: set by neural 'logic circuits' so that in some conditions a tropism is switched off, or switched from positive advancing to negative retreat. In even simple organisms, internal states are monitored in subtle ways to maintain metabolism; so senses have far more to do than appears from behaviour. This is so even for plants (which of course have no nervous system) for they have subtle detectors of gravity, humidity, and chemical senses for control of their green-blooded metabolism. Plant behaviour is indeed remarkable, from following the sun, responding to insects and even trapping them, to predicting the seasons. If they were quicker they might appear intelligent.

The eye, and ear, and other receivers of information are remarkably sensitive. The eye can respond to a flash of a few hundred quanta (the smallest unit of energy) and would be more sensitive still but for light lost in the media of the eye itself. The retinal receptors (the 'rods' and 'cones' which signal black-and-white and colour respectively) are sensitive to as little as one or two quanta - and so they have the maximum possible theoretical sensitivity. The ear also is as sensitive as it could be. It has been calculated that in the cochlea, where by a process not fully understood frequencies of air vibrations are separated spatially around its spiral structure, the basilar membrane vibrates with an amplitude half the diameter of a hydrogen atom at the faintest sound we can hear. By touch, we can feel ridges less than a thousandth of an inch in height, and the vibration sense of the skin is even more delicate. The range of intensities over which the senses work is also remarkable: the eye functions (with dark/light adaptation) over a range of a million to one intensity units, and will discriminate differences of a few per cent in intensity over most of this enormous range.

The images in the eyes do not enter the brain. Their patterns are transmitted down a bundle of nerve fibres, at about the speed of sound, by pulses of electricity giving coded messages. The basic code is: increasing frequency of pulses with increasing intensity of light. This long and complicated chain of events gives a very different notion of perception from the direct immediate knowledge we *seem* to have when we open our eyes and see the world around us. The brain has the task of reconstituting - or creating its own - reality from these pulse-coded signals which are its only messages from the outside world. When we experience colour, movement, sound, touch or smell, all that our brains receive are these chains of electrical pulses running down the millions of nerve fibres from the receptors of the various senses. The brain decodes, or 'reads', these patterns of pulses to give sensation and perception, but the signals are of no use until they are processed and read as messages.

There is an important analogy here to signals from scientific instruments. Signals of any kind are useless until they are processed to give data. Data are not physical, in the usual sense of the word, for data are given by reading and intepreting signals as symbols. This cannot be done with any instrument in the range of the physical sciences. An oscilloscope can show the signals in a nerve, but it cannot tell what the information is, or how much is being transmitted. And it certainly cannot indicate the information of *no* signals! We may recognise something from a *surprising absence* of signals. When signals or their absence are *surprising* they convey *information.* To estimate the amount of information conveyed we need to know how surprising - how unlikely - is the message or its absence. Perception is generally a matter of deciding between alternatives. The significance of alternatives is what makes perception essentially different from the physical world. The seventeenth-century physicists were concerned with what *happens* in given situations; but perception is continually concerned with what *might* happen. Perception does not merely signal what is, it generates alternative hypotheses of what might be. These hypotheses are predictive - for decisions, to be useful and have survival value, must be aimed at the future. In unusual situations - or if false assumptions are accepted - such procedures could generate errors in perception much as errors occur in science when inappropriate procedures, or false assumptions or premises, are adopted. This can happen at all stages of scientific observation, including deriving data from the signals of instruments by statistical methods. Indeed, the methods of science and the processes by which the nervous system gives us perceptual knowledge could be very similar. We may go further, to suggest that *perceptions are hypotheses of reality.* Some are no doubt true; but many (as in science) are more or less incorrect.

In some conditions a wrong alternative is accepted: then we have an illusion or an hallucination. Hallucinations are total departures from reality; illusions are discrepancies from reality - so neither are within physics.

There are many kinds of illusions, and they can tell us a lot about perception. This becomes a technical and tricky business, but the following classification of illusions may help:

(1) *Ambiguities*: such as the Necker cube, and the figure and figure/ground ambiguity of the Rubin figures.
(2) *Distortions*: such as the 'café wall', the Zöllner and Orbison figures.
(3) *Paradoxes*: such as the Penrose impossible triangle figure, and other 'impossible objects' which exist in three dimensions but appear impossible from certain points of view.

Ambiguities: two equally valid interpretations can be made, and we cannot be sure which is right. In the Necker cube, which square face is the nearer? Does the Rubin figure portray a face (white) or an old beggar woman (black)?

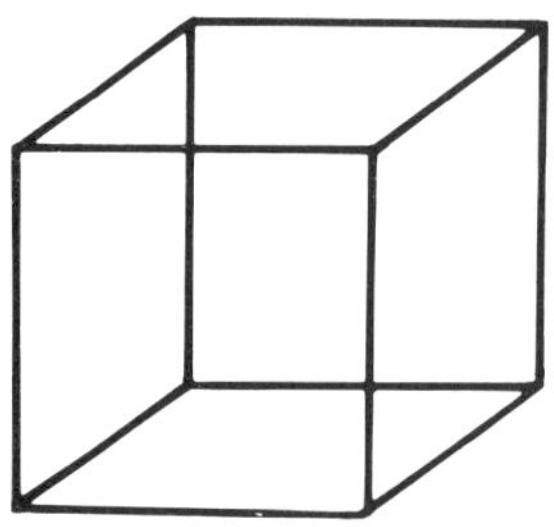

Distortions: in the 'café wall' illusion, when alternate rows are displaced, the lines between seem no longer parallel.

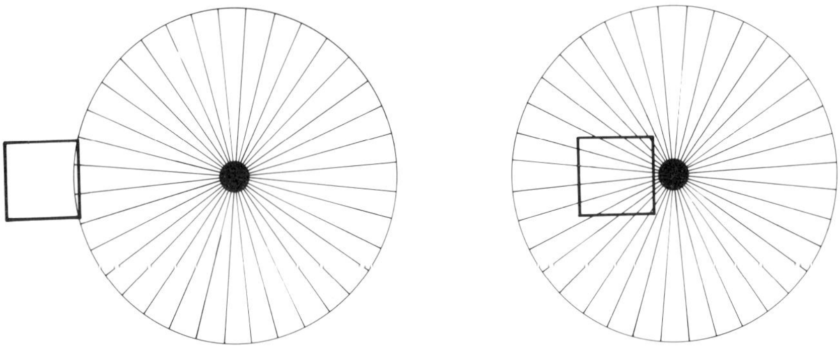

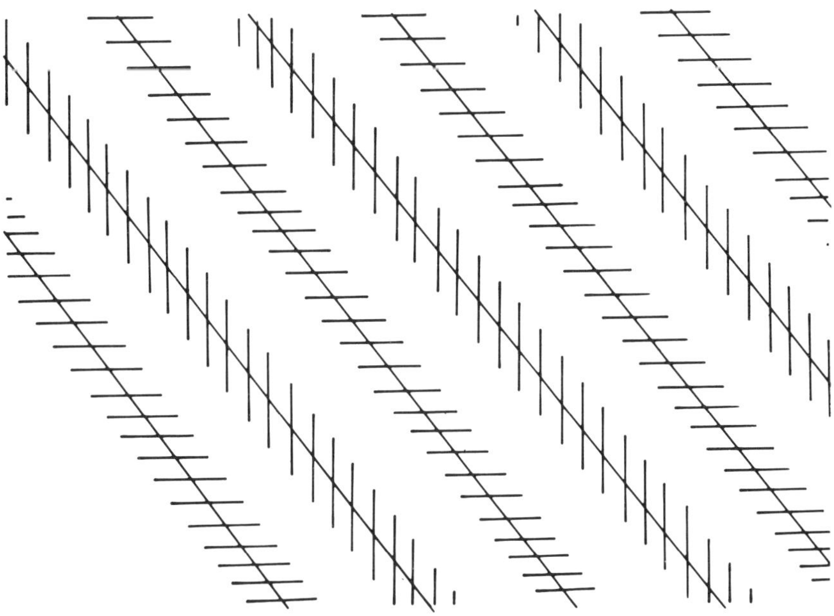

Distortions: in the Orbison figure the square seems distorted when placed over converging radii; in the Zöllner figure the long oblique lines are actually parallel.

Hypotheses are very different from reality even when they are true. They are different because they are *descriptions*, or *explanations*, rather than copies. Further, there is an endless number of possible hypotheses for any event or situation, though some will be more useful, appropriate, adequate, or true than others. It is always a question which is the best hypothesis. The number of alternatives to choose from is – for science or for perceptions – limited only by imagination. This notion of selecting between alternative hypotheses follows from the concept of perception and science as being active hypothesis generators. It leads to the recent technical account of information as selecting between alternatives. This account of information was developed by C. E. Shannon, of the Bell Telephone Laboratories, and has made it possible to quantify and measure information in communication channels and computers. Unfortunately, though, it is not very helpful as a measure for brains, because we do not know how many alternatives we have to choose from even for the simplest skill.

Each of the senses has its own kind of *receptors* which convert patterns of physical energy from the external world (times internal changes from within the organism) into the action-potential signals of nerves; but sensations are not simply related to the channels. For colour vision there are three channels (sensitive to red, green and blue light respectively) but colours as we see them are *mixtures* of these. Yellow appears as a simple colour but it is always given by a mixture of 'red' and 'green' signals. In general, sensations which seem to be simple or primary are not given by particularly simple physiological mechanisms. This very likely applies to that most basic sensation – pain – though how pain is signalled remains mysterious. It is particularly odd that pain is never elicited by direct electrical stimulation of any regions of the brain (during brain operations with conscious patients), though the other sensations are readily aroused in this way.

How are we – as observers – related to the world? The key discovery was made at the end of the tenth century by an Arabic scholar, Alhazan, who put visual perception into a clear relation with the physical world by inventing the *camera obscura.* This projects the world as an image on a screen. The principle is now so familiar, from slide projectors and cameras, that it may not look important or revolutionary, or least of all of philosophical significance. Its implications are still not fully realised even by some writers on perception. Alhazan, and later the astronomer Kepler, realised that the world is projected into the eye as an image, so that we do not have *direct* visual knowledge of the external world. We are connected visually to the physical world by a tenuous link of light-giving images very different from the objects we see and very different also from our perceptions. With the advance of the physical sciences, mathematical accounts of the universe threaten what we accept as knowledge by perception.

Physics took off from a few simple experiments in the seventeenth century, notably by Galileo, which gave insight into the kinds of things worth investigating and describing in detail, to flower in Newton's account a generation later. Astronomy gave essential keys for understanding the physical world, and for predicting and controlling a far wider range of

The Penrose Impossible Triangle

events and situations than the brain unaided by science could achieve. The success of Newton's mathematical account of the universe was, however, bought at the cost of leaving out the observer. Science very largely ceased to care about why things appear to us coloured, hard, beautiful, or frightening.

This rejection of how things *look* in favour of how they must *be* to give simple mathematical descriptions, started with the Copernican switch of thought, from the sun moving round the earth (as we see it) to the earth moving round the sun. This was mind-jolting, running against what we seem to know directly by experience from the senses. The sun is *seen* to move across the sky, the earth *feels* stationary; such scientific insights came from abandoning sight and feel. With the new insights of science our most trusted sources of knowledge as well as our strongest beliefs became suspect and sometimes trivial. Lapse into total triviality of feeling was avoided by the artists; but they too suffered from science's rejection of experience as representing important or deep truth. The *sensations* of colours were not at all explained. How we see remained mysterious and was seldom questioned. The physical sciences went from one triumph to the next, to transform the way we live and understand, but left us as observers and knowers almost entirely out of account. The unprecedented success of Galileo and Newton demoted sensation and feeling, leading to the twentieth-century psychology of Behaviourism, which altogether denied feeling and consciousness.

(From: R. L. Gregory, 'Feeling the World by Perception' in *How Does it Feel?*, Ed. Mick Csaky, Thames and Hudson, 1979)

1. 'Plant behaviour is indeed remarkable . . . If they were quicker they might appear intelligent.' (second paragraph). Can you explain why horticulturalists can entice bulbs to produce flowers by storing them in cold conditions for a short while?

2. Describe how a human being can perceive something from a 'surprising absence of signals'. (paragraph 5).

3. Are there any kinds of information about the outside world that our senses cannot signal to us?

4. 'Seeing is believing' – or is it? Look at the distortion illusions on pages 62–3. How can you convince yourself that what your eyes are 'seeing' is not necessarily the truth?

5. Use either words or diagrams, or both, to show how the human eye perceives the world.

6. 'With the advance of the physical sciences, mathematical accounts of the universe threaten what we accept as knowledge by perception.' (paragraph 9). Explain this statement and discuss its implications for both the scientist and the artist.

7. '. . . the 20th century psychology of Behaviourism, which altogether denied feeling and consciousness.' (final paragraph). Refer back to the extract on Behaviourism (A6) and decide whether or not you agree with the point Gregory makes in his final sentence.

8. 'The physical sciences went from one triumph to the next, to transform the way we live and understand, but left us as observers and knowers almost entirely out of account.' (final paragraph). Discuss the validity of this statement with regard to:
Medicine
Economics
Defence systems
Domestic mechanical appliances
Food production
Education
Production of electricity
Crime

See also Question 3 in B10.

Further Reading

R. L. Gregory, *The Intelligent Eye*, Weidenfeld & Nicholson
– a very good and well-illustrated introduction to the psychology of perception.

E. H. Gombrich, *Art and Illusion*, Phaidon
– examines the argument that art is based on illusion and that perception has perhaps more to do with selecting alternatives than reality.

Classical Logic and Probability

B3

We are concerned here with the reflective type of thinking which is ordinarily called *reasoning*, in which one step leads in an orderly way to the next step, the whole consecutive process drawing finally to a conclusion.

This kind of thinking reaches a particularly refined level in mathematics. Its precision in mathematics depends upon several things – the unambiguous way in which terms are defined, the restraint with which the definitions are obeyed, and the care with which all the rules of procedure are set out and made clear.

This kind of thinking is *logical* thinking; and logic itself can be defined as the systematic study of the conditions and procedures which permit *valid inference* – that is to say, which permit one to start with one or more statements (or 'propositions' as the experts like to say) and derive from these, or *infer* from these, one or more *new* statements or propositions which are *valid* in the sense that they are justified by, and are in strict fact consequences of, the starting statements.

It is of the highest importance to recognise that logic does not make something from nothing, that it merely unrolls out to view, so to speak, statements and propositions and relationships which were present in, although hidden within, the statements used as the starting point.

Thus what is important about a logical inference is not its *truth*, but rather its *validity*. A logical conclusion can properly merit the adjectives *correct*, *sound*, or *accurate*, all meaning that it has been dependably and properly derived from the starting material. But the fact that it has been produced by correct logical methods is of itself not the slightest evidence that it is *true*. If the starting statements were, in some way, known to be true, then the logically derived consequence would also be true. But if you are interested in truth, then either you have to go back and establish the truth of the starting statements, or, neglecting the logical process which has produced them, you have to establish the truth of the inferred statements by some method directly supplied to them.

Bertrand Russell once declared that mathematics is the subject in which you never know what you are talking about, and never know whether or not what you say is true. What we have just said should explain the final part of his description; for we have seen that validity, not truth, is the hallmark of a logical conclusion. The earlier part of Russell's somewhat mischievous but accurate definition is, incidentally, equally sound and equally important. Mathematics is so magnificently *general* a discipline, that it is literally true that one does not know, in trivial particular, what one is talking about. Thus the mathematical identity $2x+2x=4x$ is valid, even though you have no idea what x stands for.

CLASSICAL LOGIC

The type of reasoning used in geometry and algebra is that which has been developed in classical logic. It involves three steps. First, you start out with a set of *premisses* (statements, or postulates) which are, at least in that particular discussion, to be accepted without question. In modern mathematics these initial premisses are recognised to be pure assumptions. Long ago mathematics – Euclid, for example – started out with 'axioms', statements which were then presumed to be self-evidently true. But this alleged truth turned out to be a snare; for it was later found out that several of these 'self-evidently true' statements could be replaced with other statements (not necessarily at all the same) and that self-consistent, but different, theories could be developed from them. So nowadays the starting step consists of premisses simply assumed without further discussion.

The second step involved the application, to the starting premisses, of the rules of logic. The core of deductive logic is the so-called syllogism, which consists of a major premiss, a minor premiss, and a conclusion. In general terms:

Major Premiss:	Every *M* is *P*,
Minor Premiss:	*S* is *M*,
Conclusion:	Therefore *S* is *P*.

Or, to cite a particular example:

Every virtue is laudable,
Kindness is a virtue,
Therefore kindness is laudable.

It is really remarkable that from this kind of start, which seems so innocently simple, there has been developed a grand array of powerful procedures by means of which reasoning can be kept tidy and dependable.

Lewis Caroll, the author of *Alice in Wonderland* and a mathematician at Christ Church, Oxford, wrote several books and pamphlets explaining how to apply the rules of logic, and – not wholly leaving wonderland – he showed how one could, from the three premisses

1. Babies are illogical,
2. Nobody is despised who can manage a crocodile,
3. Illogical persons are despised,

derive the conclusion:

Babies cannot manage crocodiles.

In fact, since *babies are illogical* (Premiss 1) and since *illogical persons are despised* (Premiss 3) it follows that *babies are despised.* And since *despised persons cannot manage crocodiles* (Premiss 2), it follows that *babies cannot manage crocodiles.*

This example of logical reasoning indicates, incidentally, that a logical conclusion is worth just exactly what the premisses are worth. Also you will say, and properly, that you could solve this little puzzle without studying logic. But take a look at another of Lewis Carroll's examples. What is the conclusion from the following nine interlocked premisses?

1. All who neither dance on tightropes nor eat penny buns are old.
2. Pigs that are liable to giddiness are treated with respect.
3. A wise balloonist takes an umbrella with him.
4. No one ought to lunch in public who looks ridiculous and eats penny buns.
5. Young creatures who go up in balloons are liable to dizziness.
6. Fat creatures who look ridiculous may lunch in public provided they do not dance on tightropes.
7. No wise creatures dance on tightropes if liable to giddiness.
8. A pig looks ridiculous, carrying an umbrella.
9. All who do not dance on tightropes and who are treated with respect are fat.

This one takes a bit of thinking; but it is straightforward, using the procedures of logic.[. . .]

Now you may not be overwhelmed by the significance of these examples, but, on the other hand, you must admit that it is rather impressive to realise that involved and complicated premisses do in fact lead unambiguously to certain definite conclusions, and that clearly formulated procedures of logical thinking can unravel a curious mess of interlocked statements of this kind.

But the most important aspect – the third and culminating step of the classical procedure that one often first learns in geometry – is precisely that there *is* a definite conclusion, that with open-and-shut finality one can be sure that the conclusion is, under the given premisses, completely valid, and that its opposite is completely false.

Be sure you did not miss, in the preceding sentence, the critically important clause 'under the given premisses'. For this type of reasoning can, of course, produce nothing more than an 'if-then' kind of result. That is, *if* the assumptions hold, *then* the result is valid. Indeed it is then unquestionably valid, and its opposite is unquestionably false.

One can have nothing but enthusiasm and respect for the development of the rules and procedures of logic, and a university course in logic shows how complex and fascinating and dependable they can be.

With a given start, this process enables one confidently to decide that certain statements, on the basis of the given start, are *true* or *false.* To certain questions one can confidently respond 'yes' or 'no'.

But this process in its classical form (which in deference to its major originator is sometimes called Aristotelian logic) has an absolutely devastating limitation.

The trouble is that there are so very many interesting and important questions to which this logical method does not at all apply. There are so many questions which cannot possibly be answered with either yes or no. There are so very many cases in which our starting knowledge is simply not sufficiently extensive, or sufficiently reliable, to lead to a completely positive yes or a completely negative no. Much more often the answer should be, to use the phrase made famous by Sam Goldwyn, 'a definite maybe'.

In logic it is customary to speak of 'truth values'; and classical Aristotelian logic is concerned with only two truth values – absolute and perfect truth, which can be symbolised by the number 1, and absolute and total falsehood, which can be symbolised by the number 0. On that basis, classical logic puts all statements into one or another of these categories. The first category contains statements which receive the score of 1, or *true.* The second contains statements which receive the score of 0, or *false.* A third, and embarrassingly large, category contains all the statements which classical logic cannot handle at all, many of these statements presumably being neither completely true nor completely false.

A great limitation of classical logic is that there are so very many interesting and important statements which fall in the third category with which classical logic cannot deal at all.[. . .]

It is at just this point that the *logic of probability* comes to our rescue. It is capable of taking a whole series of statements, no one of which is either totally false or totally true, and of ordering these statements relative to their *degree* of truth, telling how much more or less plausible one is than another. Probability logic is not restricted to *two* truth values, 0 and 1, but makes use, as we will see, of an infinite set of truth values, expressed as numbers lying between 0 and 1.

Probability theory is capable of considering situations in which we just haven't enough information to permit the application of classical logical thinking, and it is capable of giving the best kind of answer which the incomplete evidence justifies. In a great many cases probability theory not only says, 'My advice is thus and so,' but also can tell what degree of confidence you are justified in placing in the advice given.

What we need is probabilistic thinking, which is for so many practical and serious problems the *only* realistic kind of thinking. We must be trained in the technique of weighing alternative risks. We must face the grim fact that we cannot eliminate risk. The problem, therefore, is to be able to evaluate risks, to identify a reasonable risk, and to adopt it with courage, and care, and hope.[. . .]

THE DEFINITION OF MATHEMATICAL PROBABILITY

Let us agree that we are, for the moment, thinking about an experiment or a trial which can result in N *different equally probable outcomes.* You understand that we are talking about a *general* situation, not a *specific* one; so we do not at the moment know (or care) what N is. It may be two, or six, or thirty-six, or fifty-two, or any other positive integer. Let us further agree, as a matter of general notation, that of all these N equally probable outcomes, we consider n of them (again n is a positive integer, general except for the condition that it clearly cannot exceed N) as 'favourable' in the sense that the occurrence of any one of them results in the event we are interested in, or are concerned about, or desire. Let us call this event E.

We are now ready to state the definition of the mathematical probability of an event; *The probability $P(E)$ of an event E is defined by the equation:*

$$P(E) = \frac{n}{N}$$

where N is the total number of equally probable outcomes, and n is the number of the outcomes which constitute the event E. The word 'constitute' in this definition may be used in a rather queer way. The n outcomes *constitute the event E,* in the sense that if any one of them occurs, then E is said to have occurred.

It has been for the moment assumed that both n and N are integers – whole numbers, but this definition can be generalised to cover much broader possibilities.

If the event E occurs in *all* the N outcomes which can happen – that is to say, if every outcome results in E – then $n = N$ and $P(E) = 1$. But if all possible outcomes result in E, then E is assured. A mathematical probability equal to 1 corresponds to the *certain* occurrence of the event E under consideration, or more briefly, and more generally, to *certainty.* On the other hand, if none of the N ways result in E, then $n = 0$ and $P(E) = 0$. That is to say, a mathematical probability of 0 corresponds to the *impossibility of occurrence of E,* or more briefly, to the *impossibility of E.*

The older books on probability theory often used the terminology 'the probability of success' (meaning 'the probability that the event E occurs'), and the expression 'the probability of failure' (meaning 'the probability that E does not occur'). But the event E may be the death of a certain child, or nuclear war, so it seems more sensible to use the neutral expression 'the event E occurs' rather than the loaded words 'success' or 'failure'.

In many games it is customary to speak of the *odds* for (or against) an event E, rather than the *probability* of the event E. The relation between the two terminologies is a simple one. When the probability is n/N, there are n outcomes which result in E, and $(N-n)$ which do not result in E. Thus we can make two statements:

$$P(E) = \frac{n}{N}$$

The odds in favour of E are n to $N-n$

These statements are exactly equivalent.

The equation $P(E) = \frac{1}{2} = 0.5$ says that n is exactly one-half of N, or that just one-half of the possible outcomes result in E. The statements 'the probability is 0.5', 'the odds are 1 to 1', 'the odds are even' are exactly equivalent statements.

If you are throwing a die and want an ace to show, then $n = 1$, $N = 6$, and $(N-n)$ is 5. Thus the probability of any one face's showing is $\frac{1}{6}$, whereas the *odds* in favour of an ace, say, are 1 to 5. The odds against throwing an ace are 5 to 1.

(from: W. Weaver, *Lady Luck: The Theory of Probability*, Pelican, 1977)

1. How is it possible for a *valid inference* not also to be *true*?

2. On page 68 the following syllogism was cited as an example:

   Every M is P
   S is M
   Therefore S is P

   In column *A* are four pairs of premisses. In column *B* are four possible conclusions and a case where no valid conclusion can be arrived at. Select the appropriate conclusion from column *B* for each of the pairs in column *A*.

A	*B*
(a) All P is M Some S is not M	(i) No S is P
(b) Some P is M All M is S	(ii) All S is P
(c) No M is P Some S is M	(iii) Some S is P
(d) Some P is M Some M is not S	(iv) Some S is not P
	(v) No valid conclusion possible

3. The conclusion of a syllogism is:
   Therefore: Aristotle is not a hippo.
   Which of the following pairs of premisses would imply this as a valid conclusion?

   (a) All hippos are turnips
   Aristotle is not a turnip
   (b) All turnips are hippos
   Aristotle is not a turnip
   (c) Some turnips are not hippos
   Aristotle is a turnip
   (d) No hippo is a turnip
   Aristotle is a turnip

4. Which one of the following is the conclusion that is implied by the nine premisses of the Lewis Carroll example in the passage?
   (a) Young pigs who go up in balloons are not treated with respect.
   (b) Old pigs carying umbrellas eat penny buns
   (c) No wise young pigs go up in balloons
   (d) Pigs who dance on tightropes look ridiculous

5. What is
   (a) the probability of and
   (b) the odds against *guessing* the correct answer to a multiple-choice question where there are four possible answers, only *one* of which is correct (e.g. like question 3 above)?

6. Explain why when throwing two dice, the *odds* in favour of throwing 7 before 12 are 6 to 1.

7. Using two dice, what is the *probability* of throwing 11 before 8.

8. Re-read the paragraph that begins: 'What we need is probabilistic thinking . . .'. Apply the ideas in this paragraph to one of the following: (150–200 words)
Nuclear war
Medicine: prevention and cure
Road safety
Engineering

Further Reading

A. C. Danto, *What Philosophy Is*, Penguin
– introduction to many of the central problems of philosophy.

J. Dowie and P. Lefrere (Eds.), *Risk and Chance*, Open University Press
– interdisciplinary reader on risk and chance in a variety of contexts (health, social affairs, hazards, science, literature, etc.).

B4 Digital Electronics

Electronics is the field of science and engineering concerned with the behaviour and use of the energy of electrons in devices. In contrast to electric or electrical devices, which primarily use the flow of large currents of electricity in metal conductors to produce heat and its effects or to run motors, electronic devices involve small currents for their signal-carrying capacity.

Signals can be represented in either analog or digital form. *Analog* signals are represented by a continuous flow of energy that often functions as an electrical 'copy' of the information being signified. For example, the telephone is an analog device in which sound waves are changed into electric waves. The amperage of the electric waves changes in correspondence to the variations of the sound waves. The louder the sound, the greater the amperage.

In a *digital* device, a signal is a string of *bits* – short for 'binary digits'. The term *binary* refers to a number system that uses only the two digits 1 and 0. Digital computers, for example, process numbers and letters, which are translated into binary code – strings of 1s and 0s. In contrast to a varying, continuous electric current or analog signal, the digital signal is made up of discrete, discontinuous electrical states positioned one after the other in time. Analog and digital signals can coexist in electronic systems, and conversion between the two is not uncommon.

Among the first electronic devices were *vacuum tubes*, the use of which has dwindled since the advent of transistors. Radio and TV could not have developed without the vacuum tube devices known as the *diode* (two-element circuit) and the *triode* (three-element circuit). The disadvantages of tubes are their high power consumption, their bulkiness, and their cost. In tubes, excessive power is used to 'boil off' electrons from metal plates to generate electricity in a vacuum. In radio transmission, where high power is required for radiating electromagnetic waves, tubes still play a dominant role over their semiconductor counterparts. [. . .]

The development of digital electronics and the subsequent displacement of analog devices are spurred on by the need for greater precision in signal processing. An analog signal, as a continuous flow of electricity, is vulnerable to outside interference and distortions. An analog signal can be what is called 'noisy'. Affected by nearby, spurious signals, an analog signal can fail to clearly and cleanly represent the information it is carrying. On the other hand, a digital signal is almost nondistortable. Each signal bit in a string of bits is either one of only two voltage levels. A digital signal can contain a pure representation of the information it carries. Newly available digital audio recording systems in use in recording studios are providing a purity of sound reproduction to which analog audio systems just can't compare.

Analog/digital (A/D) conversion and the reverse, D/A conversion, are common practice. To convert an analog signal to digital, distinct levels of energy within the analog signal must be identified. Each distinct level, as it is detected, is given a specific value from among a range of specified values, broad enough to encompass the highest and lowest extremes of the analog signal. The frequency rate at which detection and value notation are made must be at a rate great enough to render a 'digitised' copy of the analog signal. (See Figure 1.) Once the signal is digitised, it is coded into binary. For example, a given digitised value of a sampled segment of the analog signal is a 7 in a range of 0 to 7. With the binary number system, a three-digit number made up of 1 s and 0 s can represent all the values from 0 to 7: 000 represents 0; 001 = 1; 010 = 2; 011 = 3; 100 = 4; 101 = 5; 110 = 6; and 111 = 7. Thus, the digitised value 7 is converted to 111. Keep in mind that 1 s and 0 s represent electrical states; for instance, 1 = a specific high voltage, and 0 = a specific low voltage. Thus, a string of binary-equivalent values becomes a series of discrete high and low 'pulses' that carry the information of the original analog signal. In the conversion of digital signals to analog, the process is reversed. An example of the use of A/D and D/A conversion can be seen in studio audio recording. Microphones pick up sound, which is itself an analog signal. They transduce the sound into analog electrical signals, which are then converted to digital. For playback, the digital signals must be converted back to analog to drive the speakers.

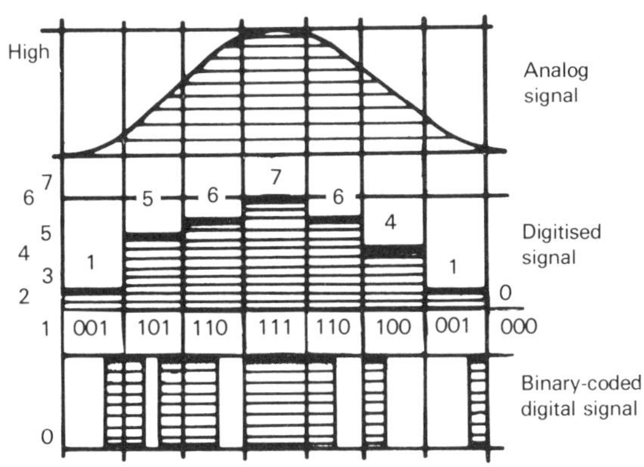

Figure 1
Analog-to-Digital Conversion

Although A/D and D/A conversions are feasible in many situations, they are not always economical. Another consideration, one that is under regular revision because of ever-upgrading circuitry, is the capacity of the medium through which the signal is sent. Digital signals require greater bandwidth, or signal-carrying capacity, than do analog signals. For instance, a television picture is transmitted in analog form. Some 7.5 million distinguishable voltage levels every second make up that signal. In the process of converting such a signal to digital form, there is an increase to 105 million distinguishable pulses per second. That signal rate happens, at present, to be beyond the capability of the conventional metal conductors used in television transmission systems.

Digital signal processing was first applied to computers. In the first written description of an electronic computer, in 1946, John von Neumann, Herman H. Goldstine, and Arthur W. Burks laid down the basics of digital operations still valid today. Their *Preliminary Discussion of the Logical Design of an Electronic Computing Instrument,* written for the U.S. Army, at the Institute for Advanced Studies at Princeton, states that such a device is made up of a collection of many two-state elements organised to represent binary numbers and coded instructions.

Boolean logic, or switching algebra, governs the way computers carry out logical operations. It stems from the work of George Boole, a nineteenth-century mathematician. To solve problems in logic, Boole created a mathematical system using symbols to represent language statements. In his system, reasoning is, in effect, turned into calculation. When statements are properly represented as prescribed by Boole, they obey certain laws of combination and thus can be added, subtracted, etc.

All statements are treated as either true or false and nothing else. True is represented by the binary digit 1; false by binary 0. For the handling of information in such a two-state format, instructions are expressed with the use of three logical operations: AND, OR, and NOT.

- AND operation: If a statement is true AND another statement (or all others) is true, then both (or all) statements together are true. If a statement in the group is false or all are false, then all statements together are false.
- OR operation: If a statement OR another (or all others) is true, then either one or both (or all) are true. If all are false, then together all are false.
- NOT operation: One statement is NOT another statement.

Figure 2
Truth Tables

Statements		Conclusions	
A	B	AND (A and B)	OR (A or B)
0	0	0	0
0	1	0	1
1	0	0	1
1	1	1	1

Statement	Conclusion
A	Not A
0	1
1	0

Truth tables are used to show the possible combinations of elements in a logic problem related to an operation. Figure 2 shows sample truth tables for AND, OR, and NOT operations using 1 s and 0 s. Note that in the AND operation, all inputs have to be 1 s to produce a 1 output. In the OR operation, only one or more inputs need be 1 to produce a 1 output. In the NOT operation, whatever the input, the output is opposite.

In the late 1930s, Claude Shannon, a graduate student at M.I.T., showed that Boolean algebra could be applied to two-state electronic devices, which opened the way for development of electronic computation as we know it today. With a simple circuit containing a switch and light bulb, 1 and 0 are represented electrically. (See Figure 3.) The 1 equates to the switch being closed and current flowing to the light bulb. The 0 equates to the switch being opened and current being prevented from reaching the light bulb. Adding a second switch in series creates an AND circuit. Both switches have to be closed if current is to reach the light bulb. If either one or both are open, no current reaches the bulb. If the second switch is added in parallel, we have an OR circuit. Only one of the two or both switches need be closed for current to reach the light bulb. Only if both (or all) are not closed is current prevented from reaching the light bulb. The NOT circuit is constructed using a switch that is normally closed. When current flows to the switch, it opens, cutting off current to the light bulb. When current ceases to flow to the switch, it closes. OR and AND circuits can be combined with NOT to make NOR and NAND circuits.

Figure 3
AND/OR Circuits

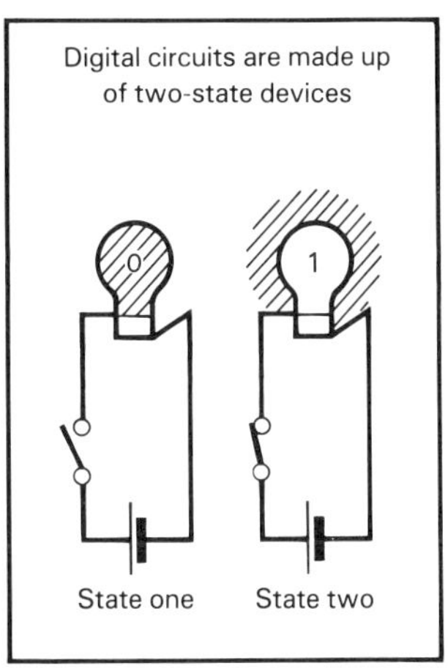

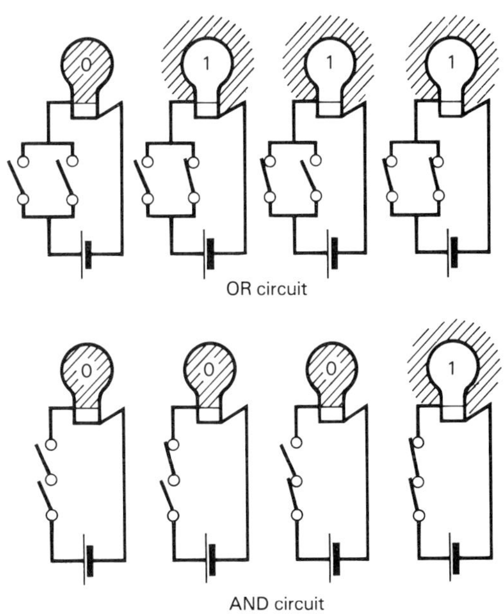

(from: K. Marsh, *The Way the New Technology Works*, Century Publishing, 1982)

1. What is a primary difference in the current flow of electronic devices compared to electric devices?

2. Distinguish between 'analog' and 'digital' signals.

3. What were the advantages of transistors over vacuum tubes?

4. As well as digital recording techniques, there are video and audio digital discs on which the digitally-encoded signal – in the form of small pits – is 'read' by laser. Explain why even with digital discs there still has to be an 'A/D' and 'D/A' conversion.

5. If a car's electrical circuit is designed to prevent the car being started if
(a) any of the doors are open, or
(b) the driver's seat belt is not fastened, is this:
 (i) an OR circuit?
 (ii) an AND circuit?
 (iii) a NOT circuit?

6. A car has an electronic alarm system that sounds the horn if a circuit is closed by opening the bonnet, boot or any of the doors. Is this:
(i) an OR circuit?
(ii) and AND circuit?
(iii) a NOT circuit?

7. In order to maximise the current available for starting, many cars incorporate a circuit that temporarily switches off the headlamps while the starter motor is being engaged. Is this:
(i) an OR circuit?
(ii) an AND circuit?
(iii) a NOT circuit?

8. Describe (or invent) an electrical circuit for a car which is either a NOR or a NAND circuit. (State which one you are describing.)

9. 'It is not so much digital electronics as the invention of the micro-chip which is revolutionising everyday life.' Discuss and illustrate with examples.

Further Reading

The Computer Book: An Introduction to Computers and Computing, BBC Publications

The Friendly Computer Book, BBC Publications
- among the clearest and best illustrated of the large number of introductory books in this field.

The BBC Computer Literacy Project, BBC Publications
- a series of programmes which are a first-class source of up-to-date information, together with support materials. The programmes cover material for absolute beginners, use of computers in office work, courses on programming in BASIC, etc. Information from:

Insight Information
BBC
London W1A 1AA

D. L. Waltz, Artificial Intelligence, *Scientific American*, October 1982
- using clear text and illustrations, this article reviews the major research over the past two decades into artificial intelligence (using the computer to develop new ways of thinking about thinking).

B5 Plate Tectonics and Earthquakes

If we were to examine the locations of the world's major earthquakes, we should find that they all fall within a marked pattern of linear zones between which lie large areas where seismic activity is minimal. Such low frequency areas are known as aseismic regions. Figure 1 shows the plotted epicentres of all the major earthquakes recorded during the year of 1970 and highlights the linearity of the global seismic zones. Clearly, the distribution of the epicentres is not a random one but is concentrated in well-defined belts such as that which marks the mid-Atlantic submarine ridge or that of the Circum-Pacific belt. The recently developed concept of *plate tectonics* explained below leaves little doubt that there is a causal relationship between the geometry of the world's tectonic plates and the geographical distribution of earthquakes.

It has been satisfactorily demonstrated by modern geologists and geophysicists that the Earth's structure is made up of a thin, rigid outer skin (some tens of kilometres thick) known as the *crust,* which is generally thicker under the continents than under the oceans. It has been calculated that below the crust there occurs a dense layer of iron- and magnesium-rich material, termed the *mantle,* which extends towards the Earth's interior to a depth of 2900 kilometres. Underlying the mantle is the *core* of the Earth, with a radius of 3490 kilometres, but this need not concern us at this juncture, for it is the composition of the mantle which is of prime importance, so far as the theory of plate tectonics is concerned. Since it was known

Figure 1
The Location of World Earthquakes in 1970 (after R. F. Legget)

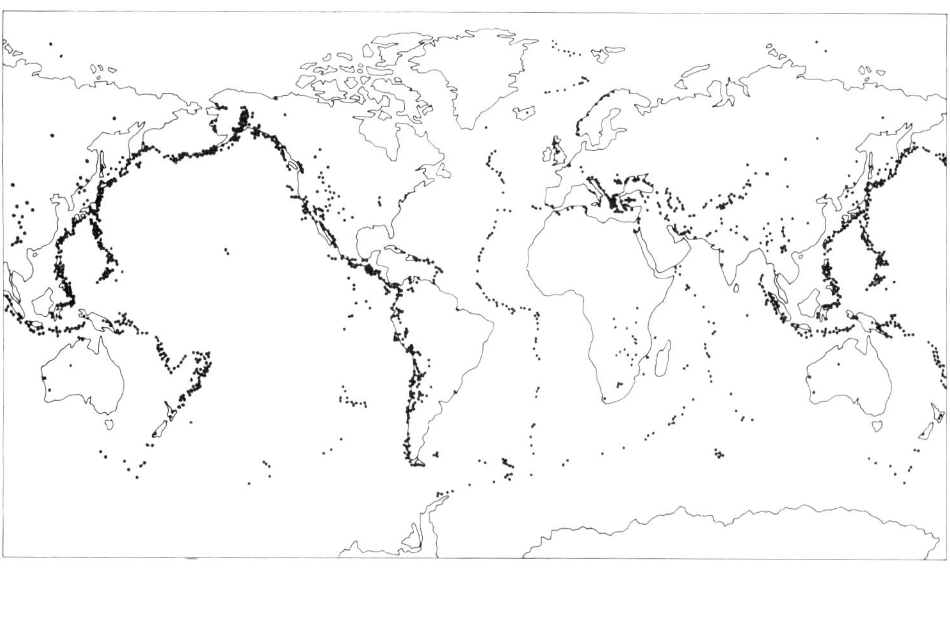

that earthquake S waves would pass through solids but not through liquids, the earliest seismic evidence seemed to suggest that the mantle was solid. Further research was able to demonstrate, however, that under certain conditions some solids begin to exhibit a plasticity and become capable of flowing. The best example to illustrate this principle of *rheidity* is that of glacier ice, which appears to possess the properties of a solid, but is also capable of flowing due to the pressure of its own weight. The same is true of the rocks of the mantle, which behave as a solid to suddenly imposed short-term shocks, such as seismic waves, but, under the sustained pressure of overlying material for millions of years, assume the properties of a liquid. Because of variations of both density and temperature within the mantle, circulatory systems similar to convection currents have developed. Thus, as hot, less-dense material rises towards the upper zone of the mantle so it will spread out just below the crust, cool down and eventually sink back into the lower mantle as its density increases.

It is now becoming clear that we have a mechanism operating in the inner layers of the mantle which is capable of carrying both the more solid upper layers of the mantle and the rigid crust horizontally across the surface of our globe. In former years this was referred to as continental drift, but it is now termed Plate Tectonics for the simple reason that it is not only the continents which are moving but the ocean floors as well. Such a mechanism has caused the Earth's crust to break up into a number of discrete plates, the edges of which rarely coincide with continental shorelines. As we shall see below, it is the plate margins which are extremely significant in earthquake studies.

Where a rising, spreading and therefore diverging, convection current occurs it is conjectured that two adjoining plates will move apart, leaving the intervening space, which is marked by a gigantic rift valley, to be filled with molten material ascending from the upper mantle. This type of tectonic movement is known as *extrusion* and the rifting is generally associated with the formation of a volcanic zone. The best example of such a plate boundary is that which forms the so-called Mid-Atlantic Ridge, marking the zone where Africa was formerly joined to South America and where Europe split off from North America some two hundred million years ago. Thus, the Atlantic Ocean has grown progressively wider throughout this period by a process termed ocean-floor spreading. A discontinuous chain of volcanic islands marks the line of the mid-oceanic rift from Tristan da Cunha in the south, through Ascension to Iceland in the north. It stands to reason, however, that if certain of the plates are moving apart then others must be moving towards each other. In order to accommodate such a movement, it becomes necessary for either one plate to over-ride another, or for a head-on collision to take place in which the frontal edge of one plate is shattered into 'flakes'. Since the latter mechanism is not clearly understood, although it may account for much of the complexity of the European Alps, we will consider only the 'over-riding' principle which is termed *subduction* (Figure 2). It is best illustrated on the western margin of South America and also around the western and northern margins of the vast Pacific Tectonic Plate, marked by the Mariana Isles and the Aleutian Isles respectively. In these

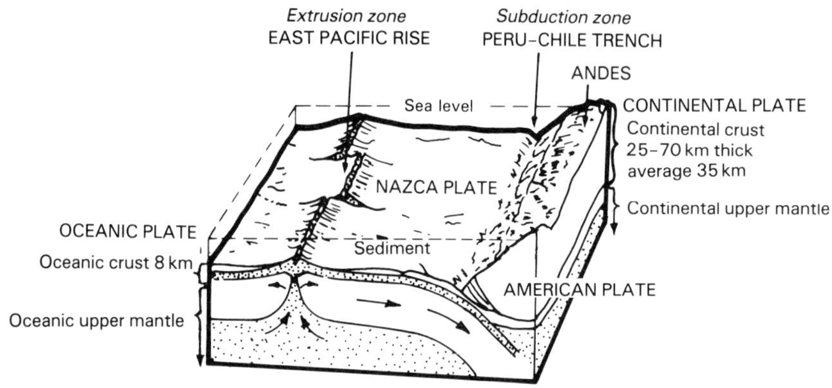

Figure 2
A Diagrammatic Representation of the South East Pacific Tectonic Plates to Illustrate the Principles of Subduction and Extrusion (after E. R. Oxburgh)

instances the Pacific Oceanic Plate is being subducted or consumed into the deeper parts of the mantle as it is gradually over-ridden by other surrounding plates. The submarine junction is generally marked by a deep oceanic trench (the Peru-Chile trench of Figure 2) beneath which is a gigantic zone of thrusting known as the Benioff zone after the well-known seismologist. On the landward side of the oceanic trenches in the northern and western Pacific lie the island arcs, so clearly illustrated in the Aleutians and the Kuril Isles. These island-chains represent the belts where the less-dense magma rises from the Benioff zone into the upper layers of the mantle before breaking sporadically through the crust as lava to build volcanic piles on the ocean floor (Figure 3). Such activity is associated with one of the Earth's most active seismic zones.

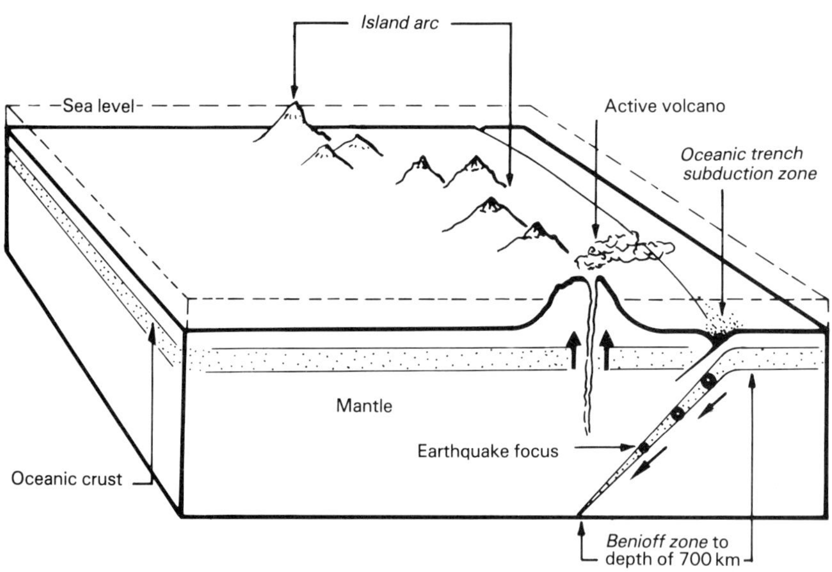

Figure 3
The Formation of Island Arcs and Oceanic Trenches (after B. A. Bolt)

So far, we have talked only in terms of *oceanic* crust and submarine plates but there are many instances where the tectonic plates coincide with *continental* blocks. When continents collide we find that instead of ocean trenches and island arcs we are faced with gigantic ranges of fold mountains.

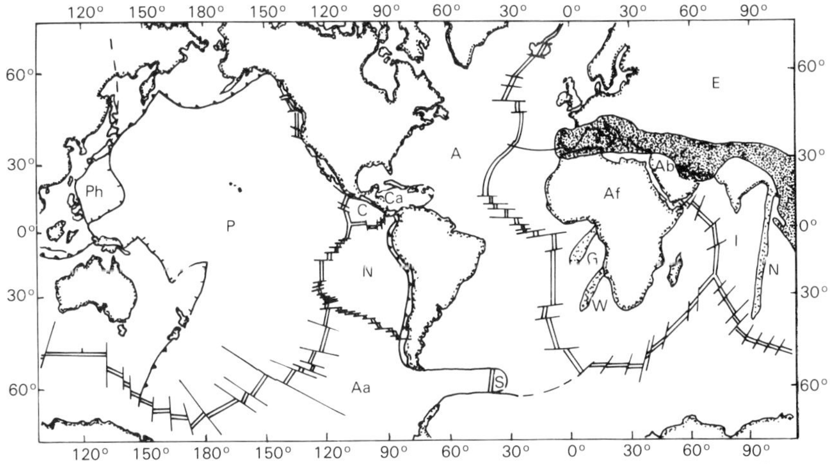

Key The present system of plates. Ridges: double lines; trenches: toothed lines; transform and strike-slip faults: single lines. A: American plate; Aa: Antarctic plate; Ab: Arabian plate; Af: African plate; C: Cocos plate; Ca: Caribbean plate; E: Eurasian plate; I: Indian plate; N: Nazca plate; P: Pacific plate; Ph: Philippine plate. The Alpine–Himalayan Tertiary collision zone is stippled. Aseismic ridges: open stipple. W: Walvis ridge; G: Cameroun line; N: ninety East Ridge; S: Scotia arc.

Figure 4
The World's Tectonic Plates (after E. R. Oxburgh)

The Himalayas are the best known example, for here the continental leading edge of the partly submerged Indian Plate has moved northwards and driven head-on into the Eurasian Plate. Figure 4 shows that the fold mountains of the Himalayan collision zone can be traced westwards into the Mediterranean basin. It also serves to illustrate the location of the eleven major plates which have so far been recognised.

A comparison between Figure 1 and Figure 4 will indicate that most of the world's major earthquakes are located along the tectonically active plate margins, being related either to the mechanisms known as extrusion and subduction, which we have already considered, or to a third type of tectonic movement known as *transcursion* in which two adjoining plates slide past each other along a series of tear faults or transcurrent faults (Figure 4). The best example of this type of junction is seen where the Pacific Plate is grinding transversely past the North American Plate, largely along the notorious San Andreas Fault of California. It will be something of a surprise to discover, therefore, that the coastal fringes of southern California do not belong to the true American continent, at least from a plate-tectonics point of view. Finally, a word of caution is necessary, for it must not be assumed that major earthquakes are to be experienced only along plate margins. Records show that severe earthquakes have also occurred in zones of weakness within the plates, as witness the severe Tangshan shock (magnitude 8.2) noted above and the damaging Meckering earthquake of 1968 (magnitude 6.8) which destroyed property near Perth in West Australia. Although these are isolated and infrequent instances, they serve to demonstrate that the plates themselves are not entirely rigid or free of locally active faults.

In summary, therefore, scientists are in general agreement that the regions of greatest tectonic instability coincide with the marginal zones of the slowly moving plates, because it is here that the crustal rocks are being subjected to enormous incessant strains as the plates travel in conflicting directions and at differing speeds. Thus, along belts of many thousands of miles, on sea-floor and on continent, rock deformation goes on unendingly, and as the deformation increases so does the stored strain energy. When the stress exceeds the strength of the rock at a particular point or even at a number of points simultaneously, often exploiting some pre-existing lithological weakness, a sudden rupture takes place. The rock on both sides of the fracture snaps back along the tearing fault and it is this sudden release of stored strain energy which produces the seismic waves and generates an earthquake. Such ruptures can occur at any point between the surface and a depth of 700 kilometres. Consequently, we read of *deep-focus* and *shallow-focus* earthquakes, the latter originating within the crust less than 40 kilometres below the surface. The shallow-focus earthquakes have been found to produce the most widespread damage and to be responsible for more than three quarters of the world's annual seismic energy release, when judged on the Richter Scale.

(from: J. Whittow, *Disasters: The Anatomy of Environmental Hazards*, Pelican, 1980)

1. What is meant by *rheidity*?
2. Explain the difference between the following types of tectonic movement:
   (a) extrusion
   (b) subduction
   (c) transcursion
3. Why is the term 'Plate Tectonics' now preferred to that of 'Continental Drift'?
4. Why are volcanoes likely to form in areas of extrusion?
5. Earthquakes along the Pacific coast of the United States are likely to be caused by which *one* of the following tectonic movements?
   (a) transcursion
   (b) extrusion
   (c) subduction
6. Alaska, in the far North West of North America, experienced a severe earthquake in 1964. This earthquake is likely to have been caused by which *one* of the following movements:
   (a) transcursion
   (b) extrusion
   (c) subduction
7. The Pacific Plate (and therefore Los Angeles and San Francisco since they are to the west of the San Andreas Fault) is moving in relation to the American Plate at an average rate of 5 centimetres a year. Looking at

Figure 4, in which direction is the Pacific Plate moving?
(a) towards the North West
or
(b) towards the South East
On what evidence in Figure 4 do you base your answer?

8. The islands that make up Japan are the world's most active seismic area. The citizens of Japan have to reconcile themselves to the inevitable recurrence of earthquakes and their related seismic sea waves (tsunamis). On the other hand, the citizens of the United States and Canada are not compelled to live in the seismically hazardous area along the western seaboard of North America. Nevertheless, the Pacific coast is a booming settlement area and includes the cities of San Diego, Los Angeles, San Francisco, Sacramento, Seattle and Vancouver (whose total populations exceed 13 million).
Why don't people abandon this area for safer parts of North America?

Further Reading

B. Bolt, *Earthquakes and Volcanoes*, Scientific American, 1980
– a collection of articles describing the nature of earthquakes and volcanoes, and the methods seismologists use to study them.

R. Redfern, *The Making of a Continent*, BBC Publications
– accompanies the television series of the same name. Notable particularly for clear illustrations of processes notoriously difficult to represent visually.

B6 Biochemistry of Freshwater Pollution

INTRODUCTION

Pollution of fresh water is one of the most serious environmental problems for the world as a whole. Unless circulation from the deep oceans is inadequate, heavy marine pollution does not extend more than a few miles offshore. The situation is very different for fresh waters, and it is difficult to see how many of the problems can, with present technology, be alleviated. We will restrict ourselves to surface waters, which may be divided into running streams, and lakes. Even in lightly-populated hard-rock areas, such as the Scottish Highlands, surface water always contains nutrients in sufficient quantities to support many kinds of life. The further a body of water (running or still) lies within a highly-populated area, the higher the concentration of nutrients that it will contain. It is not necessarily more active biologically.

Even in the absence of accidental pollution, there is not enough unused water in many temperate and tropical countries for the needs of the population. About 0.06% of the total fresh water in the world at any one time is in lakes and rivers – about 3×10^{15} litres. With a world population of 3000 million people, in theory everyone has a million litres to call his own. In practice, most of this water is not within reach of the major centres of population. In the U.S.A., the total stream flow is only 21 000 litres day^{-1} per person, and the *actual* amount withdrawn from streams is less than 4000 litres day^{-1} per person. Even the larger volume is barely capable of dissolving enough oxygen to oxidise the nitrogenous compounds which the population of the U.S.A. excretes each day, leaving nothing over for the non-nitrogenous components, or the waste products of animals or of industry. As far as possible, then, these oxidations must not be allowed to occur in lakes and streams.

Industrial processes require vast quantities of water, often for cooling, but sometimes to dilute waste products to an acceptable concentration before returning them to rivers. The very large volumes sometimes quoted for industry's requirements must be assessed with caution – the water does not simply disappear, as ultimately most of it returns to source, and the water need not be drinkable. Nevertheless, effluent water from industrial plants is always warmer than the intake, and almost always more impure. The temperature differential is often the most important factor, as explained below. Power stations, particularly nuclear plants, are especially bad sources of heat pollution.

A serious source of industrial pollution is the leaching of sulphides (particularly pyrite, FeS_2) from mine workings or dumps. Dissolved O_2 converts this to $FeSO_4$ and then to ferric sulphate, which is hydrolysed.

Ferric hydroxide ($Fe(OH)_3$) is precipitated in the stream bed, and dilute H_2SO_4 flows off. The consequent high acidity and the loss of O_2 makes the water biologically sterile, so it is both useless as a diluent, and unfit to drink. In heavily polluted waters downstream the sulphate may be reduced by anaerobic bacteria to sulphide, which is both toxic and unpleasant. Salts, especially potassium chloride from salt mines, may also cause problems.

Up to a point, river water may be re-used. Estimates have shown that much of the water running from London's taps has been taken from the Thames, purified, and returned to the river at least four times previously. On each occasion the water that is returned, although technically unobjectionable, adds a quota of nutrients, particularly nitrate, so this re-use cannot go on indefinitely without dilution by 'virgin' water.

Dilution of polluted effluent by purer water is a simple thing to specify, but the purity characteristics of the diluent water need to be discussed in some detail. Water flowing from the drains or sewage works of a town can almost always become biologically and biochemically more pure, if time is allowed for microbial action to go to completion. This requires a large volume of water so that the concentration of pollutants remains low, a relatively neutral pH, absence of obvious biochemical poisons such as cyanide, phenols, or copper salts, and abundance of dissolved O_2. In practice, the minimal diluent flow is five times the flow of effluent, if regeneration within a reasonable distance downstream is to be achieved.

Of all these requirements, the need for O_2 is the greatest. Since the solubility of gases decreases with rising temperature while the rate of biochemical activity often doubles for every 10°C rise in temperature, one may see why the temperature of water entering rivers from industrial plant is so important. Thus a large volume of effluent, even pure distilled water, coming from a power station at, say 40°C, would be disastrous. The effect of increased temperature on river life was shown in England in 1976, when prolonged drought and intense sunlight raised the temperature of many rivers to 25°C, resulting in the death of most fish. Along the S.E. coastline of the U.S.A., the summer heat and thermal pollution from industry regularly raise the temperature of rivers to 33–35°C. All living things die except a few thermophilic bacteria, which are useless for regeneration purposes.

Why is the oxygen so vital? To see this, we must consider how human effluent is dealt with in Western countries. A well-nourished adult excretes about 8 g of combined nitrogen per day. Of this about 6 g is in urea, $NH_2CO.NH_2$, 1 g in uric acid and 1 g, mostly as bacterial protein, in faeces. The latter two can fairly readily be broken down to derivatives that may be re-assimilated by growing bacteria. Urea is quickly hydrolysed by the enzyme *urease* to CO_2 and ammonia, which is toxic to most higher animals, probably because it reduces the activity of the Citric Acid Cycle in the brain. The limit of toxicity for ammonia is low and often surprisingly sharp. Trout, for instance, will die after 24 h in water containing 2 parts per million of NH_4^+ but will survive at a concentration of 1 ppm. Thus the ammonia problem may be solved by dilution (for example when untreated sewage is pumped into the sea), otherwise it must be converted into something less toxic, preferably by biological means. Fortunately there are bacteria which will convert ammonia to the far less toxic nitrite and nitrate. This solution is the one commonly adopted in inland cities of the Western world. The nitrate is very soluble and is removed from the vicinity by streams and rivers.

Conversion of NH_4^+ to NO_3^- is obviously an oxidation. In addition, human beings excrete about 100–150 g of solids each day, much of it as undigested plant polysaccharides (roughage). Microorganisms present in almost any natural water will slowly hydrolyse these polysaccharides to monosaccharides, and if an oxidising agent is available, will convert the latter to CO_2 and H_2O. This uses a lot of O_2:

$$C_6H_{12}O_6 + 6O_2 \rightarrow 6CO_2 + 6H_2O$$

Oxidation of ammonia and carbohydrate are the major chemical processes requiring dissolved O_2 in surface waters. If the oxidations can be carried out, using forced aeration, in an effluent treatment plant, this O_2 demand can be avoided. Unfortunately, treatment plants are seldom completely efficient, and the problem is made much worse if industrial effluents also contain oxidisable organic material. Among the worst offenders are industries that use polysaccharides as raw material, for example sugar refineries, paper or cellulose pulp producers and other users of wood products. These can release very large quantities of soluble carbohydrate into local rivers, to compete with the human effluent for the O_2 brought downstream. [. . .]

LAKES

The use of lakes for drinking water, and the disposal of human and industrial effluent, is no different in principle from the use of river water, and it might at first sight seem that the greater volume of water available for dilution would make pollution less formidable. There is, however, one crucial difference between rivers and lakes. The pollutants of a river will eventually flow to some unfortunate community downstream: as the Swiss export their pollution to the Germans, and the latter, with the French, burden the Dutch, by means of the Rhine as it flows from the Alps to the North Sea. The results of mismanagement of lake water stay where they are, with the community that made them. Thus Lake Erie is dead; it is unsafe to swim in, or even to sail over, but it remains obstinately outside the doors of the citizens of Detroit, and the other lakeside towns that made it so.

A lake is, in effect a trap which retains almost all the solid and dissolved matter that flows into it. Geologically speaking, lakes are temporary phenomena and they are sooner or later filled up, as the enormous sedimentary deposits of the Holocene bear witness.

There are, however, great differences in the rate at which infill takes place. Hydrologists distinguish between *oligotrophic* lakes, which lie in hardrock districts, get little soluble matter from the rocks or vegetation surrounding them, and consequently can support only a low density of plant and fish life; and *eutrophic* lakes, lying in softer rock surrounded by a more fertile soil (and usually a denser population).

The increase in the productivity (fertility) of lake water is called *eutrophication.* Human populations can speed this up to such an extent as to diminish drastically the usefulness of the lake water, and the process is almost irreversible. It is compounded by the peculiar behaviour of large volumes of water.

Lakes, unless very shallow, rarely freeze completely even when the surface temperature goes below zero for long periods, because the maximum density of water lies at 4°C, so that colder water floats to the top. The body of water which lies below the frost boundary in the surrounding soil remains at 4°C. When the air becomes warmer in the spring this lower part of the lake does not, as might be expected, become warmer. Instead a sharp temperature boundary, the thermocline, is established about 16 m down; above this level the water circulates by convection currents and is rapidly warmed by sun and air. The water in the lower layer, or *hypolimnion* (Figure 1) remains at 4°C and does not physically mix with the upper layer, or *epilimnion.* At 16 m there is very little light, even in the clearest lake, for photosynthesis, and in consequence the hypolimnion only becomes oxygenated at the two seasons in the year (spring and autumn) when the temperature of the epilimnion is also 4°C, and bulk mixing can take place. Winds, by turbulence, increase the depth at which the thermocline is found, and blur the boundary, producing an intermediate zone, or *metalimnion.* The persistence of strong winds over the open oceans helps to prevent the establishment of permanent temperature boundaries, except in the tropics.

The charge of oxygen that the hypolimnion receives in spring has thus to sustain all the aerobic activity within it, both plant and animal, until the autumn. At the same time, the hypolimnion must deal with the rain of solid matter brought in by the inflowing rivers, and also with the organic matter released on the death of organisms in the epilimnion. This will happen faster in summer, when higher temperature and abundance of sunlight provide favourable conditions. If the supply of nutrients to the epilimnion becomes too great, it is the hypolimnion which first becomes anaerobic, with serious consequences.

The nutrients required for growth and replication of organisms are nitrogen, which, as we have seen, is continuously added to rivers by human activity, together with potassium, magnesium and phosphate, and many trace elements. It is often phosphate which is the limiting ingredient and the amounts added to lakes over the last few decades from washing powders

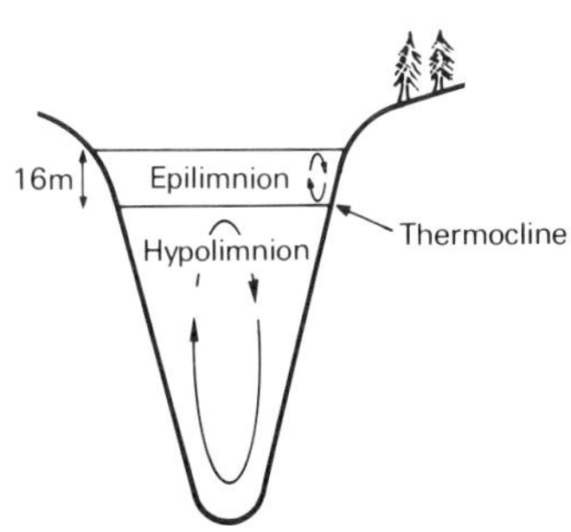

Figure 1
Temperature Boundaries in Lake Waters

and fertilisers can make a serious difference to the biological balance. In hot summer weather when the dissolved oxygen concentration is low, the epilimnion of lakes can become anaerobic; in which case shallow-water fish die. Algal blooms may form, and reduce the attractiveness of the lake waters for leisure purposes. Moreover, by-products of some algae are toxic to cattle. The water may become unpalatable for human consumption, and algal remains clog the input filters of the water purification plants.

However, anaerobiosis in the hypolimnion is more serious even than this. Debris which passes through the thermocline sinks to the bottom as a mud similar to that in a polluted river, and the nutrients in the mud support the activities of a wide range of anaerobic bacteria. Less dense products (H_2S, CO_2, CH_4, and sometimes other specialised pollutants) rise, perhaps as bubbles, through the water column back to the epilimnion. The inorganic nutrients released on the death of the bacteria remain in the mud and are taken up by new microorganisms. When a lake has reached this stage, in which both epi- and hypolimnion are anaerobic for much of the year, it is said to be 'eutrophicated'. The lake waters, previously used for drinking water by the towns on the bank, become foul-tasting, and if there is an effluent stream, it is useless as a supply of diluent for the reasons outlined in the previous section.

It is, unfortunately, almost impossible to regenerate a eutrophicated lake. Even if all pollution is prevented from entering its waters, the mud on the bottom has to be removed, which has only proved possible for small lakes. In the neighbourhood of Geneva, which depends heavily on lake water, as much as a million tonnes of oxygen per year has been pumped into the hypolimnion. This treatment has been successful, but is obviously a desperate and expensive remedy. In general, it is only possible to cut down the amount of nutrient entering the lake (particularly phosphate), and to hope that in a few decades aerobic conditions will be re-established. Some hope is provided by the partial regeneration of Lake Michigan, but Lake Erie, which is only 50 m deep, is still sterile. This is also the present state of many Swedish and Finnish lakes, eutrophicated by untreated sewage and wood pulp effluents. Further east, strict control is yet to come. Immense amounts of nutrients brought in by the Volga are rapidly eutrophicating the Caspian Sea; in addition the bottom of the southern half of this sea is said to be covered by several centimetres of tar from the oil fields of Georgia. The floor of Lake Baikal, the largest fresh-water lake in the world, is reputed to be covered by millions of tonnes of waterlogged tree trunks, lost during lumbering operations, which will provide enough oxidisable carbohydrates to keep the bottom mud anaerobic for centuries.

(from: J. H. Ottaway, *The Biochemistry of Pollution*, Arnold, 1980)

1. If only 'about 0.06% of the total fresh water in the world at any one time is in the lakes and rivers', where is some of the rest of the fresh water?
2. Give two reasons why the temperature of even clean water entering rivers from industrial plants is important.

3. What is the difference between *aerobic* and *anaerobic* bacteria?

4. (a) In what two processes is dissolved oxygen in surface water particularly important?
(b) What happens if there is insufficient dissolved oxygen?

5. In what principal way do lakes differ from rivers in the problems they pose for pollution management?

6. In the summer the warmer water floats to the top of the lake. In freezing winter conditions the colder floats to the top. How can both of these happen?

7. Which two means of oxygenation are absent from the *hypolimnion* in summer and winter?

8. Give two reasons why the *hypolimnion* is the first part of the lake to become anaerobic.

9. Why would the mud have to be removed from the bottom of a *eutrophicated* lake before it could be regenerated?

10. What can individual countries do to prevent their air and water being polluted by other countries?

11. The passage outlines some of the immense problems encountered in regenerating eutrophicated lakes. By what means could the following types of pollution be reduced or eliminated and what difficulties would such 'cleaning up' programmes face?

'Acid rain'
Oil pollution
Heavy metal, e.g. mercury in water
Lead in the atmosphere
Radioactivity

12. It is proposed to build a nuclear power station of the fast breeder type in a remote country district, which is rich in flora and fauna and is of marked natural beauty. Give the main arguments that might be advanced
(a) for, and
(b) against this proposal. Discuss their relative merits and attempt on this basis to reach a conclusion as to the wisdom of this proposal. Your discussion should cover technical, scientific, ethical and aesthetic issues and any others you consider relevant.

13. The basic premiss underlying the economic system described in passage A2 is that growth is both necessary and worthwhile. However, many theorists and observers of the late 20th century now believe that a blind pursuit of growth has led to many unforeseen and undesirable consequences. Write an essay outlining the consequences which are already with us and those which could happen in the future. (You will find it useful to refer to passage A2. See also the book by F. Capra in the Further Reading in A2.)

Further Reading

Journals like *New Scientist* and *Scientific American* regularly have articles on environmental concerns. Three examples from the former are:

C. Joyce, Can We Save Chesapeake Bay? *New Scientist*, 24 March 1983
– an account of the Chesapeake Bay Program, born in 1977 and 'one of the world's most intense examinations of marine pollution'.

M. Allaby, The Greening of the Cornish Alps, *New Scientist*, 21 April 1983
– describes the reclamation of the industrial wasteland of Cornish china clay pits.

G. Matthews, Can We Control Insect Pests? *New Scientist*, 12 May 1983
– looks at biological, cultural and chemical controls of agricultural pests.

The Physics of Music

B 7

SOUND: THE MATERIAL OF MUSIC

In the beginning, we may suppose, there was silence. There was silence because there was no motion, and therefore no vibration could move the air - a phenomenon of fundamental importance in producing sound. The creation of the world, however it came about, must have been accompanied by motion - and therefore sound. Perhaps this is why music has such magical importance for primitive peoples, often signifying life and death. Right through its history, in all its varying forms, music has kept its transcendental significance.

Sound can only be produced by a kind of motion. The motion (or *vibration*) arising from a vibrating body, for example a string, or the skin of a drum, generates waves of compression which travel through the air to our ear. The *speed* at which the sound travels from the vibratory body to the ear is about 1100 feet per second. This speed naturally changes according to the condition of the atmosphere. As well as air, there are other media capable of transmitting sound, as for example water, wood, etc., but this passage deals only with musical sound and its artistic use, so our medium is air.

If the vibration is regular, the resulting sound is musical and represents a note of a definite pitch; if it is irregular the result is noise. This phenomenon can be simply illustrated by the 'graphic' method. A needle is soldered to one prong of a tuning-fork and is placed vertically over a blackened glass so as to lightly touch it. Then the tuning-fork is made to vibrate and the glass is slowly moved forward. The result is that as the tuning-fork vibrates the needle scratches a *regular* set of curves.

Every sound has three characteristic properties. Let us take an everyday example. When walking along the street we hear several sounds at the same time; cars, motorbikes, aeroplanes, radios, people walking and talking, simultaneously produce sounds of higher and lower, louder and softer degrees. With our ear we automatically distinguish between the highness of a child's voice and the lowness of a man's, the loudness of a passing plane and the hum of traffic, and we know whether the tune coming from somebody's radio is played on a trumpet or a violin. In doing this, we are unconsciously selecting the three characteristics of a sound: *pitch*, *volume*, and *quality*.

Pitch

Perception of pitch means the ability to distinguish between the highness and the lowness of a musical sound. That its pitch is high or low depends on the *frequency* (number of vibrations per second) of the vibrating body. The higher the frequency of a sound, the higher is its pitch, the lower the frequency, the lower its pitch. Physicists demonstrate this by the following experiment. A piece of metal is fixed so that it makes contact with a cog-wheel, which is then turned, thus generating vibrations in the air. If the wheel has, for example, 128 teeth, and using an adjustable motor we make it turn twice per second, we get a sound of 256 vibrations, or cycles, per second (c/s). If we make it turn once per second we get a sound of 128 vibrations, which is lower than the former, and so on.

The downward threshold of our hearing is about 16–20 vibrations per second, the upward threshold about 20 000 vibrations per second. The limit of the normal range of musical sound is best demonstrated by the fact that a mixed choir produces sound between the frequencies 64 and 1500, and a large concert piano (with a longer keyboard than the domestic variety) ranges from about 20 c/s to 4176 c/s.

Volume

We have seen that the pitch of a note depends entirely on the *frequency* of its vibration. The *volume* of a note depends on the *amplitude* of the vibration. More (or less) intensive vibration produces louder (or softer) sounds.

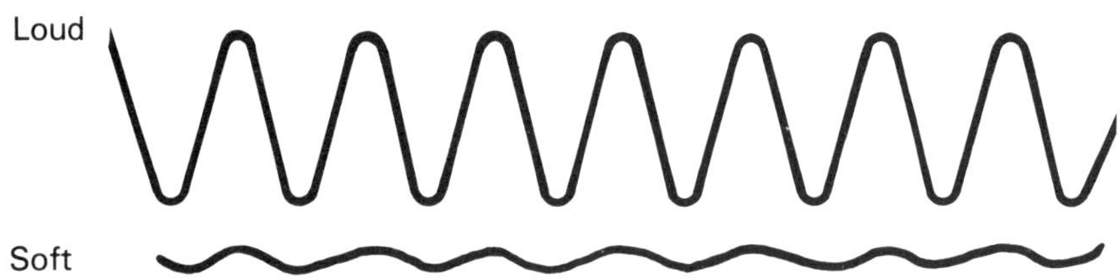

Quality

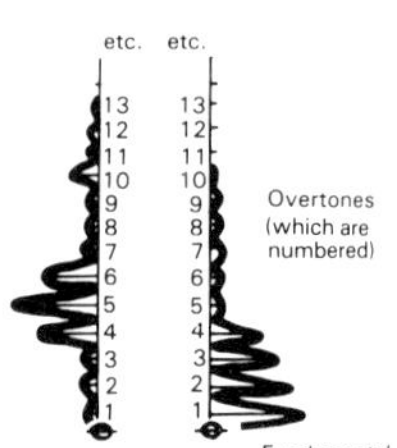

Quality (or in French, *timbre*) defines the difference in tone colour between a note played on different instruments or sung by different voices. Thus the 'colour' of a note enables us to distinguish between various instruments playing the same tune. No one will find it difficult to distinguish between the tone of a trumpet and a violin. But why? Here we come to one of the most fascinating of acoustic phenomena, the *overtones.* The characteristic frequency of a note is only the *fundamental* of a series of other notes which are simultaneously present over the basic one. These notes are called overtones (or partials, or harmonics). The reason why the overtones are not distinctly audible is that their intensity is less than that of the fundamental. But they are important because they determine the *quality* of a note, and they also give brilliance to the tone. What makes us able to distinguish between the quality of, say, an oboe and a horn, is the varying intensity of the overtones over the actual notes which they play. You can imagine what a complex wave pattern a full orchestra produces.

Before leaving the field of pure physics there are a few more points which are worth mentioning, as they are bound to crop up frequently in the listener's experience.

Standard Pitch

When we go to a concert-hall, before the concert begins we notice that at a given moment the musicians of the orchestra or ensemble adjust their instruments to a note played by the principal oboe or first violinist. They are tuning their instruments to a note which has (or should have) 440 vibrations per second. This standard pitch was accepted by most of the Western nations at an international conference in 1939.

Intonation

Good intonation, that is, being in tune (pitching the notes accurately), has of course capital importance for the musician (not to say his listeners). But what happens acoustically when we notice uneasily that something is wrong during a performance, that someone is playing too high or too low? We commonly say that the player is out of tune. What actually happens is this: if two notes have the same frequency, for example 440, we know that they have the same pitch, and so they are in unison. But if one of these is played slightly out of tune and has only 435 c/s, the result is that the former note will produce shorter waves than the latter, and these waves inevitably collide with each other, producing a pulsating effect, the number of beats produced per second being the difference between the two frequencies. In our example this would mean five beats per second. It is interesting to note that after a certain number of beats (about 30 per second) the disturbing effect diminishes.

Resonance

Some of us may have noticed that singing or whistling at a certain pitch can cause some near-by object, say, a tumbler, to resound sympathetically. This illustrates the principle of resonance: when two vibrating sources are at the same pitch, and one is set into vibration, the untouched one will take the vibration sympathetically from the other. Thus when we sing it is not our vocal cords alone which produce sound, but the sympathetic vibrations set up in the cavities of our head. The same thing happens with man-made instruments: it is the belly of the violin which actually produces the tone, by vibrating sympathetically with the bowed string. This acoustic phenomenon is very useful in reinforcing the tone of both bowed and plucked string instruments. (The viola d'amore, with its 'sympathetic' strings placed under the bowed strings, is one example of this.)

Acoustics of Auditoriums

There is another factor which very much determines, or rather modifies, the tone quality of instruments and voices. This is whether an auditorium is 'good' or 'bad' for sound, which means whether or not it possesses balanced resonance. This was instinctively felt by many composers and performers of the past, notably Bach, who, we are told, used to clap his hands and count until the sound was absorbed in order to achieve an approximate idea of the acoustics of a building where he had to play. But not till the late nineteenth century was a scientific explanation found for this phenomenon. Now we know that whether or not an auditorium is good for sound depends on the length of its 'reverberation period' (which means the length of time a sound takes to die away). Experiments have shown that the most convenient reverberation period for speech and music is between about 1 and $2\frac{1}{2}$ seconds. The acoustics of a hall can be modified by various devices, such as putting up or taking away hangings which absorb the sound.

(from: Ottó Károlyi, *Introducing Music*, Penguin, 1965)

The principles of physics described above apply not only to the *production* of music but also to the *reproduction* of music on domestic 'hi-fi' systems. You may find that you will have to do some research in order to answer all of the following questions:

1. (a) Explain the importance of the accuracy and constancy of speed of a gramophone record turntable for realistic reproduction of music.

(b) Describe at least one method by which turntable manufacturers seek to achieve these objectives.

2. How does the shape of the groove in a gramophone record change with variations in both the frequency and volume of the music recorded on it?

3. Electronic music 'synthesisers' (including the more complex 'home' electronic organs) are often used to attempt to simulate the sound of particular musical instruments (some home organs have keys marked with the names of different instruments).
Explain why it is difficult to make these 'synthesisers' sound convincingly realistic, particularly over the whole range of an instrument such as a clarinet or a piano.

4. A loudspeaker must vibrate accurately to convert electrical impulses into sound waves of 'high fidelity' ('hi-fi'). Why is it important that the loudspeaker *cabinet* does *not* vibrate with the loudspeaker?

5. When choosing and installing a domestic hi-fi system, what consideration should be given to the characteristics of the room in which it is being installed?

Further Reading

Introductory textbooks on Physics will normally have sections on sound. For example, A. F. Abbott, *Ordinary Level Physics*, Heinemann, has chapters on Longitudinal Waves and Sound, Musical Sounds and Strings and Pipes.

Cassette Tape Recording

B8

In 1963, the giant Dutch-based electrical company Philips launched a new type of tape recorder, which did away with the tedious business of threading tape on to spools and around tapes guides. They called it the Compact Cassette.

But Philips did not conceive the cassette as a medium for high fidelity music reproduction. In order to make the cassette compact, they had used tape half the width of standard recording tape, and in order to get a reasonable playing time from the Compact Cassette they had fixed on a speed half that used by most domestic reel-to-reel recorders. All other things being equal, the sound quality to be had from tape is proportionately worse the slower the tape runs and the narrower the recorded tracks. So the sound of the Compact Cassette was adequate for speech recording in business and other functional applications, but left a lot to be desired. The cassette certainly caught on quickly – largely because Philips allowed other manufacturers to produce decks and tapes without paying any licence fee, provided the technical specifications and dimensions laid down by them were adhered to – but for some years it was looked at askance by hi-fi purists.

From the hi-fi point of view, there were several points of criticism. First and most obvious was the amount of audible tape hiss which could be heard when listening to most kinds of music, but was particularly objectionable on classical music, where there might be very quiet passages or silences. Second, and related to this, was the cassette's lack of dynamic range – in other words, the cassette was incapable of realistically reproducing the range between crescendos and quiet passages because either the loud passages would overload the tape and sound distorted, or the quietest bits would be buried in the hiss.

DOLBY NOISE REDUCTION

However, one very clever innovation transformed the performance of the Compact Cassette as a recording medium, and opened the way for further developments. This was of course the Dolby *B* noise reduction system, invented by the American Ray Dolby, at the end of the 1960s.

Dolby had successfully introduced a professional noise reduction system, known as Dolby *A*, but this was too expensive and cumbersome for inclusion in domestic equipment. Dolby *B* was a very much simplified but nonetheless very effective domestic system using similar basic principles. It is impossible here to give more than a very simple idea of how the system works. Basically, the Dolby circuits operate on the audio signal both prior to recording and prior to the playback output – *processing* and *deprocessing* (or sometimes 'encoding' and 'decoding') respectively.

On record, the Dolby circuit selectively boosts low-level treble signals, leaving high-level treble signals and bass parts of the signal untouched. So when the audio signal reaches the tape, the level of the quietest treble sounds has been raised so that they will record above the intrinsic hiss level of the tape.

On replay, the signal is given the reverse treatment – those treble parts of the signal which were boosted on record are brought back down to their proper level relative to the rest of the music signal – but this automatically means that the hiss from the tape (which is mostly treble frequencies) is brought down too. When working correctly, Dolby *B* can reduce the apparent level of tape noise by 9 or 10dB, which means in practical terms the difference between quite annoying and practically inaudible amounts of hiss.

Dolby *B* is now universal on hi-fi decks, but has been effectively upgraded with the introduction of Dolby *C*. This employs the same principles, but with the processing and deprocessing in effect made twice as drastic, thus giving twice as much hiss reduction – with the benefit of improved usable dynamic range.

FURTHER DEVELOPMENT

With the inclusion of Dolby *B*, the cassette deck became, potentially at least, an important part of the hi-fi scene. Although Philips in Europe had invented the system, it was really the Japanese who raised the level of cassette technology to its current heights. During the 1970s, when Philips were only grudgingly beginning to acknowledge the existence of Dolby, the Japanese manufacturers were forging ahead with research and development programmes aimed at making cheaper and better decks (and tapes), and with the ultimate aim of making cassette performance as good as reel-to-reel tape recording. How well they succeeded will be obvious if you compare the performance and facilities on a good £100 deck of today with a machine that cost £150 five years ago – cassette decks *have* got better and cheaper, even without allowing for inflation! As for the comparison between cassette deck performance and that of reel-to-reel decks, there is no doubt that the gap has continued to narrow over the last year.

Along with the genuine advances though, there have been some innovations that turned out to be unsatisfactory in one way or another, and of course there have been some extra 'facilities' which turned out to be little more than gimmicks. It is also perhaps ironic that while the cassette was meant originally as a simple and convenient recording system which was very easy to use, some modern decks fall into the 'Concorde flight-deck' category, being covered with an excessive amount of switches and flashing lights. These will be a delight to compulsive knob-twiddlers, but a nightmare to the non-technical.

However, many of the extra controls found on cassette decks now actually are put there to make the machine easier to use. There are a number of variations on the 'programme search' theme – features designed to enable you to find the beginning or end of a piece of a music quickly and easily. Most of these work simply by detecting a gap between recorded items while fast winding or rewinding, but some decks also have complex microprocessor-based counter and 'memory' facilities to enable you to preselect particular parts of the tape and replay them as desired. These kind of options are very much a matter of personal taste, and if you are attracted to particular models because of them, do try them out in the shop before buying to make sure that the deck will really do what you want, and not just make life more complicated!

Typical Track Dimensions on Cassette Tape

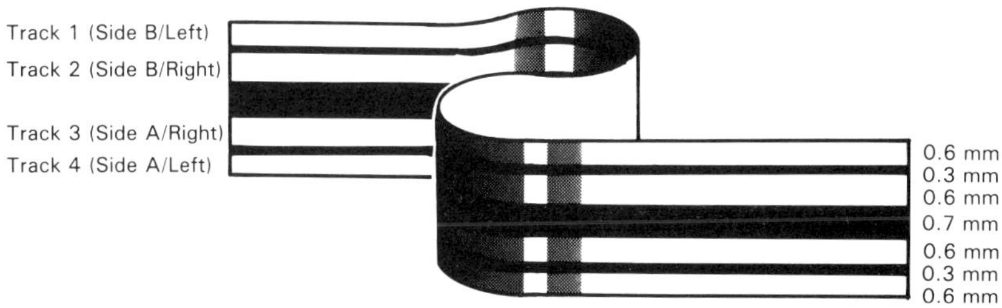

Microprocessor technology has brought another very important benefit to cassette decks, though, and that is the possibility of designing a deck to set itself up to give optimum results on whatever tape you insert into it. Several Japanese manufacturers have introduced such decks, which have proved successful. Their efforts are to be applauded, for the business of matching tapes to decks is really the bane of the serious cassette user. But to cover this subject, we had better first look at the basics of cassette recording.

HOW TAPE RECORDING WORKS

In tape recording, sound signals are stored as a magnetic pattern along the length of the tape. The tape consists of a polyester-type plastics backing layer, on which is applied a special coating with magnetic properties. This coating usually contains very tiny particles of ferric iron oxide (hence *ferric* tapes) though advanced tape types may use chromium dioxide particles (*chrome* tapes) or most recently pure or metal alloy particles instead of oxides (*metal* tapes).

Basic Operation of Recording Head

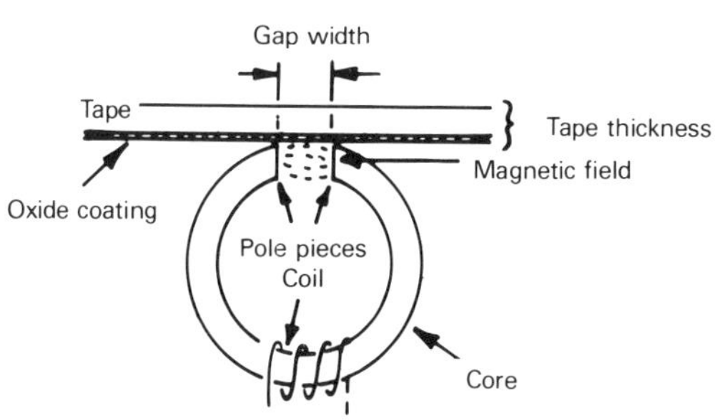

To produce a recording, the tape is pulled at constant speed past the recorder's *tape head.* This is essentially an electromagnet, in which a current passing through a coil creates a magnetic field in the core on which the coil is wound. The two ends of the core, the *pole pieces,* are brought together with only a minute *gap* between their ends, so that the magnetic flux is concentrated in and around this gap. The current fed to the record head (and hence the magnetic flux) is varied in accordance with the audio signal to be recorded, and so as the tape passes the gap a constantly varying degree of magnetisation produces a stored analogue of the original sound waveforms.

Playback may be accomplished using the same head. This time, as the tape passes over the head gap the varying magnetic field of the tape coating induces tiny currents in the coil. These can be amplified and converted back into sound by a loudspeaker or headphones.

An *erase head,* placed so that the tape goes past it just before reaching the record head, 'wipes' any previous magnetic patterns from the tape. It does this by applying to the tape a powerful magnetic field which alternates in polarity at several times the frequency of the highest audio frequencies (usually at least 80 kHz), and this effectively randomises the magnetic orientation of the particles in the coating.

Most cassette decks in use, and all non hi-fi ones such as portables, are *two-head decks,* having a single record-and-playback head, plus a separate erase head. However, there are performance advantages to be gained by having separate record and playback heads and decks which have this feature are called *three-head decks.* In a cassette deck, the size of the record/playback head assembly is strictly limited as it must be able to enter the appropriate aperture in the body of the cassette. So manufacturers of three-head cassette decks have had to use considerable ingenuity and have often used a *combination* record and playback head – this consists of separate record and replay heads built into a single body.

BIAS

If the record head was simply fed with the alternating audio signal current, the recording would be very distorted. This is because the relationship between input current and amplitude of magnetisation on the tape is non linear – in other words, a graph of input-versus-magnetisation is not a straight line going up at 45 degrees from zero, but is distinctly S-shaped.

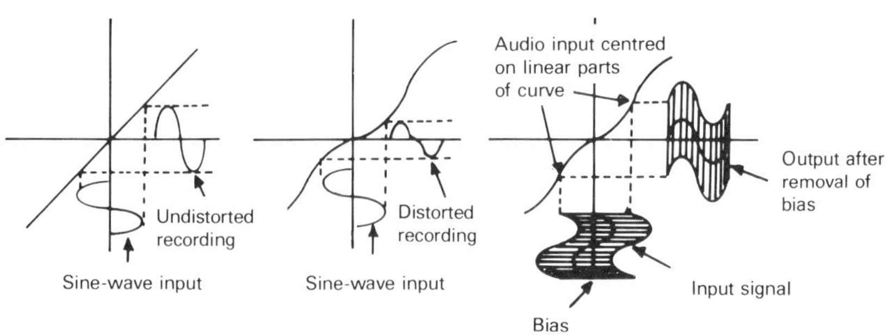

Why Bias is Needed. Left, what would happen if the input-versus-magnetisation characteristic of head and tape was perfectly linear. This can never happen in reality! Centre diagram shows what would actually happen, without bias, due to the 'kink' in the input-versus-magnetism characteristic. The output is clearly distorted. Right, the high-frequency bias current effectively 'lifts' the audio signal to a linear part of the curve. The bias frequency itself is self-erased as the tape leaves the head gap.

This non-linearity is overcome by *biasing* the audio signal. As well as the wanted audio frequency signal, the record head is fed with a carefully-controlled amount of the very high frequency alternating current used for erasing. The audio modulations are in effect super-imposed on this bias current, which thus raises them in level to a part of the input-versus-magnetisation curve which is virtually a straight line. This is shown in the diagrams. Note that the bias frequency, in any case far above the audible range, disappears from the output.

This electronic dodge would hardly concern the cassette deck user, except that different tapes need different amounts of bias to work at their best. All modern hi-fi cassette decks provide bias setting which is switchable between three positions optimised for ferric, chrome (or pseudochrome) and metal tape types.

Bias requirements vary between different brands of tape within the same category, though, and so for example the 'ferric' setting on any given machine will suit some tapes better than others. The most obvious audible results of incorrect biasing are changes in frequency response - too little bias for the tape being used will emphasise the treble and make the sound 'bright' while too much bias will make the sound lacking in treble, dull and muffled. In fact the optimisation of bias setting is a compromise between various factors.

Fortunately there now seems to be a greater effort on the part of tape manufacturers to standardise bias requirements in accordance with the stipulations of the IEC.

EQUALISATION

The term *equalisation* or 'eq' when applied to cassette decks normally means 'replay equalisation'. This describes the deliberate adjustment of frequency response in the replay amplifier, to international standards, which if the record side is set up correctly by the manufacturer, will give a flat overall response from record input to playback output.

Replay equalisation switches will be marked '120μs' (for ferric tapes) and '70μs' (for chrome, pseudochrome and metal tapes). Setting the switch in the wrong position will make the sound too bright or too dull - for example, playing back a ferric tape on 70μs will cut off too much treble, making the sound dull.

Very often bias and equalisation controls are combined as a single 'tape selector' for convenience, although of course bias acts only on record.

There are some machines which do allow adjustment of *record equalisation*, either manually or via a microprocessor-controlled automatic setting-up system, but these are a minority.

(from: *Hi-Fi Choice Cassette Decks and Tapes*, Felden Productions, 1983)

1. What were the two principal reasons why the sound quality of Compact Cassettes when first introduced was inferior to conventional 'reel-to-reel' tape recording?

2. Very simply put, how does the 'Dolby *B*' noise reduction system work? Is it:

(a) by boosting the recording of quiet, bass signals and replaying them at a higher level?

or

(b) by reducing the recording of loud treble signals and replaying them at a higher level?

or

(c) by boosting the recording of quiet treble signals and replaying them at a lower level?

or

(d) by boosting the recording of all low-level signals and replaying them at a lower level?

3. Carefully explain how it is possible to use the *same* 'head' for both recording and replay.

4. What is the reason why different types of tape may require different amounts of 'bias' during recording?

(a) their different 'replay equalisations'
(b) their different magnetisation characteristics
(c) their different speeds
(d) their different playing times

This is an illustration of the construction of a typical tape cassette (tape running from left to right).

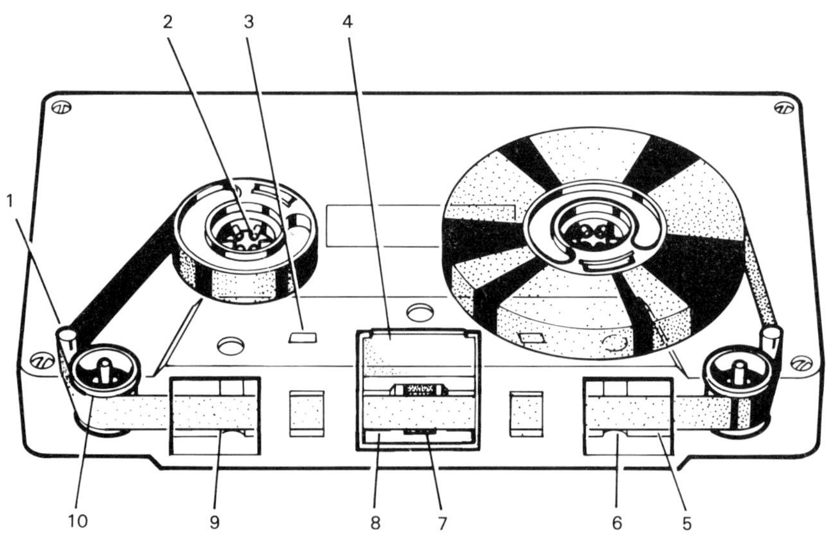

5. Match the features listed below with the numbered arrows in the illustration (if you think that arrow number 2 is the 'tape guide pin', then you would write 'C2' and so on).

A Hub: loose in cassette housing, engages splined spindle in cassette player
B Erase head enters here, wiping off previous recordings before tape reaches the record head
C Tape guide pin
D Metal hum shield: prevents stray magnetic fields from reaching head during playback
E Hole for locating peg
F Capstan (narrow revolving metal post driven by cassette deck motor) enters here. Tape driven between this and rubber pinch wheel
G Pressure pad: spring-mounted felt keeps tape in good contact with record/play head
H Tape guide roller
I Rubber pinch wheel enters here
J Record/play head enters cassette housing here

6. In the illustration opposite, on which side of the exposed length of tape is the oxide coating?

(a) the side facing outward towards the reader
(b) both sides
(c) the side facing inward towards the centre of the cassette

7. Why does the construction of the cassette have to be *symmetrical* for use in virtually all cassette players, even the most basic models?

8. In the illustration opposite, is the tape:

(a) near the beginning of play of that side?
(b) near the end of play of that side?

9. Explain the importance of precision manufacture of the cassette as well as the cassette player by indicating some of the faults that defects in tape cassette manufacture could cause (clearly indicate the manufacturing defect followed by the resultant performance fault).

B9 Extraterrestrial Life

In our history it [extra-intelligent life] was some horde of furry little mammals who hid from the dinosaurs, colonised the treetops and later scampered down to domesticate fire, invent writing, construct observatories and launch space vehicles. If things had been a little different, it might have been some other creature whose intelligence and manipulative ability would have led to comparable accomplishments. Perhaps the smart bipedal dinosaurs, or the raccoons, or the otters, or the squid. It would be nice to know how different other intelligences can be; so we study the whales and the great apes. To learn a little about what other kinds of civilisations are possible, we can study history and cultural anthropology. But we are all of us – us whales, us apes, us people – too closely related. As long as our inquiries are limited to one or two evolutionary lines on a single planet, we will remain forever ignorant of the possible range and brilliance of other intelligences and other civilisations.

On another planet, with a different sequence of random processes to make hereditary diversity and a different environment to select particular combinations of genes, the chances of finding beings who are physically very similar to us is, I believe, near zero. The chances of finding another form of intelligence is not.[. . .]

Because we inhabit the same universe as they, we and they must share some substantial information in common. If we could make contact, there is much in their brains that would be of great interest to ours. But the opposite is also true. I think extraterrestrial intelligence – even beings substantially further evolved than we – will be interested in us, in what we know, how we think, what our brains are like, the course of our evolution, the prospects for our future.

If there are intelligent beings on the planets of fairly nearby stars, could they know about us? Might they somehow have an inkling of the long evolutionary progression from genes to brains to libraries that has occurred on the obscure planet Earth? If the extraterrestrials stay at home, there are at least two ways in which they might find out about us. One way would be to listen with large radio telescopes. For billions of years they would have heard only weak and intermittent radio static caused by lightning and the trapped electrons and protons whistling with the Earth's magnetic field. Then, less than a century ago, the radio waves leaving the Earth would become stronger, louder, less like noise and more like signals. The inhabitants of Earth had finally stumbled upon radio communication. Today there is a vast international radio, television and radar communications traffic. At some radio frequencies the Earth has become by far the brightest object, the most powerful radio source, in the solar system – brighter than

Jupiter, brighter than the Sun. An extra-terrestrial civilisation monitoring the radio emission from Earth and receiving such signals could not fail to conclude that something interesting had been happening here lately.[. . .]

But is there anyone out there to talk to? With a third or half a trillion stars in our Milky Way Galaxy alone, could ours be the only one accompanied by an inhabited planet? How much more likely it is that technical civilisations are a cosmic commonplace, that the Galaxy is pulsing and humming with advanced societies, and, therefore, that the nearest such culture is not so very far away - perhaps transmitting from antennas established on a planet of a naked-eye star just next door. Perhaps when we look up at the sky at night, near one of those faint pinpoints of light is a world on which someone quite different from us is then glancing idly at a star *we* call the Sun and entertaining, for just a moment, an outrageous speculation.

It is very hard to be sure. There may be severe impediments to the evolution of a technical civilisation. Planets may be rarer than we think. Perhaps the origin of life is not so easy as our laboratory experiments suggest. Perhaps the evolution of advanced life forms is improbable. Or it may be that complex life forms evolve readily, but intelligence and technical societies require an unlikely set of coincidences - just as the evolution of the human species depended on the demise of the dinosaurs and the ice-age recession of the forests in whose trees our ancestors screeched and dimly wondered. Or perhaps civilisations arise repeatedly, inexorably, on innumerable planets in the Milky Way, but are generally unstable; so all but a tiny fraction are unable to survive their technology and succumb to greed and ignorance, pollution and nuclear war.

It is possible to explore this great issue further and make a crude estimate of N, the number of advanced technical civilisations in the Galaxy. We define an advanced civilisation as one capable of radio astronomy. This is, of course, a parochial if essential definition. There may be countless worlds on which the inhabitants are accomplished linguists or superb poets but indifferent radio astronomers. We will not hear from them. N can be written as the product or multiplication of a number of factors, each a kind of filter, every one of which must be sizable for there to be large number of civilisations:

N^*, the number of stars in the Milky Way Galaxy;
f_p, the fraction of stars that have planetary systems;
n_e, the number of planets in a given system that are ecologically suitable for life;
f_l, the fraction of otherwise suitable planets on which life actually arises;
f_i, the fraction of inhabited planets on which an intelligent form of life evolves;
f_c, the fraction of planets inhabited by intelligent beings on which a communicative technical civilisation develops;
and
f_L, the fraction of a planetary lifetime graced by a technical civilisation.

(from: Carl Sagan, *Cosmos*, Futura, 1983)

1. Suppose there is extraterrestrial life. Why should we wish to make contact with it (or it with us)?

2. 'Because we inhabit the same universe as they, we and they must share some substantial information in common.' (paragraph 3). What kinds of information would we and extraterrestrials be likely to share and what kinds would be peculiar to the planet Earth?

3. '. . . the evolution of an intelligent species from simple one-celled organisms is so improbable that we are likely to be the only intelligent species ever to exist.' (F. Tipler)
Take any of the following and use them to either support or attack the above statement.

(a) Out of the nine planets that circle our star, the Sun, certainly one, and maybe two, can support Life.

(b) There are approximately 4×10^{11} stars in the Milky Way Galaxy.

(c) For billions of years life on this planet did not evolve much beyond the blue-green algae, indicating perhaps that while the origin of life is not a difficult feat, evolution to higher and more specialised life forms is.

(d) Our present intelligence and technology have developed because of many unlikely events in our evolutionary history. For example, the destruction of the dinosaurs made way for the development of mammals, but we still don't know what destroyed them.

(e) In the DNA of a typical human cell there are 10 billion nucleotides, and therefore 10 billion chances of mutation.

4. One of the arguments against Sagan's stance that intelligent extraterrestrial life is a realistic possibility is that if 'they' existed they would already be here. Explain
(a) what is meant by this, and
(b) how such an argument could be countered.

5. The equation at the end of the extract is written out thus:

$$N = N^* f_p n_e f_l f_i f_c f_L.$$

To derive N, each of the quantities must be estimated. Some of the early factors in the equation are fairly well known (for example, the number of stars in the Milky Way Galaxy is estimated to be 4×10^{11}) but estimates of some of the later factors in the equation will be little better than guesses. Sagan himself arrives at a figure of $n = 10^7$ (approx.). What would your final figure be?

6. Why is 'an advanced civilisation one capable of radio astronomy' a 'parochial if essential definition' (paragraph 7)?

7. If an extraterrestrial civilisation were to monitor the radio emissions from Earth what would be the first definite signals they receive?

8. 'Sooner or later we will meet types of intelligence much higher than our own, yet in forms completely alien. And when that time comes, the treatment man receives from his superiors may well depend on the way he has behaved towards his own kind and the other creatures of his world.' (A. C. Clarke)

If you thought that this hypothesis was a reasonable one what areas of human behaviour would you consider needed some attention before we could face the inspection of a 'higher intelligence' without embarrassment?

9. 'We have not yet even come close to solving some of the problems posed by the inadequacies of Mankind – aggression, apathy, greed, exploitation, etc. Space exploration will merely be a means of exporting those inadequacies.' How valid an argument is this? (You will find it useful to refer also to passages A3 and A4.)

Further Reading

The idea of contact with other beings from other worlds has been extensively covered in Science Fiction. Most notable authors are: R. Bradbury, A. C. Clarke, I. Asimov and P. K. Dick.
The arrival on Earth of other inhabitants of the Galaxy has also been the subject of many films: e.g. *The War of the Worlds*, *Close Encounters of the Third Kind* and *The Andromeda Strain.*

F. Tipler, We are Alone in our Galaxy, *New Scientist*, 7 October 1982 – an idiosyncratic argument against the existence of extraterrestrial life.

B10 'Lies, Damn Lies and Statistics'

Despite its mathematical base, statistics can be as much an art as a science. It is possible to manipulate or even distort figures and yet still remain within the bounds of propriety. A statistician has to choose from among many methods the one which he will use to present his facts and that choice is a subjective process. In all forms of commercial practice, industrial relations, etc., he is more likely than not to choose a method which will give the greatest backing to the point he is trying to promote.

Below are the different cases put forward by the management and trade union during a wages dispute at a brewery which employed 1000 workers. Both cases rely on the same figures and neither of them actually tells lies – but they appear to present quite different positions. (The figures for average earnings are given below.)

Average gross weekly earnings
Basic = £55
Overtime = £20
Productivity bonuses = £5
Total = £80

Average deductions for income tax, etc.
£20

MANAGEMENT

The claim for a 15% increase in wages which is being demanded by the trade union representing the employees of this company is, we feel, both unreasonable and unrealistic.

At present the wages of employees average £80 per week – overtime is only a quarter and productivity bonuses a mere 1/16 of these average earnings.

Level of Profit for the Years 1980–1984

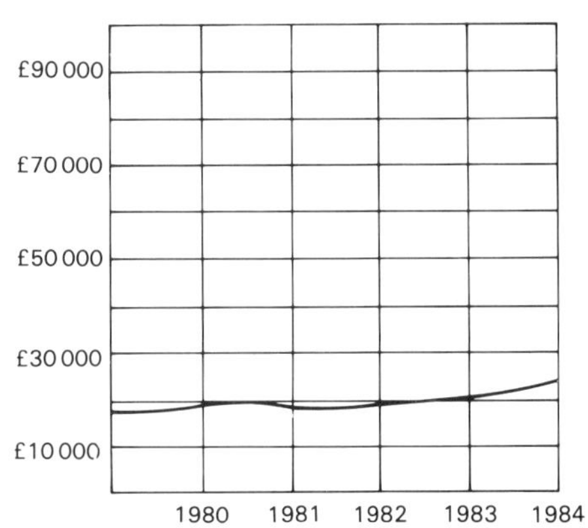

'Lies, Damn Lies and Statistics'

Like every other business we have been hit by the recession of the past few years. Only by increased levels of efficiency have we been able to maintain a certain level of profit, as is shown in the graph below. However, that level of profit cannot sustain a massive 15% wages increase.

Profits might well have been higher last year had we not lost 1000 working days through industrial stoppages.

It might have been possible to finance an increase of this size if there had been a substantial increase in levels of productivity but as can be seen from the graph below the response has been slow.

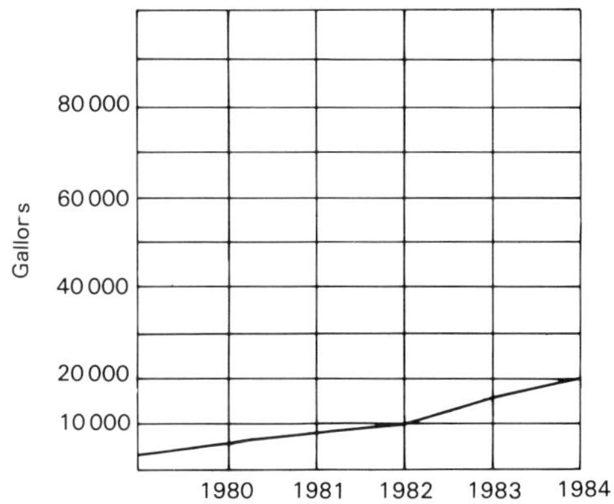

Productivity Levels for the Period 1980–1984

TRADE UNIONS

The wages of the average worker in this company are so low that men have to earn over 45% above the basic rate to end up with a mere £60 in take-home pay. The company are insisting on pay awards being linked to productivity, but productivity bonuses are already equivalent to nearly 10% on top of the basic rate.

If we examine the company's claim that low profits of the last few years mean they cannot meet the cost of a 15% rise then the graph below clearly shows the total fiction of their case. Profits have been climbing steeply for at least the past five years.

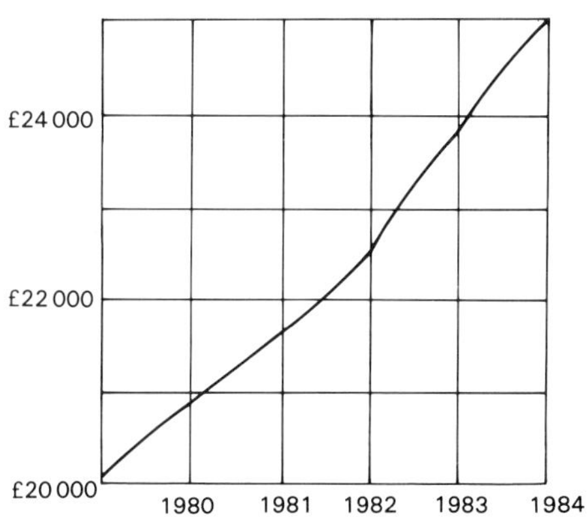

Level of Profits for the Years 1980–1984

Management also disingenuously suggest that low productivity figures are one reason why they cannot award this wage increase. But if we look at the figures it is immediately apparent that this claim is, again, a nonsense. In the period from 1980 to 1984 productivity rose by a huge 300%.

1980 5000 gallons   1982 10000 gallons   1984 20000 gallons

Finally, any claim that this company is 'plagued' by industrial disputes must be laid to rest – during the period 1983–1984, which was a typical one, industrial action consisted of a *token one-day stoppage.*

1. Examine the separate cases presented by the management and the trade union, and show how each side has managed to manipulate the available statistics to provide the greatest possible support for its position.

2. Find out the basic statistics underlying one or two current disputes, and present them as each of the parties to the dispute might present them.

3. In passage B2, R. L. Gregory talks about ways in which we apply our perception to the objective reality which we may believe to exist. Does the material in the passage above provide any evidence about perception as Gregory describes it? (You will find it useful to refer to passage B2.)

Further Reading

W. J. Reichmann, *Use and Abuse of Statistics*, Penguin
– the author shows how and for what purpose statistics may be usefully employed.

D. Huff, *How to Lie with Statistics*, Penguin
– an entertaining description of the possibilities and the detection of the misuse of statistics.

C

EXPRESSIVE MAN

Self-aware Man

C1

Man is the only animal who not only knows objects but who knows that he knows. Man is the only animal who has not only instrumental intelligence, but reason, the capacity to use his thinking to *understand* objectively – i.e. to know the nature of things as they are in themselves, and not only as means for his satisfaction. Gifted with self-awareness and reason, man is aware of himself as a being separate from nature and from others; he is aware of his powerlessness, of his ignorance; he is aware of his end: death.

Self-awareness, reason, and imagination have disrupted the 'harmony' that characterises animal existence. Their emergence has made man into an anomaly, the freak of the universe. He is part of nature, subject to her physical laws and unable to change them, yet he transcends nature. He is set apart while being a part; he is homeless, yet chained to the home he shares with all creatures. Cast into this world at an accidental place and time he is forced out of it accidentally and against his will. Being aware of himself, he realises his powerlessness and the limitations of his existence. He is never free from the dichotomy of his existence: he cannot rid himself of his mind, even if he would want to; he cannot rid himself of his body as long as he is alive – and his body makes him want to be alive.

Man's life cannot be lived by repeating the pattern of his species; *he* must live. Man is the only animal who does not feel at home in nature, who can feel evicted from paradise, the only animal for whom his own existence is a problem that he has to solve and from which he cannot escape. He cannot go back to the prehuman state of harmony with nature, and he does not know where he will arrive if he goes forward.[. . .] Man's existential, and hence unavoidable, disequilibrium can be relatively stable when he has found, with the support of his culture, a more or less adequate way of coping with his existential problems. But this relative stability does not imply that the dichotomy has disappeared; it is merely dormant and becomes manifest as soon as the conditions for this relative stability change.

Indeed, in the process of man's self-creation this relative stability is upset again and again. Man, in his history, changes his environment, and in this process he changes himself. His knowledge increases, but so does his awareness of his ignorance; he experiences himself as an individual, and not only as a member of his tribe, and with this his sense of separateness and isolation grows. He creates larger and more efficient social units, led by powerful leaders – and he becomes frightened and submissive. He attains a certain amount of freedom – and becomes afraid of this very freedom. His capacity for material production grows, but in the process he becomes greedy and egotistical, a slave of the things he has created.

Every new state of disequilibrium forces man to seek for new equilibrium. Indeed, what has often been considered man's innate drive for progress is his attempt to find a new and if possible better equilibrium.[. . .]

These considerations suggest a hypothesis as to how to define the essence or nature of man. I propose that man's nature cannot be defined in terms of a specific quality, such as love, hate, reason, good or evil, but only in terms of fundamental *contradictions* that characterise human existence and have their root in the biological dichotomy between missing instincts and self-awareness. Man's existential conflict produces certain psychic needs common to all men. He is forced to overcome the horror of separateness, of powerlessness, and of lostness, and find new forms of relating himself to the world to enable him to feel at home. I have called these psychic needs existential because they are rooted in the very conditions of human existence. They are shared by all men, and their fulfilment is as necessary for man's remaining sane as the fulfilment of organic drives is necessary for his remaining alive. But each of these needs can be satisfied in different ways, which vary according to the differences of his social condition. These different ways of satisfying the existential needs manifest themselves in passions, such as love, tenderness, striving for justice, independence, truth, hate, sadism, masochism, destructiveness, narcissism. I call them character-rooted passions – or simply human passions – because they are integrated in man's *character*.[. . .]

What all men have in common are their organic drives (even though highly modifiable by experience) and their existential needs. What they do not have in common are the kinds of passions that are dominant in their respective characters – character-rooted passions. The difference in character is largely due to the difference in social conditions (although genetically given dispositions also influence the formation of the character); for this reason one can call character-rooted passions a historical category and instincts a natural category. Yet the former are not a purely historical category either, because they are the result of the impact the various historical constellations have on the biologically given conditions of human existence.

(from: E. Fromm, 'The Anatomy of Human Destructiveness', Cape, 1974, as abridged in *Society and the Social Sciences*, D. Potter et al, RKP/OU, 1981)

1. 'Reason' (paragraph 1) is used in the sense of:
(a) justice
(b) persuasive argument
(c) understanding
(d) problem solving

2. Man is the 'freak of the universe' (paragraph 2) because he:
(i) is self-aware
(ii) uses reason
(iii) has instrumental intelligence
(iv) is imaginative

(a) (i) and (iv)
(b) (i) and (ii) and (iv)
(c) (iii) and (ii)
(d) (ii) and (iii) and (iv)

3. 'Dichotomy' (paragraph 2) is used in the sense of:
(a) uneasiness
(b) a disease which can lie dormant
(c) two parts which oppose each other
(d) a cultural solution to existential problems

4. The author believes that man's innate drive for progress comes from:
(a) powerful leaders
(b) the need to produce material goods
(c) a search for a new equilibrium
(d) the need to increase knowledge

5. 'Character-rooted passions' can be called a historical category because:
(a) they have been around for a long time
(b) they can only be understood *after* they have been formed
(c) they are formed by reaction to differing social conditions
(d) each generation will manifest the same passions

6. Fromm maintains all men experience the 'horror of separateness' and that the deepest need of man is to 'leave the prison of his aloneness'. He lists some of the ways that man satisfies this deep need: love, tenderness, striving for justice, independence, truth, hate, sadism, masochism, destructiveness, narcissism. The list contains concepts that would appear to be completely opposite in nature and yet (according to Fromm) they serve the same purpose. Take each concept in turn and discuss how (and if) man can use them to overcome the awareness of himself as being separate from nature and from others.

See also Question 7 in C3.

Further Reading

L. Stevenson, *Seven Theories of Human Nature*, Oxford University Press
– very readable, interdisciplinary introduction to what Plato, Christianity, Marx, Freud, Sartre, Skinner and Lorenz have to say about the nature of man.

A. Koestler, *The Ghost in the Machine*, Pan
– discusses the nature of a belief or a theory being held as a 'closed system'.

H. Hesse, *Narziss and Goldmund*, Penguin
– Hesse's novel deals with the dual nature of man – the flesh and the spirit.

M. Csaky (Ed.), *How Does it Feel: Exploring the World with Your Senses*, Thames and Hudson
– interdisciplinary collection of contributors on man's experience of the world.

N. A. Scott, *Mirrors of Man in Existentialism*, Collins
– overview of key figures and ideas in Existentialism.

How we Listen to Music

c2

We all listen to music according to our separate capacities. But, for the sake of analysis, the whole listening process may become clearer if we break it up into its component parts, so to speak. In a certain sense we all listen to music on three separate planes. For lack of a better terminology, one might name these:

(1) the sensuous plane,
(2) the expressive plane,
(3) the sheerly musical plane.

The only advantage to be gained from mechanically splitting up the listening process into these hypothetical planes is the clearer view to be had of the way in which we listen.

The simplest way of listening to music is to listen for the sheer pleasure of the musical sound itself. That is the sensuous plane. It is the plane on which we hear music without thinking, without considering it in any way. One turns on the radio while doing something else and absent-mindedly bathes in the sound. A kind of brainless but attractive state of mind is engendered by the mere sound appeal of the music.

You may be sitting in a room reading this book. Imagine one note struck on the piano. Immediately that one note is enough to change the atmosphere of the room - proving that the sound element in music is a powerful and mysterious agent, which it would be foolish to deride or belittle.

The surprising thing is that many people who consider themselves qualified music lovers abuse that plane in listening. They go to concerts in order to lose themselves. They use music as a consolation or an escape. They enter an ideal world where one doesn't have to think of the realities of everyday life. Of course they aren't thinking about the music either. Music allows them to leave it and they go off to a place to dream, dreaming because of and apropos of the music yet never quite listening to it.

Yes, the sound appeal of music is a potent and primitive force, but you must not allow it to usurp a disproportionate share of your interest. The sensuous plane is an important one in music, a very important one, but it does not constitute the whole story.

There is no need to digress further on the sensuous plane. Its appeal to every normal human being is self-evident. There is, however, such a thing as becoming more sensitive to the different kinds of sound stuff as used by various composers. For all composers do not use that sound stuff in the same way. Don't get the idea that the value of music is commensurate with its sensuous appeal or that the loveliest sounding music is made by the greatest composer. If that were so, Ravel would be a greater creator than Beethoven. The point is that the sound element varies with each composer, that his usage of sound forms an integral part of his style and must be taken into account when listening. The reader can see, therefore, that a more conscious approach is valuable even on this primary plane of music listening.

The second plane on which music exists is what I have called the expressive one. Here, immediately, we tread on controversial ground. Composers have a way of shying away from any discussion of music's expressive side. Did not Stravinsky himself proclaim that his music was an 'object', a 'thing', with a life of its own, and with no other meaning than its own purely musical existence? This intransigent attitude of Stravinsky's may be due to the fact that so many people have tried to read different meanings into so many pieces. Heaven knows it is difficult enough to say precisely what it is that a piece of music means, to say it definitely, to say it finally so that everyone is satisfied with your explanation. But that should not lead one to the other extreme of denying to music the right to be 'expressive'.

My own belief is that all music has an expressive power, some more and some less, but that all music has a certain meaning behind the notes and that that meaning behind the notes constitutes, after all, what the piece is saying, what the piece is about. This whole problem can be stated quite simply by asking, 'Is there a meaning to music?' My answer to that would be, 'Yes'. And 'Can you state in so many words what the meaning is?' My answer to that would be, 'No'. Therein lies the difficulty.

Simple-minded souls will never be satisfied with the answer to the second of these questions. They always want music to have a meaning, and the more concrete it is the better they like it. The more the music reminds them of a train, a storm, a funeral, or any other familiar conception the more expressive it appears to be to them. This popular idea of music's meaning – stimulated and abetted by the usual run of musical commentator – should be discouraged wherever and whenever it is met. One timid lady once confessed to me that she suspected something seriously lacking in her appreciation of music because of her inability to connect it with anything definite. That is getting the whole thing backward, of course.

Still, the question remains, How close should the intelligent music lover wish to come to pinning a definite meaning to any particular work? No closer than a general concept, I should say. Music expresses, at different moments, serenity or exuberance, regret or triumph, fury or delight. It expresses each of these moods, and many others, in a numberless variety of subtle shadings and differences. It may even express a state of meaning for which there exists no adequate word in any language. In that case, musicians often like to say that it has only a purely musical meaning. They sometimes go farther and say that *all* music has only a purely musical meaning. What they really mean is that no appropriate word can be found to express the music's meaning and that, even if it could, they do not feel the need of finding it.

But whatever the professional musician may hold, most musical novices still search for specific words with which to pin down their musical reactions. That is why they always find Tschaikovsky easier to 'understand' than Beethoven. In the first place, it is easier to pin a meaning-word on a Tschaikovsky piece than on a Beethoven one. Much easier. Moreover, with the Russian composer, every time you come back to a piece of his it almost always says the same thing to you, whereas with Beethoven it is often quite difficult to put your finger right on what he is saying. And any musician will tell you that that is why Beethoven is the greater composer. Because music which always says the same thing to you will necessarily soon become dull music, but music whose meaning is slightly different with each hearing has a greater chance of remaining alive.

Listen, if you can, to the forty-eight fugue themes of Bach's *Well Tempered Clavichord.* Listen to each theme, one after another. You will soon realise that each theme mirrors a different world of feeling. You will also soon realise that the more beautiful a theme seems to you the harder it is to find any word that will describe it to your complete satisfaction. Yes, you will certainly know whether it is a gay theme or a sad one. You will be able, in other words, in your own mind, to draw a frame of emotional feeling around your theme. Now study the sad one a little closer. Try to pin down the exact quality of its sadness. Is it pessimistically sad or resignedly sad; is it fatefully sad or smilingly sad?

Let us suppose that you are fortunate and can describe to your own satisfaction in so many words the exact meaning of your chosen theme. There is still no guarantee that anyone else will be satisfied. Nor need they be. The important thing is that each one feel for himself the specific expressive quality of a theme or, similarly, an entire piece of music. And if it is a great work of art, don't expect it to mean exactly the same thing to you each time you return to it.

Themes or pieces need not express only one emotion, of course. Take such a theme as the first main one of the *Ninth Symphony* [Beethoven's], for example. It is clearly made up of different elements. It does not say only one thing. Yet anyone hearing it immediately gets a feeling of strength, a feeling of power. It isn't a power that comes simply because the theme is played loudly. It is a power inherent in the theme itself. The extraordinary strength and vigour of the theme results in the listener's receiving an impression that a forceful statement has been made. But one should never try to boil it down to 'the fateful hammer of life,' etc. That is where the trouble begins. The musician, in his exasperation, says it means nothing but the notes themselves, whereas the nonprofessional is only too anxious to hang on to any explanation that gives him the illusion of getting closer to the music's meaning.

Now, perhaps, the reader will know better what I mean when I say that music does have an expressive meaning but that we cannot say in so many words what that meaning is.

The third plane on which music exists is the sheerly musical plane. Besides the pleasurable sound of music and the expressive feeling that if gives off, music does exist in terms of the notes themselves and of their manipulation. Most listeners are not sufficiently conscious of this third plane. It will be largely the business of this passage to make them more aware of music on this plane.

Professional musicians, on the other hand, are, if anything, too conscious of the mere notes themselves. They often fall into the error of becoming so engrossed with their arpeggios and staccatos that they forget the deeper aspects of the music they are performing. But from the layman's standpoint, it is not so much a matter of getting over bad habits on the sheerly musical plane as of increasing one's awareness of what is going on in so far as the notes are concerned.

When the man in the street listens to the 'notes themselves' with any degree of concentration, he is most likely to make some mention of the melody. Either he hears a pretty melody or he does not, and he generally lets it go at that. Rhythm is likely to gain his attention next, particularly if it seems exciting. But harmony and tone colour are generally taken for granted, if they are thought of consciously at all. As for music's having a definite form of some kind, that idea seems never to have occurred to him.

It is very important for all of us to become more alive to music on its sheerly musical plane. After all, an actual musical material is being used. The intelligent listener must be prepared to increase his awareness of the musical material and what happens to it. He must hear the melodies, the rhythms, the harmonies, the tone colours in a more conscious fashion. But above all he must, in order to follow the line of the composer's thought, know something of the principles of musical form. Listening to all of these elements is listening on the sheerly musical plane.

Let me repeat that I have split up mechanically the three separate planes on which we listen merely for the sake of greater clarity. Actually, we never listen on one or the other of these planes. What we do is to correlate them – listening in all three ways at the same time. It takes no mental effort, for we do it instinctively.

Perhaps an analogy with what happens to us when we visit the theatre will make this instinctive correlation clearer. In the theatre, you are aware of the actors and actresses, costumes and sets, sounds and movements. All these give one the sense that the theatre is a pleasant place to be in. They constitute the sensuous plane in our theatrical reactions.

The expressive plane in the theatre would be derived from the feeling that you get from what is happening on the stage. You are moved to pity, excitement, or gaiety. It is this general feeling, generated aside from the particular words being spoken, a certain emotional something which exists on the stage, that is analogous to the expressive quality in music.

The plot and plot development is equivalent to our sheerly musical plane. The playwright creates and develops a character in just the same way that a composer creates and develops a theme. According to the degree of your awareness of the way in which the artist in either field handles his material will you become a more intelligent listener.

It is easy enough to see that the theatregoer never is conscious of any of these elements separately. He is aware of them all at the same time. The same is true of music listening. We simultaneously and without thinking listen on all three planes.

In a sense, the ideal listener is both inside and outside the music at the same moment, judging it and enjoying it, wishing it would go one way and watching it go another – almost like the composer at the moment he composes it; because in order to write his music, the composer must also be inside and outside his music, carried away by it and yet coldly critical of it. A subjective and objective attitude is implied in both creating and listening to music.

What the reader should strive for, then, is a more *active* kind of listening. Whether you listen to Mozart or Duke Ellington, you can deepen your understanding of music only by being a more conscious and aware listener – not someone who is just listening, but someone who is listening *for* something.

(from: Aaron Copland, *What to Listen for in Music*, McGraw-Hill, 1957)

1. Copland talks about listening on three 'planes':
(i) the *sensuous*
(ii) the *expressive* and
(iii) the *sheerly musical.*
He maintains that we listen to 'serious' music on all three planes to varying degrees.
However, there are certain types of music and certain uses of music which involve listening almost totally on one plane only. Give examples of these with reference to each of the three 'planes' described (for example, supermarket 'muzak' is listened to primarily on the *sensuous* plane).

2. Explain how Copland's idea of the 'three planes' of listening might help you not only to distinguish a great classical composer from a mediocre one but also the 'good' in other forms of music (e.g. a 'good' blues pianist, a 'good' jazz saxophonist, a 'good' electric guitarist, a 'good' brass band, a 'good' musical, and so on). Use examples in your discussion.

3. To what extent do you agree or disagree with Copland's approach to listening to music?

4. Write a careful analysis of one piece of music with which you are familiar (whether classical, jazz, popular or other).

See also Question 6 in C7.

Further Reading

The Larousse Encyclopedia of Music, Hamlyn Paperback
– although poor on post-1960s music, this clear and well-illustrated book looks at music both historically and cross-culturally.

S. Frith, *Sound Effects: Youth, Leisure and the Politics of Rock 'n' Roll*, Constable
– looks at the cultural and economic impact of popular music and its links with youth culture.

C3 Improvisation in Jazz

'Like well man, I just blow don't I.'

This sort of answer – with variations of vocabulary depending on the background of the person involved – is often as far as you'll get when discussing with a jazz musician how he improvises. If the truth were known he doesn't really know how he does it and he rarely thinks about where it comes from.[. . .]

This question of how the jazz musician improvises is perhaps analogous to how we walk; we just put one leg in front of the other, shift the weight onto the front leg and continue ad infinitum. To improvise, the musician just plays his instrument by pressing down the correct valves or keys or strings. But to walk effectively one must be aware, usually of course in a sub-conscious way, of the hazards – the pavement, the kerbs, the traffic, other pedestrians, etc. To improvise effectively one must be aware of the supporting structure – of the harmony, melody, rhythm and mood of the piece and of the role of the other musicians in the performance.

One must also be alive to any *potential* hazards: those that are in the piece, like a strange chord or a sudden change of tempo (equivalent perhaps in our walking analogy to a broken area of pavement we have to cross each day) which we get used to though still take a little extra care, and those that come up during the improvising, like an unexpected drum fill or a strange chord voicing from the pianist. For these – and the analogy here could be the unexpected hazards of suddenly turning traffic, wayward prams, etc. – we keep our eyes and ears open and react accordingly. But of course in the same way that pedestrians stumble – sometimes for no good reason – so too do musicians.

However, given an awareness of his framework and a willingness to take chances there are in fact very few limitations on the jazz improviser. Completely different solos can be constructed on the same piece not only by different musicians (which could be expected) but by the same player at a different time. The jazz musician is quite free to express himself – to create something from himself.[. . .]

Of course, much non-western music also contains some degree of improvising. Indian classical music for example is almost completely improvised. The musicians develop very complex variations from the basic scale and an underlying rhythmic pattern, introduced as the piece evolves. This music is considered a high art in India – almost a religion – and the great sitar player Ravi Shankar spent many years studying before he was allowed to play in public.

In western music, there was, prior to the mid-nineteenth century, a tradition of improvising. We are told that Bach would improvise for hours, and soloists of that time were expected to make up their own cadenzas.

Some early violin sonatas showed only the melody and a guide to the harmonies (on the lines of a jazz chord progression) and the violinist and the accompanist were expected to improvise around the material.

This improvising has returned to some straight music in recent times although now it is often called 'aleatoric' or 'chance' music. Here though, the improvising is likely to be much more controlled by the composer than it is in jazz. The player may be given a note and told to 'play rhythmic variations on your note for twenty-five seconds, wait ten seconds and repeat'. Or he may be given a diagram

(meaning play an ascending scale, getting softer while you are doing so, then play your highest note very loud). In such music the improvising is used very much as the tool of the *composer* – the end result may be different each time but only different between certain defined limits. There is rarely the freedom of the improviser to be himself that is found in jazz.[. . .]

Contemporary popular music also has its measure of improvising and many good jazz musicians have worked in rock groups producing good jazz, improvising in the context of the strong rhythms of that kind of music. Often though, the improvising is very repetitive and derivative and has little value except to fill the gaps between the opening and closing vocal statements.

Musically, though, by its use of rhythmic syncopations over some sort of regular beat, the use of 'vocalised' sounds and the freedom of the improviser to express himself within the given structure, the improvising in contemporary rock has a great similarity to that of jazz. (By these definitions Indian improvising also has a similarity to jazz except that their tradition of altering notes is somewhat different. I have a conviction that Ravi Shankar is a great jazz musician – and it is only our insistence on jazz having an Afro-American heritage that stops this being generally recognised.)

These improvising trademarks (rhythmic syncopation and the use of vocalised sounds) allied with the individuality of the particular jazz musician are the basis of a good jazz solo. But as has been mentioned his awareness of the structure he is improvising within is very important.

To take some common jazz situations:

a trad. band playing *When The Saints Go Marching In*
a big band playing *Take the A Train*
an avant-garde group in a totally free improvisation.

All have a basic frame of reference.

With *The Saints* and *A Train* it is the original structure of melody, harmony and rhythm. With the avant-garde group it is simply the other musicians and the mood that they create once they start to play.

These elements of the other musicians involved and the created mood are important, but to a lesser degree, in *The Saints* and *A Train* examples. The mood has been set up by the original melody and the musicians involved have a prescribed role to play: that laid down by the arranger in the big band and that passed down by tradition in the dixieland group. The solos also are played within certain limits – there may not be a verbal or written agreement as to the length of solos in *The Saints* but, in that style, very long solos are, perhaps mercifully, rare. Within these limits and the context of the piece the soloist can express himself and create good music, but though I'm not denying it can be done, it might be reasonable to assume that it would take an extremely good musician to say something new on *The Saints* or *A Train*!

In the avant-garde situation there are immense responsibilities placed on the musician. He has no structure to fall back on – all he has to work from is his own reaction to what is being created around him. The results can vary. Perhaps a beautiful passage where two people create an intertwining of ideas that stays in your memory long afterwards. Or a mass improvisation – possibly ten musicians playing very loudly for twenty minutes or longer. Within that mass it may be possible to distinguish elements of sympathetic listening between the musicians and perhaps some degree of ebb and flow in intensity may come through. Perhaps it can all be seen as an expression of the twentieth-century artist's reaction to the madnesses of our civilisation. Often though it's just the musicians having a ball.

In the more normal jazz situation of a given melody in a set tempo the jazz musician builds his solo from these elements plus the additional one of created mood. He utilises the harmonic, melodic, and rhythmic elements of the tune in his solo but rarely does he concentrate on one to the exclusion of the others, though some improvisers have done so.[. . .]

When discussing the rhythmic elements of a jazz solo it is important to distinguish between the actual rhythm of the melody or the improvised solo and that of the steady pulse provided by the rhythm section. Take *The Saints* –

the actual melody rhythm is	xxx	x	xxx	x	
and the basic beat	xxxx	xxxx	xxxx	xxxx	etc.

It is this basic beat, provided essentially by the bass and drums, which anchors the solo. The soloist places his rhythms around and about the repeating sub-structure. Yehudi Menuhin, after his recordings with Stephane Grappelli, was surprised at the freedom he had over this steady pulse and likened the rhythm to 'the pillars of a building on which you can put any type of rooms'.

When considering the final element of created mood one has the mood given by the original tune and the mood that the rhythm section may develop. Of course they should be following the soloist but, whether they are or not, it is quite common for a tune which started off as a fairly slow quiet ballad to be transformed during the solos into a much more complex piece of music. Whether this is a good thing or not depends on the soloist – and the original tune!

The jazz musician's solo is, ideally, fresh each time. He is, albeit subconsciously, constantly discarding one idea and developing another: making split-second decisions as to where to go next, and his solo should contain that spark which Whitney Balliett described as 'the sound of surprise'. The recent vogue to re-issue every scrap of material ever recorded by Charlie Parker (including some tunes that break down after only one bar) gives us the chance to observe the improvising process closely. We can hear many different takes from the same recording session and see how, though still recognisably Parker, the solos do differ.

Although alternate takes of the Parker tunes were issued later, there was generally one which was considered to be the best. However while Stan Getz was recording *I'm Late, I'm Late* for the Eddie Sauter album *Focus* (Verve records) he provided two such stunning improvisations over the same string background, that it was impossible to choose between them and both were issued – simply joined together to make one long track. (The *composed* nature of the backgrounds made this joining much easier to do than if Getz had been improvising on a conventional tune.)

Naturally though, all good jazz soloists have their own style, their own way of producing a tone and their own way of dealing with certain situations and these can become formalised – can become the soloist's own clichés.[. . .]

It is not surprising, though, that given the problems of creating afresh each night some jazz solos have become formalised. (The classic example is the clarinet solo in *High Society* which was adapted by Alphonse Picou from the piccolo countermelody to the original march and is now as much a part of the performance as the main melody.) Duke Ellington said that 'all improvising is thought out beforehand – although some only a split second before' and the story is told of how Louis Armstrong and King Oliver would amaze the crowd by playing the seemingly improvised breaks note for note with each other. What they did not notice though, was Joe Oliver leaning over to Louis and silently showing him the fingerings he was planning to use in the next 'improvised' spot!

It should also be remembered that, in 'conventional' jazz, the rhythm section (nowadays most often piano, bass and drums with the possible addition of guitar) are usually improvising throughout a piece. In the written sections they may be told exactly what to play, but in the improvised sections, and possibly even in the composed parts, they will be given only a guide: for the bass and piano the chord sequence and/or the rhythmic pattern the piece is based on; for the drummer possibly just a brief indication of what's expected of him.

Working from this kind of guide the rhythm section try to create a background to the improvising which will assist the soloist and move the piece along – help it 'swing'. (John Lewis's definition of jazz as 'collective improvisation that swings' is a good one when we remember the rhythm section's role in a large proportion of the music. In some contemporary developments though, swing is not wanted and the bass, drums and piano, if used at all, become equal members of the group improvisation. There is no 'front-line and supporting rhythm section'.)

Typical Rhythm Section Guide

One quality which all good jazz musicians possess is a sense of space. He knows when to stop – when he's said all that he needs to say, neither more nor less. He also knows when to dwell on a note or take a rest and allow the rhythm section to play for a while – in other words allow the piece to breathe. It is interesting to observe through recordings the development of soloists like Milt Jackson and Miles Davis. Both learnt, after a while, to control their playing and even a player like John Coltrane – known for his 'sheets of sound' approach, where he virtually tried to play all the available notes on a given chord at once – knew when to 'lay-out' for a little while.

Possibly the most important tool of any improviser is his personal instrumental technique. To play jazz effectively he must have a great degree of control over his instrument though he need not necessarily be a perfect technician. For example, the 19-year-old Miles Davis on his first recordings with Charlie Parker showed a very limited range on his instrument. He split notes often and rarely played fast runs – and this in the bop period when the great trumpet technician Dizzy Gillespie was also playing with Parker. However Miles's strong points – his tone and the musical content of his solos – allowed him to hold his own and later to be responsible for two of jazz's most influential albums (*Birth of the Cool*, the Capitol recordings which foreshadowed the whole 'west coast' movement in jazz, and *Kind of Blue* (C.B.S.), the first album to show the possibilities of improvising with simple modes and scales). Since that time Davis has mastered his technical problems and is in complete control. But there were times on his early records when he goofed badly, yet it doesn't seem to matter, one accepts his solos as great jazz – warts and all.[. . .]

What makes a good solo?

Firstly, a sense of correctness. As Benjamin Britten said when discussing composition 'Every note must sound inevitable and right'.

Secondly, the spark of sheer inspiration – Balliett's 'sound of surprise'.

Thirdly, a sense of communication between the artist and the listener. In the same way that jazz is an individual art from the point of view of the soloist it is also an act of individual appreciation and communication from the point of view of the listener. I can catalogue what I consider to be good solos but until they touch you personally the list will mean nothing more than that *I* like them. I can only say that for me the Miles Davis version of *My Funny Valentine* on the C.B.S. Lincoln Center record is perfect. I can make particular points in relation to his use of certain notes above certain chords but when it really comes down to it, my enthusiasm about the solo is a very personal, subjective feeling. Miles communicates to me – we are on the same wavelength.

THE JAZZ MUSICIAN'S INDIVIDUALITY

All of us see things differently each time we look. We often see more a second time because, while the first look was for the outline, the second will take in more detail – and a third may be directed at some particular point which attracts us. Sometimes though, we may see less on the second look because we glance at the object without taking anything in. We think we have seen it all.

Also of course we see things differently from the next person: it may be he has more interest in that particular object – or maybe he simply looks deeper at things.

These two manifestations of individuality, when expressed in terms of improvising, are responsible for one of the great strengths of jazz and, paradoxically, are one of the major stumbling blocks to many people's appreciation. That is, jazz's capacity for change at each performance.

When you are used to a fixed-art object like a great novel or painting it will not have changed when you return to it. You may see more – your individuality is affecting it – but the object itself is not altered. Even with a symphony or concerto where a conductor or soloist can interpret the piece the basic work of art remains unchanged.

In jazz however, if you decide you like a particular band playing a particular piece then the chances are that if you see the band on four successive nights then you will hear, at least in some particulars, four different pieces of music. As was mentioned above this can be heard on certain Charlie Parker records where one can listen to several alternate takes of the same tune made in one afternoon. Some were scrapped because a musician goofed, some because Parker didn't like his solo – or because he thought he could do better. He tried, though not in a conscious manner, to start each take in a different way – to start with a fresh idea. He then developed his solo from that initial idea. If he didn't like the way a solo was developing he could, at least in the recording studio if not in public, stop the tape and try again. But each fresh start would be different.

Also of course, different musicians – even playing the same kind of instrument – who are working from exactly the same supporting structure of melody, harmony, rhythm and mood will produce different solos. Each approaches the same supporting structure in a completely different way. One may be more harmonically influenced than another or there may be a difference in basic talent and technique but more important perhaps is the musician's own personal background: the people he has listened to and played with and in some way or other, consciously or sub-consciously, been influenced by; the type of person he is – where he was born, how he thinks. In fact everything that goes to make him into a complex human being.

(from: Graham Collier, *Inside Jazz*, Quartet Books Ltd, 1973)

1. What, according to the author, is one of the great strengths of jazz when compared to other conventional art forms?
2. It would seem that jazz is the musical form allowing the musician the greatest individualism. Does this mean that the musician as an individual is less important in other forms of music?
3. To what extent could you argue that a good jazz player is not merely a *performer* but also a *composer*?
4. Performances by most of the great jazz musicians are available on records and tapes. What are the advantages and disadvantages of such recordings both for the jazz performer who makes them and for the jazz enthusiast who listens to them?
5. Examine the idea that a jazz enthusiast has to *learn* to appreciate what a good improvised jazz solo sounds like.
6. Discuss the importance of improvisation in one of the performing arts other than jazz.

Further Reading

A. Rich (Ed.), *The Simon and Schuster Listener's guide to Jazz*, Simon and Schuster (also published as *The Listener's Guide to Jazz*, Batsford) – useful introduction to key jazz figures and their best recordings.

The Miles Davis version of *My Funny Valentine* admired by the author of the extract was also re-issued five years later in 1969 on *Miles Davis' Greatest Hits*, C.B.S.

Impressionists

c4

In the spring of 1874 a group of rather unsuccessful French painters mounted an exhibition in Paris at the premises of one of their friends, a photographer called Nadar. There were some thirty exhibitors; and they included Pissarro, Sisley, Degas, Renoir, Monet, Cézanne and Berthe Morisot. The show was a failure. The general public, alternately mocking and angry, was hostile; and the press was extremely rude. One of the paintings by Monet, a view of the harbour at Le Havre at sunrise, was actually titled 'Impression'; and this gave a critic the opportunity to dismiss it as a mere 'impression' and nothing more. That is the origin of the term Impressionist, which, like the word 'Gothic', was originally used in a derogatory sense.

But that was by no means the end of the story. Impressionism and the movement that developed out of it, Post-Impressionism, prospered to the point where they have become the best loved of all schools of painting.

What can it be about the paintings of Renoir or Manet or Gauguin or Van Gogh that makes them so universally admired and loved? Why are they the chosen decoration of so many, from the housewife who buys a colour reproduction in the local supermarket to the Wall Street banker who hangs originals on the walls of his Fifth Avenue apartment?

It is worth looking at the likely reasons for their appeal because it may possibly tell us something about the nature of the art itself. And the first point is the subject matter. You will find pictures of people out for a Sunday stroll; dancing in an open-air café; at the theatre; boating; enjoying the seaside; painting out of doors; and having lunch by the river beneath a pretty striped awning. There are portraits, but of ordinary people, a postman, a peasant, a doctor. There are plenty of landscapes, some of real places, others so like a dream as to be quite unambiguously artifical. Occasionally there are non-contemporary subjects, such as young Spartan girls inciting the boys to fight, or the vision of Jacob wrestling with the Angel, but even these exert an easy appeal over and above their narrative content.

There is very little in Impressionist or Post-Impressionist painting that requires any background knowledge. You don't have to know your Bible or the Greek and Roman classics, or even generally be very well read, to enjoy a Renoir or a Van Gogh or a Seurat. There are plenty of interesting things to know about these pictures: the models were often friends or relations and the settings can often be exactly identified: but this knowledge is not essential to their enjoyment. This was a major problem in 1874, when taste in art was much more snobbish, a much more exclusive prerogative of the upper classes, and when literary content was still thought to be important. The pictures of Renoir, Pissarro, Degas and Monet were considered trivial precisely because they seemed to offer a visual impression and nothing more, no stories, no ironies, no moral overtones. But since then democratic forces have asserted themselves in the arts, as in everything else, and educational and religious values have altered. In 1874 there were still people who would have been disturbed by the idea of a large and evidently important work of art that celebrated the pleasures of the working class. Impressionism is a type of painting that needs no texts to explain it; it does not usually have complex levels of association and meaning. It is, in short, an art without an iconography. In the 1870s that was its disadvantage; in the 1970s this is its virtue.

More understandable was the feeling that the Impressionists were either incompetent or foolish because they ignored the solid, concrete nature of so many visible facts about the real world. It is hard for us now to understand that in the late nineteenth century many people still looked to painting for what – until the advent of photography at the beginning of the 1840s – had always been one of its prime functions: the recording of visual phenomena, the presentation of a reassuringly solid image of the world. The fragmentary character of the Impressionist style, the blatant patchwork of strokes, really did seem like an attack on order and stability. We no longer look to contemporary painting for this kind of reassurance because it is so much more convincingly supplied by the cinema and television.

While almost all the subjects depicted by the Impressionists belong to everyday life, the general mood is decidedly optimistic. Now anyone with the slightest experience of life knows that an objective assessment of our probable chances and expectations is not likely to be as positive. Life is full of disappointments, the slow erosion of youthful ideals. Our characters – like our bodies – seldom improve with age. The tragedies of poverty and the indecencies of excess are everywhere.

But the important thing about the Impressionists is that they were artistic, not social, realists; revolutionaries in the studio but not in the streets. They were interested in *how* things looked rather than in the social implications of those things. Furthermore, the effects of sunlight and the play of strong clear colours, which so absorbed them as painters, are just the kind of factors that make for a therapeutic, even celebratory, form of art. Even the somewhat pessimistic vision of Van Gogh and Toulouse Lautrec was softened by the very nature of their style. Van Gogh, who originally wished to be a preacher but was too unstable to bear the strain of intense missionary work, wanted his pictures to move people to pity. In the beginning, he chose serious, even harrowing subjects, like *The Potato Eaters.* Many of the paintings of his maturity still concentrate on the hard life of the peasant and the farm labourer; but the radiance of his style tends to blind one to the social implications of the theme. In the same way, the colourful distortions of Lautrec's style, the sheer buoyancy of his outlines, rob his scenes of vice of most of their squalor.

It is this combination of usually cheerful subjects with an obviously affirmative, life-enhancing style that helps to explain so much of the popularity of the Impressionists and Post-Impressionists. The great masters of earlier centuries had painted happy subjects, blissful landscapes, goddesses and bacchanalian revels, but not in such a way that we easily identify with them. But the world of Impressionism, cosy, relaxed, suburban, represents an ideal that most of us share: the pleasures of the average

Pierre-Auguste Renoir. *La loge.* Painted in 1874.

commuter, who likes a Sunday afternoon on the river, a drink at the pub, pretty barmaids and a quiet rest in the sun. Even Paul Gauguin extended the Impressionist range of subject matter in a universally popular way. The tropical island, complete with palm trees and half-dressed native girls, is one of the perennial dreams of European man. The fact that Impressionist and Post-Impressionist pictures are firmly rooted in the late nineteenth century even works to their advantage in the world of the 1970s, with its cult of nostalgia, its hotels that offer Gaiety Bars and Hansom Cab Grills, its Old-Time Music Hall where the entire audience as well as the cast are invited to dress up in the costume of the 1890s. So obvious has the Impressionist appeal become that television commercials now borrow ideas from the pictures, taking from Renoir the image of a pretty girl tripping gaily through a sunlit meadow to advertise a shampoo, or from *At the Moulin de la Galette* the vision of young couples dancing under the trees, to promote a popular aperitif.

As has often been pointed out, the Impressionists invented very few of their subjects. 'Modern' themes had been depicted earlier. Ballet, picnics, boating scenes, simple landscapes with cornfields – they had all been painted before. Major nineteenth-century French precursors, like Corot and Courbet, had shown the way: Corot through his miraculous rendering of the effects of light – which becomes the real subject of many of his pictures – and Courbet through his dogmatic, much advertised belief in realism, a belief that drove him to paint scenes from the classics or the reign of Napoleon. The Impressionists brought the various strands together in the late 1860s and early 1870s and created a new style and a new vision.

And the nature of that style is another element in their popularity. To explain this more fully, it is necessary to think back to the grand landscapes of seventeenth-century painters such as Rubens, Claude and Poussin. Most of their compositions are elaborate, with framing elements (trees, rocks, buildings) at the sides, sweeping vistas and a route through the scenery, which is mostly fanciful and contains a great quantity of detail. The eye is invited to travel from the plants and grasses in the foreground, obviously only a few feet away, to a horizon that may be several miles distant. The variety of detail symbolises the abundance of nature (which is part of the subject of the pictures) and the point of focus has constantly to be changed as the eye of the spectator goes from one part of the painting to another. These shifts in focus are reconciled by means of the elaborate design.

Seventeenth-century principles of landscape generally held firm throughout the eighteenth century, resulting in a large quantity of agreeable pictures by artists such as Richard Wilson, Vernet, Gainsborough, Boucher and Zuccarelli. But in the early nineteenth century serious problems began to arise. John Constable, for example, who died in 1837 – three years before Monet was born – was a great admirer of the work of Claude, Poussin, Rubens, Ruisdael and Cuyp; and many of his big, six-foot canvases (such as *The Hay Wain*; *The Leaping Horse*; *Salisbury Cathedral from the Meadows* or *The Lock*) are as ambitious. But beautiful though they are, these large paintings tend to highlight the contradictory elements inherent in Constable's art. He wanted his paintings to have the visual stability and comprehensiveness of the Old Masters; at the same time, as his exquisite oil sketches from nature show so well, he valued as highly the direct response to what he could actually see happening in nature: changes of light and atmosphere, the sudden shaft of sunlight piercing fragmented cloud. This heightened reaction to the natural world was a characteristic phenomenon of the Romantic Period. It subtly shifted the balance in landscape painting, making the traditional formulae that much harder to use. And that is the problem with some – though by no means all – of Constable's more ambitious works. The comprehensive landscape of knowledge, incorporating what the mind knows to be in a given scene, is at odds with the landscape of observation, the sweeping view of what can be observed by the eye at any one moment.

What the Impressionists did to this tradition (which remained in force in academic circles throughout the century) was to abolish the framework. The composition of the average Impressionist landscape is very simple. There are no artfully placed trees at either side to frame the view, no minutely painted flowers and plants in the foreground. More important still, a single focus takes in the whole scene at once.

And this brings us back to one of the main points about the popularity of the Impressionists. In the landscapes of the great seventeenth-century masters all the features are interdependent. In a Claude, the visual climax, the sunlit distance, is both led up to and set off by the rest of the composition. The construction, to adopt a rather loose musical analogy, is symphonic. And as with symphonies, a certain amount of patience is necessary for their enjoyment. But the typical Impressionist landscape is like a single melody. You can grasp the picture at once. It is all tune. Now I am not for a moment suggesting that the Impressionists deliberately lowered their sights to court immediate popularity – the very opposite was the case – but it was in the nature of the Impressionist programme to concentrate on straightforward and immediately comprehensible effects.

This programme was all very well while Impressionism was at its height – roughly from about 1866 to 1876, with some fine works by Manet and Renoir from a few years later. But like all movements in art, Impressionism succumbed to internal pressures, the perennial desire to do something different, to try something new. By the late 1870s and the early 1880s a certain impatience had developed with the 'classic' doctrine of Impressionism, crudely but neatly summed up in the remark that Cézanne is supposed to have made about Monet: 'only an eye, but my God what an eye!'

In other words, Impressionism was lacking in content. It was not just the old Academic principle of telling effective stories in paint but subtler issues of what a picture could be made to suggest. Paul Gauguin, who had begun as an Impressionist, and who of the Post-Impressionists was to go farthest in his pursuit of poetic overtones, wrote in 1888: 'I love Brittany. I find wildness and primitiveness here. When my wooden shoes ring on this granite, I hear the muffled, dull and powerful tone which I try to achieve in painting.' In Gauguin's hands Impressionism was transformed into a major expression of Symbolism, the movement that dominated the arts in the late 1880s and 1890s. Van Gogh was the other major figure who moved away from the relatively naturalistic style of his early period to the more consciously artificial idiom of his last years. Many of these mature pictures have a tension that does not arise from the subject matter but which Van Gogh imposes on it; and in this way many of his paintings reveal Symbolist tendencies, though less overtly than Gauguin's work.

Impressionism also came under attack on the grounds that the pursuit of the instantaneous effect led to looseness of pictorial structure. There is some truth in this argument, when we look not only at an obvious case, like Renoir's *At the Moulin de la Galette*, with its poorly constructed space and anatomical weaknesses, but also at a subtler example, such as Manet's *Road-Menders*, where the delicate observation of light holds together an otherwise flimsy interpretation of form. One false step, one minor inaccuracy in the tones, and the picture would fall apart.

The major artists who make up the Post-Impressionist group solved the dilemma in a variety of ways. Cézanne came to observe nature in a much more analytical way, breaking down forms into facets with which he could then build up his picture. Seurat's method was to treat colour analytically. He reduced all forms to a series of spots of colour, which he so applied to the canvas that they create the desired image when seen by the spectator from a certain distance. This system, usually known as *pointillism*, enabled him to create superbly ordered images of the world around him, still full of the Impressionist feeling for sunlight and loyal to their democratic subject matter but less immediate, less infectiously joyful. *Sunday Afternoon on the Île de la Grande Jatte* is as stately as an Italian Renaissance fresco.

The other way was to stress the non-naturalistic qualities of line and colour, which acquire expressive qualities of their own, over and above their purely descriptive role in a picture. This was the method adopted by Gauguin, who used it to create Symbolist pictures, and by Lautrec, who found in it a means of heightening the naturalistic Impressionist style of Degas. In Lautrec's drawings, paintings and posters, line is used much as Oscar Wilde used conversation: to show off, mock, deflate, outrage, satirise and as a vehicle for wit.

Although the Impressionists and Post-Impressionists were all very different as individuals, and though they came to interpret artistic problems differently, thus destroying the initial coherence that held the movement together in the early 1870s, they were united in their belief that art was a form of commitment to high ideals of what painting was about and even of what life was about, and not just a form of business with 'lines' to meet the taste of complacent customers. And that is why their work has lasted so well. They have become universal favourites not because they painted 'popular pictures' but because they gave a uniquely exciting visual expression to facts and feelings, ideas and dreams, that are popular because they are universal.

(from: K. Roberts, *The Impressionists*, Phaidon, 1975)

1. Why are the pictures of the Impressionists 'so universally admired and loved'? (paragraph 3) (300 words).

2. Explain in your own words the meaning of: 'an art without an iconography'. (paragraph 5).
3. What differences are there between the landscapes of Impressionist painters and those painted by artists of the 17th and 18th centuries?
4. How does Cezanne's supposed remark about Monet, 'Only an eye, but my God what an eye!' (paragraph 15) sum up the classic doctrine of Impressionism?
5. What, eventually, were the shortcomings of Impressionism and by what means did the Post-Impressionists try to overcome them?
6. At first glance the methods and objectives of Impressionism and photography would seem to be totally opposed to each other – yet they were both products of the same age. Are there, in fact, any ways in which these two arts resemble each other?
7. How do you recognise a masterpiece?
8. 'Art, music and other forms of human expression can rarely be separated from each other – there are nearly always points of contact.' Discuss what those points of contact may have been for each of the following groups:
   (a) Constable; Turner; Delacroix; Berlioz; Chopin; Mendelssohn.
   (b) Freud; Jung; Magritte; Dali; Bartok.
   (c) Hogarth; Fragonard; Gainsborough; Mozart; Haydn.
   (d) Now devise your own shortlist of artistic creators of the modern age, making sure that you are aware of the points of contact between them.

Further Reading

E. H. Gombrich, *The Story of Art*, Phaidon
– thoroughly comprehensive – the book spans the entire history of artistic creation.

c5 Henri Cartier-Bresson

'We are passive onlookers in a world that moves perpetually. Our only moment of creation is that 1/125 of a second when the shutter clicks.'

Henri Cartier-Bresson was born in Chantaloup, France in 1908, originally studying painting until becoming seriously interested in photography in 1930. After travelling until 1936, Cartier-Bresson returned to France and became involved in film-making, making, among others, a documentary on the Spanish Civil War. From the late 1940s, the name Henri Cartier-Bresson has been virtually synonymous with photography. His reputation was fully confirmed in 1952 with the publication of his first major book *Images a la Sauvette, (The Decisive Moment).* In 1955 *Les Européens (The Europeans)* was published, and in the same year his photographs were exhibited at the Pavillon de Marsan at the Louvre. Shortly afterwards came books on

Place de l'Europe (1932) A sprightly figure leaping lightly on a poster mocks this bulky figure about to lurch into the wet. In the 1930s, and after, French photographers believed that it was possible to have insights into the hopes and fears of other people, as well as into the conduct of their daily life. Henri Cartier-Bresson delights in insight. Here, he shows that the marooned man has done his best, even if hopelessly, to escape the flood.

Moscow (*Moscou*, 1955) and China *D'Une Chine à l'Autre*, 1955 *(Photographs of China)*. During the 1960s he was revered by a younger generation of photographers. Joel Meyerowitz, in the introduction to his book *Cape Light* (1978), recalls spotting him for the first time at a St Patrick's Day parade in New York City in 1963: 'I saw a man jumping around, bobbing and weaving, twisting and turning, dancing: he was just terrific . . . I was shaking: I was *shaking*! I couldn't believe that we would have the luck to meet the master in this situation,'

Cartier-Bresson is a 'human interest' photographer, and was the first to give a full account of his practice. In his foreword to *The Decisive Moment*, he strongly emphasises the importance of being in the middle of things, absorbed by events. He virtually disclaims responsibility and suggests that it is the events themselves which provoke 'the organic rhythm of forms'. According to Cartier-Bresson, a photographer able to work in unison with

The Banks of The Loire (Seine et Marne) (c. 1965) Photographers did not invent a modern idea of Frenchness all by themselves. They were part of a movement which included film-makers René Clair and Jean Renoir. Yet they were enormously important in establishing an idea of the French as a fundamentally traditional people, under their modern trappings. Cartier-Bresson's city men attend absorbed to their angling, despite the imminent ruination of a pair of shoes.

this rhythm will find a moment when form fits its subject matter. In this respect he is following Surrealist procedures; they too believed that the artist should be absorbed in the 'creative process' and carried along by the organic rhythm of forms.

At the same time, 'the decisive moment' had a prototype in photography itself. During the late 1920s, manoeuverable lightweight cameras such as the Ermanox and the Leica, which Cartier-Bresson uses, made possible a new and dynamic type of sports photography. Reporters scrutinised sporting events for 'the psychological moment' and watched for 'effort at the moment of maximum intensity'. These phrases are taken from the sports pages of *Vu* magazine, the French illustrated weekly paper founded in 1928, in which Cartier-Bresson published his first pictures. He took the idea of 'the psychological moment' and applied it to society at large, and, in so doing wrought a great transformation in the role of the photojournalist, who formerly had been expected to work according to well-established pictorial stereotypes. Surrealist beliefs, lightweight cameras and new ideas in sports photography all helped to liberate photojournalism.

In addition, Cartier-Bresson had the example of André Kertész. Kertész had moved to Paris from Budapest in 1925 and became one of the principal photographers for *Vu* magazine to which he brought irreverence and a taste for the peripheral pleasures of life. Cartier-Bresson, who acknowledges the influence of Kertész on him, also brings the peripheral into the foreground; he works with the audience rather than with the parade, and watches for incidental details which might be symptomatic of some greater cultural whole.

Château Biron, Dordogne (1969). Europeans who survived the Second World War returned with relief to their traditional ways. French photography after 1945 shows an ancient land, imbued with tradition and peopled by timeless cultivators. This picture of Old France is one of the most complete images within the traditional mode; it shows France conceived as it had been in the fifteenth century by the illustrator of the 'Très Riches Heures of the Duc de Berry' – as a land of seasonal labour and settled society.

Moreover, Cartier-Bresson comes from a society which attaches importance to psychological realism in its art, and thinks in terms of insight into others. For example, the stories of the French realist writers like Guy de Maupassant show people as knowable, as possessors of secrets, aspirations and cherished habits. Cartier-Bresson's photographs are elaborate essays on this same understanding but in a different and newer medium. Some of his greatest pictures are extraordinarily revealing. One such, published wherever the photography of Cartier-Bresson is mentioned, is *Sunday on the*

Banks of the Marne, 1938. Two family groups picnic on the shelving bank of the river. They look towards the water and their elegant boat and, with their faces hidden, give nothing away. Yet the picture is redolent with clues. Costume, position and gesture all point to a rich story. The foreground figure, in a dark hat and braces on a warm, summer's day, is an embodiment of prudence, positioned towards the crest of the bank, safe from spillage and inconvenience.

Matisse à Saint-Jean-Cap-Ferrat (1952). French photographers were appreciative of French painters. They understood what they were up to. As in so many of Henri Matisse's own paintings a mirror doubles the image. It holds a picture of the vase just as the painter himself recreates the curve of the bowl and the curve of a buttock with a gesture of his hand. Picasso, Bonnard, Braque and Matisse were much photographed in the years of peace after 1945 – they represented civilisation saved.

Cartier-Bresson relishes such signs of prudence. His people manage as best they can, keeping their wits about them and avoiding difficult situations. They defer to uniforms and to Party bosses and, even when in the tender throes of love, make sure that lighted cigarettes are kept out of harm's way.

One of the most influential of all photographers, Cartier-Bresson has never been outdone: no other photographer offers a comparable degree of insight into the lives of others. Remarkably, in a profession where careers are often short and brilliant, he has maintained a consistent level of achievement for over half a century. Clearly, human prudence is endlessly fascinating, and the minor pleasures of life countless.

Cartier-Bresson's greatest achievement might well have been the creation, or at least establishment, of a particular image of France as a land peopled by singular personalities: crabbed and lined peasants, shrewd *bourgeoisie*, vivid children. During 1936 and 1937 he worked as an assistant director to the film-maker Jean Renoir in the making of *Une Partie de Campagne* and *La Règle du Jeu* (*Rules of the Game*). Renoir's vision of France, and of human nature, was in many ways very like Cartier-Bresson's.

Sunday on the Banks of the Marne, 1938.

Perhaps more importantly, Cartier-Bresson gave Europeans suffering from the ruination of war a rich vision of what settled domesticity could be like. His France is a land of milk and honey, vines and orderly farms. Moreover, it is a strongly traditional land in which café life flourishes and the business of small towns proceeds in a classical and undisturbed environment. Cartier-Bresson brought the same message from abroad, finding signs of worship, devotion and tradition wherever he went, be it China, India, Indonesia or the Soviet Union. Overseas, however, he had less access to psychological and social truths. In the East he found great formal beauty, but few of the intensely revealing signs which mark his French pictures.

Henri Cartier-Bresson

Taking his cue from Kertész in the early 1930s, Cartier-Bresson became France's greatest photojournalist. Britain, leaning towards a more theatrical idea of social life, produced no major photojournalist in this vein; nor did the United States, where a taste for activism and a romantic regard for the primacy of feeling led to an altogether different type of photo-reportage. The peers of Cartier-Bresson are French photographers who learned from his example: Willy Ronis, one of photography's most benign artists, who worked emphatically to project a picture of domestic tranquillity; Robert Doisneau, responsible for a wealth of genial insights into the many-sided French. But it is Cartier-Bresson above all who recalled the intense pleasures to be found along the way; either in daily life or after the parade's gone by.

(from: B. Coe et al, *Techniques of the World's Great Photographers*, Phaidon, 1981)

1. Explain carefully the ideas and innovations which contributed to Cartier-Bresson's use of the 'decisive moment' in photography.
2. How did the Surrealists believe an artist should approach his work? In what ways does this differ from the work of representational artists of the previous two centuries?
3. Photographers, film makers and novelists are all image makers and in their own fields Maupassant, Cartier-Bresson and Renoir have contributed to a particular image of French life. Use the information in the passage to describe what that image is.
4. Why are Cartier-Bresson's French pictures reckoned to be his best?
5. What kinds of pictures would you expect a 'liberated photojournalist' to take? What effects do you think these pictures have on the millions of people who see them in newspapers and magazines?
6. In what ways could photojournalism (e.g. in war reporting) be biased or propagandist?

Further Reading

H. Evans, *Eyewitness*, Penguin
– a collection of the most outstanding, moving and disturbing products of photojournalism from the last twenty-five years.

P. Pollack, *The Picture History of Photography*, Adams, New York
– history of photography; the men, their techniques and pictures.

M. Freeman, *Photoschool*, Papermac
– practical techniques of the craft of the modern photographer.

P. Brassaï, *The Secret Paris of the '30s*, Thames and Hudson
– fascinating example of photography as both art and social documentation.

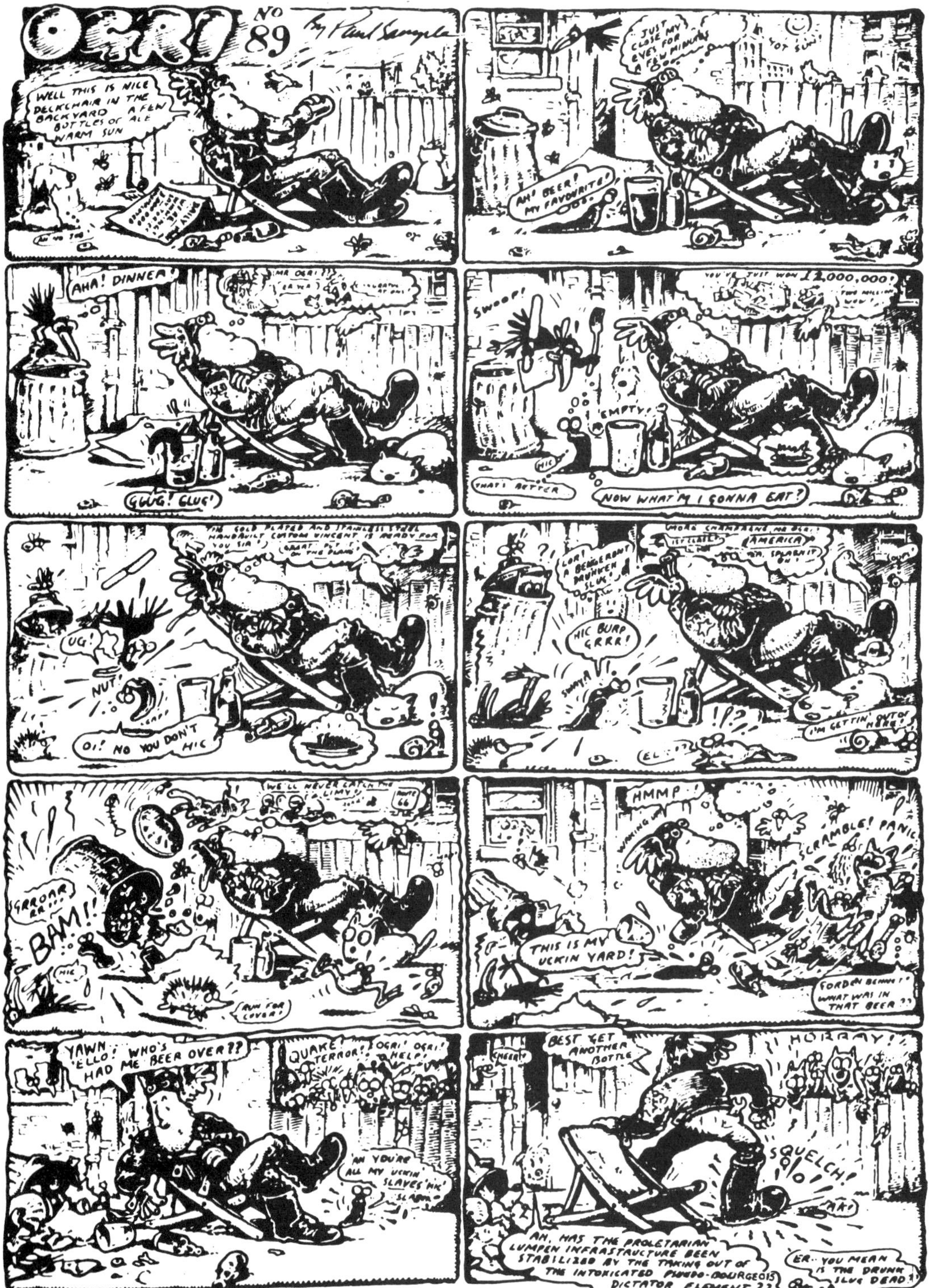

 (from: P. Sample, *The Ogri Omnibus*, Dalkeith Press Ltd, 1981)

Strip Cartoons

C6

'Ogri' is a regular strip cartoon that has appeared in 'Bike' magazine since 1972.

1. Cartoonists depend heavily on exaggerated or caricatured aspects of their subjects. In what ways is the Ogri character a caricature of a motorcyclist?
2. Many forms of humour, including the strip cartoon, make use of stereotypes. What is particularly 'British' about parts of this cartoon?
3. Anthropomorphism is to attribute a human personality to animals or inanimate objects. Point out two separate instances of anthropomorphism, apart from the drunken slug, in the cartoon.
4. Choose a well-known animal character from an animated cartoon film (e.g. Mickey Mouse, Donald Duck). How does the artist achieve a human-like appearance and personality for his character?
5. The cartoon has long been a method of political comment. What makes it so effective? Are there any dangers in using cartoons for political purposes?
6. In the last frame does the dog mean merely 'is the drunk slug dead'?
7. From the slug's point of view his destruction is dispensed by an immense, powerful figure who is indifferent to his existence. Is there a parallel to this in human life?

c7 The Empty Space

We are on the verge of a formula, an equation that reads *Theatre = R r a*. To arrive at these letters we are forced to draw from an unexpected source. The French language does not contain the words adequate for the translation of Shakespeare, yet strangely it is just in this language that we find three words used every day which reflect the problems and the possibilities of the theatre event.

Repetition, representation, assistance. The words work just as well in English. But we normally speak of a rehearsal: *répétition* say the French, and their word conjures up the mechanical side of the process. Week after week, day after day, hour after hour, practice makes perfect. It is a drudge, a grind, a discipline; it is a dull action that leads to a good result. As every athlete knows, repetition eventually brings about change: harnessed to an aim, driven by a will, repetition is creative. There are cabaret singers who practise a new song again and again for a year or more before venturing to perform it in public: then they may repeat this song to audiences for a further fifty years. Laurence Olivier repeats lines of dialogue to himself again and again until he conditions his tongue muscles to a point of absolute obedience – and so gains total freedom. No clown, no acrobat, no dancer would question that repetition is the only way certain actions become possible, and anyone who refuses the challenge of repetition knows that certain regions of expression are automatically barred to him. At the same time, repetition is a word with no glamour; it is a concept without warmth; the immediate association is a deadly one. Repetition is the piano lessons we remember from childhood, the repeated scales; repetition is the touring musical comedy repeating automatically, with its fifteenth cast, actions that have lost their meaning and lost their savour. Repetition is what leads to all that is meaningless in tradition: the soul-destroying long run, the understudy rehearsals, all that sensitive actors dread. These carbon-copy imitations are lifeless. Repetition denies the living. It is as though in one word we see the essential contradiction in the theatre form. To evolve, something needs to be prepared and the preparation often involves going over the same ground again and again. Once completed, this needs to be seen and may evoke a legitimate demand to be repeated again and again. In this repetition, lie the seeds of decay.

What can reconcile this contradiction? Here, the French word for performance – *représentation* – contains an answer. A representation is the occasion when something is re-presented, when something from the past is shown again – something that once was, now is. For representation is not an imitation or description of a past event, a representation denies time. It abolishes that difference between yesterday and today. It takes yesterday's action and makes it live again in every one of its aspects – including its immediacy. In other words, a representation is what it claims to be – a making present. We can see how this is the renewal of the life that repetition denies and it applies as much to rehearsal as to performance.

The study of what exactly this means opens a rich field. It compels us to see what living action means, what constitutes a real gesture in the immediate present, what forms the fakes assume, what is partially alive, what is completely artificial – until slowly we can begin to define the actual factors that make the act of representation so difficult. And the more we study this the more we see that for a repetition to evolve into a representation, something further is called for. The making present will not happen by itself, help is needed. This help is not always there: yet without this true aid, the true making present will not take place. We wonder what this necessary ingredient could be, and we look at a rehearsal, watching the actors toiling away at their painful repetitions. We realise that in a vacuum their work would be meaningless. Here we find a clue. It leads us naturally to the idea of an audience; we see that without an audience there is no goal, no sense. What is an audience? In the French language amongst the different terms for those who watch, for public, for spectator, one word stands out, is different in quality from the rest. *Assistance* – I watch a play: *j'assiste à une pièce.* To assist – the word is simple: it is the key. An actor prepares, he enters into a process that can turn lifeless at any point. He sets out to capture something, to make it incarnate. In rehearsal, the vital element of assistance comes from the director, who is there to aid by watching. When the actor goes in front of an audience, he finds that the magic transformation does not work by magic. The spectators may just stare at the spectacle, expecting the actor to do all the work and before a passive gaze he may find that all he can offer is a repetition of rehearsals. This may disturb him deeply, he may put all his goodwill, integrity, ardour into working up liveliness and yet he senses all the time a lack. He talks abut a 'bad' house. Occasionally, on what he calls a 'good night', he encounters an audience that by chance brings an active interest and life to its watching role – this audience assists. With this assistance, the assistance of eyes and focus and desires and enjoyment and concentration, repetition turns into representation. Then the word representation no longer separates actor and audience, show and public: it envelops them: what is present for one is present for the other. The audience too has undergone a change. It has come from a life outside the theatre that is essentially repetitive to a special arena in which each moment is lived more clearly and more tensely. The audience assists the actor, and at the same time for the audience itself assistance comes back from the stage.

Repetition, representation, assistance. These words sum up the three elements, each of which is needed for the event to come to life. But the essence is still lacking, because any three words are static, any formula is inevitably an attempt to capture a truth for all time. Truth in the theatre is always on the move.

(from: P. Brook, *The Empty Space*, Pelican, 1968)

1. In what ways can rehearsal or 'répétition' be either creative or deadening?

2. Explain clearly the effect a 'bad' and a 'good' audience can have on the performance of a play.

3. There are film and television versions of many stage plays, (e.g. *Hamlet, Othello, A Man for All Seasons, Equus,* etc.) What would be the advantages and disadvantages of using film for:
(a) actors
(b) directors
(c) audiences

4. Much of our everyday behaviour can be likened to acting a part in a play. How far can you apply Peter Brook's formula, 'répétition, représentation, assistance' to the role of each of the following:
(a) barrister in court
(b) teacher in a classroom
(c) confidence trickster

5. 'A play should entertain – just that.' Discuss.

6. Aaron Copland talks of the three separate planes on which we listen to music: the sensuous, the expressive and the sheerly musical. He maintains that someone watching a theatre performance also operates on the equivalent of these three planes. Describe, in terms of Copland's three planes, a play that you have seen. (You will find it useful to refer also to passage C2.)

Further Reading

P. Hall, *Diaries*, Hamilton
– personal account of life behind the scenes of Britain's most prestigious theatre.

Le Corbusier

c8

In 1920 Le Corbusier had published *Towards a New Architecture (Vers une Architecture)* in which he had called for a modern architecture appropriate to the 'machine age'. Buildings should be designed in a modern and functional way just as ships, racing cars, lorries and aeroplanes were. 'A chair', he wrote, 'is a machine for sitting on'. Similarly, 'a house is a machine for living in'. Houses, like cars, should be mass-produced, standardised industrial products, rather than one-off objects, laboriously and inefficiently put together outside in all weathers. He also argued that the 'question of building is at the root of the social unrest of today', because he believed that everyone had a 'primordial instinct' for shelter and the various social classes no longer had dwellings 'adapted to their needs'. The choice was 'Architecture or Revolution'.

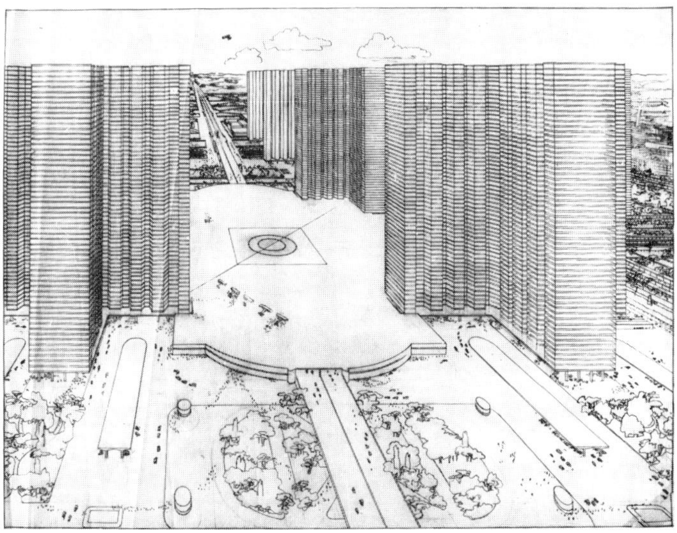

City for Three Million. This view shows the central station and airport with adjacent office buildings.

This was certainly a magnificent way to sell an architectural programme, with political unrest throughout Europe and the example of the Russian revolution fresh in people's minds, and it was inevitable that he should apply himself to the problem of the city. This he did in 1922 on a massive scale, in his project for 'a contemporary city for three million', which contains most of the ideas later developed in *The Radiant City*.

Just as a house is a machine for living in, so 'a town is a tool' for an ordered, stratified, efficient, modern life, provided for people who are fully adapted to industrial society. A city is 'the grip of man on nature', he said, 'a human operation directed against nature, a human organism both for protection and for work'. Its characteristic was 'order', represented in geometry, and the straight line as well as the functional separation of its parts.

> Man, by reason of his very nature, practises order . . . his actions and thoughts are dictated by the straight line and the right angle . . . the straight line is instinctive to him and his mind apprehends it as a lofty object . . . he walks in a straight line because he has a goal and knows where he is going . . . the modern city lives by the straight line, inevitably; for the construction of buildings, sewers and tunnels, highways and pavements. The circulation of traffic demands the straight line: it is the proper thing for the heart of the city. The curve is ruinous, difficult and dangerous; it is a paralysing thing. The straight line enters into all human history, into all human aims into every human act . . . geometry is the foundation . . . the material basis on which we build those symbols which represent to us perfection and the divine. . . .

Le Corbusier was very fond of the straight line at this stage of his career, seeing it as the inevitable and symptomatic result of machine production, and its use as a symbol of civilisation.

Orthogonal (right-angled) planning was as significant to him as concentric circular plans had been to Campanella when he designed the City of the Sun as an analogy of the solar system. Where Campanella has a temple and observatory in the centre, the centre of the highly civilised city for three million contains the administrative and commercial district. Its 24 gigantic cross-shaped skyscrapers 'contain the city's brains, the brains of the whole nation'.

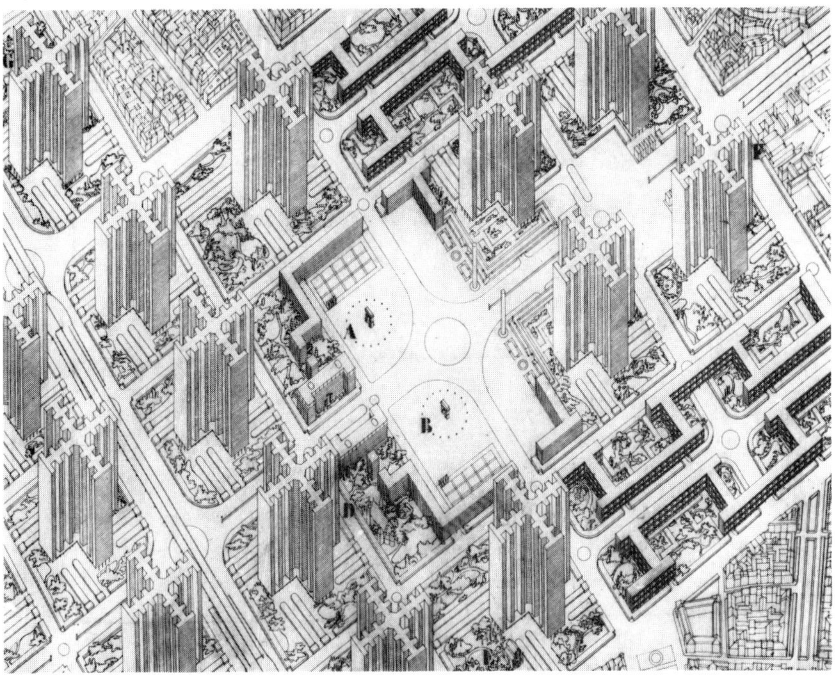

In the 'Plan Voisin', Le Corbusier applied the techniques of the city of three million to Paris (1925).

They stand for all the careful working-out and organisation on which the general activity is based. Everything is concentrated in them: apparatus for abolishing time and space, telephones, cable, wireless, the banks and business affairs, the control of industry, finance, commerce, specialisation.

However, in the very heart of the city, the altar of the temple as it were, lies the multi-level traffic interchange, containing motorways, railway station, bus station, and on top, between the skyscrapers, an airport. All of this expresses the importance and virtue of speed and mobility in the modern city. 'The city of speed', Le Corbusier wrote, 'is the city of success'. Adjacent to the administrative areas lies a cultural and civic centre in its own park. Both are surrounded by the housing zone.

Le Corbusier felt that the skyscraper was not really appropriate for family life, and that 'its internal economy demands so elaborate a system that if one of those structures is to pay, only business can afford the cost'. The family should have all the benefits of sun, light and air, greenery, privacy, vistas, freedom from high-speed traffic and open space. Since only 15 per cent of the ground area is built over, there is plenty of space for garages, gardens, parks, nurseries, playing fields and swimming pools. Even the roofs of the building are used for recreation, and the housing area as a whole is surrounded by a wide green belt, separating it from the factories, giving a city zoned into four main areas - housing, factories, culture and administration.

Le Corbusier developed these ideas in a series of projects both for actual cities and the ideal. The plan Voisin of 1925 shows 'the city of three million' applied to a huge area of Paris, with giant skyscrapers, motorways and a super population density of around 13 000 people per acre. In the plans for Algiers, the housing strip is developed into a linear city with the motorway on top of the building. But the clearest statement of his ideas is in *The Radiant City (La Ville Radieuse)*, compiled in response to a questionnaire from city officials in Russia asking for suggestions on the replanning of Moscow. Like many technocrats, Le Corbusier claimed that his work was above politics, merely the logical rational outcome of the modern world.

In this world, production was in factories, and it was mass-production. The factories were operated by a proletariat who required standardised mass housing and they were administered by an intellectual élite who required an administrative centre. The working day was to be reduced - another advantage of mass-production - to five hours per day, so cultural and leisure facilities would be needed. Finally a transportation system was needed to link up, like a nerve system, the various parts of the body industrial. As long as these are the ingredients, and politics is just a matter of who holds authority, then it is true that 'plans are not politics' and the solutions of technocrats are independent of the ambitions of politicians.

Thus *The Radiant City* is dedicated to 'Authority', and it did not particularly matter to Le Corbusier whether it was the authority of party bureaucrats or the authority of industrialists and bankers, though he used to claim that 'town planning is a way of making money'. What mattered was that the authority was strong enough to carry out the plan - he greatly admired Napoleon III under whose organisation Haussmann had transformed Paris. For the 'plan' was all important.

> The plan is dictator! Let each specialist establish the plans which are in conformity with the new times . . . once these plans are made, discussion is closed, doubt swept away, certainty assured. . . . Plans are the rational and poetic monument set up in the midst of contingencies. Contingencies are the environment: places, peoples, cultures, topographies, climates. They are furthermore, the resources liberated by modern techniques. The latter are universal.

The plan of the Radiant City, as the direct consequence of these 'universal modern techniques', is the urban equivalent of factory production. In the factory the stages of manufacture are separated out and rationalised, so in the city the activities of life are separated into discrete parts. In turn, the parts are standardised – administration into skyscrapers and housing into slabs – because standardisation too was seen as a characteristic and beneficial result of mass-production. Through it, the city would be a place of order, with 'a universal standard and complete uniformity in detail. Under such conditions the mind is calm.' The Radiant City represents the division of labour on a metropolitan scale, as a city planning technique, with the transportation system in the position of the assembly line, that brings all the fragmented 'parts' together as a final product.

However it has become a truism that the division of labour, for all its 'efficiency', not only divides the work, but also divides the worker who has to live with it. Similarly the Radiant City divides the life of the city dweller into standardised parts, with housing in one place, work in another and leisure somewhere else. It has proved more difficult to draw together a fragmented life than it is to assemble an industrial product. Thus the subsequent success of the Radiant City as a model for city planning has meant that the alienation of industrial capitalism has been reproduced, literally, in the physical arrangements of our environment. This model of the ideal city, which had become orthodox by the end of the World War II, was based on the myth that industrial mass-production could be applied to everything, and that this would lead to untold benefits for all.

(from: I. Tod & M. Wheeler, *Utopia*, Orbis, 1978)

1. Le Corbusier stressed the modern, functional nature of machines ('a chair is a machine for sitting on'; 'a house is a machine for living in'). Would you say that a modern car is merely a 'machine for travelling in'? Explain your answer.
2. Why might a city plan based on straight lines and right angles symbolise 'the grip of man on nature'?
3. In your own words explain the sentence: 'Like many technocrats, Le Corbusier claimed his work was above politics, merely the logical, rational outcome of the modern world.' (paragraph 10).
4. Give reasons why Le Corbusier might either approve or disapprove of democratic consultation in the planning process.
5. Explain carefully what is meant by this sentence in the last paragraph: 'Thus the subsequent success of the Radiant City as a model for city planning has meant that the alienation of industrial capitalism has been reproduced, literally, in the physical arrangements of our environment.'

6. Examine the reasoning underlying *one* of the following developments. Evaluate critically the positive and negative aspects of the chosen development. (400–500 words)

(a) 'high-rise' council flat schemes
(b) housing estates with large numbers of near identical houses
(c) 'New Towns' (e.g. Stevenage, Runcorn)
(d) city centre re-development (e.g. Birmingham, Leeds)

7. Refer to the extract *Economies of Scale* (A2). What would be the economies and the diseconomies of scale to be found in Le Corbusier's 'Radiant city'?

8. CIAM (Congrès Internationaux d'Architecture Moderne) was set up in 1928 to try to solve collectively some of the dominant problems of modern architecture – problems which were seen as moral rather than stylistic. CIAM has not met since the Dubrovnik meeting of 1956 which concluded that 'cluster planning' was more acceptable than overall planning. 'Cluster planning' is where a town or a building complex is set up by the accumulation of elements, each of which is viable in itself, a concept which is perhaps closer to traditional town planning. Discuss the social, financial and ethical reasons why overall planning of the Le Corbusier type has fallen from favour.

Further Reading

N. Pevsner, *An Outline of European Architecture*, Penguin

E. M. Forster, 'The Machine Stops' in *Short Stories of E. M. Forster*, Penguin
– the story deals with the awful results of complete dependency on a 'machine to live in'.

c9

Aspects of the Novel

Since the novelist is himself a human being, there is an affinity between him and his subject-matter which is absent in many other forms of art. The historian is also linked, though as we shall see, less intimately. The painter and sculptor need not be linked: that is to say they need not represent human beings unless they wish, no more need the poet, while the musician cannot represent them even if he wishes, without the help of a programme. The novelist, unlike many of his colleagues, makes up a number of word-masses roughly describing himself (roughly: niceties shall come later), gives them names and sex, assigns them plausible gestures, and causes them to speak by the use of inverted commas, and perhaps to behave consistently. These word-masses are his characters. They do not come thus coldly to his mind, they may be created in delirious excitement, still, their nature is conditioned by what he guesses about other people, and about himself, and is further modified by the other aspects of his work. This last point – the relation of characters to the other aspects of the novel – will form the subject of a future inquiry. At present we are occupied with their relation to actual life. What is the difference between people in a novel and people like the novelist or like you, or like me, or Queen Victoria?

There is bound to be a difference. If a character in a novel is exactly like Queen Victoria – not rather like but exactly like – then it actually is Queen Victoria, and the novel, or all of it that the character touches, becomes a memoir. A memoir is history, it is based on evidence. A novel is based on evidence + or $-x$, the unknown quantity being the temperament of the novelist, and the unknown quantity always modifies the effect of the evidence, and sometimes transforms it entirely.

The historian deals with actions, and with the characters of men only so far as he can deduce them from their actions. He is quite as much concerned with character as the novelist, but he can only know of its existence when it shows on the surface. If Queen Victoria had not said, 'We are not amused', her neighbours at table would not have known she was not amused, and her ennui could never have been announced to the public. She might have frowned, so that they would have deduced her state from that – looks and gestures are also historical evidence. But if she remained impassive – what would any one know? The hidden life is, by definition, hidden. The hidden life that appears in external signs is hidden no longer, has entered the realm of action. And it is the function of the novelist to reveal the hidden life at its source: to tell us more about Queen Victoria than could be known, and thus to produce a character who is not the Queen Victoria of history.[. . .]

For human intercourse, as soon as we look at it for its own sake and not as a social adjunct, is seen to be haunted by a spectre. We cannot understand each other, except in a rough and ready way; we cannot reveal ourselves, even when we want to; what we call intimacy is only a makeshift; perfect knowledge is an illusion. But in the novel we can know people perfectly, and, apart from the general pleasure of reading, we can find here a compensation for their dimness in life. In this direction fiction is truer than history, because it goes beyond the evidence, and each of us knows from his own experience that there is something beyond the evidence, and even if the novelist has not got it correctly, well – he has tried. He can post his people in as babies, he can cause them to go on without sleep or food, he can make them be in love, love and nothing but love, provided he seems to know everything about them, provided they are his creations. That is why Moll Flanders cannot be here, that is one of the reasons why Amelia and Emma cannot be here. They are people whose secret lives are visible or might be visible: we are people whose secret lives are invisible.

And that is why novels, even when they are about wicked people, can solace us; they suggest a more comprehensible and thus a more manageable human race, they give us the illusion of perspicacity and of power.

(from: E. M. Forster, *Aspects of the Novel*, Pelican, 1962)

1. What, according to the author, is the difference between 'people in a novel and people like the novelist or like you, or like me, or like Queen Victoria'?

2. Explain: 'novels . . . give us the illusion of perspicacity and of power'. (final paragraph).

3. 'The novelists can teach you more about human nature than the psychologists.' Some critics would agree with this assertion, pointing out the very limited number of people whose inner lives and motivations are known to us; while others would maintain that people in novels can never be *real* people because they are a creation born of only one aspect of the author's mind. Which view would you support?

4. 'The teaching of History should provoke on the part of the pupil a real sense of involvement and sympathy with the people of the past . . . but empathetic writing in History should not indulge the imagination at the expense of the historical facts. There is a discipline in writing empathetically.' (J. Hull in *Teaching History*, No. 28, Oct. 1980)
In looking at real people in the past, is this discipline essential? If, as Forster says, 'the function of the novelist is . . . to tell us more about Queen Victoria than could be known, and thus to produce a character who is not the Queen Victoria of history', is that a legitimate and valuable thing to do? Or might it distort reality in an unacceptable way?

5. (a) The word 'fiction' can be taken as meaning the opposite of 'truth'.

(b) Increasingly, in an age of science, truth is only that which can be publicly verified.

(c) Truth is stranger than fiction.

(d) Literature presents, 'for inspection, imaginary gardens with real toads in them'.

Take each statement in turn and explain it in your own words; then, using all, some or none of the ideas, write either a defence or a condemnation of the novel as a valid art form.

6. Has literature a use, a job, which nothing else can do so well? Or is its function purely to entertain?

7. You have been asked to give a talk to your fellow students on two books, one that you have enjoyed reading and one which you disliked. Prepare your speech.

Further Reading

A. Kettle, *Introduction to the Novel*, Penguin
– an examination of the literary, social and political factors which lay behind the emergence of the novel in the late 18th century, plus critical analyses of six major novelists.

G. Josipovici, *The World and the Book*, Macmillan
– a critical study of modern fiction by a writer who is himself a novelist.

SUPPORT MATERIAL

FILMSTRIPS AND TAPES

There are a number of suppliers of relevant materials. For example, EAV (distributed by Mary Glasgow Publications Ltd, Brookhampton Lane, Kineton, Warwick) include such titles as the following in their catalogue:

Economics and the Global Society
The Ideas of Karl Marx
The Scientific Revolution
Man and Space
Electronic Music
Listening to Jazz
The Right to Pollute
The Energy Crisis
The Comics – a Cultural History
Modern British Literature

FILMS AND VIDEOS

Films are readily available from many sources. The following major agencies can supply feature films, film study extracts and educational and general information films.

Concord Films Council (201 Felixstow Road, Ipswich, Suffolk)

The Open University Library (Guild Sound and Vision Ltd, 85–129 Oundle Rd, Peterborough PE2 9PZ)

The Central Film Library (Government Buildings, Bromyard Ave. London W3 7JB) – can supply many Government information films.

NB. Many video libraries can supply copies of feature films much more cheaply than film hire agencies.

SIMULATION GAMES

Many issues can be structured for use as a role playing game where the participants discuss and consider the issues involved. Some are available through commercial distributors:

Star Power – G. Shirts. (from: Simile II, PO Box 910, Del Mar, California)

The Star River Project – I. Waddington (ESSO Petroleum Co)
– a situation which might arise in an industrially developing river valley – users have to plan and resolve problems of conflicting demands on resources.

Other sources of both made-up gaming sets and information about how to develop your own are:

Media Resources Centre. ILEA, Highbury Station Road, London N1 1SB

SAGE, 44 Hatton Garden, London EC1N 8ER